THE FIRST LADIES OF ROME

Annelise Freisenbruch was born in 1977 in Paget, Bermuda, and moved to the UK at the age of eight. She studied Classics to postgraduate level at Newnham College, Cambridge, receiving a PhD in 2004. For five of the last ten years, she has taught Classics at The Leys school in Cambridge. During that time, she has also worked as a research assistant on a number of popular books and films about the ancient world, and as a research officer exploring the interface between the arts and the law, at the King's College Research Centre in Cambridge. She now lives in Dorset, where she teaches Latin. *The First Ladies of Rome* is her first book.

ANNELISE FREISENBRUCH

The First Ladies of Rome

The Women Behind the Caesars

VINTAGE BOOKS
London

Published by Vintage 2011

10 9

Copyright © Annelise Freisenbruch 2010

Annelise Freisenbruch has asserted her right under
the Copyright, Designs and Patents Act 1988 to be identified
as the author of this work

First published in Great Britain in 2010 by
Jonathan Cape

Vintage
Random House, 20 Vauxhall Bridge Road,
London SW1V 2SA

www.vintage-books.co.uk

Addresses for companies within The Random House Group
Limited can be found at: www.randomhouse.co.uk/offices.htm

The Random House Group Limited Reg. No. 954009

A CIP catalogue record for this book
is available from the British Library

ISBN 9780099523932

Typeset in Dante MT by Palimpsest Book Production Limited,
Falkirk, Stirlingshire

Penguin Random House is committed to a sustainable future for
our business, our readers and our planet. This book is made from
Forest Stewardship Council® certified paper.

Printed and bound in Great Britain by Clays Ltd, Elcograf S.p.A.

For my parents

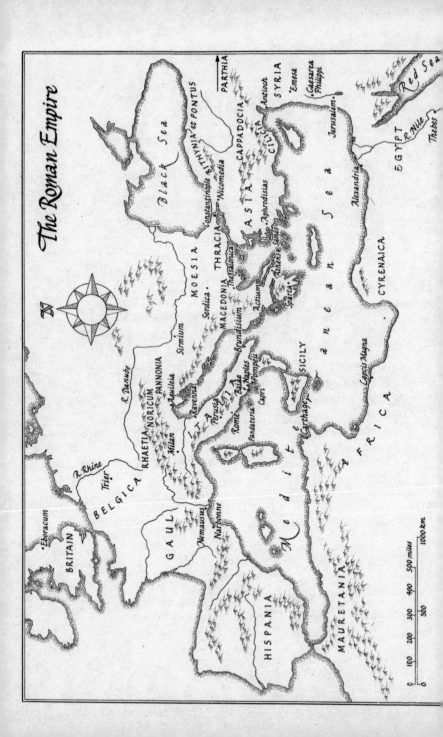

The Roman Empire

Contents

List of Illustrations

15. Relief depicting delivery of a baby (© photo SCALA. Ostia Antica, Museo Ostiense. © 2010)

16. Ivory doll (Roma, Musei Capitolini. Archivio Fotografico dei Musei Capitolini)

17. Jewellery (©The Trustees of the British Museum)

18. Fayum mummy-portrait (©The Trustees of the British Museum)

19. Ivory comb (©The Trustees of the British Museum)

20. Bust of Livia (© Ny Carlsberg Glyptotek, Copenhagen)

21. Bust of Agrippina Maior (Roma, Musei Capitolini. Archivio Fotografico dei Musei Capitolini)

22. Bust of Flavian woman (courtesy of the San Antonio Museum of Art)

23. Bust of Plotina (© Soprintendenza Speciale per i Beni Archeologici di Roma)

24. Bust of Julia Mamaea (Louvre, Paris, France/Giraudon/The Bridgeman Art Library)

25. Front cover of *Agrippa's Daughter* by Howard Fast (reproduced by kind permission of the Syndics of the University of Cambridge Library)

26. Apotheosis of Antoninus Pius and Annia Galeria Faustina (© photo SCALA. Vatican, Courtyard of the Corazze. © 2010. Photo Scala, Florence)

27. Berlin tondo of Septimius Severus, Julia Domna and their two sons (Staatliche Museen, Berlin, Germany/The Bridgeman Art Library)

28. Paolo Veronese's *The Dream of St Helena* (© National Gallery, London)

29. Helena's discovery of the True Cross (© British Library Board – Add.30038, f.237)

30. Sarcophagus of St Helena (Vatican Museums and Galleries, Vatican City, Italy/Alinari/The Bridgeman Art Library)

31. Stilicho, Serena and Eucherius (Basilica di San Giovanni Battista, Monza, Italy/The Bridgeman Art Library)

32. Coin featuring Pulcheria (©The Trustees of the British Museum)

33. Galla Placidia praying to St John the Evangelist (Ravenna, Biblioteca Classense, cod. 406, n.138, ord. B, lettra O)

34. Mausoleum of Galla Placidia (© photo SCALA. Ravenna, Mausoleum of Galla Placidia. © 2010. Photo Scala, Florence)

THE JULIO-CLAUDIAN DYNASTY

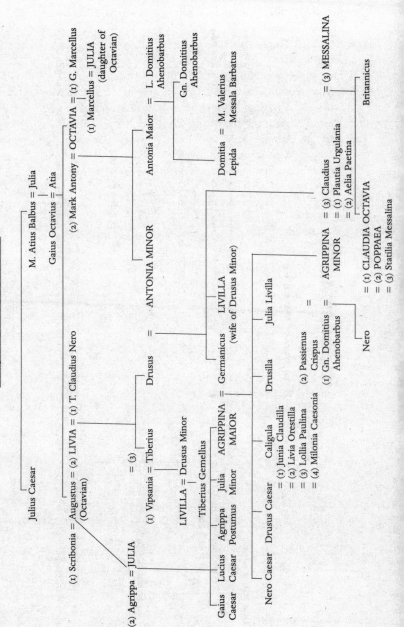

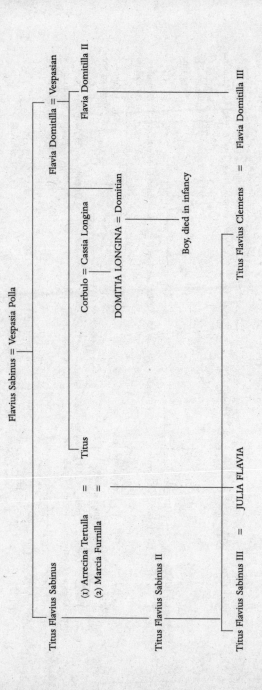

THE FLAVIAN DYNASTY

Flavius Sabinus = Vespasia Polla

Titus Flavius Sabinus

(1) Arrecina Tertulla
(2) Marcia Furnilla

Titus Flavius Sabinus II

Titus Flavius Sabinus III = JULIA FLAVIA

Flavia Domitilla = Vespasian

Titus

Flavia Domitilla II

Flavia Domitilla III

Corbulo = Cassia Longina

DOMITIA LONGINA = Domitian

Boy, died in infancy

Titus Flavius Clemens = Flavia Domitilla III

THE FAMILIES OF TRAJAN, HADRIAN AND THE ANTONINES

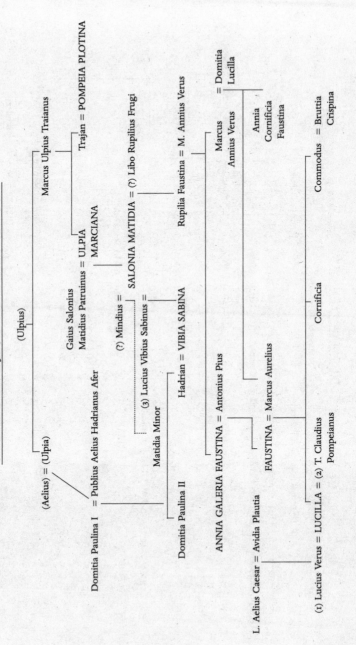

THE SEVERAN DYNASTY

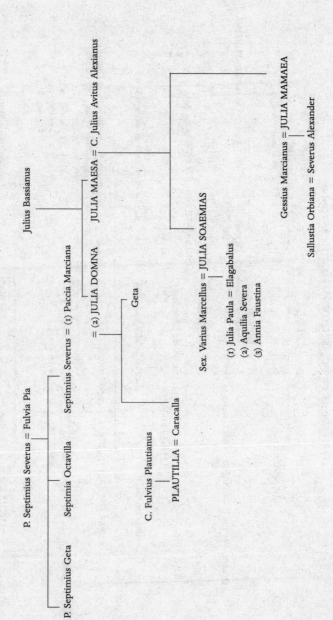

THE TETRARCHS AND THE CONSTANTINIAN DYNASTY

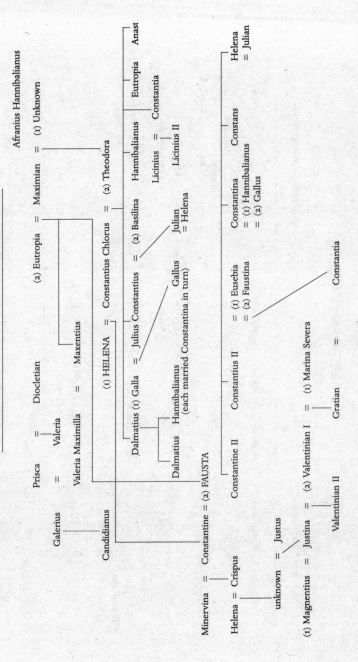

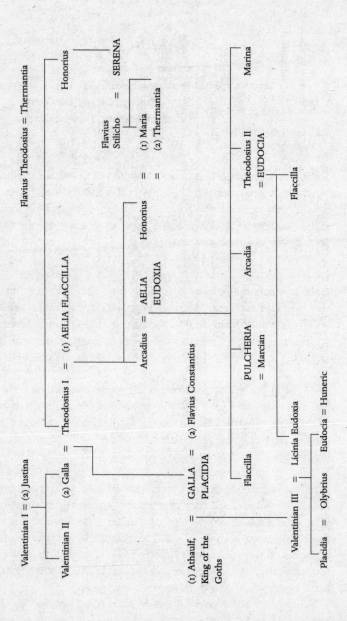

THE THEODOSIAN DYNASTY

INTRODUCTION

I, Claudia . . .

Caesar's wife must be above reproach.
Plutarch, *Life of Julius Caesar*
Mrs Landingham, *The West Wing*[1]

Visitors to Cambridge University's Museum of Classical Archaeology
might be forgiven for thinking they had wandered into a reclusive
art collector's private playground. Stroll through this long, echoing
gallery with its high, beam-latticed glass roof, a rustling soundtrack
provided by the brush and claw of sketching artists' pencils, and one
is treated to a parade of over 400 of the most iconic and instantly
recognised images from the classical world. There are the friezes
and pediments removed by Lord Elgin from the Parthenon; there is
the Apollo Belvedere, once worshipped as the most beautiful
surviving statue from antiquity; there is the Vatican's harrowing
sculpture of tragic Laocoön and his sons being dragged to their
watery grave by two strangling serpents, before the doomed walls
of Troy.

As we arrive in the final bay of the museum's circuit, a Roman
hall of fame greets us, a disembodied line-up of the portrait heads
of the men who ruled Rome. Most of the big names are here, their
marble physiognomies conjuring up their well-known historical
personalities: a pudgy, youthful Nero, a wizened, bullish Vespasian,
a cultured, bearded Hadrian, and a pinched, discontented Commodus.
Huddled in the back row of this illustrious gallery of grey patrician
heads, the smooth, pale face of a woman sits slightly incongruously.
Her name is printed simply on a card underneath: *Faustina Minor;* no
more, no less. It is an airbrushed, bloodless mask of a face, expres-
sionless and unreadable, the ripples of her combed hair carefully
regulated, the shells of her almond eyes gazing blankly at something
behind us.[2]

What is left to us of who this woman once was, in this chalk-
white echo? For an echo is all it is, not simply because it's inanimate,
but because, like most other things in this museum, it is a copy, a

plaster reconstruction created from the original more than a century ago, when such cast collections, and indeed the study of classical art, were particularly fashionable. In the uncertain business of identifying faces from the ancient world, it is not even a certainty that it really is Faustina Minor, a name that is unlikely to evoke many flickers of recognition though she was in fact the wife of the much-admired sixteenth emperor of Rome, Marcus Aurelius. How should we go about imagining the life of the woman behind this enigmatic plaster shell, who looked out at an empire over her husband's shoulder, yet about whose life comparatively little evidence survives?

The temptation to play Pygmalion, to bring Faustina and the other great women of imperial Rome to life according to one's fantasy, is incredibly tempting, and has indeed proved so for many artists and writers. Perhaps the most influential of all modern portraits is that created by the British author Robert Graves, who in August 1933, while living in exile in the sleepy Majorcan village of Deya, dispatched his latest manuscript to his London publishers, hoping disconsolately that it would enable him to pay off a £4,000 debt on his house. The book was *I, Claudius*, an account of the first imperial dynasty of the Roman Empire told from the perspective of its stammering, eponymous narrator Claudius, Rome's fourth emperor. Graves professed scorn for the work, calling it a 'literary conjuring trick', yet both it and its sequel *Claudius the God* proved huge commercial and critical successes, and the novels were eventually adapted for television screens in Britain and the US in 1976. The thirteen-episode saga, sold under the tagline 'The family whose business was ruling the world', quickly became the *Sopranos* of its day, winning acclaim for its all-star British cast and topping viewing figures for the networks. But in a shift in emphasis from the narrative focus of Graves's books, the real stars of the show – the ones who dominated most of the scenes, attracted much of the reviewers' attention and whose faces became the defining promotional image for the programme – were the women in Claudius's life, in particular his grandmother Livia, the wife of Rome's first emperor Augustus, and Claudius's third and fourth wives, Messalina and Agrippina. These women formed a dangerous trio: Livia a Machiavellian who eliminated all rivals to her son Tiberius with cold-blooded insouciance; Messalina a murderous tease who cuckolded and humiliated her elderly husband; Agrippina a black widow whose hand was ultimately behind Claudius's demise.[3]

The long shadow cast by *I, Claudius* was well illustrated in the recent popular HBO series *Rome*, which chose Julius Caesar's niece Atia for its most malevolent and memorable character. Even though there is barely any historical evidence for Atia's life beyond the suggestion that she was a devoted and morally upstanding mother to her son Octavian, she was played here with scene-stealing brio as a cunning, amoral temptress – a clear cultural hangover from the series' 1970s televisual predecessor. However, Graves's own unflattering portrait of Rome's leading women did not spring unaided from the creative mists of the author's imagination. He simply chose to co-operate, for the most part, with the descriptions of them written by ancient Rome's best-known and most revered commentators, and, indeed, made a virtue of doing so. 'I have nowhere *gone against* history . . .', he wrote in his defence of the books' themes, citing the likes of the ancient Roman historians Tacitus and Suetonius as corroborators of his depiction of the women of Rome's first imperial dynasty.[4]

Reading through the ancient literary accounts that inspired Graves, his characterisations seem on the face of things to be entirely appropriate. Besides Livia, Messalina and Agrippina, a sample of the potted biographies of the women of the Roman imperial age includes a wisecracking daughter who disgraced her father by getting drunk in the Roman forum and then having sex with strangers on the speaker's platform; a vain and beautiful mistress who persuaded the emperor to kill his mother in order that he might marry her; a wife who committed adultery with an actor before conspiring in her husband's assassination; and a stepmother who tried to seduce her own stepson and then engineered his execution before herself being boiled to death as punishment. Julia, Poppaea, Domitia and Fausta – these are just a few of the women whose reputations are responsible for the largely hostile historical reaction to the women of Rome throughout history. So vilified are they that their names have been invoked by many as justifications for denying women a share in political power through the ages, their faces held up – quite literally in some cases – as malignant and universal spectres of murderous delinquency, promiscuity and criminality.[5]

For Graves was by no means the first to exhume the women of antiquity from the pages of Tacitus and his Roman contemporaries.

Far from it. The image of Rome's imperial women had already run the gauntlet of centuries of post-classical western cultural production via a kaleidoscopic spectrum of plays, histories, novels, operas, films, poems, pornographic compendiums, paintings, prints, sculptures, manuscript illustrations and even playing-card illustrations and other novelty curios. Since the fourteenth century, when the first biographical catalogues of notorious women from history began to appear, beginning with Giovanni Boccaccio's *De claris mulieribus* (*On Famous Women*) in 1374, Roman ladies made regular appearances in such lists, held up in a few isolated cases as role models of female stoicism and patriotism, but more often than not touted as sternly worded cautionary tales to rebellious-minded young ladies in volumes that enjoyed a wide readership in their day such as Scottish clergyman James Fordyce's 1766 tome, *Sermons to Young Women*. In history and literature, their names have been recycled as pseudonyms for other famous – and controversial – women: Catherine the Great, Anne Boleyn, Mary Queen of Scots, Lucrezia Borgia, Catherine de Medici, Eleanor of Aquitaine, Marie Antoinette and Josephine Bonaparte, to name a handful, have all been compared at one time or other to female counterparts from the Roman Empire. At a more home-grown level, there was even a 'Messalina of Ilford', twenty-nine-year-old Edith Thompson, who in January 1923 became the first woman to be hanged in Britain for fifteen years for her alleged part in the murder of her husband. Many have since called the verdict into question, but press reports at the time did not hesitate to cite the erotic content of Thompson's letters to her lover and co-accused Frederick Bywaters as justification for naming her after Claudius's nymphomaniacal and murderous third bride.[6]

Not all reviews of the women connected to the Roman imperial houses have proved negative, however. Several enjoy relatively favourable reputations both in the literary sources of antiquity and posthumous legend, including Agrippina Maior ('Agrippina the Elder'), mother of the Emperor Nero's infamous parent Agrippina Minor ('Agrippina the Younger'). After being widowed in the year 19 by the suspicious death of her popular husband Germanicus, the elder Agrippina became a rallying figure of sympathy for those who suspected the fell hand of the ruling emperor Tiberius and his mother Livia in Germanicus's murder. Caenis and Berenice, mistresses respectively of father-and-son team Vespasian and Titus, have both featured as the heroines of popular plays and novels, while Helena, mother of the Roman Empire's first Christian emperor, Constantine, was even granted entry to the sainthood. Yet it is undoubtedly their more notorious, unchaste and dictatorial female counterparts who, assisted by popular fictionalisations of their lives, have come to dominate the popular conception of what Rome's imperial women were really like, and even the saintly examples seem like cardboard-cut-out gynoids, the ancient equivalent of Stepford wives.

This book reopens the case file on Livia and her fellow Roman 'first ladies', aiming to reveal something more about them than their static, cartoonish stereotypes allow. But the question of how we speak for and about them has its own complications. Rome was a man's world, no two ways about it. Roman identity was defined exclusively in terms of achievement in the male spheres of militarism and politics, from which its female citizens were shut out. Even the Roman word *virtus*, meaning 'courage', was rooted in the word for man – *vir* . Women could not hold political office at any point in Roman history. They could not command armies, they could not vote in elections, they had relatively few rights under the law and overall played a limited and heavily prescribed role in Roman public life, certainly in comparison to their husbands, brothers, fathers and sons. Despite occasional evidence of female rebellion against unpopular laws, and of debate among jurists and philosophers about the privileges that should be afforded Roman women in the realm of education or property inheritance, there was certainly no such thing as a women's rights movement in antiquity. Most (though not all) of the Roman first ladies discussed here would never have come to historical notice if it were not for the men they married or the sons they gave birth to, and their biographies were invariably constructed in the shadow and reflection of those of their male relatives.

One of the principal conundrums for the modern historian of the women of ancient Rome is that virtually no writing by a woman, let alone a woman of the imperial family, survives in the historical record, with the exception of a few fragmentary scraps of poetry, letter writing and graffiti. Whereas today's political wives can give interviews or write memoirs to set the record straight on their lives, the only known female autobiography of antiquity, written by Nero's mother Agrippina Minor, has fallen prey somewhere along the line to history's censoring hand, along with any other female-authored works that may or may not have once existed. Men of antiquity as well as women have also been victim to such literary accidents and sabotages – the writings of Claudius, for example, have not survived, works which may well have exerted a restraining influence on the popular verdict that Rome's fourth emperor was an ineffectual and comical figure.[7] But the systematic blackout imposed on the voices of women from ancient history reflects more general prejudices about women, and the value or desirability of hearing about them in the first place. As a result, we can never see the women of antiquity except through the eyes of those who were often writing about them decades, or even centuries, after their deaths and who were often less interested in them as individuals than as extras and supporting players in the narratives of their male relatives' lives.

Perhaps the greatest dilemma of all, though, lies in steering a course through the hazard-strewn literary terrain that we rely on for the vast majority of our impressions of Rome's imperial women. How do we choose, for example, between the contrasting versions of Livia that coexist in the uncomplimentary descriptions of her as an unruly bully by the great Roman historian and fierce Julio-Claudian critic Tacitus, the sly flattery of her as a chaste matron with the beauty of Venus by the poet Ovid, and the appreciation of her stoic fortitude in the face of bereavement by the philosopher Seneca? Ancient sources are often a bewildering and frustrating Gordian knot of contradiction, bet-hedging, gossip, insinuation and red herring. They do not moreover share the same biographical preoccupations as we do, such as character development and psychological motivation, something that is especially true of their descriptions of female characters. Instead they tend to paint their subjects in brash, surface-deep primary colours, assigning them moral 'types' into which they can be pigeon-holed – as conniving stepmothers, for example (Livia, Agrippina Minor and to some extent Trajan's wife Plotina would belong to this category), or wronged wives (Augustus's sister Octavia or Nero's first wife Claudia Octavia).[8]

Faced with such dilemmas, the temptation is to pick and choose which parts of the stories about the women of antiquity sound most plausible – usually by the measuring stick of which seem the least lurid – and then to resort to psychoanalysis and intuition to fill in the rest. But the task of deciding definitively which elements in these crude character sketches are true and which are false is, in the majority of cases, a hopeless task. No historian has a privileged antenna to the past and it would be disingenuous to claim that we can ventriloquise for these women in the absence of their own voices and other pieces of their lives. This book does not pretend to do so, nor does it claim to be a 'biography' of these women in any conventional sense – it cannot get inside these women's heads, it cannot provide us with a complete A–Z of their lives.[9]

Instead, what is needed is an agnostic approach to the eclectic array of narrative choices and prototypes of Roman first lady that face us. For it is precisely the sense of fighting a historical multi-personality disorder when it comes to pinning down the real Roman women behind the masks and caricatures of their ancient depictions that in fact is the key to our understanding of their place in Roman society. It is my argument that the identities of Rome's first ladies seem so fluid, contradictory and contentious because they were dictated by the political agenda and reputation of the emperor to whom they were married or related, as well as the critical reaction to his reign. In general, emperors aimed to project an image of themselves as strong family men, and their female relatives would be deployed as good-will ambassadors and models of familial propriety, propping up that image. But of course, in the hands of an emperor's opponents, or a succeeding dynasty keen to sever ties and extinguish memories of their predecessors, his wife's depiction could be wildly different.

This is why my use of the term 'first lady' in the book's title and text feels apposite. It is in part a nod to the description of Livia on more than one occasion in the literature of antiquity as *femina princeps* – a feminised version of her husband Augustus's chosen title of *princeps*, meaning 'chief' or 'leading citizen' – which loosely translates to 'first lady'.[10] But it also invites attention to the inescapable, and sometimes startling, similarities between the key parts played by these women of ancient Rome and their modern political counterparts in 'selling' a domestic image of their husbands – for husbands rather than wives they still usually are – to their public, while helping to further their political agenda, as I argue that Livia and her fellow Roman first ladies did.

So we shall see, for example, how individual Roman emperors' wives were praised for stances such as adopting an approachable, open-house attitude to their subjects, sacrificing clothes and posses-sions to help raise funds for the Roman army, and cultivating a frugal lifestyle, all in the aid of their ruling emperor's image. If we consider some of the women for whom the term 'first lady' was originally coined, we see such model actions reverberating through the ages with exactly the same purpose. For instance, America's first presidential spouse Martha Washington began a much-copied tradition of opening the official residence to callers on certain days, a suitable gesture from the wife of one of America's republican founding fathers; Edith Wilson auctioned off the wool from a flock of Shropshire sheep and donated the proceeds to the First World War effort during the presidency of her husband Woodrow; and Michelle Obama has followed in the practical footsteps of Andrew Johnson's daughter Martha Johnson Patterson, and Rutherford B. Hayes's wife Lucy – the first of whom grazed milk cows on the White House lawn, the second of whom kept her clothing receipts for inspection – by planting a vegetable garden, a politically savvy move in the eco-conscious, economically perilous times in which her husband was sworn in.

Conversely, just as certain Roman empresses were pilloried as spend-thrifts or accused of interfering in politics by their husband's opponents, similar criticisms have dogged many modern first ladies. Mary Lincoln and Nancy Reagan both landed in hot water for their lavish spending – the former for her unpaid clothing bills, at a time when families were mourning relatives lost in the American Civil War; the latter when an announcement was made early in her husband's first term of the purchase of more than $200,000-worth of new china for the White House, the day before her husband's administration was due to announce plans to lower nutrition standards for school lunches programmes. In an illustration of how positive and negative stereotypes can be attached to the same first lady, Michelle Obama is just the latest in a long line of presidents' wives who have raised hackles by expressing strident personal political opinions, leading in her case to the cultivation of her softer, 'Mom-in-Chief' role, in order not to risk alienating conservative-minded voters.[11] Even though ancient and modern political consorts are unquestionably worlds apart in terms of the political and social opportunities open to her, the models of femininity that have been passed down through the ages are in many ways unchanged.

This book begins on the eve of the imperial age, just as Livia's husband Augustus stood on the verge of becoming Rome's first emperor and she its first empress, and proceeds to ghost the footsteps of a selection of the women who followed Livia in the role from the first century through to the fifth century, culminating in the death of one of the last empresses of Rome's western empire, Galla Placidia. Not every imperial woman of that long period of history can be included, but I have chosen to focus on those about whom the richest tradition survives and whose stories are the most important within the unfurling narrative of Roman history. Imperial wives are the focus of most chapters, but, in many cases, the daughters, sisters, mothers and other female family members of the emperors play just as key a role – as indeed they have during the course of the history of America's first ladies, notably in the nineteenth century, when a president's nieces, sisters and daughters-in-law were frequently called upon to serve as surrogate consorts and hostesses at the White House, in the face of reluctance from the president's own wife.[12]

Looking back into the past can often be like peering through a frosted pane of glass, beyond which indistinct shapes and colours move in blurred slow motion. That is very much the experience of trying to see into the world of the women of Rome. Yet occasionally, images and shapes come nearer the glass, closer into focus, making us squint harder in our desire to see them clearly. We all have our longings to satisfy in this regard, a sense of need to make contact with the past, to stand where someone once stood, to touch something she or he once touched. We can never know exactly who the 'real' Livia, Messalina, Agrippina and company were, what they thought, what they felt, whether they were every bit as black or as saintly as they were painted. But this can never repress the frisson we feel at moments of discovery which seem to bring us one tantalising step nearer to them: the cremated remains of some of the slaves who once folded Livia's clothes and poured out her favourite glass of red wine; the richly decorated house in which Augustus's disgraced daughter Julia once lived; a jointed ivory doll that a girl growing up in the imperial household might once have played with; or a letter written by a young Roman emperor, reminiscing about long evening talks with his mother, as she sat at the end of his bed.

It is at moments such as these, coupled with our increasing willingness to reflect on the vital role that the women of Rome played on Rome's great stage, that that pale, blank-eyed museum portrait begins to come alive again.

Ulysses in a Dress: The Making of a Roman First Lady

> The characteristic of the Roman nation was grandeur: its virtues, its vices, its prosperity, its misfortunes, its glory, its infamy, its rise and fall, were alike great. Even the women, disdaining the limits which barbarism and ignorance had, in other nations, assigned to their sex, emulated the heroism and daring of man.
>
> Mary Hays, *Female Biography* (1801)[1]

The blaze had seemed to come out of nowhere, and it caught unawares those trapped in its path, scything a lethal swathe through the olive groves and pinewoods of Sparta. As tongues of flame billowed into the night air, filling it with the acrid smell of burning tree sap, the dry sounds of crackling branches were layered with panicked shouts and laboured breathing. A man and a woman were hurrying through a burning forest. The going was perilous, so much so that at one point the woman's hair and the trailing hem of her dress were singed. But there was little time to inspect the damage. Enemy forces were hard on their heels, and had been harrying them for some time now. Weeks earlier, the fugitive couple and their travelling companions had nearly been apprehended as they tried secretly to board a vessel out of the port of Naples – the fractious wails of their baby son almost giving the game away. The man's name was Tiberius Claudius Nero, and the woman was his seventeen-year-old wife Livia Drusilla.[2]

The year was 41 BC. Three years earlier, the assassination of the dictator Julius Caesar by dissidents acting in the name of liberty had plunged the Roman Republic into civil war, dividing its elite ruling classes into two bitterly opposed camps of supporters, those backing the assassins Brutus and Cassius, and those who had chosen to throw their weight behind Caesar's self-appointed champions, namely his eighteen-year-old great-nephew and nominated heir, Gaius Octavius, and his lieutenant Marcus Antonius – otherwise known as Octavian and Mark Antony. Together with ex-consul Marcus Lepidus, these self-appointed musketeers had formed a brittle three-way power-sharing agreement known as the triumvirate and proceeded to crush Brutus and Cassius at the battle of Philippi in October of 42 BC.

But with Octavian and Antony soon at loggerheads, the Roman elite had found itself being forced to declare its loyalties once more, triggering violent clashes between rival supporters in Italy a year later, clashes which had forced the noble Tiberius Nero – who had chosen to side with Antony – and his young wife Livia into their desperate flight. A ten-year countdown was now in motion, with the courses of all parties set for the battle of Actium in 31 BC, the great sea fight at which Antony, bankrolled by his Egyptian lover Cleopatra, would square off against Octavian and the fate of the Roman Empire would be decided once and for all.

As the first act of this grand drama began, Livia Drusilla was still just an extra in the crowd, an invisible character in a society where few women were permitted to make a name for themselves as public figures. But the events of the second act, in which the man whose troops were pursuing her through Sparta replaced Tiberius Nero as her husband, propelled her to leading-lady status, and by the time the play reached its grand finale, Livia stood on the verge of becoming the 'first lady' of the dawning imperial age, and the founding mother of the Julio-Claudian dynasty that inaugurated it. Arguably the most powerful, certainly one of the most controversial and formidable women ever to occupy the role – her grandson Caligula later bestowed on her the sobriquet *Ulixes stolatus* ('Ulysses in a dress'), a hybrid reference to the Greek warrior known for his cunning, and the *stola* gown worn by upstanding Roman matrons – Livia was the model against whom all subsequent wives of Roman emperors would have to measure themselves.[3] No woman was to epitomise the pitfalls and paradoxes involved in being a Roman woman in public life better than she.

Unlike her Egyptian opposite number Cleopatra, to whom she was forced to play the part of understudy both over the next decade and in historical memory, Livia Drusilla was not bred into the role of imperial dynast, though nor was she an outsider to the Roman political establishment. Born on 30 January 58 BC into the distinguished patrician family of the Claudii, who boastfully claimed descent from Trojan war refugee Aeneas – one of the mythical founders of the Roman race – Livia was fourteen when Julius Caesar's assassination on 15 March

44 BC triggered civil war among the Roman elite.[4] The Claudian clan, from which she was descended on her father's side – her mother Alfidia was from a well-heeled but less aristocratic family based in the Italian coastal town of Fundi – had been a towering presence on the political scene since the early days of the Roman Republic in the fifth century BC, boasting no fewer than twenty-eight consulships, five dictatorships and six triumphs (public honours for successful generals) between them. An additional connection through her father to the illustrious Livian family – one of whose members, Marcus Livius Drusus, had become a populist hero to Italian communities clamouring for Roman citizenship in the early first century BC – also brought with it immense kudos.[5] Such a glittering pedigree marked out the young Livia as a great matrimonial asset to any aspirant to political power and a successful suitor duly presented himself in 43 BC.[6]

Tiberius Claudius Nero, himself a member of a slightly less exalted branch of the Claudian clan, was cut from the same political cloth as Livia's wealthy father Marcus Livius Drusus Claudianus, who would a year later find himself on the losing side at Philippi. Described in a letter by the great Roman statesman Cicero as 'a nobly born, talented and self-controlling young man', Tiberius Nero had enjoyed a reasonably auspicious run up the Roman ladder of advancement during the 40s, holding first the quaestorship and later the praetorship, one rung below the highest possible political rank of consul.[7] Having enjoyed some favour under Julius Caesar, whose fleet he successfully commanded during the Alexandrian war, he nevertheless switched allegiances in the wake of Caesar's murder, opting, like his future father-in-law, to support the assassins Brutus and Cassius, but later transferred his loyalties once more, this time to Mark Antony.

Rome's political hierarchy was still in disarray following the death of Julius Caesar when Tiberius Nero, thwarted of an earlier desire in 50 BC to marry Cicero's daughter Tullia, instead opted for a wedding with his kinswoman Livia, who at the age of fifteen was probably around twenty years his junior, a common age-gap between prospective spouses in Roman society.[8] The marriage would most likely have been arranged for Livia by her father, though Roman mothers could evidently have some say in such matchmaking – the union of Tiberius Nero's first-choice bride Tullia to her third husband Dolabella, for example, was facilitated by her mother Terentia with the resigned acquiescence of Cicero.[9] Legally though, almost every Roman woman, with the exception of the six Vestal Virgin priestesses who tended the hearth of the goddess Vesta, was subject to the total authority of her father or *paterfamilias* as long as he was alive, and from the first century BC onwards, most remained so even after marriage to their husbands. This was thanks to the increasing prevalence from that date of marriages without *manus* (*manus* here having the sense of possession or power), in other words marriages where a woman, and more importantly her dowry in the form of cash and property, remained under the legal jurisdiction of her father rather than her spouse. Such arrangements became the norm thanks to the desire of wealthy clans such as Livia's to keep their estates intact and preserve the integrity of their families by not allowing members to come under the control of another *paterfamilias*.[10]

A girl in Livia's position would technically have been free to refuse to marry, but only in the event that she could have proved that her father's choice of fiancé was a man of bad character, an option that few girls probably felt able or inclined to take advantage of. Marriage was the only respectable occupation for a free Roman woman, but it was also the social grease and glue of Rome's political hierarchy. An aristocratic young girl such as Livia, who had few opportunities to make acquaintances male or female outside of her restricted family circle, could very conceivably expect to be married more than once in her lifetime, in an elite culture where marriage was often not so much a romantic union as a facilitator of social and political alliances between ambitious families, alliances which might well rest on shifting sands.[11]

On the eve of a lavish high-society wedding such as hers, Livia would have undertaken the first of a series of ceremonial procedures symbolising her graduation from childhood to adulthood, and her transition from her father's house to her husband's. First, a Roman bride put away childish things – her toys and the miniature-sized toga she had worn throughout infancy and childhood – and dressed herself in a straight white woollen dress (*tunica recta*) that she had woven herself on a special loom. The next day, this simple white bridal tunic was cinched in at the waist with a woollen girdle whose complicated 'Herculanean' knot would eventually have to be untied by her husband. Her long hair, which had been confined overnight in a yellow hairnet, was arranged in an austere style involving the peculiar use of a sharp spear to separate the hair into six tight braids before they were secured with woollen ribbons.[12]

The groom and guests typically arrived at the bride's father's house in the afternoon. Though Roman weddings were not a religious compact, various ceremonial gestures took place on the day, including a sacrifice of a pig to ensure good omens for the union. Words of consent were exchanged between the betrothed couple, and the marriage was sealed when a married female guest, or *pronuba*, took the right hands of the bride and groom and joined them together. A contract may have been witnessed and signed, the couple toasted with the salutation *Feliciter* ('Good luck') and a wedding feast then preceded the bride's final escort to her new home, where her husband had gone ahead to await her. We can imagine the scene as the distant sounds of singing echoed across the city, just above the evening traffic and the babble of traders shutting up shop for the night. Snaking along a route thickly scented with burning pine torches, flute-players piped musical accompaniment as the raucous crowd, well-oiled by the wedding feast they had just left, tramped along in high gig, singing the traditional wedding refrains of 'Hymen Hymenae!' and 'Talasio!', and tossing handfuls of nuts to scampering children and curious local residents who had come out to watch the cavalcade go by.

In the middle of the crush, Livia's striking egg-yolk-coloured wedding veil, or *flammeum* flared like a beacon in the darkness, draped over a wreath of verbena and sweet marjoram. Matching yellow slippers or *socci*, perhaps embroidered with pearls, slipped in and out of view beneath her belted tunic as she was swept along by the two young boys holding her hands, chosen from the offspring of married family friends as hopeful harbingers of the children she would one day bear. A third boy marched ahead with a pine torch, and instead of a bouquet, a spindle was carried for her along the route, a symbol of her new domestic duties. Despite the presence of these innocuous symbols of respectable wedded life, the atmosphere was thick with well-intentioned but ribald humour, and a gauntlet of risqué jokes and innuendo-laden songs had to be endured before the bride could reach her new marital home. When at last Livia's noisy escorts delivered her up to Tiberius Nero's front door, she found it judiciously garlanded with flowers by her waiting groom. As was required of her, she ceremoniously daubed the doorposts with animal fat and affixed skeins of uncombed wool to them, rituals designed to guarantee wealth and plenty to herself and her new husband in their married life. Finally she was carefully lifted over the threshold by her young male attendants. Caution was necessary. For any bride to trip as she was admitted through the doorway of her new husband's home was considered an ill omen. Once inside, after being presented with gifts of fire (a torch) and water (in a jug or vessel) from her husband, symbolising her wifely responsibility for cooking and washing and the overseeing of the household, she was led away by another married woman who escorted her to her new bedroom before admitting the groom for consummation to take place.[13]

Livia's status as a teenage bride was entirely normal. Upper-class girls in the late Roman Republic typically embarked on their first marriage in their early teens, sometimes as early as twelve. This capitalised on their most fertile, child-bearing years in a climate where infant mortality rates were high. The production of children, the asset for which Roman women were most publicly valued, was an imperative for a woman in Livia's position, and sterility, the blame for which was invariably pinned on the wife rather than the husband, could be cited as grounds for divorce. It comes as no surprise then that the date 16 November 42 BC marks the spot on the Roman time-line on which Livia leaves her first footprint, with the official documentation of the birth of her eldest son, Tiberius, the boy whose cries would later nearly spoil his parents' cover as they fled through the Greek city-state of Sparta, and who would one day become emperor of Rome.[14]

Tiberius's birth took place at home on the Palatine hill, the most exclusive residential district in Rome. Thanks to its close access to the Roman forum, the hub of the city, and its sacred associations with key moments in Rome's mythical past, such as the birth of the city's twin founders Romulus and Remus, the Palatine was the ideal home for an ambitious politico like Tiberius Nero. A veritable *Who's Who* of late republican movers and shakers had also chosen to make it their base, from Cicero to Octavian and Mark Antony, and Livia had probably grown up there herself in her father's house.[15]

Childbirth for a woman in the Roman world was a closely scrutinised business. From the moment of conception to the feeding and weaning stages, a barrage of advice was on offer to expectant mothers – some of it based on the theories of respected medical practitioners, some of it rooted in superstitious quackery. Prior to baby Tiberius's arrival, Livia herself was said to have employed various old wives' techniques to try and ensure the birth of a son, including one where she incubated a hen's egg by cupping it in her hands and keeping it warm in the folds of her dress, where it would eventually hatch into a proud-combed cock-chick, in supposed premonition of a baby boy.[16]

The more pragmatic, though equally unscientific, advice of medical experts like Soranus, writing some years later in the second century, recommended that the best time for conception was towards the end of menstruation, and after a light meal and a massage.

Home births were the only kind available, and a wealthy mother-to-be such as Livia was attended by a roomful of females, including several midwives, who were kept on permanent staff by the richest households. Husbands were not present in the delivery room – though Octavian's father Gaius Octavius had reportedly been late for a Senate vote in 62 BC when his wife Atia went into labour – while male attending physicians were almost unheard of. A remarkable terracotta tombstone from Isola Sacra, near the Roman port of Ostia, offers us an extraordinary snapshot of a Roman woman in the process of parturition. A midwife (probably the dedicatee of this roughly hewn funerary relief) crouches on a low stool before a labouring woman who is naked, and gripping tightly to the armrests of a birthing chair, her upper torso supported by another woman standing behind her. From other medical sources, we know what the relief does not show – that there was a crescent-shaped hole in the seat of such chairs, through which the baby would be delivered by the squatting midwife.[17] An unpleasant-looking vaginal speculum made of bronze was discovered in the ruins of Pompeii; such contraptions may have been used to examine the birth canal in the event of complications. If the advice recorded by Soranus was followed, hot oil, water and compresses were on hand, and the air scented with herbs such as minty pennyroyal and fresh citrus, to soothe the exhausted mother.[18]

Giving birth was a dangerous experience in antiquity both for mother and child. It is estimated that about a quarter of infants died before their first birthday, and funerary epitaphs offer many mournful paeans to mothers who died in labour.[19] But in the event of a successful outcome, such as sixteen-year-old Livia's safe delivery of little Tiberius, the house was soon flooded with congratulatory, back-slapping friends of the proud father, and there is literary evidence that women had post-partum support from female members of their own families too.[20] Nine days after the birth, a day of ceremonial cleansing rites called the *lustratio* was held for the baby, during which he or she was officially named.[21] Public scrutiny of the child's upbringing did not stop there, however. Despite the fact that most members of the elite apparently handed their children over to wet-nurses for suckling, many ancient sources criticised the practice, and insisted that women should breast-feed their own infants themselves. A description from the second century recalls a philosophising visitor named Favorinus criticising a girl's mother for trying to spare her daughter the exigencies of breast-feeding so soon after giving birth, insisting that the child's moral character would be harmed by the milk of foreign, servile wet-nurses who might well be addicted to the bottle to boot. He follows the point home:

> For what kind of unnatural, imperfect and half-motherhood is it to bear a child and at once send it away from her? . . . Or do you perhaps think . . . that nature gave women nipples as a kind of beauty-spot, not for the purpose of nourishing their children, but as an adornment of their breast?[22]

Even though such intellectual critiques failed to stop elite mothers in Livia's day from handing over their babies for weaning, and Soranus's gynaecological compendium actually recommended the employ of a wet-nurse for exhausted mothers, the satirising of females who did not want to endure the trials and damage to the figure caused by child-birth played well to auditors with long, rose-tinted memories. For such female narcissism was portrayed by critics of the society in which Livia grew up as a revealing contrast to the good old days of Rome's earlier history, a period inhabited by female nonpareils such as Cornelia, a much-fêted matriarch of the second century BC who was said to have dispensed with hired help and brought up her children 'at her breast' and 'on her lap'.[23]

An ancient biography of Tiberius preserves the information that Livia herself employed a wet-nurse or *nutrix* to look after her son, one of the very few glimpses we have of this period of her life.[24] Yet it is important. For it plugs directly into Roman thinking about the ideal woman, a yardstick against which Livia and her successors as Roman first lady would be judged. Women rarely won praise in the writings of antiquity for acting in their own interests, rather, they were praised for facilitating the interests of their husbands and their sons, and, through them, furthering the glory of Rome. Cornelia, as the mother of populist politician brothers Tiberius and Gaius Gracchus, was celebrated for her stewardship of their childhood, bringing them up to be eloquent orators and morally upstanding young men fed on a diet of mother's milk. In the same way, details of Livia's upbringing of Tiberius survive because the ancient biographers in question were interested not in Livia per se, but in how her upbringing of young Tiberius might have impacted on the grown man – and emperor – that he would eventually become.

Those reviews were still unwritten. At this stage, despite her impressive family tree, Livia was still very much one of the giant cast of extras in the grand historical narrative of this tumultuous period in Roman history. But unravelling political events and the aspirations of her husband soon propelled her closer to the centre of the action.

In the wake of their joint victory over Brutus and Cassius at Philippi in 42 BC – the victory which resulted in the suicide of Livia's father – the honeymoon period for arch rivals Mark Antony and Octavian did not last long. The relationship between this charismatic veteran warhorse and ambitious political wunderkind had always been a marriage of convenience. On their return from the scene of their victory, Antony had departed to oversee his allocated share of territory in the eastern Roman Empire. This left the third triumvir Lepidus with responsibility for the province of Africa and Octavian with jurisdiction over Italy, and the unpopular task of repossessing land and redistributing it among the military troops who had been promised a reward for supporting the triumvirs against Brutus and Cassius. Very soon, a cold war set in between Octavian's and Antony's camps which showed few signs of thawing over the next decade.

With Lepidus increasingly sidelined, the battle-weary Roman ruling classes found themselves under pressure to declare their allegiance between two rival candidates for overall power, and soon Tiberius Nero made his choice, deciding to nail his colours to the mast of Antony. Smuggling Livia and their newborn son out of Rome in 41 BC, they made for Perusia (modern Perugia) in central Italy, where they found Antony's wife Fulvia and his brother Lucius spearheading attempts to foment popular discontent against Octavian among those Italians whose land had been repossessed.[25]

Antony's third wife Fulvia was a highly controversial figure in his campaign, and one whose character assassination in ancient sources gives us a taster of what was in store for the *femmes dangereuses* of the imperial era. Rome was an aggressively militarist society, one that configured war as a critically – and exclusively – masculine sphere of achievement. The presence of a woman on the front line was anathema, making Fulvia a prime target for Antony's opponents, who made political capital out of the spectre of a woman managing her husband's operations in the field. Recent archaeological discoveries at Perugia of missiles thrown during stand-offs between the opposing sides give us a flavour of the kind of rhetoric employed. The finds included slingshots on which derogatory insults aimed at Fulvia had been scratched – slogans such as 'I'm aiming for Fulvia's cunt', and 'Baldy Lucius Antonius and Fulvia, open your arses'.[26] Her press in the annals of Roman history is scarcely more flattering than these crude graffiti.[27] For one ancient historian, Fulvia's macabre pleasure in the death of Antony's harshest critic Cicero, whose head she demanded to be brought before her in order that she might stab the great orator's quicksilver but now lifeless tongue with a gold hairpin – a feminine variant on a dagger or sword – crystallised her reputation as a terrible hybrid of male and female characteristics; while Octavian himself was the alleged author of an obscene poem about her, in which he claimed that Fulvia, frustrated by Antony's affairs with other women, had adjured Octavian to 'fight me or fuck me', an invitation which he mockingly declined.[28]

For a Roman woman to stray into traditionally male territory, as Fulvia was seen to be doing, did not automatically have to lead to her condemnation. The city's richly idealised history of its own mythical past was punctuated by stories of females like Cloelia, a young girl lauded for rescuing a group of female hostages from the Etruscan king Porsenna by swimming with them across the Tiber through a hail of enemy spears, and publicly thanked with the erection of a statue on the Appian Way, an honour otherwise afforded almost exclusively to men during the republic. Other women, both fictional and real, were praised for their 'masculine' bravery in suicide. Most notable among this group was Lucretia, whose rape by Sextus Tarquinius, the son of the Roman king Tarquinius Superbus, was the catalyst for the overthrow of monarchical rule in 509 BC, and the founding of the republic, on ostensibly democratic principles. Lucretia won everlasting praise as a role model for Roman women for stabbing herself in the heart after her rape, rather than allow her compromised chastity to bring dishonour on her father and her husband. Then there were the ladies who directly intervened to broker peace between warring male factions, like Veturia and Volumnia, who in response to a plea from other Roman matrons inside the city, negotiated the about-turn from the city gates of their respective son and husband, Coriolanus, when he threatened to invade Rome in the fifth century BC; and the Sabine women, whose abduction by the earliest Roman settlers threatened to spark war between the newcomers and their Sabine neighbours, but whose pleas for reconciliation led to peace. All of these stories were set at times of severe flux in Roman history, as tyrants were overthrown or thwarted, and ages of peace restored. The message was, if only all women were as chaste as Lucretia, as brave as Cloelia, and as wise as Veturia and Volumnia, then Rome would never fall into the traps of vice, corruption and despotism that had afflicted it at various points in its historical trajectory.[29]

As a rule though, women like Fulvia, and later Antony's lover Cleopatra, who meddled in the exclusive political and military territory of men, were more usually categorised as harbingers of a world turned upside down. The dividing line between the female sphere of domestic life and the public world of men was a fixed one, and woe betide any woman perceived to have overstepped it. One such straw woman of the republican era was Clodia Metelli, cited during a lawcourt speech delivered in 56 BC by Cicero, when he was defending her former lover Caelius Rufus on a charge of attempting to murder her. Cicero, who claimed that the allegation had been cooked up by Clodia's brother Clodius, with whom Cicero had a long-standing feud, undermined Clodia as a witness by claiming that she was a member of a rowdy, drunken and sexually promiscuous social set who hung out at the popular seaside resort of Baiae, south of Rome. The damning word he used was that she was 'notorious', implying that Clodia had broken the unwritten rule of Roman society which dictated that a woman's place was to be seen and not heard.[30]

The real targets of such vilification, however, were usually the men who tolerated a woman's incursion into the public sphere in the first place, and who, according to Roman definitions of masculinity, were thus to be regarded as weak and feminine themselves, unable to keep their own house in order. These at least were the sentiments behind Plutarch's description of Fulvia as 'a woman who cared nothing for spinning or housework, and was not interested in having power over a husband who was just a private citizen, but wanted to rule a ruler and command a commander – and consequently Cleopatra owed Fulvia the fee for teaching Antony to submit to a woman'.[31] In stark contrast, funerary epitaphs on the tombs of women of the period painted sepia-toned portraits of the occupants as domestic role models who without exception bore children, loved their husbands, kept house, spun wool and could hold a conversation but knew their place.[32] To the Roman way of thinking, this wool-working housewife was the ideal woman, moulded in the image of the heroic martyr Lucretia, who had been engaged in spinning at her loom when her rapist Sextus Tarquinius first saw her. The contrast between her and the brazen Fulvia could not have been more acute.

In the end, Fulvia's and Lucius's campaign to drum up opposition to Octavian in favour of Antony was scuppered in early 40 BC when Octavian's forces laid siege to their camp, forcing the rebels into a chaotic exodus in which Tiberius Nero and Livia were caught up. The next year of their lives was spent in peripatetic exile, and the timing of their various movements from this point becomes uncertain. Forced to make first for the resort of Praeneste, east of Rome, they went from there to Naples where they had a close shave with Octavian's forces because of the crying of Tiberius, who had to be passed from hand to hand between Livia, his nurse and their other travelling companions in a bid to quiet him, as they surreptitiously threaded their way down to the port. On arrival in Sicily, the hopes of Livia's husband that they would receive the protection of another renegade, Sextus Pompeius, who had used the island as his base since fleeing the scene of his father Pompey's defeat at the hands of Julius Caesar, were dashed when Octavian began to make peace overtures to Sextus Pompeius. Livia and Tiberius Nero made next for Greece, where Sparta seems to have afforded the émigré couple a warm welcome at least, thanks probably to the doors opened by the Claudian family name, which had vested interests in the region. But their hiding place was discovered, forcing them into their swift and hazardous night-time exit through the Spartan forest fire.[33]

Such was the tumultuous nature of Livia's first trip into the internecine landscape of the late republic. In its more colourful details, such as the singeing of her dress and hair as she ran through that burning Spartan forest and her frantic attempts to silence her crying son, it reads almost as the autobiographical back story of an aspiring political candidate, a *Biography* channel voiceover narrative of an underdog's struggle against the odds. It is impossible not to wonder what the young Livia made of her situation. In the absence of first- or even second-hand testimony, we can never know whether she was a willing abettor in Tiberius Nero's political objectives or simply a passive accomplice whose only option was to follow dutifully in her husband's footsteps. Graffiti from Pompeii dating to the first century, in which Roman women, though deprived of voting rights themselves, urged support for certain electoral candidates, along with the active example set by republican matrons such as Fulvia, illustrate that women could and did promote the political causes of their menfolk.[34] Despite the Roman conception of public speaking as another of the key building blocks of masculine identity, to the exclusion of women, female protest and rebellion on their own behalf was also not unheard of – the most famous incidence coming a year before the siege of Perusia in 42 BC when Hortensia, the daughter of one of the great orators of the day, Hortensius, delivered a speech against the triumvirs' imposition of a tax on Rome's wealthiest women to help pay for the war with Brutus and Cassius, a tax that was later partially repealed. Livia herself, now that her father was dead and she was *sui iuris* – independent, save for the supervision of a guardian who oversaw certain of her affairs – was legally free to leave Tiberius Nero if she wanted to. Instead, by staying with her husband, she was actually acting in a way that even those who reviled Livia in later life recognised was an honourable part for a woman to play, as the historian Tacitus acknowledged when he wrote approvingly of the virtue displayed by women in other turbulent times who 'accompanied their children in flight' and 'followed their husbands into exile'.[35]

Nevertheless, it is clear that if circumstances had not intervened, a prolonged marriage to Tiberius Nero, for all his impressive credentials, would never have brought Livia more than fleeting recognition at best in the annals of Rome's history. Instead, while she and her husband licked their wounds, it was another woman who found herself in the temporary glow of the public spotlight.

In a bid to patch over the cracks in their fragile alliance, Octavian and Antony now agreed to put the Perusine wars behind them and call a truce. At the harbour of Brundisium (Brindisi) on the Adriatic coast of Italy, the terms of a treaty were agreed in October 40 BC, which confirmed the awards of the eastern provinces of the empire to Antony and the western provinces to Octavian, while third-wheel Lepidus was dispatched to the province of Africa, well away from the centre of the action. To seal the deal, Octavian took a page out of the negotiation handbook of his great-uncle Julius Caesar. He offered up his recently widowed elder sister Octavia – who thirteen years earlier had been the bait in a similar bargain offered by Caesar to his rival Pompey (though she was rejected by the latter) – in marriage to his opponent. The death from illness earlier that year of Fulvia, as she tried to join up with Antony in Greece, had removed any obstacle on his side, and though Roman protocol recommended that ten months' mourning should have followed the death in May of Octavia's previous husband, Gaius Claudius Marcellus, before she married again, her brother's political needs could not wait. The treaty and attendant wedding duly cemented peace between Antony and Octavian, with twenty-nine-year-old Octavia as the glue holding it together.[36]

Octavia was in some ways the quiet woman of this era in Roman politics, remembered now chiefly as a passive bystander forced to play second fiddle to her more exotic rival for Antony's affections, Cleopatra. In her incarnation in Shakespeare's tragedy *Antony and Cleopatra,* she is described as being of 'a holy, cold, and still conversation' whose frigidity would drive Antony into the arms of his 'Egyptian dish', while a recent television drama about the Roman Empire portrayed her as a plaintive wet-blanket, a prostituted pawn in the plans of her scheming mother, Atia.[37] Octavia's reputation in antiquity was rather more impressive. As well as inspiring declarations of devotion from her brother Octavian, she was presented as someone whose beauty, honour and prudence might successfully tame the roving eye of roué Antony. Above all, she won plaudits as a mother. In the three years after Brundisium, she gave birth to two daughters, Antonia Maior and Antonia Minor, whom she raised alongside her son and two daughters from her first marriage, as well as her two stepsons from Antony's relationship with Fulvia, a brood of seven in total.[38] In short, Octavia figured in the Roman mindset as the perfect, passive, dutiful antidote to 'bad women' like Cleopatra and Fulvia – a maternal paragon in the mould of Cornelia, and someone whose example other women of her generation would be encouraged to follow.

But there was one important way in which the role created for Octavia on her marriage to Antony represented a break with the past. Shortly after their wedding, Antony commissioned a series of gold, silver and bronze coins from mints operating in various eastern cities under his control, depicting himself and his new bride. Tiny, fingernail-sized examples of these coin issues survive, showing Octavia's and Antony's heads in tandem, the couple's portraits stamped either individually on the reverse and obverse sides, or in 'jugate' form – that is to say, with their profiles overlapping side by side. The issue of these coins was a powerful gesture. For as well as advertising the new dynastic alliance binding two halves of the empire in ostensibly blissful harmony, they made Octavia the first clearly identifiable living woman to appear on official Roman coinage in her own right, and this was the first time that a Roman woman's image is known to have been used alongside that of her husband to bolster his political credentials.[39]

The choice of a coin as the medium for a Roman woman's visual debut as a public icon was particularly forceful. Coins allowed replicas of the image to be duplicated and distributed on a huge scale, finding their way into the palms and pouches of a ruler's subjects quickly. At one level, Octavia's first public portrait was a resolutely traditional affair, personifying her as the good and faithful wife of Roman legend, a serene support to her husband. Even her hairstyle was on message – a meticulously combed arrangement known as the *nodus* (literally meaning 'knot'), in reference to the distinctive roll of hair swept up harshly above the forehead. This rigid pompadour was highly fashionable among both well-to-do and less well-heeled women of the first century BC, its demure austerity projecting the appropriate image for the respectable Roman wife and mother, and it was a style from which Octavia never deviated during her lifetime, at least in her official portraits.[40] But despite the comfortable familiarity of the *nodus*, the post-Brundisium coins confounded the status quo that had previously refused to contemplate the sight of a living woman on state-sponsored iconography. Portraits of women had appeared on coins in the empire's eastern provinces, but never on ones directly issued by Rome itself.[41] For the Senate to sanction the image of a woman on a coin issued to represent the government of Rome to its subjects was a striking innovation. It was also one that Octavian would use before long to turn the tables on his opponent.[42]

For now though, the intended effect was still to remind the subject ruminatively or unconsciously fingering that small coin of the unity of the couple depicted and the unity at the heart of the triumvirate with Octavia as the linchpin holding the whole edifice together. For a time at least, the illusion of these two bitter former rivals playing happy families seems to have stuck, and the truce agreed at Brundisium poured oil on the troubled waters of Mediterranean politics. As part of the terms of a separate deal struck by Antony and Octavian with the Sicily-based Sextus Pompeius, those who had supported this outlaw against the triumvirs were permitted to return from exile without reprisals, an amnesty which finally permitted Livia, her husband and son to abandon their uncomfortable life on the run. They returned to Rome in 39 BC. As a punishment for disloyalty, however, some of the triumvirs' opponents would be returned only a quarter of their confiscated assets. Tiberius Nero was among those to whom this punishment was meted out. It surely spelled the end of any prospects of a glittering political career for Livia's husband, as obscure retirement beckoned for the former praetor. As far as Livia herself was concerned, though, fate was about to take a surprising hand.[43]

While Antony departed for the east that October with new wife in tow, his young brother-in-law was reassessing his own marital options. The son of a respectable but unremarkable equestrian clan whose ties to Julius Caesar through his mother Atia were his only claim to fame, an advantageous marriage was more important to the highly ambitious Octavian than most. His decision a year earlier in 40 BC to marry Scribonia, a twice-divorced woman some ten years his senior, had been motivated by her family's close connections to the Sicilian renegade Sextus Pompeius, with whom the triumvirate were at the time trying to come to terms. It was Octavian's second marriage, and was the follow-up to his termination of a brief – and, so he claimed, unconsummated – union with Fulvia's daughter Claudia, which had been dissolved when he initially fell out with Claudia's stepfather Antony. Prior to this, Octavian also had at least one broken engagement to his name, underlining the speed and ease of betrothal, divorce and remarriage among the Roman elite in a climate where husbands, fathers and brothers needing to forge alliances with influential families used their female relatives as a vital currency.[44]

But before the year 39 BC was out, in a ruthless demonstration of how easily these alliances could be made and broken, Octavian had divorced Scribonia – just hours after she had given birth to their only daughter, Julia – and invited the pregnant ex-wife of one of his political opponents to move in with him, as a prelude to marrying her. The pregnant woman in question was Livia. A year which she began as a political exile ended with her as consort to one of the two most powerful men in the world.[45]

How this pair met and came to abandon their respective spouses has been the subject of considerable confusion and controversy. Octavian later wrote of his abrupt decision to divorce Scribonia after just a year of marriage: 'I could not bear the way she nagged at me'.[46] His critics, such as Tacitus – looking back on events from the vantage point of the following century – claimed that on the contrary, Octavian was fascinated and tempted by Livia's beauty and had stolen her from Tiberius Nero by force. Barbed letters from Antony to his rival, as preserved by imperial biographer Suetonius, insinuated that Scribonia had been shown the door for having objected too loudly to having a rival, and that Octavian was so lecherous that he had once seduced a fellow guest's wife – possibly Livia, though it is left unclear – at a dinner party, dishevelling her hair and returning her pink-faced to the table.[47] Other sources, however, portray Tiberius Nero less as a cuckold than as a willing accomplice, saying that he even gave away his ex-wife in lieu of her father at the marriage ceremony, and then joined in with the wedding feast afterwards.[48]

Further intrigue surrounds the fact that at the time of her second betrothal, in the autumn of 39 BC, Livia was already six months pregnant with her second son Drusus, to whom she gave birth while living under Octavian's roof on 14 January 38 BC. She had only three days to recover from the delivery before the marriage ceremony took place on 17 January.[49] Predictably, Livia's pregnancy set tongues wagging. Octavian's reported anxiety for the proprieties, even pausing to consult priests about the permissibility of marrying a pregnant woman, did not stop the inevitable speculation over Drusus's paternity, summed up in a sarcastically witty epigram which enjoyed much popularity:

> How fortunate those parents are for whom
> Their child is only three months in the womb![50]

It is a perplexing set of anecdotes to sift through, and several theories have been put forward in a bid to untangle the story's narrative knot. There is the suggestion, for example, that mischievous satellites of Antony were the ones stoking the rumours of Drusus's illegitimacy. Others argue that Tiberius Nero's own sons had in adulthood tried to smother suggestions that their father was in any way a hapless cuckold by claiming his acquiescence in all the arrangements.[51] Both ideas are plausible, given the Roman establishment's propensity for casting smokescreens over uncomfortable historical episodes. However, there is clearly another agenda at stake behind the preservation of these stories. Those who read or listened to accounts of Octavian's seizure of Livia from Tiberius Nero were being invited to scrutinise the masculine credentials of the rivals, the axis on which all Roman political battles were fought. Some wanted to portray Tiberius Nero as the occupant of the moral high ground, others were being prodded to draw the conclusion that Octavian was the more manly of the two.[52]

At least one secure conclusion about the motives for Octavian's and

Livia's marriage can be drawn. Livia's proven fertility and family tree would have been absolutely priceless assets to her new husband. Octavian's relationship to the assassinated dictator Julius Caesar had opened a lot of doors in his rise up the ladder of public life, but the origins of his own immediate family were resolutely middle-class, laying him open to scorn from Rome's political aristocracy, quick to detect the scent of the bourgeois. Marriage to Livia, with her impeccable family lineage linking her to two of Rome's greatest and most revered political dynasties, the Claudians and the Livians, could silence those critics very effectively. To the ruthlessly ambitious Octavian, such considerations cannot have been far from his mind in turning his attentions to the wife of one of his opponents.

Whether or not Tiberius Nero objected to being supplanted at his wife's side by his younger rival, it would have done him little good to protest. His star was on the wane, his political credit was more or less used up in Rome and he had lost most of his property to the proscriptions – a stark contrast to the stratospheric rise of Octavian, now just one step away from holding all the aces in the imperial deck. Giving in with good grace was probably the best option open to him. He lived in quiet retirement for another five years after the divorce, before dying around the year 32 BC, after naming Octavian as guardian to both his sons. They had lived with Tiberius Nero since their parents' split, as prescribed by Roman law which usually granted custody of children to fathers after a divorce.[53] It was nine-year-old Tiberius who ultimately clambered on to the speaker's platform in the Roman forum to deliver his father's funeral eulogy.

Scribonia retreated into the shadows and seems never to have remarried though she lived well into her eighties, a grand old age in antiquity. It is unclear whether her little girl Julia was allowed to remain with her or went with her father – though the law automatically granted guardianship of her to Octavian, children were allowed to remain with their mothers when convenient. Given Julia's infancy and Octavian's political schedule, it is most likely that the girl stayed in her mother's care for the time being.[54] Scribonia's story, however, would intersect dramatically with Julia's further down the line. Octavian's hostile portrait of his ex-wife as a nagging shrew remains the most influential description of her, but others in antiquity were more admiring, the philosopher Seneca calling her a *gravis femina* (a 'serious' or 'dignified' woman) for her robust advice given many years later to a disgraced great-nephew on how to face his punishment like a man. Elsewhere the elegist of one of her daughters by an earlier marriage referred to her flatteringly as 'sweet mother Scribonia'.[55] It was a stock epithet of the obituarist's vocabulary. Yet Scribonia's unstinting loyalty as a mother was indeed in the end to be her most remarkable legacy.

Home for Livia's sons Tiberius and five-year-old Drusus after their father's death in 32 BC reverted to an elegant if relatively modest grey stone property on the Palatine hill, occupied by their now twenty-six-year-old mother and new stepfather since the occasion of their marriage. The house had been confiscated by Octavian during the wave of proscriptions in the aftermath of the battle of Philippi from the family of Quintus Hortensius, the famous orator and great rival of Cicero's who had amassed a fortune from his legal career and subsequently bequeathed the villa to his daughter Hortensia and son Quintus Hortensius Hortalus. Both these children were bitter opponents of Octavian – Hortensia, who as we have seen had inherited her father's gift for oratory, became a heroine to republican-minded women of the eighteenth century such as the British historian Catherine Macaulay for her stand against Octavian and his plans to tax wealthy Roman women in 42 BC. Hortensia's brother died at Philippi, fighting for Brutus and Cassius. By adopting their family home as his own, Octavian not only rubbed salt into their wound, but advertised the spoils of his victory at Philippi in the most blatant manner possible.[56]

Scant traces survive recording Livia's footsteps as Octavian's wife over the next decade. But we can sketch a picture of the luxurious lifestyle she, as a Roman matron moving in the first circles of republican Roman society, had access to, thanks to sources such as the correspondence of Cicero, whose letters yield an impression both of the domestic pleasantries and of the glamorous social scene on offer to fashionable, well-connected women like his own wife Terentia – whose enormous personal fortune was used to help bankroll Cicero's political career – and his daughter Tullia, the one-time object of Tiberius Nero's courtship.[57]

Written in the two decades prior to his brutal assassination in 43 BC, Cicero's letters, addressed chiefly to his close confidant Atticus, paint a self-gratifying portrait of idyllic family life. On the one hand, we hear references to Terentia and Tullia making long leisurely summer tours of the family's well-staffed seaside properties in coastal resorts such as Antium, to the south of Rome, a holiday destination

particularly popular with the empire's plutocrats. City life offered
plenty of distractions too. Though banned from entering public buildings of office such as the Senate, Roman women had relative freedom
of movement, certainly compared to their sequestered Athenian female
forebears. Besides women-only religious gatherings, such as the rites
of the goddess Bona Dea, there were also plenty of entertainments
to attend, plays and public games at which, unlike in later years, women
were still allowed to sit with the men. Such occasions were opportunities to socialise with friends as well as watch the shows, as the
subversive poet Ovid playfully observed in a poem some years later
when he said that the circus was a good place to start an affair and
advised his male readers to try fanning the object of their affection
with a racing programme to win her smiles.[58]

Then there were dinner parties to plan, host and attend, where
unlike their classical Athenian sisters, respectable Roman women ate
side by side on reclining couches with the men – though excessive
wine consumption was frowned upon for females.[59] One of our few
references to Livia's whereabouts during the 30s tells us that in 36 BC,
she, her children and Octavian were given permission to hold an annual
state banquet celebrating final victory over Sextus Pompeius, with
whom any illusion of a truce had since been shattered by Octavian's
divorce of Scribonia. Several naval clashes ensued before Sextus's defeat
by Octavian's lieutenant Marcus Agrippa at the battle of Naulochus.
If the celebratory banquet in question had followed traditional dinner-
party protocol, then Livia would have invited the female guests, and
Octavian the male guests.[60] Since men could attend parties on their
own with propriety but women had to be accompanied by a male
chaperone, male guests probably often outnumbered female guests,
and like their counterparts at mixed dinner parties in the nineteenth
century, for example, women were encouraged to confine their remarks
to acceptable subjects, and not attempt to muscle in on male conver-
sational topics such as the work of the latest poets. But they were
sometimes permitted to stay for after-dinner entertainments such as
literary recitations, magicians or even appearances by dwarves, though
there was disapproval in some quarters of women being allowed to
watch these spectacles.[61]

Like Terentia's, Livia's daily routine would have revolved to a large
extent around her husband's, which was dominated at least during
the first half of the day by the *salutatio*, the obligatory all-male daily
levee which started at dawn and witnessed a steady stream of friends

and clients trooping across the thresholds of prominent men like Cicero and Octavian, seeking their help or advice in various personal and business matters. Cicero himself claimed to hate these daily duties, protesting to Atticus that the only repose he had was with his wife and children. In the meantime, elite women were expected to spend the morning delegating tasks to the staff and supervising the running of the household. It is not known for certain if during the late republic women of Livia's and Terentia's standing received their own deputations of visitors during the morning *salutatio*, although Livia certainly did during the imperial era. But we do know of invitations extended by women to other women to pay courtesy-calls, and that occasionally women even received trusted male visitors unchaperoned, as Atticus's wife Pilia did when she borrowed Cicero's villa on the Lucrine Lake one summer for a vacation without her husband and daughter.[62]

Rome's fashionable families typically maintained several properties for their private use, moving out from their winter townhouses in early spring to their luxurious seaside villas on the shores of fashionable resorts such as Antium, and retreating in the sweltering summer months to the cool of the Alban and Sabine hills around Rome, whose slopes were flecked with the summer hideaways of the privileged.[63] As Cicero's letters illustrate, travel around Italy between family homes without the escort of one's husband was perfectly de rigueur for the respectable Roman matron, and certain wealthy Roman women of the period, including Terentia, Fulvia and Livia herself, are known to have been considerable property owners in their own right. The jewel in Livia's own impressive portfolio, probably inherited from her father after his death, was a magnificent rural villa at a locality known today as Prima Porta, 9 miles (14.4 km) outside the city on the Via Flaminia, one of the main arterial roads leading north out of Rome, and a key anecdote locates her here not long after her marriage to Octavian.

It was not until excavations of the skeleton of this villa, first discovered in 1596, were made in the late nineteenth century that the connection between it and a property known to have belonged to Livia in the region was made, validated in part by the discovery there of the so-called Prima Porta Augustus, the most famous statue in existence of Livia's husband.[64] Set high on a hill, the estate boasted beautiful gardens and breathtaking views of the local countryside from the terrace, with a magnificent vista across the valley of the River Tiber towards Rome in the distance and the Alban mountains whose slopes were littered with sacred shrines. Thanks to the rust-red tufa of the rocky local terrain, which was also used in the masonry of Livia's house, Prima Porta was once called *Saxa Rubra* or 'Red Rocks' in antiquity, while ancients knew the villa itself by the name *ad Gallinas Albas*, which translates colloquially as 'White Hen House'.[65]

Roman villa owners placed a premium on cool and shade in their hillside homes. Cascading fountains and fragrant gardens provided a refreshing oasis in the heat, and there was a preference for placing bedrooms and eating areas in the middle of the house away from the warmth of the exterior walls.[66] But there were still ways to let the outside in, as proven by the remarkable 1863 discovery at Livia's villa of a large underground summer dining-room (*triclinium*), measuring a little under 6 metres by 12 metres (19½ by 39 feet). Here the walls were painted with the miraculous indoor illusion of a Mediterranean garden paradise, richly planted with poppies, damask roses, periwinkles and chrysanthemums. Against a background palette of warm turquoise, blackbirds, nightingales, partridges and thrushes flit among the branches of lemon, orange, pomegranate and cypress trees, and there is even a birdcage perched on a marble balustrade, and a neat lawn enclosed by a cane-and-wicker fence. Cocooned from the scorching summer heat by this cool subterranean bower, which was accessible by a steep staircase, Livia would once have played the part of political hostess to guests of her husband's who had either come over from neighbouring villas or travelled the distance from nearby Rome, and she may even have been responsible for commissioning the unique design and decoration of the *triclinium*.[67]

Visitors peering closer at this lush botanical and ornithological mural, now illuminated in the cool, air-conditioned museum setting of the Museo Nazionale in Rome, will find an intriguing detail. Nestled among the palms and pines painstakingly re-created on the room's walls are laurel trees, a common enough sight in a Roman garden but one with a particular resonance in this case. For the presence of laurels in the decoration scheme, coupled with the referencing of 'white hens' in the villa's name, echoes a famous omen said to have befallen Livia while in residence, one that formed a key part of her husband's self-glorifying winner's story in the years after Actium.

The story goes, as told by more than one source from antiquity, that one day shortly after her marriage to Octavian, Livia was returning to the villa when suddenly a snow-white hen-chick, dropped from the beak of an eagle flying overhead, fell from the sky into her lap. Clutched in the chick's mouth was a twig of laurel wood, which Livia removed and decided to plant in the ground, on the advice of augurs. While the hen-chick produced a healthy brood of chicks, the laurel twig multiplied into a thriving grove of trees. The bird plummeting from the sky into Livia's lap sounds a little too good to be true, but recent excavations at Livia's villa indicate that the laurel grove was perhaps less mythical. Perforated earthenware planting pots, ideally suited for growing laurel trees, have been found on the south-west corner of the hillside at Prima Porta, fired from the villa's own kilns.[68]

Though the laurel grove itself still eludes excavators to this day, the idea of its existence served as a powerful talisman to generations of Livia's and Octavian's heirs. In later years, when Roman emperors descended from Octavian and Livia rode in triumphal processions, they carried and were garlanded with laurel branches which were said to have been plucked from the villa's grove.[69] As long as the laurels still grew at Livia's villa, the dynasty spearheaded by her husband would continue to thrive, and the laurel – a tree associated with the Roman god Apollo – would become Octavian's insignia, a logo for his divinely granted right to rule. Thus Livia, still just a sapling herself in historical terms, was given her first role of importance to play as a chatelaine in her husband's victory myth. She would imprint herself more and more in the Roman public's psyche over the coming years.

However, as the decade wore on, Livia continued to play a backseat role to her sister-in-law as far as the annals of the period were concerned. Octavia was still garnering plaudits for her role as mediator between the most powerful men of empire. In the spring of 37 BC, around the time that she was pregnant with her younger daughter Antonia Minor, she was called upon to douse another flare-up between her husband and her brother and act as go-between in a renegotiation of their power-sharing agreement at the Gulf of Tarentum in southern Italy.[70] Recalling the role played by legendary female peacemakers Veturia, Volumnia and the Sabines, ancient commentators on the new treaty report that it was only through the calm diplomacy of Octavia that an acceptable compromise was brokered, in which Antony and Octavian agreed to lend each other ships and soldiers for their respective military campaigns against Parthia and Sicily. In tribute, Octavia was toasted as 'a marvel of womankind'.[71] The celebration of her role as peacemaker led to her appearing once more on her husband's currency, this time with Antony's and Octavian's heads conjoined like Siamese twins and facing her profile – the reverse showed an image of three galleys with sails billowing. Other surviving bronze examples display the eroded features of Antony and Octavia facing each other on the reverse side of the coin while on the obverse we can just make out a couple cast in the role of the sea-god Neptune and his wife Amphitrite, riding in a chariot drawn by hippocamps, embracing each other on the waves.[72]

But this romantic tableau was little more than a charade. With matters wrapped up satisfactorily at Tarentum, including the renewal of the triumvirs' power-sharing agreement for another five years, Antony departed Italy once more in the autumn of 37 and returned to the east. Octavia usually spent winters with her husband in Athens, but this time he left his wife and children behind at Rome in the care of Octavian. As an excuse, he offered the pretext of keeping them out of harm's way while he continued a long-standing campaign against the Parthian Empire in the east. Yet it was less than the truth. In the words of Plutarch, 'an awful calamity which had been dormant for a long time' was due to reawaken.[73] Rome's uneasy political and domestic alliance was about to be irrevocably blown apart and the fragile foundations of Antony's and Octavia's union fully exposed. To borrow the phrase of another disillusioned royal wife, one might say there were three of them in this marriage.

The last and most famous incumbent of a Macedonian dynasty of pharaohs who had ruled Egypt for almost three centuries since its conquest by Alexander the Great, Cleopatra VII, queen of Egypt, had inherited her throne in 51 BC at the age of seventeen. She spent the next decade wrestling with internal family feuds provoked in some part by her willingness to do business with Roman leaders to whom she pledged military and financial support in return for territorial guarantees. During this period she formed a particularly close alliance with Julius Caesar, whose mistress she became, their union producing a son, Caesarion. After two years as a guest in his house on the Tiber, provoking mutterings of disapproval from Cicero, who in a letter to his old friend Atticus wrote that the queen's arrogance while in residence 'makes my blood boil', Caesar's assassination drove her back to Egypt.[74] Three years later, in 41 BC, Cleopatra was visited by a messenger inviting her to diplomatic talks in the city of Tarsus in southern Asia Minor with the triumvir Antony, who had taken charge of the Roman Empire's eastern holdings as part of his power-sharing agreement with Octavian and Lepidus. The rest – well, the rest was history.[75]

Antony's and Cleopatra's affair, which began while the former was still married to Fulvia, has been reimagined and re-enacted on countless occasions in literature, art and film, perhaps most notoriously and certainly most expensively in Joseph L. Mankiewicz's 1963 film production, *Cleopatra*, starring Elizabeth Taylor and Richard Burton.[76] Other incarnations range from the great eighteenth-century canvases of Renaissance painter Giovanni Battista Tiepolo, to silver watch-casings, snuff-boxes and kitsch, gaudy enamel figurines manufactured between the seventeenth and nineteenth centuries.[77] Amongst the literary reconstructions, Shakespeare's *Antony and Cleopatra* of course stands out, though there are also famous retellings from the likes of Chaucer, Boccaccio and Dryden. The principal source for Shakespeare's play though was an English translation of the account written at the beginning of the second century by Antony's biographer Plutarch.[78]

Although Plutarch had consulted earlier accounts including that of Quintus Dellius, an eye-witness to Antony and Cleopatra's first meeting, he clearly also relied on his imagination in the telling of the couple's tale, plugging gaps in his source material with his own fiction, describing scenes when no one but the protagonists were in the room or putting long speeches in the mouths of characters which could never have been recorded for posterity.[79] It is essential both to the history of Antony's and Octavian's clash at Actium, and to understanding the stories of the first Roman empresses who rise to prominence in the aftermath of her death, to recognise that Cleopatra, the original model for a kaleidoscopic array of medieval and modern copies of the Egyptian queen, is herself a composite, woven from a miscellany of different sources and judgements crafted, edited and disseminated in the climate of Rome's victory over Egypt at the battle of Actium and fostered by Cleopatra's eventual conqueror Octavian. The Cleopatra we know today, summed up by one ancient author as a woman prepared to use her *artes meretricae* ('whoreish arts') to get her way with the Roman Antony, is in fact a wraith, the echo of a phantasm created and sustained by the publicity machine of Octavian, who was intent on casting Cleopatra as the embodiment of barbarian feminine values whom it was Octavian's duty and destiny to crush, and in the process, win a moral victory both for the masculine Roman values of *virtus* ('courage') and *pietas* ('piety') which he claimed to represent, and for the traditional feminine traits of fidelity and chastity epitomised by his wife Livia and sister Octavia.

In the tale as told by Plutarch, Cleopatra's spectacular arrival in

Tarsus in 41 BC was followed by an exchange of competitive hospitality between herself and Antony, as each attempted to outdo the other by hosting lavish banquets, an encounter in which Antony came off looking the worst. Cleopatra's company at the dinner table was nonetheless sufficient to captivate him so thoroughly that she was able to whisk him off to Alexandria for the winter, all thought of his military duties abandoned. A recital of Antony's Egyptian sojourn follows, an eccentric catalogue of whimsical anecdotes and exploits portraying the couple as inveterate pleasure-seekers and pranksters. Cleopatra encouraged Antony in all manner of pastimes, including gambling and hunting, and they were even said to have formed a drinking club called the 'Society of Inimitable Livers', and to have dressed up as slaves to go gallivanting through the streets of Alexandria, much to the delight of the population. They spent money like water, ordering feasts for a party of twelve that would better have fed a hundred. The pair also played practical jokes. Annoyed at his lack of success fishing in the harbour of Alexandria one day while Cleopatra was watching, Antony told one of his slaves to swim underwater and attach some previously caught fish to the end of his line which he duly hauled up in triumph. Cleopatra turned the tables the next day, in front of a large audience of her friends whom she had forewarned, by ordering one of her own slaves to attach a fish clearly not native to the Mediterranean to Antony's hook, much to his embarrassment when he reeled it in.[80]

Whether rumour or fact, tales like this were priceless ammunition for Octavian over in Italy. In 40 BC, Cleopatra gave birth to twins, Alexander Helios and Cleopatra Selene, but news of Lucius's and Fulvia's rout by Octavian's forces in Perusia had already drawn Antony away from his Egyptian second family, back to Italy and his confrontation with Octavian. The result was the pact at Brundisium, ratified by Antony's marriage to Octavia. Cleopatra was suddenly out of the picture and remained so for the next three years, as Antony, tempted back into line alongside his rival, directed military operations against the Parthians from Athens, where he had set up home with Octavia.

But then in the autumn of 37 BC, while Octavia was still receiving praise for her role in brokering peace between her husband and her brother at Tarentum, Antony headed back to the east for a reunion with Cleopatra. He proceeded to attempt an invasion of Parthia in 36 BC, with Cleopatra as his financial backer, but was driven into a calamitous retreat, tarnishing his military reputation. Meanwhile

Octavian had killed two birds with one stone by defeating the triumvirs' old enemy Sextus Pompeius at the battle of Naulochus on 3 September and simultaneously ousting the hapless Lepidus from the third spot at the triumvirate's table on a charge of trying to usurp Octavian's authority in the battle for Sicily. Three had become two and the deck was steadily stacking in Octavian's favour.

The ace up Octavian's sleeve was Octavia. Just as she had been an instrument for peace, she was now to become an instrument for war. In the summer of 35 BC, not long after Antony had suffered his humiliating reversal in the Parthian campaign, Octavia travelled from Rome to her old marital home in Athens, taking with her money, army supplies and troop reinforcements for her husband. Plutarch is again our reporter, describing first Octavia's reception in Athens, where she found letters from Antony forbidding her from proceeding further, and her self-restraint despite her anger at his dissembling. He then sketches Cleopatra's mental turmoil at the thought that 'Octavia was coming to take her on in hand-to-hand combat' and her strategy of shamming illness as though grief-stricken at the thought of losing Antony. Reproached by Cleopatra's aides who plaintively censured him for neglecting the woman who loved him so much, Antony was said to have become 'so soft and effeminate' that he was persuaded to abandon his latest military project and return to her side in Alexandria. Octavia was forced to return to Rome but refused to leave the home she shared there with her husband, against the wishes of her brother. She elected to remain there caring both for her own children and for Antony's offspring with Fulvia, continuing to welcome his friends, and in the process 'hurting Antony without meaning to, because he became hated for wronging a woman of her fine quality'.[81]

The portrait of Cleopatra as a deceitful manipulator, of Antony as soft and effeminate and of Octavia as a faithful, wronged wife were all hallmarks of Octavian's increasingly vociferous campaign to persuade the Roman public that he was the only man to lead them. With typical tactical savvy, he seized with relish the opportunity to make serious political capital out of the trouble in his sister's marriage, and threw all of his weight behind a strategy aimed at boosting his credentials as a champion of old-fashioned conservative morality while painting Antony as the emasculated puppet of a foreign queen. In the process, a glass ceiling of sorts was broken for women in Roman public life, as Livia and Octavia became increasingly important in helping define Octavian's image as devoted husband, brother and family man.

The year 35 BC was the watershed. In a bid to ratchet up his campaign to sell the Roman public an image of his wife and sister as the new Cornelias for their age, Octavian approved the special grant of a series of remarkable honours and privileges to Octavia and Livia. Their new entitlements were threefold: first, they were awarded a protection known as *sacrosanctitas*, making it an offence to utter verbal insults against them. Secondly, they were given immunity from *tutela* – male guardianship – which effectively meant they had the freedom to manage their own financial affairs. Thirdly, statuary portraits of Octavia and Livia were to be commissioned for public display.[82]

These three marks of distinction put the two women in an extra-ordinary and unprecedented position. The right of *sacrosanctitas* was a concession reserved exclusively for the publicly elected male political class of tribunes. The granting of it to Octavia and Livia acknow-ledged their emergence into a position of public political significance hitherto closed off to women. It also suggests that there had been an escalation of the war of words between Antony's and Octavian's camps of supporters, which had led to retaliatory insults being directed at Livia and Octavia – or at least, that that was the impression Octavian *wanted* to create. The award of *tutela* was not completely innovatory, as it was a right that had long been shared by the Vestal Virgins. But all other Roman women, even those whose fathers and husbands were dead, were required to accept the supervision of a *tutor* or guardian, and the honour by association with the Vestals was clear. Octavia and Livia were to be treated on a par with the most revered group of women in Roman society.[83]

The grant of statues was potentially even more significant, however. Politicians of the Roman Republic had long proved themselves staunch opponents of the idea of allowing a woman to be venerated in public sculpture. In 184 BC, a speech by the great orator and moral stickler Cato the Elder had caustically disparaged the idea, and prior to Octavian's announcement in 35 BC, we hear of only a single other example where a real-life Roman woman was publicly honoured in the city with a statue in her likeness – who else but Cornelia, commem-orated for her role as mother of the Gracchi with the dedication of a bronze statue which is unfortunately lost.[84] But that exception notwithstanding, the idea of women taking their place in the male public gallery of portraits honouring Rome's mythological and historical leaders was still deeply alien to a senatorial class notoriously wary of permitting women to cross the threshold of politics.

Octavia of course already had a public portrait profile of sorts in the east, thanks to the coins issued by Greek and Asian mints under her husband Antony's jurisdiction during the more peaceful years of their marriage. Moreover, while statues of women were taboo in the city of Rome itself, it was not uncommon to erect statues of the wives, daughters and mothers of high-ranking men in the Greek eastern areas of empire. The royal houses of the east also displayed few qualms about granting space to their female dynasts on coins and statuary. In keeping with the portrait practices of the Ptolemies, Cleopatra herself projected her own image across her kingdom, in statuary, on temple reliefs and coins. Perhaps this was the key to Octavian's motivation in sanctioning such statues of his sister and wife in Rome. In giving the nod to a sculpture programme featuring Octavia and Livia, Octavian was pointedly setting up the women of his own family in direct competition with their eastern counterpart.[85]

But there were risks attached to such a ploy, given that public statuary of female family members in the east commonly went hand in hand with kingship, and might lay their sponsor open to the accusation of dynastic aspirations, a touchy subject in republican Rome. Octavian had to tread carefully. His gesture meant that in a single stroke, Octavia and Livia were emancipated from many of the usual supervisory restrictions on their gender, and simultaneously became the most scrutinised women in the entire city. Therefore, Octavian had to get these portraits just right, so as not to offend the traditionalists whose support he needed.

We cannot identify for certain which, if any, of the catalogue of surviving portraits we have of Livia and Octavia may be prototypes of these earliest statues, but one of the best contenders can be found on the ground floor of the Museo Nazionale in Rome.[86] A slightly pockmarked marble bust, just under 40 cm (15¾ inches) high, the face is of a serenely beautiful woman with regular symmetrical features and large heavy-lidded eyes, her neatly combed locks meticulously arranged into the quiff-like *nodus* hairstyle, with just a few tendrils allowed to escape from the hairline above her ears. Found at Velletri, south-east of Rome, it has been widely accepted as a portrait of Octavia, whose family originated from that region, and the identification is bolstered by the facial similarity to portraits of her brother

Octavian and comparisons to her own profile on coins. Moreover, the more old-fashioned style of her *nodus,* the hair whipped up into a higher peak than was the fashion in subsequent decades, supports the suggestion that this portrait may indeed be a close relative of those original sculptures commissioned of Octavia in 35 BC.[87]

The Velletri bust is the most commonly reproduced image of Octavia today. A far larger number and variety of ancient portraits survive for her sister-in-law Livia, thanks to the latter's greater longevity in the spotlight, but during this teething period for female sculpture, the portraits of both women were so similar that distinguishing them with any confidence is sometimes impossible. Coin and statuary portraits do not, regrettably, give us anything like a photographic facsimile of how Livia, Julia and other imperial women actually looked in real life, any more than portraits of Roman men do. Individual facial quirks do sometimes creep in, which can help with identification – for example, some of Livia's round-cheeked, thin-lipped early portraits betray a slight overbite shared by other members of the Claudian family, while Octavia has the serious expression and aristocratic bone structure which characterise portraits of her brother. But by and large, these were idealised images whose sponsors were less concerned with getting a good likeness than with projecting a blandly appropriate image that could be uniformly produced by artists and sculptors across the empire. This stern regularity in itself articulated the key message being silently preached.[88] By portraying Livia and Octavia in inscrutable, perfectly *nodus*-coiffed uniformity in their early portraits, a vindication of the virtues of traditional, decorous Roman womanhood was proclaimed, and a dignified reproof offered to Antony's desertion of his Roman wife for Egyptian Cleopatra.

We should not imagine that the empire's streets were suddenly flooded with images of women – that would have been to risk offending traditional ideas of a woman's place in the public sphere. But with a few strategically placed commissions, Octavian issued the Roman world with a clarion call, inviting them to see his wife and sister as muses for his project to resurrect a long-lost golden age of Roman history. A golden age when legendary women like Lucretia sacrificed themselves on the altar of duty. A golden age for which Octavian was tacitly offering himself up as the architect of restoration.

While Octavian set about projecting images of Octavia and Livia in marble as paradigms of feminine modesty to citizens of Rome,

Cleopatra replaced Octavia as the face of Antony's Roman coinage, issued by mints under his control. Surviving records of one issue of around 33 or 32 BC show that huge numbers of silver *denarii*, the currency of Rome, were commissioned on Antony's orders after he finally achieved some military success in the east by defeating Armenia with Cleopatra's financial help. These coins feature Antony on one side, and Cleopatra on the other, a ship's prow in the forefront to signal her contribution of naval power towards the victory.[89]

Despite the concession of statues to Livia and Octavia, the inclusion of a foreign queen on the official coinage of a Roman general was completely unprecedented and deeply provocative in a political culture so ideologically opposed both to the idea of a woman near the heart of power – a foreign one at that – and to the principle of monarchical government. In 34 BC, Antony took his victory celebrations further by staging a lavish Roman-style triumph in Cleopatra's home city of Alexandria, during which he was said to have formally given Cleopatra and her children vast gifts of territory, now known as the 'Donations of Alexandria'. Octavian knew exactly which button to press to make the Roman political classes nervous about what was happening in Alexandria. By playing on long-held Roman prejudices against the feminine, weak, immoral, servile and barbarous orient, he continued to aggressively portray Antony as a turncoat against traditional, male, Roman values, a poodle in Cleopatra's lap.

Antony directly rebutted at least one of the many charges Octavian levelled at him, that of being a drunkard, a common stereotype of the east, writing an essay titled 'On his Drunkenness', which has since been lost. In letters to his former brother-in-law, he also accused Octavian of hypocrisy for trying to score points off him on the grounds of sexual morality by recalling Octavian's own affairs:

> What has come over you? Do you object to my sleeping with Cleopatra? . . . what about you? Are you faithful to Livia Drusilla? My congratulations if, when this letter arrives, you have not been in bed with Tertullia, or Terentilla, or Rufilla, or Salvia Titsenia – or all of them. Does it really matter so much where, or with whom, you perform the sexual act?[90]

Harking back to his opponent's nuptials, Antony also claimed that his rival's marriage to Livia had been conducted 'in indecent haste', and reminded Octavian of times when his friends used to arrange for him line-ups of women and girls, stripped naked for his inspection, as though at a slave market.[91]

Just as in modern electioneering, making political capital out of the peccadilloes of one's opponents was a common tactic employed by rivals for office in republican Rome. The most famous grandees of this period – Cicero, Pompey, Julius Caesar – were all accused of seducing other men's wives at one time or another, so Antony's charge that Octavian had been unfaithful to Livia was nothing out of the ordinary. But it did need refuting if Octavian was explicitly setting himself up against Antony as the moral guardian of Roman values, and his first-century biographer Suetonius cites the excuses given by Octavian's friends, who, while admitting his infidelities, claimed none were motivated by unthinking lust. Instead, by tapping up the wives and daughters of his enemies, he was getting inside information that would help his political campaign, and thus defending Roman interests.[92]

Many of the most notorious Roman accounts of Cleopatra's infamy are preserved from poems and stories recorded after the final confrontation between the two sides at Actium. But they give us a flavour of the sort of invective that was aimed against her in the years before, including charges of sexual and culinary gluttony. Pliny the Elder, in the first century, wrote that Antony and Cleopatra had once challenged each other to see who could stage the most lavishly expensive banquet, and that Cleopatra had won the wager by tossing one of her pearl earrings into a goblet of vinegar, letting it dissolve and then nonchalantly swallowing it.[93] The story certainly captured the imagination and was one of the most popularly re-created episodes of art from the Renaissance to the eighteenth century. Such tales reflect a long-standing preoccupation on the part of Roman moralists who bemoaned the gluttonous materialism of pleasure-seeking plutocrats both among their own contemporaries and in previous eras. Pliny the Elder himself lamented that in his day, Romans spent over 100 million sesterces a year on pearls and perfumes imported from the east. Over-expenditure on food was a particular source of outrage.[94] Salacious stories of Antony's and Cleopatra's gluttonous banquets and wastefulness with money appealed to this moralising streak in Rome's conscience. Probably one of the most well-known habits of Cleopatra is that she liked to bathe in asses' milk, to keep her skin soft. The fact that the same bathing habit was said to have been shared by later Roman women who were regarded as profligate and corrupting, such as Nero's second wife Poppaea, may suggest that the practice was commonly attributed to any woman who was seen to offend morality. [95]

In the summer of 32 BC, after a year or two more of this cat-and-mouse baiting, Antony finally divorced the hapless Octavia, ordering some of his men to go to Rome and evict her tearfully from his house, and Octavian's propaganda machine swiftly whirred into overdrive.[96] He dispatched a delegation to the Vestal Virgins, who commonly acted as keepers of citizens' important papers, with orders to fetch Antony's will. When the Vestals refused to give it up, Octavian came to fetch the document himself, already primed as to its contents by two of Antony's supporters who had witnessed it and then subsequently defected. Once he had his hands on the will, Octavian called meetings of the Senate and the popular assembly, and proceeded to read it out. Among the passages he highlighted was the revelation that Antony was leaving vast sums of money to his children with Cleopatra, and, most devastatingly, that Antony had requested that he should be buried alongside the Egyptian queen in Alexandria.[97]

Octavian's action in publicising another man's will was illegal and there are different accounts of the Roman reaction to it. Some say Octavian's claims were treated with unease and some scepticism while others recount that it convinced everyone, even Antony's closest friends, of their worst fears that Antony was completely under a woman's thumb and even planning to move the headquarters of Roman government to the Nile.[98] But the outcome was the same. Tales of Antony, a Roman general, dressing in oriental clothing and walking behind the litter of a woman in company with her eunuchs could not be stomached. In October, a resolution was passed declaring war. Because Octavian did not want to incur the charge of starting a civil war, however, the official target of his declaration was not Antony, who was after all a fellow Roman citizen, but Cleopatra herself, forcing Antony to show his hand in opting to fight on the side of Egypt.[99]

The next few months were spent in preparation for battle. Armies were raised, war chests filled and allegiances traded with promises of land and rewards. On both sides the ongoing battle for the right to claim just cause continued over the autumn and winter of 32 BC. Stories of portents and omens predicting defeat for Antony were circulated, probably by Octavian's agents. Octavian himself publicly claimed that Antony was on drugs and that when it came to the fight their opponents would be Cleopatra's hairdresser, her eunuch and her ladies-in-waiting.[100] In fact Antony, with the wealthy Cleopatra as his financial backer, started out with a greater number of troops and funds at his disposal.[101] But, thanks to the superior stewardship of Octavian's lieutenant Agrippa, Antony's advantage was eaten into during initial engagements over the spring and summer of 31 BC. Finally, the bulk of Antony's naval fleet were pegged back to an anchorage just off Actium, at the narrow mouth of the Ambracian Gulf. On the afternoon of 2 September, after several days of skirmishing and stand-offs, the two opposing fleets steadily advanced towards each other across the glimmering blue surface of the Ionian Sea to decide the destiny of the Roman Empire.[102]

> . . . on one side was Augustus Caesar, leading the men of Italy into battle alongside the Senate and the People of Rome, its gods of home and its great gods . . . on the other side, with the wealth of the barbarian world . . . came Antony in triumph . . . with him sailed Egypt and the power of the East from as far as distant Bactria, and there bringing up the rear was the greatest outrage of all, his Egyptian wife! On they came at speed, all together, and the whole surface of the sea was churned to foam by the pull of their oars and the bow-waves from their triple beaks . . . fresh blood began to redden the furrows of Neptune's fields . . . But high on the headland of Actium, Apollo saw it all and was drawing his bow. In terror at the sight the whole of Egypt and of India, all the Arabians and all the Shebans were turning tail and the queen herself could be seen calling for winds and setting her sails by them. She had untied the sail-ropes and was even now paying them out.[103]

Years after the battle of Actium, the image of Cleopatra hoisting her purple sails and lamely fleeing the scene of the fight with Antony in hot pursuit was an abiding theme of literature written in honour of Octavian's victory. Actium did not bring down the final curtain, and in fact relatively few casualties were suffered, but it was the pivot on which the fate of Octavian's and Antony's contest was decided. After escaping with some of their ships still intact, Antony and Cleopatra resumed life in Alexandria, where they remained for another year until Octavian arrived in the summer of 30 BC and dealt a final knockout blow to their land and sea forces. The final act of Antony's and Cleopatra's story became the stuff of legend. After a despondent Antony took his own life and bled to death in Cleopatra's arms, the Egyptian queen managed to convince Octavian of her pliability, even offering gifts to Octavia and Livia to earn their goodwill. She thus earned permission to visit Antony's tomb, where she was later found dead on a golden couch, through self-inflicted poisoning either by asp bite, as the most popular report had it, or by a vial of venom secreted in one of her hairpins. One of her dying ladies-in-waiting, Charmion, who had also ingested poison, had the breath to hiss, in response to an angry reproach from one Roman soldier, 'It is no more than this lady, the descendant of so many kings, deserves', a line borrowed sixteen centuries later by Shakespeare, in his own staging of the scene.[104] Thwarted of his hopes to carry his illustrious prisoner of war back to Rome, Octavian later had an image of Cleopatra carried through the city streets in his triumphal procession, an image which was said to have featured a snake clinging by its jaw to the dead queen.

The last political rivalry of the republic was over. Unlike her father and ex-husband, Livia had backed the right horse.

Livia did not find herself empress of Rome overnight. The transformation from republic to monarchy in the aftermath of Antony's and Cleopatra's deaths was not instantaneous: Rome was still raw and bloodied from decades of civil war, and Octavian understood the need to tread carefully, all too aware of the fate of his great-uncle Julius Caesar, whose attempts to strong-arm the state into accepting autocratic rule had resulted in his assassination. In 27 BC, three years after the deaths of Antony and Cleopatra, Octavian made a great show of renouncing the extraordinary dictatorial powers granted him as a triumvir, pledging to restore the republic and declining the trappings of despotic kingship. In return for this self-effacing gesture, the Senate, its palm greased by the promised restoration of its former constitutional powers, urged Octavian to become consul-for-life and pressed on him the appellations of *Augustus*, meaning 'divinely favoured one', and *princeps* or 'first citizen', an epithet familiarly used in the republic for a leading statesman. Effectively, they handed him the keys to the empire, a mandate for absolute power carefully cloaked in traditional republican language in order to oil the wheels of transition.

Livia herself received no official title for the time being. Augustus shied away from giving his wife an honorific name equivalent to his and it was not until after his death almost forty years later that her role in the dynastic set-up was recognised with a variant of his own *cognomen*, *Augusta*. The word 'empress' is now accepted shorthand for the woman married to the Roman emperor, but there is no equivalent for it in Latin. The Roman public had apparently voiced no opposition to having portraits of Livia on display in public spaces since the grant of 35 BC. But to accord her official status akin to that enjoyed by queens of the eastern royal families, in a society still getting acclimatised to the idea of one-man-rule, where the memory of Cleopatra was still very raw, was one step too far.[105]

Augustus's victory had been won on the back of a campaign promise to clean up Rome, not just its streets and public spaces but its heart and soul. Having castigated Antony and Cleopatra as denizens of the corrupting vice and moral laxity that had so weakened the old republic, Rome's new ruler pledged himself as the defender of the old-fashioned virtues of a rose-tinted past, an age when men put down their ploughs to go to war and women would die rather than betray their marriage vows. If that illusion was to work, the emperor's own family closet had to be skeleton-free. Thus while Augustus set about rebuilding neglected temples and passing legislation that promised to restore decency, his elder sister Octavia, his daughter Julia and his wife Livia would be enlisted as faithful reincarnations of the virtuous women of that golden age, the Lucretias, Veturias and Volumnias whose chaste, wise ideals had helped in the past to save Rome.

But at least one of these women was to prove a far less malleable recruit to the cause than the others. Augustus, as one scholar has phrased it, may have 'self-consciously fashioned a family legacy as compelling as Jackie Kennedy's Camelot'.[106] But like Camelot, the dream turned sour, the mirage shimmered and faded.

First Family: Augustus's Women

The political agenda of Rome's first emperor began, quite literally, at home. Determined to prove to his public that he really was 'first among equals', a man of the people, a regular Joe just like them, Augustus declined the opportunity of moving to a rich palace in the style of an eastern dynast like Cleopatra, opting instead to remain with his family in their old house on the exclusive but densely populated Palatine hill, where the public could walk right past their front door – the ancient equivalent of a modern media-savvy politician leaving his name in the public telephone directory.[2]

Laurel trees flanked the entrance of the emperor's front door, perhaps grown from cuttings taken from Livia's Prima Porta estate in an advertisement of the empress's role as the bountiful chatelaine of the new imperial headquarters. Otherwise an oak wreath given to Augustus by a grateful state was all that outwardly distinguished the house from its neighbours. The egalitarian façade was kept up on the inside, and with its stone-grey minimalist interior and plain furnishings, the home where Rome's 'first family' lived certainly struck at least one future Roman visitor as modest in comparison to the grandiose residences of later emperors:

> [Augustus's] new palace was remarkable neither for size nor for elegance;
> the courts being supported by squat columns of peperino stone, and
> the living rooms innocent of marble or elaborately tessellated floors
> ... how simply Augustus's palace was furnished may be deduced by
> examining the couches and tables still preserved, many of which would
> hardly be considered fit for a private citizen.[3]

Suetonius, the author of this description, had the opportunity of visiting the house only decades after Livia's and Augustus's occupancy. His description of its relative lack of luxury can be corroborated today thanks to excavations on the Palatine hill between 1861 and 1870 by Pietro Rosa, an Italian architect and topographer who was working under the commission of Napoleon III – himself the scion of an imperial dynasty and obsessed with finding the palaces of the Caesars.[4] Rosa's discovery in 1869 of part of Augustus's house – thought perhaps to have been the personal quarters of Livia herself, thanks to the uncovering of a lead water pipe inscribed with her name – proved that it was indeed paved in black and white mosaic rather than the more expensive option of imported marble, a canny use of local stone that eloquently conveyed the modest tastes of the new imperial family to the Roman public.[5]

Admittedly, the old estate confiscated from Hortensius had expanded in the last decade. Two years after his marriage to Livia, Augustus had acquired a neighbouring property, a villa formerly belonging to the Roman senator Catulus, once one of the richest men in Rome. The purchase made Augustus the largest landowner on the Palatine, and the combined buildings now did not just house the apparatus of imperial government but provided living accommodation to the entire family circle. Gorgeous wall paintings of mythological characters and rural landscapes in a rich palette dominated by expensive red cinnabar and yellow, advertised the family's importance and social prominence, albeit in a way that toed the fine line between good taste and offensive ostentation. On becoming *princeps*, Augustus also added an extension to his home in the form of a temple to his patron god Apollo which covered an area half the size of a football pitch. With a deity living next door, Augustus took care to affect a sober personal aesthetic, encouraging his family members to do the same.

So while Augustus's own abstemious personal habits were broadcast for scrutiny, including the information that he slept in the same bedroom on a low bed with simple coverings regardless of the season, subsisted on a frugal diet of coarse bread, fish, cheese and figs and spurned the silks and fine linens worn by plutocrats, new empress Livia also affected to have little time for fussing about her appearance and was said to have shadowed her husband's example by dressing in an unobtrusive style and avoiding personal adornment.[6] This aped the dictum of the admired Cornelia, who had once famously retorted to a female companion showing off her jewels that she herself had no need of such finery, asserting magnificently: 'My jewels are my children.'[7] Even the recipe Livia purportedly used for toothpowder was a frugal concoction said to have been in common use, consisting of dried common garden nettles (a particular species chosen for its gritty, abrasive quality) soaked in brine and baked with rock salt until charred, an unappetising-sounding concoction, albeit one scented in her case with exotic imported spikenard oil.[8]

Another of the populist fiats issued from the Palatine was that the emperor's simple woollen gowns were made personally by Livia, Octavia, Julia, or in later life, one of his granddaughters. Wool-working was thought of as the ideal pastime for a Roman matron, as reflected in Rome's legends of virtuous women busy at their looms and spindles, and in the custom of draping uncombed wool around the doorway when a bride was led across the marital threshold for the first time.[9] Augustus's encouragement of his wife's, sister's and daughter's cultivation of the skill fostered the illusion of a household of unassuming domestic tranquillity and reassuring moral propriety. Looms were typically set up in the atrium, the most public place in the house, where, in wealthy households like this, slaves would have the best light to work in under the watchful eye of their mistress. Visitors and curious passers-by loitering in the busy street outside the emperor's home, peering through the large double doors – which were kept permanently and purposely open – would thus apparently have been treated to the sight of the empress and her female cohort in the dark, cool atrium, engaged in this homely act.[10]

Augustus's attempts to paint his female relatives as rustic sisters of the loom, were hard to square with the fact that the Palatine household was staffed by a cast of hundreds, to some of whom was surely delegated the task of making Augustus's clothes. In fact, we can probably even put a name to at least one of the individuals involved. For in 1726, an extraordinary building was excavated on Rome's Appian Way, the discovery of which permitted the reconstruction of an almost forensic profile of the staff – mostly male as it turns out – who did the Augustan family's daily bidding.

The building was the *Monumentum Liviae*, a *columbarium* or funerary vault built near the end of Augustus's reign. It contained the cremated remains of over a thousand Roman slaves and freedmen, their ashes packed in row upon row of *ollae* (burial jars) stacked in tiny niches around the vault, like pigeon-holes – hence the name *columbarium*, which literally means 'dovecote'. Most of those entombed here worked for the imperial household, and thanks to invaluable recent research into the marble plaques beneath each niche, we now know that approximately ninety of the individuals whose ashes were found worked for Livia herself, making her the principal patron of the vault. Hairdressers, masseuses, doorkeepers, copyists and clerks, accountants, footmen, wool-weighers, window-cleaners, shoemakers, builders, plumbers, furniture-polishers, goldsmiths, silversmiths, bakers, catering-managers, medical staff, wet-nurses, even someone to set her pearls – individuals employed by Livia in all these occupations and more are recorded here. Amongst those recorded by name, we know of a freedman called Auctus, whose job as a *lanipendius* was to weigh and dole out wool to the slave women of the imperial house to use at their looms.[11]

The remains in the *Monumentum Liviae* represent only a sample of the staff who worked in Livia's Roman establishment, and do not include those who worked in her various other properties such as the Prima Porta villa. Only the wealthiest in Roman society could afford to keep such staff numbers, and the highly specialised nature of the tasks they performed testified to the wealth and prestige of their owner. Livia's wardrobe was so bureaucratised that she had two attendants to look after her ceremonial dress, another to put her clothes away, and another, called Parmeno, in charge of just her purple garments. Lochias the *sarcinatrix* mended her clothes; Menophilus the shoemaker – *calciator* – kept the empress shod in the thonged sandals and cork-soled shoe-boots commonly worn by Roman women; and the job-title of Eutactus the *capsarius* suggests his duty was to watch over a box of some sort, either a storage-chest for Livia's clothes, or a more portable receptacle that served as the empress's 'handbag'.[12]

We should probably take the image of Livia and Octavia sitting in full view of passing members of the Roman populace lovingly weaving togas for Augustus at the same face value as the cookie-bake-off competition held every four years between potential American presidential spouses.[13] Given Augustus's talent for spin, it is not hard to imagine that the scene of his wife and sister weaving was choreographed on occasion to keep the public entertained and to attempt to convince them that the first family practised what they preached, though the Roman populace would surely have taken the image with a pinch of salt.

But for all this careful stagecraft, transparency was the watchword of the day. Indeed, so keen was Augustus's concern on this point that he was still repeating it in his old age, reputedly forbidding his only daughter Julia and his granddaughters 'to say or do anything underhand or which might not be reported in the daily chronicles' – the bulletin of daily news issued from the Palatine to the public.[14]

In Julia's case, it was to prove a hollow warning.

We last saw Julia when she was a squalling day-old infant, newly delivered by her mother Scribonia's midwives on the eve of Augustus's departure to set up home with Livia. By the time her father became the ruler of the Roman Empire, she had reached the age of ten and been welcomed into the happy family tableau that Augustus was so eager to promote. On the Palatine, she was not short of playmates, surrounded by a house full of cousins and stepsiblings fairly close to her in age, including her stepbrothers Tiberius and Drusus, her cousin Antonia Minor – the youngest of Octavia's four daughters – and Octavia's son Marcellus, the latter three years Julia's senior.[15]

Although we are often told in ancient imperial biographies about the salad days of the boys who grew up to be emperor, the same Roman chroniclers were uninterested in the formative years of their female sisters and cousins like Julia. Based on accounts of the upbringing of other Roman girls of her milieu, we know that childhood for a girl like Julia was over all too quickly. In an illustration of the abrupt transition between infancy and adulthood, bypassing adolescence, if a girl died before reaching marriageable age – which was set at a legal minimum of twelve by Julia's father – her favourite toys might be buried with her, toys that served as learning aids instilling in a girl the ideal to which she should aspire in adult life. Jointed dolls of ivory and bone have been found in the coffins of young Roman girls, dolls with full child-bearing hips quite unlike the proportions of, say, a modern Barbie, and with their hair styled in the fashions in vogue among elite women of the time.[16]

As a child, Julia's hair would have been styled more simply than this adult alter ego, tied back with woollen bands or *vittae* until it was long enough to be pinned up in the stiff *nodus* favoured by her stepmother and aunt, which would have happened just as she was nearing the age of marriage. A long, simple, sleeved tunic bordered with a purple stripe was the standard uniform for both freeborn boys and girls at Rome, and a protective neckchain called a *bulla* in the case of boys and a moon-shaped *lunula* for girls (the moon being the symbol of Diana, the Roman goddess of chastity) their only adornment. Despite the Roman fixation on roomy female hips, underneath the tunic girls also wore a breastband or *strophium*, whose purpose was

to strap down their budding breasts, in a bid to make them conform
to the otherwise slender Roman ideal for women's bodies.[17]

Prior to marriage, a girl's upbringing varied widely from household to household, depending on the wealth and inclination of her
family. Basic literary skills in reading and writing were taught to most
girls of the upper classes but few progressed to the more advanced
education in rhetoric and philosophy provided for their male siblings
beyond the age of ten or eleven. Instead, as underlined by Augustus's
own educative recommendations to the women of his family, a
premium was placed on domestic talents useful in marriage. A slave
girl born within her mistress's house – like Livia's hairdresser Dorcas
– might also be given an education, but of a vocational kind.[18]

The education of women was a controversial subject during the
early imperial period. Some philosophers argued that girls should
receive a similar schooling to boys, but a more vocal, traditionally
minded seam of opinion deplored the notion and predicted that women
who were given too much education either became pretentious
witterers or amoral hussies.[19] A few elite families however, particularly those with a proud intellectual tradition such as the families of
Quintus Hortensius or Cicero, nevertheless encouraged their daughters as well as their sons to emulate their forebear's educational achievements. Augustus's old *bête noire* Hortensia, who famously took on the
triumvirs from the rostrum in 42 BC, may have been one of the only
women ever to win fame as a public speaker, but tutors in grammar
were employed for others such as Caecilia, a daughter of Cicero's
friend Atticus, while the great Cornelia wrote letters which were
published as acclaimed pattern-plates of style. Music lessons, once
frowned on as inappropriate, crept onto the curriculum in a few households, and some girls learnt to read and write in Greek as well as
Latin. Providing such an all-round education was not, however, motivated by any progressive pedagogical philosophy but by the very traditionally minded desire to ensure that girls destined to be the wives of
prominent politicians would make suitable partners and hostesses for
their husbands in their careers, and good guardians of the education
of their sons, which they were expected to oversee.

Given the evidence that private tutors were employed for privileged
girls such as Caecilia, Julia herself in all likelihood benefited from the
tuition of Marcus Verrius Flaccus, the grammarian whom Augustus
imported into his house at the enormous annual salary of 100,000
sesterces to teach the young male personnel of the Palatine household,

though she would certainly have spent some time acquiring the more domestic skills that her father was so determined the women of his family should be seen to have.[20] We know that at least one of Julia's daughters received a literary education and when one also considers Julia's privileged situation, living in a house that was visited daily by the greatest cultural ambassadors of the day including Horace and Virgil, and with access to the newly built imperial library on the Palatine, it is no wonder that centuries later she was remembered as having had a 'love of letters and a considerable store of learning – not hard to come by in her home'.[21]

But reservations about the extent to which a woman should be educated did not go away. All too often, the description of a girl as *docta*, or 'clever', was a euphemism for something far less respectable. In Julia's case, this would turn out to be painfully true.

For the first half of Augustus's reign, the women of the imperial household remain safely out of the literary headlines. For the vast majority of the Roman Empire's residents, public portraits were their only point of visible connection with the emperor and his family. Official prototype sculptures of the imperial family were commissioned and created at Rome and then dispatched to the provinces where they served as a model for local sculptors, workshops and coin die-cutters to copy. Variations might result when individual artists or mints took creative liberties, but the basic portrait type remained the same.[22] Once publicly displayed in town forums, temple porches or even wealthy private homes, these silent portraits served as a reminder to the empire's female population of the role models they should be looking to emulate. As she came of age, portraits of the emperor's daughter Julia showed her with her hair twisted into the same stiff, controlled *nodus* favoured by her stepmother and aunt, under whose aegis she was now being brought up.[23] The overall effect was of conformity with good old republican maxims of domestic purity and faithfulness, albeit advertised through a far from traditional medium.

Under the radar, however, and despite continuing to model the stay-at-home-matron look in her own public portraits, Livia herself at least was steadily and unobtrusively making a name for herself. Augustus spent much of the period between 27 and 19 BC abroad, touring his imperial holdings in first Gaul and Spain, and then later in the east. Even though a conservative seam of Roman opinion frowned at the prospect of women accompanying their husbands on overseas travel, Livia accompanied the emperor, underlining the importance Augustus was placing on his wife in projecting his image abroad. Though her presence received little acknowledgement from the major ancient historians of Augustus's reign, the silent testimony of objects dedicated by Livia in the region – including a curious and unexplained gold epsilon (the Greek letter 'E') at Delphi in Greece – suggests that she fulfilled various ceremonial duties of dedication roughly equivalent to the ribbon-cutting ceremonies that the wife of a visiting head of state might be expected to perform today.[24]

To some extent, Livia was there simply to see and be seen by the crowds who came out to watch the vast, canopied, silk-upholstered imperial litter as it trundled by at a leisurely 20-mile (32-km) a day speed, tracing an itinerary that included appearances at notable tourist sites such as the oracle at Delphi. Roman emperors liked to travel in style, and Augustus's litter trailed an army of mule-drawn wagons carrying slaves for every contingency, including cooks, maids, doctors and hairdressers. One successor to Augustus went so far as to have a game board fitted in his carriage, and another equipped his with swivelling seats.[25] Despite the taboo on travelling females, Augustus's huge entourage in all certainty contained ladies-in-waiting to act as chaperones to his wife, while more stimulating female companionship was provided by counterparts in the empire's dependent territories, women such as King Herod of Judaea's wife Salome, who was to become a lifelong friend and correspondent. Certain stop-offs even resembled something of a homecoming. During one of Augustus's trips to Greece in the late 20s, the emperor paid the Spartans the tribute of attending their public mess, apparently in recognition of their aid to Livia when she took refuge there with Tiberius Nero, ironically of course while hiding from Augustus himself.[26]

Yet Livia's presence on these trips was about far more than window-dressing, as proven by the evidence of a letter written by Augustus to the Greek islanders of Samos, which was found inscribed into the marble of an archive-holding wall during excavations of the Turkish ancient city of Aphrodisias in 1967. Some time during the early part of Augustus's reign, the Samos islanders had written to the emperor requesting their independence from imperial control. In his preserved reply, Augustus apologetically explains to the islanders why he must refuse a privilege he had granted to no one but the people of Aphrodisias. He had taken his decision reluctantly, he tells the Samians, despite the vigorous canvassing efforts on their behalf by Livia:

I am well disposed to you and should like to do a favour to my wife
who is active in your behalf, but not to the point of breaking my
custom.[27]

Livia may have failed at the first attempt. But evidently she could be
a persuasive negotiator. For after Augustus's travelling party spent two
winters on Samos between 21 and 19 BC, he finally granted them their
independence. That the Samos islanders recognised the empress's
efforts on their behalf is suggested by the fact that statues dedicated
to Livia have been found on the island.[28]

That a woman could serve as a gatekeeper controlling access to
her husband was in one sense nothing new to Roman politics. During
the republican era, several elite women did indeed act as patrons and
intermediaries between their husbands and outside parties. Cicero, for
example, applied to Mucia Tertia when seeking an alliance with her
husband Pompey, and even Cleopatra was said to have attempted to
get Livia and Octavia onside during her negotiations after Actium with
her captor Augustus, offering them a gift of jewellery and expressing
the hope that they would be sympathetic towards her.[29] But such
arrangements had always been conducted very much behind closed
doors, and women like Mucia Tertia would never have dreamed of
being accorded public recognition for their efforts with the award
of statues or other official honours.

Livia was now acting out a traditional female role in a *public* political
context, and gaining kudos and publicity for doing so. She and her
imperial female counterparts were being granted a key role as goodwill
ambassadors, promoting the moral values of the new regime through
their decorous displays of traditional female behaviour, while simultaneously gaining unprecedented publicity as mediators between the
emperor and his subjects. While his first answer to the people of
Samos's plea for independence was no, by publicly advertising Livia's
efforts on their behalf, Augustus hoped to sweeten the pill of his refusal
and prevent too large a drop in his popularity among the islanders.

This apparent willingness to advertise his wife's role in his affairs
testifies to Augustus's determination to politicise his private life.
According to his ancient biographers, his obsession on this point even
extended to his writing down all his private conversations in one of
the notebooks he habitually carried about his person, including the
more 'serious' ones he had with Livia, so keenly conscious was he of
how his private life might reflect on his public persona. In one such

'recorded' conversation that was later widely published, Livia even offered a sleep-deprived and stressed Augustus lengthy advice on how to deal with a conspiracy led by Pompey the Great's grandson Cornelius Cinna to depose him, urging him to waive the punishment of death in order to avoid incurring a charge of despotism from the public, advice which Augustus duly follows:

> I have some advice to give you, – that is, if you are willing to receive it, and will not censure me because I, though a woman, dare suggest to you something which no one else, even of your most intimate friends, would dare to suggest . . . I have an equal share in your blessings and your ills, and as long as you are safe I also have my part in reigning, whereas if you come to any harm (may the gods forbid), I shall perish with you . . . I . . . give you my opinion to the effect that you should not inflict the death penalty [on these men] . . . the sword, surely, cannot accomplish everything for you . . . for people do not become more attached to anyone because of the vengeance they see meted out to others, but they become more hostile because of their fears . . . heed me, therefore, dearest, and change your course . . . it is impossible for a man to guide so great a city from democracy to monarchy and make the change without bloodshed, – but if you continue in your old policy, you will be thought to have done these unpleasant things deliberately.[30]

The intended effect of preserving her speech may have been to make Livia seem like the voice of feminine compassion, intervening to bring a peaceful conclusion to a potentially violent stand-off, just as Roman heroines of the past had once done.[31] But intriguingly, it is clearly also a portrait of a woman with a shrewd political brain, and a canny awareness of what would play best to her husband's audience.

Given that she was portrayed as so influential a figure in his life, Livia's and Augustus's real personal relationship is naturally a source of fascination. But with only the contradictory evidence of the emperor's biographers to go on, it is not an easy one to fathom. As we have seen, marriage was typically arranged for prosaic rather than romantic motives in Roman society. Nevertheless, married love was celebrated on funerary epitaphs, and, more convincingly, published letters, for all their rhetorical formality, yield glimpses of close, affec-tionate, even passionate relationships between couples, and devastated grief at separations caused by death.[32] Augustus's and Livia's own marriage, embarked on in such controversial circumstances, was one of the longest recorded in Roman history, lasting more than fifty years in total. Predictably, it was advertised in public art and some of the more adulatory literature of the time as a model of marital concord. However, some literary sources suggest that Augustus used his overseas trips as an excuse to make assignations with the wife of his friend and cultural adviser Maecenas, lending weight to Antony's jibes about his enemy's hypocrisy in reproaching him for his affair with Cleopatra. One Roman historian writes of Augustus that Livia was 'the one woman whom he truly loved until his death', yet intriguingly also includes the information that in his old age Livia herself enabled her husband's philandering by providing him with virgins, whom he had a passion for deflowering.[33] This particular anecdote was the inspiration for a mischievous entry in a 1787 pornographic compendium compiled by the pseudonymous society adventurer Baron d'Hancarville, the *Monumens du culte secret des dames romaines*, which features a mocked-up Roman cameo image of a naked Livia performing a sex act on Augustus, with the caption: 'The complaisance of this princess for her husband was extraordinary. Not content with searching everywhere for beautiful girls to amuse him, she also did not refuse to use her beautiful hand for the pleasure and lubrication of the emperor.'[34]

Towards the end of her life, Livia was said to have offered up the following explanation to an interviewer asking how she had obtained so much influence over Augustus, saying that she had done so 'by being scrupulously chaste herself, doing gladly whatever pleased him, not meddling with any of his affairs, and, in particular, by pretending neither to hear or to notice the favourites that were the objects of his passion'.[35] Whether we can trust this or any of her lengthy sermon on the Cinna conspiracy as a direct quote from her lips must remain an unanswered question, but as a blueprint for the role of dutiful, chaste politician's wife that she certainly affected, this matter-of-fact statement could not be bettered, winning her the plaudits of loyalists who called her a worthy successor to the women of Rome's golden age, and inspiring an anecdote that she once intervened to spare the lives of some men who were going to be put to death for straying into her line of sight while they were naked, saying that for a chaste woman such as herself, naked men were no different from statues.[36]

But not everyone, it seems, admired Livia in the role of consort and confidante to the emperor. 'I have my part in reigning . . .' she is supposed to have said in her conversation with Augustus about the

Cinna conspiracy. It was a sentiment that was to prove a red rag to a bull for some.[37]

One source of disappointment in Livia's and Augustus's marriage could not be disguised by any amount of obfuscation. Although both had produced offspring with their previous partners, their own union was destined to remain childless, despite it being the emperor's 'dearest wish', wrote Suetonius, that they should conceive together. A child born prematurely did not survive, prompting Pliny the Elder to claim that theirs was one of those rare unions that had 'a certain physical incongruity between them', allowing them to produce children with others but not with each other.[38] The couple's sterility was a piece of ill-fortune mocked by Cleopatra during the war of words in the run up to Actium, and although it may sound like a cheap shot, Livia's and Augustus's childlessness had serious and long-term repercussions both for the Julio-Claudian dynasty and the principle of future imperial succession.[39]

For dynasties need heirs. Although he was destined to live to a great old age, Augustus's famously weak constitution drove him repeatedly to his sickbed throughout the first decade of his reign, lending particular urgency to the dilemma of which of his relatives would ultimately replace him. Female primogeniture was out of the question, ruling out Augustus's only biological child, Julia. Two leading candidates were left – Tiberius, Livia's eldest son from her marriage to Tiberius Nero, or Marcellus, the eldest son of the emperor's sister Octavia.

Octavia had not been forgotten in Augustus's plans since his succession, far from it. Now in her forties, since the dissolution of her marriage to Antony, she had been living with her brother and sister-in-law on the Palatine, where she had assumed the duty of bringing up at least nine children, not just her own son and four daughters by her marriages to Claudius Marcellus and Antony, but also Antony's four surviving children sired with Fulvia and Cleopatra.[40] As mother to such a vast brood, she evoked the example of that paragon of motherhood Cornelia, herself the mother of twelve, and it was an association that Augustus explicitly encouraged.

One of the most important legacies of Augustus's forty-one year reign was his physical transformation of the Roman city skyline. He famously boasted that he had discovered Rome a city of brick and left it a city of marble, and Octavia was to feature significantly within this process.[41] During this period, Rome's narrow streets and tenement blocks were almost constantly choked with the dust and clattering din of construction work, on projects such as the new Julio-Claudian family mausoleum on the banks of the River Tiber, a vast circular tomb of white travertine whose fat concrete belly was destined to become the eternal resting place for the ashes of the emperor and his successors. Augustus's self-aggrandising zeal for building was, however, balanced by a commitment to undertake that building work in accordance with his moral revolution. So luxury villas and buildings that went up during the competitive era of the republic for the benefit of the wealthy few were gradually replaced or rebranded as spaces for common use. One such construction project initiated not long after 27 BC was the Portico of Octavia, a public colonnade named for the emperor's sister and remodelled on the footprint of a previous version constructed more than a century earlier by a wealthy grandee named Caecilius Metellus. Visiting the portico now, one finds only a fragile shadow of its glorious former self. The site fell into sorry neglect post-antiquity, housing a bustling fish market from the medieval period through to the end of the nineteenth century, and today its battered frontage serves as a nesting spot for pigeons and rooks. But once upon a time, this nondescript ruin was an elegant courtyard with cascading fountains and a garden that played host to a gallery of valuable paintings and sculpture.[42]

Pride of place was given to a seated statue of Octavia's chosen role model Cornelia. Based on the testimony of one tourist, Pliny the Elder, who observed the statue some years later and recorded it as having resided 'formerly in the portico of Metellus, now the buildings of Octavia', it used to be thought that when Augustus commandeered the portico for Octavia, the statue was already *in situ*, explaining perhaps why Augustus chose this particular site as a showcase for his sister.[43] Since its existence in Metellus's day would in fact make it the only known statue of a historical Roman woman in the city before the revolutionary grant to Octavia and Livia in 35 BC, Pliny's testimony is extremely important. But a new theory suggests that Pliny may have been labouring under a misapprehension. In 1878, excavations at the Portico of Octavia unearthed the large marble slab on which this statue of Cornelia rested, inscribed with the words *Cornelia Africani f. Gracchorum* – 'Cornelia, daughter of Africanus, mother of the Gracchi'. Recent re-examinations of this inscription suggest that the label shows signs of being a recut of a different original, the implication being that Augustus had another female statue – of a classical goddess, since a seated pose usually denotes divine status in ancient statuary – relabelled as Cornelia and added it to his sister's revamped portico to underline a connection between them. A statue that Pliny assumed had been in place since Metellus's day thus may only have been there since the 20s BC.[44]

The sponsorship of Roman public buildings was an act that prior to Augustus's reign had been the sole preserve of men in Roman society. In another example of the way that traditional female values were now being broadcast from very untraditional platforms, the Julio-Claudian era saw the practice of female sponsorship take off in a big way, and Octavia's portico was the blueprint for several of the female-sponsored buildings that followed. She also acted as a conduit between Augustus and the great Roman architect, engineer and historian Vitruvius, whose highly influential treatise On Architecture contained an acknowledgement of gratitude to the emperor's sister for recommending his employment to Augustus, a note that makes it clear it was not just Livia who was a useful contact in the emperor's circle. Livia would later overtake Octavia as the more prolific patron of public building works, but for the time being, it was Octavia, with her more visible role in the physical fabric of the city, whose star was arguably the higher in the firmament.

When Octavia's son Marcellus and Livia's son Tiberius emerged as the front runners to succeed Augustus, it looked at first glance as though there was little to choose between them. Both were much the same age and had been given equal billing in their youth. Indeed, they were both chosen to ride the trace-horses of Augustus's chariot during the triumphal celebrations after Actium. Marcellus, though, said to have been 'a young man of noble qualities, cheerful in mind and disposition' in contrast to his pale, silent cousin, had the advantage of being related to the emperor by blood and it was he who enjoyed the faster-tracked career.[45] In 25 BC, the Julio-Claudian dynasty celebrated its first 'royal wedding' with the marriage of seventeen-year-old Marcellus to his fourteen-year-old cousin Julia.[46] The father of the bride could not himself be present, as he was still away on his foreign tour, and so – in a piece of irony that would only be realised later – Augustus's military supremo Agrippa was commissioned to act in loco parentis.[47]

With Julia's donning of the yellow wedding veil and slippers, the status of Octavia's son as favourite for the purple was confirmed, elevating Octavia herself to the prestigious if unofficial position of mother to the heir-apparent. But the bubble burst all too quickly. Two years later in the autumn of 23 BC, while the now forty-year-old Augustus struggled to recover from a near-fatal illness, Marcellus himself died suddenly of a mysterious sickness at the age of twenty, widowing Julia and unexpectedly becoming the first occupant of the brand-new family mausoleum, now looming like a 40-metre-high (130-feet-high) wedding cake over the city. Public mourning for the boy was extravagant, and Octavia's devastation widely broadcast.[48] Burying herself in seclusion, she was said to have forbidden all mention of her son's name thereafter, giving way to her grief only during an audience with Virgil, the great poet and friend of the family, while he read her a passage from his epic poem, the *Aeneid*, in which the Roman founding father Aeneas, whom Augustus's family claimed as an ancestor, saw a vision of Marcellus's ghost in a parade of Roman heroes in the underworld. In his early-nineteenth-century work *Virgil Reading the Aeneid to Livia, Octavia and Augustus*, the French artist Jean Auguste Dominique Ingres captures in oils the moment recorded by Virgil's ancient biographer, when Octavia swoons in Augustus's lap at hearing the part of the poem that mentioned her son, her face sallow with loss.[49]

Yet Ingres adds another figure to the scene, one whose presence is unreported in the account of Octavia's faint given by Virgil's fourth-century biographer Donatus. As Augustus cradles his swooning sister and holds up a hand in signal to the poet to stop, Octavia's other companion Livia looks on poker-faced. Her hooded eyes betray no emotion as she cups her sister-in-law's head with one hand and drapes the other languidly over the back of her chair, contemplating with detached interest the grief-stricken face before her, the greys and blues of her clothing reflecting her icy demeanour in contrast to the warm pinks and reds sported by her companions. In a later version of the painting, two anonymous figures stare thoughtfully at Livia from the shadows, their suspicions apparently awakened by her utterly unconcerned demeanour.[50]

Ingres's composition reflects a well-known report that in the wake of Marcellus's death, ugly rumours were swirling around Rome. Surreptitious fingers of blame were being pointed at Livia, claming that she had a hand in Marcellus's death, motivated by jealousy at seeing her own son Tiberius passed over for the succession. Even though our source for the rumours, Cassius Dio, notes that the accusation was dismissed out of hand by many who pointed out the high incidence of fatal airborne disease in the city that year, nevertheless, some of the mud stuck and still has not come off. Robert Graves's novel *I Claudius* alludes delicately to Livia's 'unremitting attention' to her nephew, while in the television series based on the book, the camera lingers on Livia's malevolent expression as she promises to take care of the boy on his sickbed.[51]

Ingres was never quite satisfied with his composition. He reworked it several times, and his indecision mirrors the inconclusiveness of the ancient accusations against Livia.[52] Marcellus's death was nevertheless just the first of a series of murders by poison that would be laid at her door during the course of her career. While it would be a futile task to try to prove or disprove her guilt in this or any other case, we would do well to remember that the stereotype of the poisoning woman was a stock character in ancient myth and history, epitomised by Cleopatra, the bogeywoman of imperial Roman imagination who not only employed poison to effect her own suicide but tested her medicine cabinet of lethal potions on prisoners of war. Indeed her example influenced the portrait of later *femmes fatales* like Lucrezia Borgia.[53] The image of sorceresses like Medea and Circe, who used their drugs and potions to control and terrorise mankind, helped to establish a fine line between the ministering and murdering female stereotypes, and it was one that Livia would continue to skirt precariously as her profile on the Roman radar steadily rose. Women were the guardians of the domestic realm and keepers of the keys to the kitchen cabinets, and Roman satire caricatured them as the enemy within, knowledgeable in the poisons needed to induce abortions, drug their husbands or eliminate inconvenient rivals to their own sons' chances of inheritance:

> You fatherless orphans too, who are rather well off, I warn you – watch out for your lives and don't trust a single dish. Those pastries are steaming darkly with maternal poison. Get someone else to taste first anything that's offered to you by the woman who bore you.[54]

Women's pharmacological skills could also be directed to positive ends, making medicines that healed rather than harmed. The *De Medicamentis Liber*, an extraordinary compilation of traditional Roman remedies assembled in the fifth century by a medical writer from Bordeaux, even preserves for us what it claims were the favourite medical recipes of Livia and Octavia themselves, rather like the Hippocratic equivalent of a modern celebrity cookery book. Drawing on the writings of Scribonius Largus, a physician who served the imperial court during the reign of Livia's great-grandson Claudius, it records that Livia herself recommended a linctus including saffron, cinnamon, coriander, opium and honey to soothe a sore throat, and also kept a salve of marjoram, rosemary, fenugreek, wine and oil in a jar by her bed to soothe chills and nervous tension, an ancient version of Vicks VapoRub. As well as telling us of Livia's toothpaste formula, it is also our source for Octavia's own prescription for *dentifricium*, which like her sister-in-law's was a simple abrasive blend consisting of rock salt, vinegar, honey and barley-flour, baked into charred dumplings and scented, again like Livia's, with spikenard.[55]

Octavia's profile spiked briefly in the aftermath of Marcellus's death. Despite her vow that she would make no public appearances, she emerged from the shadows to dedicate a library to her dead son in her eponymous portico – while Augustus established a nearby theatre in his name, the Theatre of Marcellus – and she continued to make periodic appearances in art commissioned by her brother. But the damage was done. It was said that she never recovered, either politically or personally, from Marcellus's death, and wore mourning clothes for the last decade of her life. Amid the chorus of ancient approval that paints her as one of the best, most modest and praiseworthy of Roman women, a dissenting voice appeared some decades later in the person of Seneca, a member of the Emperor Nero's inner circle who said that Octavia had grieved too incontinently for her son, contrasting her behaviour unfavourably with the restrained conduct of Livia when she had her own maternal sorrows to bear.

Of course, the differences between the two women ran far deeper than their respective experiences of grief. According to Seneca, they fell out badly after Marcellus's death. Octavia was said to have nursed a hatred for her sister-in-law, suspecting that now she would get her long-standing wish of seeing one of her own sons succeed Augustus. If Livia did cherish such maternal ambitions, though, they would have to wait a little longer.[56]

Augustus was forced to rethink his plans quickly in the aftermath of the events of 23 BC. Marcellus's death had not only created a vacancy in the dynastic pecking order, it left his teenaged daughter Julia without a husband. To permit his only daughter to remain single for any length of time would have been contrary to the civic ideals that Augustus actively sought to promote – under legislation passed by him within the next few years, one year was the maximum time a woman was allowed to remain an unattached widow before she was expected to remarry.[57] But Augustus did not turn to either of his stepsons by Livia, even though as a general rule he tended to keep things in the family as far as the marriages of the children of the imperial household went. Instead in 21 BC, apparently heeding the advice of his friend Maecenas, who advised Augustus that he had elevated his lieutenant Agrippa to so powerful a position that 'he must either become your son-in-law or be slain', he married the now eighteen-year-old Julia to the forty-two-year-old architect of the victory at Actium, who in turn divorced Octavia's eldest daughter Claudia Marcella Maior to make way for his new bride, a marital reshuffle to which Octavia apparently gave her blessing.[58]

In 1902, railway workers building a track between Boscotrecase and Torre Annunziata happened to uncover the remains of a magnificent country residence where Agrippa and Julia spent at least some of their married life. Set into a hillside near the ill-fated city of Pompeii, the villa commanded a panoramic south-facing view of the Gulf of Naples, an area littered with the country retreats of the Roman glitterati. Excavations were cut short by the 1906 eruption of Mount Vesuvius which covered the villa's all too briefly exposed skeleton, but graffiti on amphorae and tiles found in the remains were enough to confirm the property's original ownership. Thanks to the painting style of the interior decoration, the so-called 'Third Style' which was popularised after 15 BC and was characterised by delicate decorative schemes on monochrome backgrounds, it is thought construction work on the villa probably began in the early years of Agrippa's and Julia's marriage.[59]

The Villa Boscotrecase was one of the most impressive houses of its day, testifying to the enormous wealth and prestige its owner had acquired since Actium. Words can scarcely do justice to the brilliant frescoes that were found inside, and which are today divided between the Metropolitan Museum of Art in New York and the Muzeo Nazionale in Naples. Colour poured through the house like a liquid rainbow, flooding the walls with a richly polychromatic palette inspired by nature: red cinnabar, yellow ochre, turquoise, lime-white, violet and green. Whisper-fine pastoral vignettes chequered the walls of the so-called 'Red Room'; painted candelabra served as pedestals for landscape 'postcards' on the sober walls of the 'Black Room'; and two paintings 5 and 6 feet high (1.5–1.8 m) depicted the rescue of Andromeda from a sea-monster by Perseus and the one-eyed Cylops Polyphemus's love for the sea-nymph Galatea in the 'Mythological Room'. The cool marine greens and blues of their composition lent a sense of peace, tranquillity and fantasy to the ambience of this otherwise red-painted chamber, which may have been a bedroom given that this was often the *locus* for mythological scenes.[60]

We cannot tell if any of these rooms were intended for Julia's or any other female resident's personal use. One of the key distinguishing features between Roman houses and Greek houses is that they show no signs of segregation along gender lines. Nothing in the decoration, layout or archaeological remains of Roman houses indicates which if any rooms were given over to solely male or female use. We do not even have clues such as toy remnants that might identify children's nurseries.[61] Instead, while their Athenian counterparts were almost permanently confined to secluded areas of their homes, Julia and her fellow Roman matrons were expected to make themselves visible, albeit in strictly domestic occupations in the *atrium* where their activities would be on full view, thanks to the open-door policy which Roman male grandees employed to show off their status and encourage the assumption that they had nothing to hide in their personal lives. This principle applied even at their homes outside the metropolis. Thus the Villa Boscotrecase functioned as an extension of Agrippa's personal political empire in the city, a rural show home where, aided by Julia, he might entertain friends, receive clients and continue to flourish his plumage. However, such sociability only extended so far. Both town and country villas were divided into subtly graduated areas of public and private, the *cubiculum* ('bedroom') being the most private, and the atrium being the least private. The more special and privileged the visitor, the more private and richly decorated the room to which he was admitted. It was a mark of Livia's unusually elevated status, and the rank of visitor she therefore received, that the empress herself maintained a staff of *cubicularii*, or bedroom attendants, whose task it was to supervise admittance to her inner sanctum.[62]

Such rich gorgeousness as we find in these rooms at Boscotrecase may seem curiously at odds with the mantra of moral austerity so rigorously espoused by Augustus. Like any society, the Romans had their own unwritten codes of conduct, an unspoken understanding of where the line between vulgarity and acceptable ostentation lay, and with its delicate pastoral and mythological decoration themes, Agrippa's and Julia's home was in fact quite in keeping with the elegant but restrained style of the imperial residence on the Palatine. Nevertheless, Augustus had serious reservations about the luxurious country mansions that some Romans built for themselves, taking care to advertise the fact that he himself did not decorate his own modest country places with painted panels and statuary but let natural features such as terraces and plantations do the work, and when, many years later, one of his granddaughters, Julia Minor, built a lavish country palace that did not accord with his moral precepts, he had it demolished, an ominous warning sign, if ever it were needed, that Augustus would not tolerate moral hypocrisy in his own family.[63]

Julia Minor was one of a tally of five children to whom Julia gave birth during her nine-year union to Agrippa, rewarding the hopes of the Julio-Claudian dynasty which seemed now to have settled on Julia and Agrippa as the guardians of its legacy. The eldest, a son named Gaius, was born in 20 BC, followed three years later by a younger brother Lucius, and in a clear signal of intent to groom them as the front runners to their grandfather's throne, Augustus officially adopted both of them as his own sons. Adoption, whereby one *paterfamilias* legally took another man's child, or even another *paterfamilias*, into his own family, was a long-standing Roman practice, often employed by those unable to produce heirs of their own – Augustus himself owed much of his rise to his adoption as a seventeen-year-old by his great-uncle Julius Caesar.[64] In 13 BC, once Gaius and Lucius had reached the age of seven and four respectively, the Roman mint issued a coin featuring the emperor on one side, and on the other, a tiny fleshy-featured bust of Julia, her hair neatly arranged in the *nodus*, and flanked by the heads of her two infant boys. Julia thus became the only woman to appear on a coin issued by the Roman mint during her father's reign. Above her portrait hovered the *corona civica*, the crown of oak leaves that along with the laurel was Augustus's own particular crest; it marked Julia out as the new queen-mother-in-waiting, just as Octavia, mother of Marcellus, had been before her.[65]

The birth of two girls, Julia Minor and her younger sister Agrippina Maior, intersected those of Gaius and Lucius, and finally another boy came along, named Agrippa Postumus in recognition of the fact that he was born after Agrippa's death.[66] Like her stepmother Livia, Julia spent much of her time accompanying her husband on foreign tours, and her daughter Agrippina is thought to have been born on the island of Lesbos, near the Turkish coast. Inscriptions and statues along the route that Agrippa and Julia took paid homage to the fertility of the emperor's visiting daughter, such as one in the Greek city of Priene labelling her *kalliteknos*, meaning 'bearer of beautiful children'.[67]

Three years into Julia's marriage to Agrippa, in 18 BC, Augustus's reforming zeal led him to introduce a highly controversial new set of laws that were designed in part to promote Julia's child-bearing example to others while purporting to deliver a sharp, self-righteous prod of moral reproof to the soft, lazy and licentious underbelly of the Roman aristocracy. The *leges Iuliae*, or 'Julian laws', were introduced in apparent response to a dwindling marriage rate among the Roman elite, and contained strict new measures aimed at cracking down on such laxity while offering economic incentives to marry and procreate. There was clearly also a related agenda of firming up the social hierarchy by preserving the purity and financial integrity of upper-class families, as demonstrated by restrictions the laws imposed both on marriage between unequal class groupings such as senators and freedwomen (former slave women who had won their liberty), and on testamentary bequests made outside the family.[68] The centrepiece of the new legislation was the *lex Iulia de adulteriis*, which made adultery a criminal offence for the first time and prescribed the exact punishment procedure for those caught in the act. In a display of stark inequality, the brunt of these legal repercussions was to be borne by women.

Under the new laws, a woman was guilty of adultery if she had sex with anyone but her husband, but a man was guilty of the offence only if the woman he was involved with was married. Slave girls, prostitutes, concubines and single women were fair game, for the key consideration was to ensure that a man's paternity of his own children was not in doubt. The law also stated that a married woman caught *in flagrante* could be killed by her father, along with her lover, while a cuckolded husband, although not allowed to kill his wife himself and subject to punishment if he did so, was obligated to divorce her immediately. Once divorced, the woman and her lover would be tried in a special court of law and, if found guilty, faced exile as the most likely punishment. Any man who failed to divorce a disgraced wife could be charged with 'pimping' for her, drawing an equivalence between an adulterous woman and a prostitute. A later revision of the law also forbade an adulteress ever to remarry a freeborn Roman male, and confiscated half her dowry and a third of her property, again underlining the fact that these laws were aimed chiefly at the wealthier classes of Roman society.[69] Widows and women between the ages of twenty and fifty, who were not guilty of the sin of adultery but had divorced for other reasons, were required by law to remarry within a year and six months respectively.[70]

The new marital legislation waved the carrot as well as the stick, offering tax breaks to members of the Roman senatorial classes who married and produced children, while penalties, such as the forfeiture of inheritance rights, were imposed on men aged 25–60 and women aged 20–50 who remained unmarried or childless.[71] Women who fulfilled their child-producing obligations under the law also gained the chance to win a certain measure of independence. Freeborn women who gave birth to three children or more were exempted from male guardianship (four children or more were required for freedwomen to be eligible) thanks to the *ius trium liberorum* – 'the three child rule'. Women who conformed to this ideal were held up as examples to their peers, and one particularly fertile slave woman was even honoured with a statue by the emperor.[72] In sum, the 'Julian laws', named after the emperor's own family, promised a return to old-fashioned family values, and the 'good old days' of Rome's past, an imaginary time when women were chaste and adultery an aberration. As Augustus himself wrote in his documentary account of his reign, *Res Gestae* ('My Achievements'): 'Through new laws passed on my proposal, I brought back many of the exemplary practices of our ancestors which were falling into neglect.'[73]

But the surface portrait painted by Augustus of the happy results of his own handiwork masked a murkier, more fractious and ambivalent reality. For a start, the close correlation in our literary sources between accusations of adultery against married women and attempts to portray their cuckolded husbands as politically impotent make it apparent that some charges were motivated by personal rivalries. Also, the extent to which Augustus's legislation was actually enforced or enforceable is a grey area.[74] There was no Crown Prosecution Service at Rome, and many husbands and wives probably preferred not to go through the public embarrassment and inconvenience of a trial. There were public demonstrations in favour of the laws' repeal, and one woman named Vistilia apparently even registered herself as a prostitute in order to get off an adultery charge, a loophole closed under Augustus's successors.[75]

One of the most subversive voices in the ongoing debate surrounding the Julian laws was that of the poet Ovid, who thrust a witty spoke in the wheel of the emperor's marital reforms. As well as advising men on how to chat up women at chariot races – the only sporting event given immunity from new rules that relegated all women, with the sole exception of the Vestal Virgins and the women

of the emperor's family, to the back seats of the theatre and gladiatorial arena – his poetry offered wives tips on how to deceive their
husbands while flirting with their lover at dinner parties:

> When he pats the couch, put on your Respectable Wife expression,
> And take your place beside him – but nudge my foot
> As you're passing by. Watch out for my nods and eye-talk,
> Pick up my stealthy messages, send replies.
> I shall speak whole silent volumes with one raised eyebrow,
> Words will spring from my fingers, words traced in wine.
> When you're thinking about the last time we made love together,
> Touch your rosy cheek with one elegant thumb.[76]

Ovid's persistent mockery later contributed to his exile on the Black
Sea in the year 8.

But Augustus's biggest nemesis of all was his own daughter. In a
piece of supreme irony, the demure poster-girl of the Augustan ideal
of womanhood, the only woman to appear thus far on coins minted
at Rome, and the mother of two of Augustus's would-be successors,
was turning out to be the Dorothy Parker of her generation, a popular
good-time girl with a steady stream of witty one-liners on the edge
of her tongue, a woman who privately chafed at the shackles imposed
on her by her conservative father. That is the portrait at least that
emerges from a fictional dinner-party conversation about Julia's jokes
and sayings in a fifth-century work called the *Saturnalia*. The author,
Macrobius, culled his material from a collection of witticisms edited
in the first century by one Domitius Marsus, who, as a protégé of
Augustan socialite Maecenas, was presumably repeating stories that
were doing the rounds of Roman court gossip at the time.[77]

The first blots on the portrait of Julia as a paragon of maternal
rectitude came with whispers about the paternity of her children. Infidelities during her marriage to Agrippa were alleged with figures such
as Sempronius Gracchus, a member of the famous Gracchi clan, and
though her father shrugged off these suspicions, her closest friends
apparently knew better. When Julia was asked how it was that all her
children by Agrippa resembled him when she had so many other
lovers, she is said to have made the pert reply, 'Passengers are never
allowed on board until the hold is full', implying that she only let
others into her bed once she was safely pregnant by her husband.[78]

Nonetheless, Julia was apparently a popular figure with the public on account of her 'gentle humanity and kindly disposition . . . those who were aware of her faults were astonished at the contradiction which her qualities implied'.[79] According to the stories repeated in the *Saturnalia*, Augustus adopted an indulgent rather than a stern attitude to his daughter at first, advising her to moderate 'the extravagance of her dress and the notoriety of her companions'. He was offended when one day she came into his presence in a risqué costume. The next day she came in wearing a demure dress and a prim expression, and embraced her father who was delighted at this show of respectable decorum. 'This dress,' he remarked, 'is much more becoming in the daughter of Augustus.' Julia had a reply ready. 'Yes,' she said, 'for today I am dressed to meet my father's eyes; yesterday it was for my husband's.'[80]

Dress, for a Roman woman, was a social, as well as sartorial, minefield. Although Livia and other exalted females were often portrayed in statuary wearing the traditional *stola* – a pinafore-like gown with a V-shaped neckline that constituted the female equivalent of the male toga and the standard uniform of the republican Roman female citizen – it was no longer everyday wear in Julia's lifetime, although donning it might well have added an extra veneer of pious respectability for her father's benefit. Instead, a long gap-sleeved tunic and *palla* (mantle) were typically worn by wealthy matrons from the first century BC onwards. An enveloping costume, with the tunic's wide elbow-length sleeves and high neckline, and the voluminous folds of the *palla*, which was draped in complicated fashion around one's body and drawn up over the head when one ventured out of doors, it clearly distinguished Rome's female leisured classes from their social inferiors, who could never have performed their daily tasks in so hot and restrictive a set of garments – poorer women wore shorter, unbelted tunics. The amount of material involved also ensured the cost of such a get-up put it beyond the reach of all but the well-heeled.[81]

Although the overall shape of female dress remained unchanged for centuries, Roman women did find ways to express both their status and sense of style. The whitewashed remains of ancient statuary give little sense of the colours women once wore, but traces of pigment on the marble of such sculptures, and painted portraits from Egypt and other provinces of the empire, vindicate literary testimony that a rich palette of dyed hues was available, from sky-blue (*aer*), sea-blue (*unda*), dark green (*Paphiae myrti*) and amethyst (*purpurae amethysti*) to saffron-yellow (*croceus*), pale pink (*albentes rosae*), dark grey (*pullus*) and chestnut-brown (*glandes*) – all colours selected by Ovid to flatter a girl's complexion. Conversely, to choose certain colours, such as cherry-red (*cerasinus*) and greenish-yellow (*galbinus*) was to mark one out as vulgar, while the exorbitantly expensive pigment purple increasingly became the exclusive preserve of the emperor and his family.[82] One's *palla* could be dyed to match the tunic underneath, while patterns and striped borders in complementary hues were popular too. Dyed and jewel-encrusted sandals (*soleae*) and shoe-boots (*calcei*) also helped women feel superior to less fortunate females. Fans (*flabellae*) fashioned from vellum or peacock feathers and closed with ivory handles; parasols (*umbraculae*) dangling tassels; high-waisted belts made of twisted cord and in a contrasting colour to the tunic underneath – all these completed the well-to-do Roman woman's wardrobe.[83]

The cost of importing the material and dye needed to make this clothing was astronomical. Although some Roman commentators argued that an expensively turned-out woman was a credit to the wealth and public standing of her husband, there were also voices of disapproval at the kind of conspicuous sartorial consumption that saw some women shunning homespun fabrics like wool or linen and instead requesting silk, a material that had to be imported into the empire at vast expense from China. Special condemnation was reserved for a type called 'Coan silk' – a flimsy, diaphanous material woven by women on the island of Cos, which was apparently all the rage among Roman women of the upper classes, yet frowned upon by some as a transparent fabric suitable only for a prostitute or a loose woman. It was just such a gown that would have inflamed Augustus's disapproval, if he had seen it being worn by his daughter.[84]

Several other reported confrontations took place between father and daughter over the issue of her dress and deportment. On a separate occasion, he arrived to visit her only to witness her maids plucking out her prematurely greying hairs. He was frustrated by such vanity, and after enquiring whether she would prefer to be bald or grey-haired, and receiving the response that she would rather go grey, he was said to have replied acidly, 'Why then are these women of yours in such a hurry to make you bald?'[85] Roman literature abounds with both plausible and preposterous-sounding stories of the lengths to which women went to adhere to an ideal – treating spots with chicken fat and onion; vanishing wrinkles with axle-grease; applying face-packs made from bread, barley, myrrh or rose leaves; whitening skin with chalk dust, lead or even crocodile dung to achieve the much sought-after pale complexion; exfoliating with ground oyster shells; scraping away body hair with a pumice stone. For Julia's own problem of greying hair, an alternative treatment of earthworms mixed with oil was recommended.[86]

Although certain of these more grotesque beauty recipes, such as the recommended use of crocodile excrement to lighten the complexion, derive from sources more concerned with sending up women's attempts to stave off the hand of time, it is nevertheless clear from multiple archaeological discoveries of cosmetic tubes and containers, including a perfectly preserved jar of face cream made from animal fat, starch and tin, that the elite Roman woman's dressing table was richly loaded, and the cosmetics industry a thriving concern.[87] Julia's preoccupation with her personal appearance may have been at odds with her disapproving father's mantra of frugal adornment and moral irreproachability, but it placed her in company with many other Roman women.

Nevertheless, as societal disapproval of Coan silk and satirical diatribes about more elaborate forms of beauty regimen demonstrated, it was easy to fall foul of the dividing line between acceptable self-embellishment and what was seen to be over-extravagant narcissism. With her sharp-tongued cracks, her relationships with undesirable men, and her racy clothes, Julia was coming to embody all of the characteristics that made Romans anxious about women, and threatening to undermine Augustus's new moral order from within. It was a dangerous game to play, especially when one's father was so public and powerful a figure.[88]

In 12 BC, the death of fifty-one-year-old Agrippa at his country estate in Naples while Julia was pregnant with their last child, Agrippa Postumus, left the emperor's only daughter a widow for the second time at the age of twenty-seven. As the mother of five children, she was now technically eligible to benefit from the clause in her father's legislation that permitted women with three children or more to be excused the protection of a husband or male guardian. Instead, perhaps wary of Julia's potential to cause him embarrassment, but also looking to provide himself with options in the succession stakes, Augustus decided that Julia should now after all marry Livia's eldest son, thirty-year-old Tiberius, who along with his younger brother Drusus had recently been winning great kudos on military campaigns around the Alps. If Augustus was toying with the idea of making his stepson his heir, an interim candidate perhaps until Gaius or Lucius could take over, he kept his audience in the dark. But his decision meant that Tiberius had to divorce his wife Vipsania, who ironically, as the daughter of the deceased Agrippa, was Julia's own stepdaughter. It was an unhappy arrangement, one that Tiberius at least was said to have raged at. He was devoted to Vipsania, the mother of his son Drusus Minor, and the sight of her in the street one day after their divorce is said to have reduced him to tears. He also heartily disapproved of his stepsister Julia, who was whispered to have long harboured feelings for him which he did not reciprocate.

Octavia, maintaining her low profile since the demise of Marcellus, lived long enough to see her former daughter-in-law Julia married to Tiberius. If Seneca's report that Octavia feared this to be Livia's ambition all along is to be believed, the sight would have been mortifying to her. Her death came soon enough, in 11 BC, reputedly of a broken heart, the ideal mother to the end.[89] A grieving Augustus delivered his sister's funeral oration himself, and in a simple ceremony she was interred alongside Marcellus in the mausoleum by the Tiber. The tombstone that she shared with her son was discovered during excavations in 1927.[90]

Two years after Octavia's funeral, on 30 January 9 BC, the new-look Julio-Claudian family gathered together for a magnificent ceremony to mark the dedication, not far from the mausoleum, of the Ara Pacis ('Altar of Peace'), one of the showpieces of Augustus's self-glorifying programme of public art, built to celebrate the emperor's recent triumphant return from Gaul and Spain and to proclaim the age of Augustus and his family as an age of peace.

It was, significantly, also Livia's fiftieth birthday. Though her role as a conduit between her husband and his subjects had been well established over the past twenty years, Livia was the only one of the three leading women of the imperial household thus far not to have been recognised on a coin of the Roman mint or with a major public building or monument in the city. That year marked her debut at last with her depiction alongside her husband on the Ara Pacis, in the most elevated and flattering guise in which she had yet appeared. Gone was the prim *nodus*, and instead her long hair was parted in the centre and allowed to fall loose under a veil, in a deliberate echo of the statuary poses of classical goddesses. Her husband also stood veiled and garlanded beside her, casting the pair as the benevolent patriarch and matriarch of the empire, a veritable Jupiter and Juno on earth.

The Ara Pacis was the first Roman state monument on which

women and children had featured. This was both a sign of the Augustan regime's growing confidence with giving the women of the imperial household a public role, and a further indication of Augustus's desire to make his family-man image a integral part of his public persona. Later that year, a banquet was held for the Senate on the Capitoline hill in honour of the military successes of Tiberius over the Dalmatians and Pannonians, and both Livia and Julia were given the distinct honour of presiding as joint hostesses over a separate feast attended by the leading women of the city – the first time that women are known to have been given a leading role in celebrating a triumph for a male relative.[91] As mother of Gaius and Lucius, and wife of the guest of honour Tiberius, Julia enjoyed exalted public status, although her complicated private life was conceivably already prompting curious whispers among the guests. Marriage to Tiberius, which had initially been conducted with a semblance of amity, had hit choppy waters, with the couple rumoured to be sleeping in separate beds. This was said to be Tiberius's decision, following the death of their infant first-born in the Italian city of Aquileia.[92]

It is difficult to gauge the depth of the attachments between Roman parents and their children without naturally bringing our own emotional expectations to bear. Mothers like Julia, who had already produced five healthy children, could expect to suffer the loss of at least one child in infancy. It is estimated that perhaps 5 per cent of all live-born Roman babies died in their first month, and that almost a quarter of infants died before their first birthdays. The inevitability of such losses perhaps explains why children of this age rarely received funerary monuments, though the evidence of letters such as that between the second-century rhetorician Fronto and the then-emperor Antoninus Pius, on the loss of the former's three-year-old grandson, indicates that the death of very young children was still an occasion for great grief:

> Be the immortality of the soul ever so established, that will be a theme
> for the disputations of philosophers, it will never assuage the yearning
> of a parent . . . I seem to see a copy of his face and fancy that I hear
> the very echo of his voice. This is the picture that my grief conjures
> up of itself.[93]

The connection made by Tiberius's biographer between the death of their child and the breakdown of marital relations with Julia does indicate that this loss was heartbreaking enough to put the final nail in the coffin of their marriage. The death of her grandchild notwithstanding, Livia on the other hand had good reason to be pleased with life in 9 BC as she looked out over the scene of the Capitoline banquet with all Rome's aristocracy gathered to celebrate the triumph of her offspring, and the city below resounding to the hubbub of ordinary people enjoying their own celebratory feasts. Her sons were bringing home victory after victory from Pannonia, Germany and the Balkans, to great adulation. Drusus in particular was a popular favourite with the Roman public, and his marriage to Octavia's younger daughter Antonia Minor, which had produced two young sons and a daughter – Germanicus, Claudius and Livilla – had tightened the knot between the Julian and Claudian branches still more securely, cementing Livia's place as the linchpin between them. With the vaunting of her image as Rome's *materfamilias*-in-chief on the nearby Ara Pacis, life must have seemed very sweet just now, particularly if her mind chanced to wander back to her precarious days on the run with Tiberius Nero.

Tragedy rudely interrupted in September that year, though, with the news of the premature death of Drusus in a riding accident, just as a celebratory banquet was being prepared by his mother Livia and wife Antonia to celebrate his military successes.[94] Accompanied by her husband, Livia went as far as the city of Ticinum (Pavia) to meet the procession bringing Drusus's body home from the campaign trail in Germany, their route illuminated by pyres lit throughout the country to signal Rome's great mourning for so popular a son. There they met a grief-stricken Tiberius, who had ridden almost 300 kilometres (185 miles) to reach his younger brother's deathbed, and had led the cortège home. A poem of condolence, the *Consolatio ad Liviam*, which was written and addressed to Livia by an anonymous figure, re-creates the scene of Drusus's sad homecoming and funeral, portraying Livia as the epitome of devastated motherhood as she grieves for her youngest boy: 'Is this the reward for piety? . . . Can I bear to look at you lying there, cursed wretch that I am? . . . Now, in my misery, I hold you and look upon you for the last time . . .'[95]

Unlike Octavia, however, for Livia the loss of her beloved son did not result in a maudlin retreat from public life. In step with the *Consolatio*'s advice that she should master her feelings, she adopted a stiff-upper-lip attitude that won her applause. While Octavia had recoiled from the prospect of seeing images of her son, unable to bear the sight of her dead child's features set in marble, Livia went the other way, commissioning her own statues of Drusus.[96] Livia's fortitude placed her in excellent company. In an essay written in the 40s, while he was in temporary exile under the reign of the Emperor Nero, the Stoic philosopher Seneca commanded his mother Helvia not to be one of those women who grieves for the rest of her life, recommending she take the great Cornelia for her example, who had refused to give in to tears and recriminations after the death of her sons.[97]

More public statues of Livia herself were also ordered by the Senate as a sign of respect. As well as acting as a public reminder of the legal incentives offered by the Julian laws to women who produced three children or more, these statues of Livia carried a new significance, because they were awarded in specific recognition of her contribution as a mother. They were accompanied by the symbolic conferral on the empress of the privileges of the 'three child rule' (despite the fact that even before Drusus's death, Livia had only two children still living). Whereas honorary statues such as these, intended for public display and granted by senatorial decree, had once been the sole preserve of men who had performed great services to the state, now a mother's contribution of children to society was portrayed as bearing comparison to male achievements in public service, a recognition of the new importance of women and the family in the Roman artistic gallery of power.[98]

Livia was also beginning to lend both her name and support to numerous public-building projects that were to become iconic landmarks throughout the city.[99] Although Octavia and a few other women had already broken ground here, including Agrippa's sister Vipsania Polla, who had also had a portico named after her and apparently took a hand in designing a local racecourse, Livia soon left her female contemporaries far behind.[100] As part of Augustus's religious regeneration of the city and its sacred precincts, she was put in charge – at least nominally – of overseeing the rebuilding of certain temples and shrines that had slumped into disuse. Easing her emergence into public life with an emphasis on her role as traditional wife and mother, the temples to receive her patronage honoured goddesses associated with women and the family. Thus under Livia's aegis, the temples of the goddess Bona Dea Subsaxana and of Fortuna Muliebris were restored, both religious complexes associated with female virtues of fertility and wifely support – Bona Dea was a fertility and healing goddess worshipped in exclusively female religious festivals, while the temple of Fortuna Muliebris ('The Fortune of Women') had in fact been built in tribute to Rome's fifth-century female saviours, Veturia and Volumnia.[101] Shrines to Pudicitia Plebeia and Pudicitia Patricia, cults of chastity, are also thought to have been dedicated by Livia, and she gave her name to non-religious edifices such as the public market, the Macellum Liviae, another appropriate commission given its association with domestic management, the Roman housewife's arena of responsibility.[102]

The showpiece of Livia's building programme though was the Porticus Liviae ('Portico of Livia'). This was one of the places to see and be seen in the city, described by an ancient tourist as amongst the great spectacles of Rome.[103] Like Octavia's portico, the plot of land on which it was erected had once belonged to a republican fat cat, in this instance a wealthy aristocrat of freedman stock named Vedius Pollio, a financial adviser of Augustus's who had earned himself a reputation for questionable business practices and feeding unfortunate slaves who incurred his wrath to his pet fish. On his death, Pollio had bequeathed a portion of his estate to the emperor, grandly expressing the wish that it should be used as the site for a magnificent building to benefit the people of Rome. Instead, Augustus ordered Pollio's sprawling private temple to excess, located within the warren-like residential district of the Subura on the Esquiline hill, to be flattened and replaced with a portico named after Livia, an oasis of sunlit gardens, artworks and colonnaded walkways shaded by thick fragrant grape-vines clambering over trellises, which soon became a popular meeting point for the inhabitants of the otherwise crowdy, smelly Subura. Ovid even cheekily recommended it in his pre-exile days as a good spot to meet girls, not quite the message Augustus had in mind.[104]

The extent to which Livia – or indeed Octavia and Vipsania Polla – was actively involved in the planning of such building projects cannot be known, but the portico was yet another instance of the way in which Livia had become a key figure in the emperor's propaganda. A handful of women outside the imperial family was inspired by her example. Eumachia, a public priestess and wealthy member of an old Pompeian family who, after her father's death, had taken on the management of his wine, amphora and tile export business, used the Porticus Liviae as a blueprint for the construction of a huge portico paid for out of her own funds and bordering the forum of Pompeii, the entrance to which still stands.[105] Livia was now clearly a role model for the women of the elite.

The Porticus Liviae was completed in 7 BC, and its dedication presided over by Livia herself. Also housed in the portico was a shrine devoted to *Concordia*, a cult in honour of marital harmony, which Livia is thought to have added as a special tribute to her husband on 11 June, a date which was celebrated as a kind of Mother's Day in the Roman calendar.[106] Highly ironic then, given the theme, that also at her side for the dedication was her son Tiberius, still basking in the glory of his first triumph and his appointment to the consulship, but whose unhappy marriage was about to drive him to commit career suicide, to the great consternation of his mother. When in 6 BC, his stepfather offered him a prestigious five-year posting to the eastern province of Armenia, Tiberius rejected it and instead requested leave to withdraw from public life and retire to the island of Rhodes. He excused his decision on the grounds that he was tired of public office, and wished to step aside in favour of Gaius and Lucius. His announcement, however, caused a rift with Augustus, who condemned his stepson's decision in the Senate, calling it an act of desertion. Livia is said to have strained every sinew to induce her son to change his mind. But he would not be persuaded, and left Rome by the port of Ostia without a word to most of his friends, spending the next seven years in quiet sanctum, attending the lectures of various professors of philosophy.[107]

Some ancient biographers insisted that Tiberius was indeed motivated by a genuine desire to advance the interests of Julia's boys.[108] Other reports claimed that he was in fact piqued at their precocious rise through the political ranks and had flounced off to Rhodes in a fit of the sullens. The most popular theory of all though was that in isolating himself on Rhodes, Tiberius was determined to put as many miles as possible between himself and Julia, whose company he could no longer endure.

How do you solve a problem like Julia? The question was beginning to cause a real headache for Augustus. He was increasingly exasperated at his daughter's recalcitrance, his sentiments on the matter summarised in a comment made to friends one day that 'he had two spoiled daughters to put up with – Rome and Julia'. In his determination to steer her on to a more respectable path, he wrote urging Julia to learn from the example set by her stepmother Livia, after differences between the two women's companions at a recent gladiatorial contest were commented on by bystanders – Livia's circle of distinguished middle-aged statesmen forming a stark contrast to Julia's entourage of dissipated young men. But in retort to her father's aspersions on her friends, Julia wrote impudently – according, once again, to Macrobius's *Saturnalia*: 'These friends of mine will be old men too when I am old.' In the face of all of Augustus's critiques, of her immodest dress sense, her rowdy circle of friends, even her vanity-driven habit of plucking grey hairs from her head, Julia refused to conform to the austere living example set by her father, apparently retorting to an entreaty by a friend: 'He forgets that he is Caesar, but I remember that I am Caesar's daughter.'[109]

Several, or even all, of these pithy sayings attributed to Julia could of course be the invention of Macrobius or his first-century source Domitius Marsus. But they are nonetheless indicative of the terms in which the rift between Julia and her father was perceived, and when the end finally came, Julia's fall from grace was truly spectacular and left no room for doubt as to the seriousness of her offences. The year 2 BC, in which the blow fell, began auspiciously enough. It marked the twenty-fifth anniversary of Augustus's formal assumption of the mantle of *princeps*, and pseudo-restoration of 'the republic'. On 5 February, the emperor was named *pater patriae* ('Father of the Country') by the Senate, and in August, lavish celebrations were held to mark the dedication of the Forum of Augustus. Alongside bronze statues of the great and the good was a magnificent temple to Mars the Avenger, in which was housed a trinity of deities claimed as patron gods by the Julian family – Mars, Venus Genetrix, and Divus Julius. The latter represented the deified Julius Caesar, who had been consecrated as a god in 42 BC, thus conveniently allowing his great-nephew to call himself 'son of a god'.[110]

But a dark cloud loomed over the pageant. Barely was the dedication over, than Augustus issued a statement to be read out to the Senate. The enraged emperor, it was announced, had publicly disowned his daughter Julia, word having reached him that she was suspected of drinking and committing adultery with a series of men. The charge-sheet included the torrid accusation that she had even had sex on the Rostra, the platform from which orators spoke to the crowds in the forum and from which her father had proclaimed his laws on marriage and adultery in 18 BC. There were even fruitier allegations, quoted later from Augustus's anguished personal correspondence, that a garland had been hung on the statue of the satyr Marsyas in the forum, next to which Julia had turned prostitute and offered to take on all comers, including strangers. Such was Augustus's shame, that when a freedwoman of Julia's named Phoebe hanged herself in the wake of the scandal, he is said to have observed that he would rather have been Phoebe's father.[III]

The scandal dealt a devastating blow to Augustus's attempts to present his family as above suspicion in the moral purity stakes. The penalty for adultery laid down by Augustus's own legislation was exile. Such was his fury that he was said to have considered killing his daughter, though in the end he contented himself with having her banished to the tiny windswept island of Pandateria, off Italy's western coast. The fact that he treated her case at the level of treason, referring it to the Senate, reflects the level of betrayal that Augustus felt at her failure to live up to the standards he had set his family.

Today, the island of Pandateria goes by the name of Ventotene. At a mere 3 kilometres (1.8 miles) long, its pink and white houses and sparkling navy-blue harbours make it popular with holidaymakers. Once, though, it was a place of bleak exile, home to a prison fortress as recently as 1965. Julia was confined to a lonely existence here for the next five years. Forbidden all sumptuary pleasures including wine and male visitors, she was now forced to live in accordance with her father's political and moral precepts – though she was not quite without company. At her own insistence, we are told, Scribonia, the wife Augustus discarded in favour of Livia, loyally accompanied her daughter into exile. As already alluded to in the case of Livia's own faithful shadowing of Tiberius Nero, such acts by women in support of banished husbands or children were much admired in Roman literature of the imperial period. Scribonia's act thus cast her not as the nagging harridan of Augustus's correspondence, but as a woman who conceived of her duty and most important role in life as that of being a mother to her child.[112]

Over the last two centuries, the case against Julia has been reopened, and many classical scholars are now convinced that the charges of sexual immorality laid against her were in fact a cover-up for something more sinister.[113] Based on hints dropped by ancient writers such as Pliny and Seneca, it has been deduced that Julia's real crime was not adultery, but involvement in a political plot against her father. Five men were named as Julia's partners in adultery – Iullus Antonius, Quintus Crispinus, Appius Claudius, Sempronius Gracchus and Scipio – all of them from noted aristocratic families. One possibility is that their real offence was conspiring in an attempt at regime change, of which there were several during the first emperor's reign. If this theory is correct, the name of Iullus Antonius – Antony's and Fulvia's son, who had been charitably brought up by his stepmother Octavia in the aftermath of his father's death – must have sent the greatest shiver down the emperor's spine. The pairing of Augustus's daughter and the son of his greatest enemy was an irony not lost years later on Seneca, who referred to Julia as 'once again a woman to be feared with an Antony'.[114]

The evidence that Julia was plotting the overthrow of her father is thin at best. But it was nevertheless impossible to separate the political from the sexual implications of her crimes. Whether true or false, an accusation of adultery against Julia, the offspring of the man who had espoused puritanical new laws against such immorality, carried with it consequences far more serious than mere personal embarrassment, and could never have been stomached by the emperor.[115] All the same, angry protests are said to have greeted the well-liked Julia's banishment. They stirred Augustus to angry retort in the popular assembly, but he did relent after a few years, permitting his daughter's return to the mainland, though confining her to the city of Regium, on the toe of Italy. In Regium, Julia was at least allowed to venture out into the town and provided with a house and an annual allowance by her father. However, Augustus was never reunited with his daughter, and she remained in his black books to the end. Her father's will later stipulated that neither she nor her daughter Julia Minor – who was to be exiled for adultery ten years later – should be permitted burial in the family mausoleum, a punishment which, as one writer has put it, 'constituted a posthumous and highly symbolic revocation of membership in the Julian *gens*'.[116] He also disinherited her, and on his death, the share of his estate that she as a daughter would have been legally entitled to passed instead solely to Livia and Tiberius.[117] Although she did not suffer the punishment known as *damnatio memoriae*, which would have immediately condemned all existing sculptures and artistic images of her throughout the empire to the scrapheap, no images of her survive that can be dated after 2 BC, the year of her banishment.[118]

Rome's attempts to airbrush certain citizens from its memory in this way usually leave telltale traces, obvious scars where someone's name or image has been erased from a monument. In Julia's case there is little sign of that happening. Her existing public portraits were probably allowed to remain, given that she was the mother of the still-in-favour Gaius and Lucius. Their removal would have spoilt the balance and aesthetic appeal of group family portraits in which she already featured prominently. But a quiet word from on high seems to have been dropped in the ear of artists and town-planners around the empire, and an unofficial moratorium issued on further production of portraits of the emperor's disgraced daughter, while her existing portraits may later have been recycled, remodelled and relabelled to fit the image of other, later imperial women.[119] This would explain why the coin issued for her and her two sons in 13–12 BC is the only securely identifiable portrait that survives of her, a woman who was once the centrefold of her family dynasty. Lead theatre tickets from Rome, and bone gaming tokens from Oxyrhyncus in Egypt, featuring images of a woman resembling the coin portrait, have been found, but we cannot tell for sure if they are Julia.[120]

Julia was the first woman in the Julio-Claudian dynasty's young history to suffer such a downfall and condemnation. She was not the last. Her fate had exposed irreparable cracks in the seemingly impenetrable façade of this new, morally rejuvenated golden age of Rome, cracks that would prove difficult to repair.[121]

When Tiberius, taking a break from his daily diet of study in self-imposed exile in Rhodes, heard of his wife's fate, the news apparently delighted him – although he had been writing to Augustus, half-heartedly urging a reconciliation between father and estranged daughter, perhaps in the hope of wheedling his way back into the emperor's good graces. Nevertheless, the irreconcilable breakdown of Tiberius's marriage had weakened any claim he might have had to succeed his stepfather as emperor. When his subsequent requests to return to Rome were eventually granted in the year 2 by an unwilling Augustus, egged on by pleading from Livia, Tiberius settled down to what should have been a life of political seclusion, decamping to an out-of-the-way house in the Gardens of Maecenas.[122]

Despite their mother's scandalous exit from Rome, Julia's sons Gaius and Lucius were still riding the crest of a great wave of popularity as the de facto heirs to Augustus. Both had long since shed the childish tunics of their boyhood and graduated to the *toga virilis*, the dress adopted by young men on reaching sexual maturity.[123] In 1 BC, shortly before the twenty-two-year old Gaius departed for a career-building posting in the eastern provinces, the Julio-Claudian house had celebrated its first imperial wedding in a decade, with Gaius's marriage to his cousin Livilla, daughter of Antonia Minor and the deceased Drusus, and thus granddaughter to both Livia and Octavia. All seemed set for the inevitable coronation of Gaius or his younger brother Lucius as successors to their grandfather's dignities.[124]

Yet within two years of Tiberius's return to Rome, Augustus's dynastic blueprint was in tatters. On 20 August 2, Lucius died of a sudden illness at Marseilles while en route to an army posting in Spain. The same year, Gaius received a wound during a siege at Artagira in Armenia, which ultimately resulted in his death eighteen months later on 21 February 4, while attempting to make the journey back to Italy.[125] The premature demise of these two popular young men left Julia's and Agrippa's last surviving son, the sixteen-year-old Agrippa Postumus, as the emperor's one surviving male grandchild. Augustus could not rest all his hopes on the shoulders of an inexperienced teenage heir, and bowed to the inevitable. On 26 June, four months after the death of Gaius, he officially adopted forty-four-year-old Tiberius, moving his wife's son to the head of the Julio-Claudian line of succession. As a pre-condition of his promotion, Tiberius was compelled to adopt in turn his seventeen-year-old nephew Germanicus, the eldest son of Drusus and Antonia. Leaving nothing to chance, Augustus also adopted Agrippa Postumus, providing another option in the succession stakes, should it be needed. The pieces on the Julio-Claudian chessboard had shifted dramatically. The next emperor of Rome would now in all likelihood come from the family of Livia and not Augustus.

In August 14, at the age of seventy-five, Augustus set out from Rome on his last journey, attended by Livia. His purpose was to accompany Tiberius, who was being dispatched to Illyricum on official imperial business, as far as the town of Beneventum, south of Rome. The last decade of Augustus's rule had been dogged by setbacks, culminating in a disastrous defeat for the Roman legions in Germany at the battle of Teutoburg Forest five years previously, which effectively curtailed further Roman territorial expansion for the time being. The empire's borders were now delineated by the Rhine and Danube rivers in Europe, the Euphrates in the east and the Sahara in Africa, and few new territorial gains would be made during the remaining course of empire.[126]

The trip did not begin auspiciously. The emperor, always a poor traveller, contracted diarrhoea during the sea voyage off the coast of Campania. The imperial party broke their journey at the emperor's

villa on Capri to allow the emperor a few days to rest, before continuing to Beneventum via Naples. Having parted company with Tiberius,
Augustus, who was still suffering from his stomach complaint, turned
around and began the return leg of the journey back to Rome with
Livia. But Augustus never made it home. On 19 August, at about three
o'clock in the afternoon, according to official reports, Rome's first
emperor died at his family's estate in the Campanian town of Nola,
not far from Mount Vesuvius. His last words were to his wife of fifty-
two years, whom he is said to have kissed and adjured, 'Live mindful
of our marriage, Livia, and farewell', before his eyes closed in death.[127]

For five days while Augustus's body burned on a pyre in the Campus
Martius, Livia did not leave his side, but remained rooted to the spot
in silent grieving vigil long after the senatorial mourners and their
wives had gone home. Traditionally, the task of washing and caring
for the bodies of the dead before burial fell to Roman women, but
Livia's commitment was unusual. To a witness who claimed (in what
was probably a pre-choreographed statement) to have seen Augustus's
spirit soaring out of the flames to the heavens, Livia paid a reward of
1,000,000 sesterces to show her gratitude. Afterwards, accompanied
by leading members of the equestrian order, she completed her duties
by scooping up his bones from the fire, and laid them in his purpose-
built mausoleum by the Tiber, where the remains of Marcellus, Agrippa
and Augustus's sister Octavia already rested.[128]

That is one version of what happened. But in a pattern that will
become all too familiar as this history of Rome's imperial women
unfurls, another tradition exists, one which casts Livia in an entirely
different light. Anxious that Augustus was about to renege on his choice
of Tiberius as his designated heir, and anoint Julia's last surviving son,
Agrippa Postumus, his successor instead, it is suggested in some historical sources that Livia had in fact disposed of her husband by smearing
poison on the ripe green figs which the clean-living emperor liked to
pluck from the trees around his house and then suppressed the news
of his death until Tiberius could reach Nola. Thus the announcement
of Augustus's death could be followed seamlessly by an on-the-spot
proclamation of Tiberius as the new emperor, obviating any delays
and ensuring a smooth transition of power from father to adopted son.
Agrippa Postumus, Julia's youngest son and the last potential obstacle
to the succession, was murdered immediately after Tiberius's investiture.
There was confusion about who had given the order.[129]

Livia the devout wife at her husband's deathbed, or Livia the manipulative cold-blooded political operative? Which portrait should we believe? It is a dilemma all too common to the study of these women, and is not a question that can be answered with any satisfying degree of certainty. Livia was not the last empress to be accused of murdering her husband. Indeed, the striking plot similarities between Livia's reported actions following Augustus's death and accounts written by the same historians of the behaviour of at least two future empresses should make us at least sceptical of taking such accusations at face value.[130]

But there is a bigger point at stake in the recycling of these stories about Rome's first empress. They speak to the profound anxiety sparked amongst the Roman elite by the increased visibility of women in Roman public life under Augustus. Where power had once been located firmly in the Senate, and distributed among its patrician members, now, for the first time in its history, Rome had its own first family, a dynastic clan from which the rulers of empire were exclusively chosen, and which celebrated the female guarantors of that progression with unprecedented amounts of exposure. Moreover, the designation on the Palatine of an imperial residence equivalent to a White House or a 10 Downing Street meant that women now presided over a household that also served as the headquarters of government, bringing them closer than ever to the epicentre of political power, both literally and figuratively. From that privileged position, they enjoyed the kind of access to the emperor that others could only dream of: as Nancy Reagan once said of her relationship with her presidential husband: 'For eight years, I was sleeping with the president, and if that doesn't give you special access, I don't know what does.'[131] Wherever the truth lies of Livia's involvement in Augustus's death, the question of how much and what kind of influence should be wielded by her and other Roman first ladies, was to be a key battleground of imperial politics over the coming decades.

3

Family Feud: The People's Princess and the Women of Tiberius's Reign

Everyone called Agrippina the honour of her country, the blood of Augustus, the only and last example of the ancient Roman Vertue: And everyone prayed the Gods that they would preserve her Race, and make her live beyond, and after the entire ruin of these wicked men.

Madeleine de Scudéry, *Les femmes illustres* (1642)[1]

On a winter's day in the year 19, a packed crowd of spectators stood shoulder to shoulder at the harbour of Brundisium (Brindisi) on Italy's southern-eastern heel, awaiting the return from overseas of one of Rome's favourite daughters. Brundisium was the gateway to Italy for travellers from Greece and Asia Minor. A bustling port usually clogged with merchant ships unloading their wares, it was here in 40 BC that Octavian and Antony had held their peace summit and toasted it with the latter's wedding to Octavia. But on this day, almost sixty years since that ill-starred treaty, the stage of Brundisium was set for a wake, not a marriage feast.

As all eyes strained across the truculent grey winter sea, some of those present waded into the cool shallows in their eagerness to catch sight of the lady's ship, already looming over the horizon from the direction of Corcyra (Corfu). Others squatted on nearby rooftops and walls, like rooks silhouetted against the sky. The mood was subdued, according to Tacitus, with people wondering 'whether they ought to receive her landing in silence or with some utterance. As they still hesitated about the appropriate course, the fleet gradually came nearer. There was none of the usual brisk rowing, but every deliberate sign of grief.' When at last the ship had laboured into port and the lady stepped down the gangplank on to dry land, barely able to meet the eyes of her well-wishers, it was seen that she was accompanied by two of her children, and that she carried 'the urn of death in her hands. Her companions were worn out by prolonged grieving; so the sorrow of the fresh mourners who now met her was more demonstrative. Otherwise everyone's feelings were indistinguishable; the cries of men and women, relatives and strangers, blended in a single universal groan.'[2]

The ship's passenger was not Julia. Augustus's daughter was, alas, long dead, perishing in exile of malnutrition just a few months after her father's passing five years previously, her death a direct result of her ex-husband Tiberius vengefully cutting off all financial support to her. Her aged mother Scribonia had since returned to Rome – whether she was still alive or not at this point is unknown.[3] The grieving newcomer was in fact Agrippina Maior, Julia's younger daughter from her marriage to Agrippa, and the urn she carried bore the ashes not of her ill-fated mother, but of her immensely popular thirty-four-year-old husband Germanicus, the eldest product of the marriage between Octavia's daughter Antonia and Livia's boy Drusus, and one of the great hopes of the Julio-Claudian dynasty.[4] Germanicus had died weeks earlier in Syria. The circumstances were mysterious, his body so ravaged by the effects of poison, some said, that his skin was covered in dark stains and his mouth flecked with foam.

The journey from Brundisium to Rome along the 370 miles (600 kilometres) of Rome's oldest highway, the Appian Way, typically took travellers anything from a week to a fortnight. As Agrippina and her husband's funerary cortège proceeded slowly towards the capital, where Germanicus's ashes were destined for the family mausoleum, mourners in their black and purple weeds watched their sad progress, and the air, usually ripe with the odour of the mosquito-dwelling swamps which plagued travellers along this route, was instead thick with the scent of perfumes and burnt offerings made by each settlement along the way. At the coastal town of Tarracina just short of Rome, the procession was met by Germanicus's younger brother Claudius, and some of the deceased's children. Inside the capital, they found a city in mourning, so lost to grief that people were not even observing the public holiday which should have been given over to feasting and celebration in honour of the Saturnalia festival that took place every December.[5]

But amidst the lamentation, there was another current running through the grieving crowds – one of anger and suspicion. It had not gone unnoticed that at least two mourners were highly conspicuous by their absence. Where, people demanded, was the Emperor Tiberius? Where was his mother Livia? Why had they not come out to mourn the people's prince?

The twenty-three-year reign of Rome's unlikely second emperor

Tiberius was a chequered stewardship. Not the first or even the second choice for the job, Tiberius's undoubted competence as a general was not matched by his skills as a politician. A reserved, dour figure, lacking the charisma and populist antennae of his stepfather Augustus, who was said to have been reluctant to hand over the reins of empire to someone with such 'slow-grinding jaws', Tiberius wore the purple awkwardly. His reign was characterised as a penny-pinching, indecisive era of government, dogged by tensions between the emperor and the senatorial classes, which eventually descended into outright despotism and vice.[6]

This hostility between emperor and Senate was mirrored by feuding within the imperial family itself. It centred in part on Tiberius's souring relationship with his elderly mother Livia, whose prominence in his administration was a source of great friction between mother and son and a target of hostility from the jury of ancient historians sitting in judgement on Tiberius, who perceived the pre-eminence of a woman in public life as a symptom of the political chaos said to characterise the Julio-Claudian era after Augustus. Germanicus's death, however, was the most serious crisis of Tiberius's reign. As well as sparking accusations of a cover-up against the emperor and his mother, it fuelled a simmering row between Tiberius and the widowed Agrippina, and raised new questions about the appropriate role of women in public life, questions that dogged the footsteps of every generation of imperial women who followed in their wake.

Livia had now embarked on the final chapter of her life. It was just over fifty years since marriage to Octavian had plucked her from relative obscurity and set her on the path to becoming empress. Just as she had been the first woman to define that role, the accession of her son Tiberius following the death of Augustus in 14 meant that she now became Rome's first dowager empress and entered uncharted waters once more.

Attempts were made to clarify Livia's new role in the guise of 'queen mother' even before her husband's lavish state funeral had begun, with the public reading in the Senate of his will, which Augustus had painstakingly copied into two notebooks just over a year before his death.[7] In the first instance, it confirmed that Livia and her son had been nominated as the chief beneficiaries in Augustus's estate, which in total amounted to a value of 150 million sesterces. Tiberius received two-thirds of this, while the other third went to Livia herself.

It was a vast sum. Females were usually subject to strict limits on the amount that they could inherit thanks to the *Lex Voconia*, a law which had been on the statute books since 169 BC and which still prohibited women from receiving bequests from those whose wealth was estimated at more than 100,000 asses (an as being a unit of Roman currency).[8] A special waiver from the Senate, however, now permitted Livia to inherit a fortune that made her one of the richest women in Rome, supplementing the income from the farming estates, brick-works and copper mines she owned in Italy, Gaul and Asia Minor, and Egypt, where she had a large papyrus marsh, vineyards, farms, olive presses and winepresses, possibly allotted to her after her husband's defeat of Cleopatra at Actium.[9] Livia had also recently been a major beneficiary in the will of her good friend Queen Salome of Judaea, who bequeathed the empress the territories of Jamnia, Phasalis and lush Archaelais, an area to the west of the River Jordan, renowned for its palm groves and high-quality dates.

More importantly though, in terms of the public role envisaged for her in the new imperial set-up, Augustus's will also stipulated that Livia should be adopted into his own Julian family clan. This was a gesture from a husband to his wife without historic precedent. In addition, having for so long held off giving her an honorific name or title equiv-alent to his own, Augustus's will stated that Livia should henceforth be known as Julia Augusta. Her new *cognomen* represented an official elevation in status, and laid down yet another new marker – no other woman before this is known to have received a feminised version of an honorary title held by her husband.[10] Subsequently, *Augusta* became the official moniker for many of Livia's successors whose sons acceded to the throne, just as *Augustus* became part of every Roman emperor's own title.[11]

Augustus was not, as some have speculated, granting his wife equal billing with Tiberius by giving her the feminine version of his own name.[12] Like all other Roman women, Livia was still barred from the all-male political arenas of the Senate, the army camps and the assem-blies, and had no official role in Palatine politics. In the latter sense, she had something in common with the modern presidential spouse, whose role is also constitutionally undefined. But she was now, without question, the closest thing to a queen that Rome had ever had, and this soon posed a dilemma for her newly invested son that was compounded when the Senate proposed to bestow tributes on her over and above the ones granted in Augustus's will.

The least contentious motion, which was duly passed, was that Livia be appointed priestess of her husband's cult – Augustus had been posthumously consecrated as a god on 17 September, thus allowing him to be worshipped in the guise of 'the Divine Augustus'. Religion was one of the few spheres in which Roman women were previously allowed to play any kind of official public role, as attendants in religious ceremonies or mouthpieces of public grief. But with the exception of the Vestal Virgins, no woman was permitted to hold any of the major priesthoods in Rome. In her groundbreaking new capacity, Livia was permitted to call on the services of a lictor, an official usually assigned to act as a minder to magistrates when they were moving through the city. Yet it was only when the Senate also suggested that Livia henceforth be known as *mater patriae* ('Mother of our Country') – a play on the title *pater patriae* granted a decade previously to Augustus – and, more provocatively, that Tiberius's official title should be qualified by the description 'son of Julia' or 'son of Livia' that the new emperor was moved to use his imperial veto.

Tiberius excused his refusal on the grounds of modesty, and asserted that 'only reasonable honours must be paid to women', pointing out that he would also be declining gratuitous tributes on his own behalf. He had good reason to be concerned. Overexposure of Livia's name and image could, as Augustus himself had realised during his own lifetime, have antagonised traditionalist critics still hankering after the republic. They would be quick to detect the whiff of eastern-style monarchism in the Julio-Claudian regime's self-presentation. There are those, we are told, who were already complaining at having to be 'slaves to a woman'. Few doubted though that what really bothered Tiberius was irritation and resentment at what he saw as the promotion of his mother at the expense of his own authority.[13] There was no getting around the fact that Livia was Tiberius's sole legitimising link to his stepfather and predecessor, and it was not just the Senate but the provinces who insisted on reminding Tiberius of this fact. Several showed no compunction in labelling Livia's portraits with the title that Tiberius himself had officially denied her.[14] Thus began Tiberius's constant struggle to define and regulate the role of his mother within his regime.

In some respects, the redoubtable Livia carried on just as she had before, showing few signs during the early years of her son's reign of relinquishing the role of gatekeeper to the emperor that she had played under Augustus. If anything, her presence was felt in the corridors of power even more. She conducted her own correspondence with client kings such as Archelaus of Cappadocia, and official letters and communications to Tiberius from the provinces were addressed to his mother as well as to himself. In one instance, Livia's old friends the Spartans wrote separately to her and her son, advising them of their plans to inaugurate a festival in honour of the divine Augustus and his family, to which Tiberius in his reply wrote that he would leave it to his mother to respond herself.[15] Since before Augustus's death, Livia had also held her own version of the men's morning *salutatio*, which gave her opportunities to bend the ear of senators as well as listen to petitions and requests from clients and friends. If she, as a woman, could not go to the Senate, then they would come to her.[16] The *Monumentum Liviae* was found to contain the ashes of support staff – doorkeepers (*ostiarii*) and greeters (*salutatores*) – whose job it was to filter these dignitaries and petitioners seeking entry to the empress's presence, and though we do not have a specific record of one, a *nomenclator* may also have been needed to help Livia remember the names of all of these guests.[17]

From his exiled vantage point on the Black Sea, Ovid, the poetic *bête noire* of the Augustan regime, once gave a memorable description of one of these audiences, in a letter to his wife back in Rome. Begging her to go to Livia, whom he gushingly described as having the ethereal beauty of Venus, the character of Jupiter and the virtue of a woman of olden times, and intercede with the emperor on his behalf, he advised his wife to choose her time of approach carefully: 'If she's busy with something more important, put off your attempt and be careful not to spoil my hopes by being too hasty. But I would urge you not to wait until she is completely at leisure; she scarcely has time for the care of her own person.' Reading between the lines of Ovid's honeyed paean, it becomes clear that the poet is in fact mischievously satirising Livia's formidable reputation, breezily scoffing at what he anticipates will be his wife's fears that she may be entering the den of a monster, while managing insidiously to compare Livia to a catalogue of she-monsters from myth: 'She isn't wicked Procne or Medea or savage Clytemnestra, or Scylla, or Circe . . . or Medusa with snakes knotted into her hair . . .'[18]

Recently discovered copies of a document issued by the Roman Senate in the year 19 reveal that Livia was publicly thanked in the official record for her personal favours towards men of every rank.[19] This concurs with other literary testimony besides Ovid's that Livia was a useful benefactress to many in the senatorial classes. As well as lending money to those who were too cash-strapped to pay for their daughters' wedding dowries, she brought up the children of some families under her own aegis, an arrangement presumably seen as of great social advantage to those boys – for boys they seem to have invariably been. But Livia's habit of summoning senators to her own house clearly set backs up in other quarters, where it was viewed less as the prerogative of a respected matriarch than as the self-important act of an interfering female:

> For she had become puffed up to an enormous extent, surpassing all women before her, and would even make a regular habit of receiving in her house any of the Senate and people who wanted. This is a fact that was entered in the public records . . .[20]

It was Tiberius, however, who struggled most with Livia's accumulating public importance. Early on in his reign, he vetoed her attempts to invite the senators, members of the equestrian classes and their wives to a banquet she proposed to host in honour of the deceased Augustus. Women typically only invited the female guests at dinner parties, and Tiberius was thus actually just restricting her to the role she had played at state banquets under Augustus's aegis.[21] On another occasion though, two years after his accession, he reprimanded his mother for taking charge of efforts to douse a fire which was threatening the temple of Vesta. Tiberius was said to have been angered by news that Livia was herself personally directing not just the ordinary populace but also the soldiers – always a sensitive topic where a woman's remit was concerned. She had done so moreover without consulting him, as if Augustus was still the emperor and not his stepson.[22]

For all this, Tiberius was all too well aware of Livia's importance to him as the link that bound him to Augustus. It is for this reason that more portraits of Livia survive from the years of her son's reign than from that of her husband, and as Livia's public role underwent a metamorphosis, so too did her official portrait. In spite of the fact that she was over seventy years of age when Tiberius became emperor, in dedicated artwork Livia was getting progressively younger.[23] Slowly but surely, the round-faced visage of her earlier public portraits underwent a facelift, the severe *nodus* hairstyle with its bulky pompadour gradually replaced with a softer, more graceful centre parting, her wrinkles filled in, her skin made smoother, her expression calmer and more serene.

In part, this change was due to a dramatic shift in portraiture styles generally since the republican period. Before the Augustan age, the more crumpled and 'realistic' the features of the sitter, the more *gravitas* and standing conferred on the subject. Now, though, there was a return to the youthful, idealising contours of earlier Greek and Hellenistic statuary, ensuring that the faces the imperial family presented to the world never grew old. This sold the notion of the current era as perfectly and reassuringly suspended in time, a visual representation of Virgil's description of the Augustan age as *imperium sine fine* – 'power without end'.[24]

Livia now appeared on coins of the Roman mint for the first time, with her hair restyled in the new centre parting, a mode usually seen only on statues of goddesses. In fact, one of the most striking differences between male and female imperial portraiture from this point was that while most emperors avoided attracting accusations of egocentric posturing by insisting on sculptures of themselves – at least while still alive – depicting them in their 'work' uniform of toga or breastplate, their female dependants were increasingly shown in the regalia of state goddesses connected with motherhood and fertility such as Juno and Ceres, a contrast that presumably found favour because it suggested a blander, more universal, less troublingly individualised role for women in the imperial set-up. Sculptors and gem-cutters across the empire latched on to this trend, assimilating the features of the emperor's wife with those of favourite divinities. A sardonyx cameo for example, probably a privately owned trinket in antiquity though now in the collection of the Kunsthistorisches Museum in Vienna, represents Livia wearing the costume of the cultic mother-goddess Cybele over her *stola*, and contemplating a miniature bust of her deified husband, which she holds in her right hand. In her left, she clutches an ear of corn, a symbol of fecundity associated with Ceres, the Roman goddess of the harvest.[25]

Tiberius needed people to accept Livia as both kingmaker and Roman *materfamilias* par excellence. So although he turned down some more honours for his mother, such as an attempt by the Senate to have the month of October renamed Livius, he did allow her birthday to be observed on the official Roman calendar, an unusual honour for a woman. An inscription from Forum Clodii, a village just outside Rome, records that honeyed wine and little pastries were distributed from the temple of the Bona Dea to women from neighbouring villages, to mark Livia's birthday on this date, 30 January.[26]

Since Tiberius never remarried after the death of Julia, remaining a bachelor emperor for the whole of his twenty-three-year reign, Livia in effect filled the vacancy for an imperial consort. That a woman other than the wife of a head of state should take the leading role in his household is a recognisable concept. Within the historical tradition of modern American first ladies, for example, several American presidents, bachelors and widowers or even just those with reclusive wives, turned to their daughters, daughters-in-law and nieces to act as primary hostesses of the White House.[27] Livia herself had no peer within the Roman imperial household. The most long-standing female resident of the Palatine besides herself these days was her widowed daughter-in-law Antonia, who some time since had colonised the role of grieving maternal paragon vacated by her mother Octavia.

Born on 31 January 36 BC, shortly before her parents' marriage broke up, Antonia could not have had many memories of her absentee father Antony, who died in his lover Cleopatra's arms in Egypt when she was just six years old.[28] Growing up under the roof of her uncle Augustus, alongside a noisy assortment of cousins and siblings, she had been a contemporary of Julia's, and near the date of her seventeenth birthday, she was married off to Livia's younger son Drusus – a union celebrated in a court poem by the Greek Crinagoras and unaccompanied by any of the scandalous *on dits* that dogged the marriages of her risqué older cousin Julia. The partnership produced two sons and a daughter born between 15 and 10 BC – Germanicus, Livilla and Claudius.

Drusus's untimely death in 9 BC when the youngest boy Claudius was just a year old, left Antonia a widow at the age of twenty-seven. Her intense reaction, according to the author of the *Consolatio* written for Livia, was not unlike her mother Octavia's at the death of Marcellus.[29] Unusually and surprisingly, given the social expectation placed on Roman women by her uncle Augustus's marital legislation to find new husbands as soon as possible after divorce or widowhood, Antonia never remarried, choosing instead to remain, without censure, an *univira* – literally, a one-man woman. She did, however, have a good precedent for doing so, copying the example set by Cornelia, the highest exemplar of republican womanhood, and since she had already produced the mandatory three children required to benefit from the privileges of the rule of *ius liberorum*, she could afford to live a relatively independent life, excused from the necessity for male guardianship and the financial scrutiny that went with it.[30]

Antonia nevertheless remained on the Palatine, acting as a companion to her venerable mother-in-law.[31] Like Livia, she is known to have had her own apartments and highly specialised staff, dozens of whose remains were buried alongside those of Livia's slaves and freedmen in the *Monumentum Liviae*, thus affording us a through-the-keyhole look at Antonia's daily routine. They tell us that she was helped with her toilet by an *ornatrix* (a dresser) called Pamphilia and that a *sarcinatrix* (craftswoman) called Athenais mended her clothes. A personal physician, Celadus, tended to her medical well-being, and Eros, a *lecticarius* (a litter-bearer), chauffeured her about the city. Cold drinks were served to her by a cupbearer named Liarus while a chanteuse called Quintia serenaded her, accompanied in a duet perhaps by a male singer called Tertius. Another key member of her household was the freedwoman Caenis, who acted as her secretary, a woman who was to make far more of an impact on Roman imperial history than her modest origins might predict.[32]

Antonia also kept slaves outside Rome and was a considerable landowner in her own right, benefiting from bequests made by wealthy family friends such as Berenice I of Judaea, and also from her father's career in the east. Papyri miraculously preserved in the dry sands of Egypt testify that Antonia owned estates in the Arsinoite district of that country, possibly received courtesy of the division of Antony's assets there.[33] These same dusty fragments also provide insights into the kind of day-to-day disputes that took place on these estates. In one case, a bailiff called Dionysius complained to local authorities that a neighbouring landowner's sheep had caused damages to wheat stores on Antonia's estate, while in a document dated to 14 November 36, a farmer in her employ who signs himself 'Aunes, aged 35 [years] with a scar on his left thumb', reports the loss of his red-skinned pig.[34]

We have no first-hand correspondence to suggest whether or not Antonia concerned herself much with mundane disputes such as missing pigs, but through the letters of male family members, we do get a sense of her everyday responsibilities on the domestic front, chief of which was the shared education with Livia of the various children living on the Palatine under these two matriarchs' protection.[35] As well as the youngest members of the Julio-Claudian dynasty and the children of senatorial families growing up under Livia's supervision, their charges included young princes and princesses from the royal families of Armenia, Thrace, Commagene and Parthia who made long visits to Rome in a show of *entente cordiale* between the Mediterranean superpowers.[36] One such protégé was a grandson of King Herod the Great and the heir to the kingdom of Judaea, Marcus Julius Agrippa. His mother, Berenice, was a great friend of Antonia's, and consequently Julius Agrippa was sent as a child to be brought up by Antonia alongside her own son of the same age, Claudius. He remained a fixture in Roman circles until 23.[37]

Such arrangements made great PR for the Julio-Claudian regime, reinforcing their territorial authority as well as earning Livia and Antonia veneration as the maternal figureheads of the empire. But official praise for the pair as benevolent patrons of other people's children is offset by the less than rosy descriptions of their treatment of Claudius recorded by the latter's biographers.[38] Famously characterised as the downtrodden, imbecilic black sheep of his illustrious family, Claudius was hampered from childhood by disabilities including a limp and physical tremors, the effects, it is now surmised, of cerebral palsy. An earnest student of literature, yet requiring the constant, much resented chaperonage of a tutor, Claudius cut a fragile figure on public occasions, swathed chin to toe in a thick cloak, and his appearances had to be carefully choreographed.[39] That this involved careful consultation with the boy's mother and grandmother is revealed by a rare preserved letter from Augustus to Livia, dating from around two years before the former's death and apparently part of an ongoing correspondence between them on the matter. In the following extract, Augustus debates whether Claudius should be allowed to appear with the family at the upcoming Games of Mars, and in the process permits us an intriguing glimpse of Julio-Claudian family politics at work, for his postscript makes clear that the rearing of children within the Palatine household was very much a family affair, and that while Antonia was permitted to be privy to the arrangements for her son, decisions about him rested principally with Augustus, in close consultation with Livia:

My dear Livia,

As you suggested, I have now discussed with Tiberius what we should do about your grandson Claudius at the coming Games of Mars. We both agreed that a decision ought to be taken once and for all. The question is whether he has – shall I say? – full command of all his senses.

If so, I can see nothing against sending him through the same degrees of office as his brother; but should he be deemed physically and mentally deficient, the public (which always likes to scoff and mock at such things) must not be given a chance of laughing at him and us. I fear that we shall find ourselves in constant trouble if the question of his fitness to officiate in this or that capacity keeps cropping up . . .

As regards the immediate question in your last letter, I have no objection to his taking charge of the priests' banquet at the Festival of Mars, if he lets his relative, the son of Silvanus, stand by to see that he does not make a fool of himself. But I am against his watching the Games in the Circus from the imperial box, where the eyes of the whole audience would be on him . . . in short, my dear Livia, I am anxious that a decision should be reached on this matter once and for all, to save us from further alternations of hope and despair. You are at liberty to show this part of my letter to our kinswoman Antonia for her perusal . . .[40]

Though Augustus later revised his unflattering view of his grandson's qualities, commenting in another letter to Livia that he had actually been impressed by the boy's skills as an orator, Claudius's disabilities apparently attracted the withering scorn of his female elders, not just his grandmother Livia and sister Livilla, but Antonia herself, who was reported to have disparagingly referred to her younger son as a fool and 'a monster: a man whom Nature had not finished but had merely begun'.[41] Livia meanwhile was said to have avoided communication with him except through brief notes, and joined forces with Antonia in stopping the budding young scholar from writing a history of the civil war that preceded Augustus's inauguration.[42]

In this last respect, Livia and Antonia were in fact doing nothing less than what every good Roman mother was expected to do for her sons. Although affectionate relationships between mothers and sons were by no means unheard of – as letters between second-century emperor Marcus Aurelius and his mother Domitia Lucilla will later demonstrate – Roman women did not generally receive praise in the ancient historical record for being doting and sensitive. Remember Seneca's disapproval of Octavia for being too emotional over the death of Marcellus. In the eyes of Roman moralists, the best thing a mother could do for her son, apart from breastfeeding him herself, was to steer him towards suitable intellectual pursuits, and away from potentially dangerous and corrosive areas of study. It was an achievement that Cornelia, among others, had been fêted for, and one that future mothers of Roman emperors would also try to emulate. In an illustration of the disconnect between the colourful behind-the-scenes portraits of life on the Palatine painted by biographers like Suetonius, and the officially disseminated ideal of a woman's role, Livia actually received praise in official documents posted later in Tiberius's reign on account of her rigorous supervision of Claudius's education.[43]

Though Livia's accomplice in this and other respects, Antonia understandably had a far more modest public portrait profile than her mother-in-law, reflecting her lesser importance to the men of her family. While over 100 statues and coins survive that can be identified with some confidence as Livia, the same can be said for only thirteen portraits of Antonia, and in contrast to Livia's ever-metamorphosing public image, they survive in only one relatively static prototype.[44] The master portrait for this group is the so-called 'Wilton House Antonia', named in honour of the residence of its owner, Thomas Herbert, eighth Earl of Pembroke and Montgomery. When Herbert bought the bust in 1678, so close was the resemblance to ancient coin portraits of Antonia that the name 'Antonia' had already been scratched onto its left shoulder, immortalising its identity.[45] The head, which is now in the Sackler Museum at Harvard, depicts a woman past her first youth – though still heavily idealised, given that Antonia was well into her fifties at the time of its creation – with strong individualised features, thin pursed lips and a chin which recedes slightly when viewed from the side.[46]

A portrait of Antonia conforming to the 'Wilton House' example came to light during excavations of the forum of the ancient North African city of Lepcis Magna in modern Libya. Thanks to the 1934 discovery of an accompanying inscription written in neo-Punic, we can deduce that it belonged to an imposing statue group honouring the imperial family set up on the platform of the town's temple of Augustus and Roma during the 20s. Though the sculpture of Antonia is one of the few originals that have been found from this cluster, the inscription allows the reconstruction of the original composition of the group, which at first glance appears to have been a magnificent snapshot of the new look Julio-Claudian dynasty under Tiberius, untrammelled by tensions and showing a united front. Dominating the centre was a chariot occupied by Germanicus and Drusus Minor, the adoptive and biological sons and heirs respectively of Tiberius. It in turn was flanked by life-sized statues of the two young men's mothers and wives, so that Germanicus was accompanied by his mother Antonia and wife Agrippina Maior on one side. At the heirs' back, towering over the junior members of the family group, were four larger-than-life statues of Livia, Tiberius, the deified Augustus and the goddess Roma. The surviving head of Livia's statue measures 68 cm (27 inches) in height, and that of her dead husband Augustus an even more gargantuan 92 cm (36 inches), giving some idea of the colossal scale, and leaving no doubt of their seniority.[47]

In showing two budding statesmen, Germanicus and Drusus Minor, accompanied by their mothers rather than by their fathers, the Lepcis Magna group was highly unusual.[48] Its primary function was to honour these two great hopes of the Julio-Claudian dynasty, born to two women from opposite branches of it. But there is another story here. If the whole survived today, the Lepcis Magna group would capture perfectly in marble the complex, interbred tangle of relationships, rivalries and resentments that were to wreck Augustus's and Livia's dynastic legacy and tear the family apart.

The seeds of this division had been sown back in the year 4, when Augustus reshuffled the dynastic pack and forced Tiberius to adopt Antonia's eldest son Germanicus as a condition of his eventual succession. Barely out of his teens, yet already a dashing contrast to his unfortunate younger brother Claudius, Germanicus had gone on in the year 5 to form what would prove a pivotal union with his cousin Agrippina Maior, the daughter of Julia and Agrippa, who was then around nineteen years old – a relatively late age for a girl of the imperial family to be wed for the first time.[49] The marriage temporarily unified the two branches of the Julio-Claudian family, since any offspring it produced would be the great-grandchildren of both Augustus and Livia.

Effectively orphaned at the age of twelve when Julia was banished to Pandateria in 2 BC, Agrippina managed to avoid the scandalous pitfalls which befell her mother and younger sister Julia Minor. Growing up, she was known to have been a great favourite of her grandfather Augustus, who maintained an affectionate correspondence with her, and praised her in a letter for her intelligence though he also advised her to adopt a plainer style of writing and speaking, such as he favoured himself.[50] For many ancient – and modern – observers, Agrippina, in contrast to her disgraced mother, represented much of what was admirable in the ideal Roman matron. Tacitus's description of her as 'determined and rather excitable' was tempered by his acknowledgement of her 'devoted faithfulness to her husband', while to the nineteenth-century historian Elizabeth Hamilton, who wrote a three-volume history of Agrippina's life in 1804, her subject exemplified the value of an educated woman to society, although the author did not approve of what she portrayed as Agrippina's ambition to share her husband's fame.[51]

In a storyline that bears strong resemblance to the first marriage of her mother Julia to Marcellus, Agrippina and Germanicus quickly became the golden couple of the Julio-Claudian dynasty. Although Germanicus's fellow heir Drusus acquired a wife in his adoptive brother's sister Livilla, they lacked the glamour of their counterparts, Germanicus a popular paragon of handsome chivalry, and Agrippina proving herself a fine advertisement for motherhood, giving birth in due course to no fewer than nine children, six of whom survived infancy.[52] They included two siblings who would eventually rank among the *enfants terribles* of Roman history – a son Gaius, better known as Caligula, and a daughter, Agrippina Minor ('Agrippina the Younger').

Germanicus enjoyed a meteoric rise through the political and military ranks, earning appointment to the consulship in 12 at the precocious age of twenty-six, and subsequently the proconsular command of legions stationed in Gaul and Germany. Agrippina herself accompanied him to his posting, where they were later joined by two-year-old Gaius, who received his nickname Caligula, meaning 'Little Boot', from his father's troops. A few months before Augustus's death, the old emperor had written a letter to his beloved granddaughter, in which he advised her of the arrangements he had personally made for Caligula's safe passage in the wake of her departure: 'I am . . . sending with him one of my slaves, a doctor who, as I have told Germanicus in a letter, need not be returned to me if he proves of use to you. Goodbye, my dear Agrippina! Keep well on the way back to your Germanicus.'[53]

In 14, the news of Augustus's death filtered through to troops patrolling the Rhine and Danube borders. It sparked a mutiny. Soldiers declared their loyalty to Germanicus over Tiberius while at the same time demanding better pay and conditions. Amid the chaos, Germanicus was urged to send his pregnant wife and son to a position of safety. Yet Agrippina was said to have disdainfully rejected the suggestion that she should flee, reminding her husband 'that she was of the blood of the divine Augustus and would live up to it, whatever the danger.' On finally being persuaded to go by a tearful Germanicus, she left in a convoy with other soldiers' wives, little Caligula in her arms, and her departure shamed into obeisance the wayward soldiers, stirred by the memory of her illustrious lineage and her 'impressive record as wife and mother', and embarrassed by the prospect of Roman women needing to seek asylum elsewhere. The immediate crisis was over, and the story served to confirm Agrippina as an heiress to the legacy of female peacemaker occupied most recently by Octavia.[54]

However, troubles flared up again the following year during a glory-seeking bid by Germanicus to breach German territory and extend the empire's frontiers. Panic spread as the invading Roman troops were surrounded and the counter-attacking German army threatened to swarm across the bridge the Romans had built over the Rhine. Once more, though, Agrippina saved the day, holding the fort and acting as a nurse to the wounded, all the while pregnant with her daughter Agrippina Minor:[55]

> Some, in panic, envisaged the disgraceful idea of demolishing the bridge. But Agrippina put a stop to it. In those days this great-hearted woman acted as commander. She herself dispensed clothes to needy soldiers, and dressed the wounded. Pliny the Elder, the historian of the German campaigns, writes that she stood at the bridge-head to thank and congratulate the returning column.[56]

A cinematic treatment of Agrippina's life would inevitably cast her as the plucky heroine. But to a Roman audience, the sight of a soldier's wife and would-be empress following the drum, directing military operations on behalf of her husband and helping forestall military embarrassment in the process, aroused more ambivalent emotions. For a start, there was the issue of Agrippina travelling abroad so freely. The question of whether women should be permitted to accompany their husbands to the front line or to political postings, had long provoked strong feelings among certain members of the ruling elite. During a debate in the Senate five years later, while discussing the choice of new governors for Africa and Asia, the senator Aulus Caecina Severus had introduced a sidebar, proposing that no appointee to a governorship should be allowed to take his wife along with him:

> The rule which forbade women to be taken to provinces or foreign countries was salutary. A female entourage stimulates extravagance in peacetime and timidity in war. Women are not only frail and easily

tired. Relax control, and they become ferocious, ambitious schemers, circulating among the soldiers, ordering company-commanders about. Recently a woman conducted battalion parades and brigade exercises! . . . They have burst through the old legal restrictions of the Oppian and other laws, and are rulers everywhere – at home, in the courts and now in the army.[57]

Severus's cantankerous tirade was swiftly rebutted, one of his inter-locutors insisting that the inability of a few husbands to control their wives was no reason to deprive all of them of conjugal company, and Drusus Minor himself pointed out that Augustus had often travelled east and west with Livia. But although Severus's concerns received little support from his listeners, the debaters did acknowledge that part of the reason for keeping women close by was to maintain a careful watch on the weaker sex: 'Marriages scarcely survive with the keeper on the spot,' it was pointed out, 'whatever would happen with some years of virtual divorce to efface them?'[58]

Then there was the question of Agrippina actually directing troops on the battlefield. Severus's outraged description in the Senate debate of 'a woman' recently conducting military exercises may not have been a reference to Agrippina herself, but there were other women of course, such as Antony's wife Fulvia, who in recent years had been the target of such vilification. These prejudices against women on the front line of war were often intricately wound up with fears that women would start making similar incursions into the political arena.[59]

That the thought occurred to Tiberius too was reflected in reports of his indignant and suspicious reaction to Agrippina's one-woman rescue mission on the German frontier:

There was something behind these attentions to the army, he felt; they were not simply because of the foreign enemy. 'The commanding officer's job', he reflected, 'is a sinecure when a woman inspects units and exhibits herself before the standards with plans for money-distributions' . . . Agrippina's position in the army already seemed to outshine generals and commanding officers; and she, a woman, had suppressed a mutiny which the emperor's own signature had failed to check.[60]

Over the next four years, the flames of Tiberius's animosity and jealousy towards his popular young ward and prospective heir continued to smoulder. Germanicus remained on the Rhine for the next two years, inflicting a series of military defeats against the Germans until recalled by the emperor to Rome to celebrate his triumph in a processional through the city on 26 May 17, which the whole population is said to have come on to the streets to witness. An old republican tradition was observed, which decreed that the sons of the triumphant commander should accompany their father in the parade. But in a novel amendment, the daughters of the *triumphator*, in this case sixteen-month-old Agrippina Minor and her baby sister Drusilla, who were both born on Germanicus's campaign trail, now rode in their father's chariot as well, alongside their three brothers.[61] It was a clever magnification of Augustus's old strategy of presenting himself as both a family man and strong protector of the state.

Tiberius's subsequent decision to dispatch Germanicus, accompanied by Agrippina and other members of his family, on a diplomatic tour of the empire's eastern provinces with a Senate-approved mandate of *maius imperium* – supreme authority – over all provincial governors in the region, was interpreted as an attempt to sideline his rival and detach him from his faithful legions.[62] The legacy of Actium should surely have warned against encouraging one's opponents to establish rival authority in the east, and soon the memory of that battle reared its head ominously, when in 18 the imperial entourage made a stop at the site of the great sea fight, so that Germanicus could make a pilgrimage to the location of his grandfather Antony's camp. Later they visited Cleopatra's old domain of Egypt and took a cruise up the Nile, taking in views of the pyramids, the Colossus of Memnon – a statue that 'sang' when the sun's rays passed over it – and other remnants of the ancient civilisation of Thebes. Germanicus also enacted popular measures such as lowering the price of corn while on a walkabout tour of Alexandria, and privately commissioned inscriptions dedicated to Antonia have been found along the route they took, honouring her for 'having provided the fullest and greatest principles of the most divine family', suggesting that perhaps she formed part of the family party too.[63]

It is hard to avoid the suspicion that the image of three generations of Augustus's arch-rival Antony sightseeing at iconic locations in their infamous relative's old hunting-ground was deliberately designed to enrage Tiberius.[64] It certainly left the latter distinctly unamused, provoking him to issue a reprimand against Germanicus for infringing a command that no senator or knight should enter Egypt without permission from the emperor.[65] Leaving Actium, the party soon stopped at the island of Lesbos, where early in 18, Agrippina gave birth to her third daughter and last child, Julia Livilla. The moment recalled her own delivery in the region just over thirty years earlier, when her mother Julia had accompanied Agrippa on his travels, and in a poignant echo of her mother's footprint around the Mediterranean, inscriptions have been found in the area of Lesbos, giving Agrippina titles in praise of her child-bearing prowess, such as *karphoros*, or 'fruit-bearing', just as Julia had received.[66]

Agrippina's fertility was a great selling point for the regime, one expressed in portraits showing a woman with strong, regular facial features, a determined chin and full-lipped mouth, her face framed by a hairstyle that deviated significantly from the vogue established by her female forebears. The middle parting made fashionable by Livia's late, classicising portrait was still in place, but the rest of Agrippina's hairstyle was quite different, her thick locks swept outwards into arched waves which were then arranged in thickly clustering ringlets around her temples, like piped curls of cream. These ringlets, each carefully coiffed coil punctured in the centre by the sculptor's drill to give it definition, were a technical tour de force, but curly hair also stood for youth, vibrancy and fecundity in the classical sculptural tradition, and was thus the perfect way to immortalise a celebrated mother of six, one of whom would in all likelihood prove the keeper of the Julio-Claudian flame.[67]

Livia and Agrippina, the two leading female lights of their generations of the Julio-Claudian family, were said to have disliked each other intensely, a piece of gossip reported by Tacitus, whose access to the lost memoirs of Agrippina's daughter Agrippina Minor lends credibility to the report.[68] The appearance of striking new portraits dedicated to Agrippina would not have eased such tensions. Through the smokescreen of our sources, it is difficult to ascertain which members of the Julio-Claudian household genuinely got on with each other. Livia obviously had day-to-day dealings with Antonia over the education of the children under their joint aegis, and was said to have been close to her granddaughter Livilla.[69] She also accumulated a wider circle of female friends, women such as Salome of Judaea, to whom she had once given pragmatic counsel when the latter expressed a reluctance to marry a man chosen for her by her brother King Herod. Livia advised her friend to abandon thoughts of marrying the man she really desired, the Arab Syllaeus, in order to avoid a serious rift within the Herodian royal family, evidence of a pragmatic strain in Livia that may have represented a lesson well learned in childhood from the Sabine women – those heroines of Rome's early history who accepted their own forced marriage rather than being the cause of war between their male kin.[70]

Livia's protection had proved an incredibly useful asset over the years to other women who found themselves in awkward situations. Two years after Augustus's death, the empress had intervened in a dispute between her friend Plautia Urgulania and a former consul named Lucius Calpurnius Piso, an outspoken critic of corruption in the courts and to whom Urgulania owed money. Urgulania took refuge with Livia on the Palatine rather than obey a summons to court from Lucius, and a stand-off which threatened to embarrass Tiberius was averted only when Livia paid the fine on Urgulania's behalf.[71] Her friendship with Livia afforded Urgulania great kudos, a fact that her own grandson Plautius Silvanus later discovered to his cost when he tried ineptly to conceal his murder of his wife Apronia, whom he had thrown out of a window. After judges were appointed to hear the case, Silvanus was sent a dagger by Urgulania. Owing to his grandmother's close friendship with the *Augusta*, Silvanus interpreted this as a message from the highest level that he should bring the matter to an end, and used the dagger on himself.[72]

From a modern feminist perspective, some have chosen to see in Livia a champion of her sex, shielding her friends from partisan witch-hunts, rather than an abuser of her position as mother of the emperor. But the sterner view of ancient commentators such as Tacitus was that Livia's close bond with women such as Urgulania placed her friends above the law. It was a damaging observation, particularly in the light of the scandal about to unfold.[73]

Despite the enthusiasm with which Germanicus and Agrippina were greeted on their various stops along their eastern tour, a simmering row brewing back in Syria, one of the provinces under Germanicus's supervision, was threatening to sour the whole trip.

Syria had recently been placed under new management with Tiberius's appointment of governor Calpurnius Piso, whose wealthy wife Munatia Plancina was, like Urgulania, an old friend of Livia's. Piso had been appointed by Tiberius ostensibly as an aide to Germanicus while he carried out his eastern duties but according to the account of Tacitus, it was whispered in some quarters that he was really there to thrust a spoke in Germanicus's wheel, and that Plancina had been primed by Livia, 'whose feminine jealousy was set on persecuting Agrippina'. Consequently, the relationship between their camps was fractious. Piso showed scant respect for Germanicus's authority while Plancina, who apparently 'went beyond feminine respectability by attending cavalry exercises', was reported to have got involved by verbally abusing her opposite number. When Germanicus returned to Syria after concluding his tour of Egypt, their long-running feud was reignited over Piso's failure to follow Germanicus's commands.[74]

In the autumn of 19, while still quartered in Antioch, Germanicus suddenly fell ill. Suspecting that Piso had poisoned him and convinced that curses had been placed around his sickbed, Germanicus summoned his friends to his bedside and accused the Syrian governor and his wife, singling out Plancina for special blame in lamenting, obscurely, that he had 'fallen to a woman's treachery'. Finally, he bade farewell to his wife Agrippina, begging her 'by her memories of himself and by their children, to forget her pride, submit to cruel fortune, and, back in Rome, to avoid provoking those stronger than herself by competing for their power'. In a private aside, he also warned her to beware Tiberius. On 10 October, at the age of thirty-three, Germanicus died, and the news of his illness and death, which took some weeks to reach Rome, sent shock waves of confusion and grief through the city, sparking angry demonstrations from those who suspected foul play, their fury fanned by claims that Plancina had celebrated Germanicus's demise by putting on festive clothing, in contrast to the sombre hues required of mourners. Agrippina made her way slowly back to the coast of Italy across the cold winter sea, finally disembarking before the sorrowing and sympathetic audience of Germanicus's colleagues and admirers at the port of Brundisium, clutching the urn with the cremated remains of her husband. In Tacitus's words, she was 'exhausted by grief and unwell, but impatient of anything that postponed revenge'.[75]

When the conspicuous absence of either the emperor or his mother from the mourners provoked disquiet from the crowds, Tiberius was forced to issue a statement urging people to conduct themselves with dignity in their grief. The climate remained rife with suspicion. People remembered the death of Germanicus's father Drusus, and stirred up old rumours by surmising that Germanicus had been killed because he was planning to restore the republic. Livia meanwhile was said to have had mysterious 'private talks' with Plancina. Also absent from the funerary ceremonies was the deceased's mother, Antonia, at least according to Tacitus, who reports that he found no record in official journals or histories of her being present. He puts the circumstance down to Tiberius's and Livia's making her stay inside, so as not to make their own absence seem more noticeable.[76]

Piso was indeed accused of murder and eventually forced to stand trial in Rome. Any hopes he had that Tiberius might intervene to save him were dashed, and he was found with his throat cut before a verdict could be reached. For Plancina, however, it was a different story. Livia's patronage evidently counted for a great deal. Plancina was as much loathed as her husband, but 'she had more influence' and 'it was doubted how far Tiberius could act against her'. After a two-day 'sham investigation' into her part in the affair, Plancina was spared as a result of Livia's private appeals on her behalf.[77]

Thanks to remarkable separate discoveries in the 1980s, two vital new pieces of evidence have resurfaced which shed fresh insight into this whole episode. Our comparing them to the account given by Tacitus allows us to reconstruct a more forensic picture of the events of 19-20, including the role of Livia, Agrippina and Antonia in the affair. The first of these exhibits came to light in 1982 when a fractured bronze tablet was recovered with the use of metal detectors in the Roman province of Baetica (Andalusia) in southern Spain. Dubbed the *Tabula Siarensis*, it was found to be inscribed with passages from two decrees issued by the Roman Senate in December of 19, two months after the death of Germanicus, which listed the posthumous honours that should be paid to him. Six years after this retrieval, the searchers struck gold (or bronze) once more in the same region, coaxing yet more tablets out of the soil, this time preserving several copies of one of the most important Roman inscriptions ever discovered – the complete 176-line text of another decree of the Senate, dated to 10 December 20, a year after Germanicus's death. The second find was titled the *Senatus Consultum de Cn. Pisone patre*, and announced to the empire's provincial audience the outcome of the trial of Piso and Plancina for the murder of Germanicus.[78]

In their essentials, both the *Senatus Consultum de Cn. Pisone patre* (abbreviated henceforth to *SC*), which was posted in provincial capital cities and in the headquarters of the army's legions, and the *Tabula Siarensis* vindicate Tacitus's outline of events, although the latter slightly modifies Tacitus's conclusion that Germanicus's mother Antonia was excluded from the funeral rituals.[79] The *SC*, though, provides an intriguing insight into the role of Livia in the outcome of Plancina's trial. Writing of Livia's private intervention on behalf of Plancina, Tacitus noted that 'All decent people were, in private, increasingly violent critics of the *Augusta* – a grandmother who was apparently entitled to see and talk to her grandson's murderess, and rescue her from the senate'.[80] It is a strong accusation. But the *SC* in fact proves that the Senate acknowledged openly and publicly that Livia's request to Tiberius was indeed the reason for Plancina's acquittal:

> . . . our *Princeps* has often and pressingly requested from the House that the Senate be satisfied with the punishment of Cn. Piso Senior and spare his wife as it spared his son M[arcus], and pleaded himself for Plancina at the request of his mother and had very just reasons presented to him by her for wanting to secure her request . . . the Senate believes that to Iulia Aug[usta], who had served the common-wealth superlatively in giving birth to our *Princeps* but also through her many great favours towards men of every rank, and who rightly and deservedly could have supreme influence in what she asked from the senate, but who used that influence sparingly, and to the supreme piety of our *Princeps* towards his mother, support and indulgence should be accorded and has decided that the punishment of Plancina should be waived.[81]

These few lines inscribed on bronze are among the most impor-tant pieces of evidence in existence of Livia's position in Roman public life. While it would be unwise to assume that the Senate's grandilo-quent blandishments referring to her 'supreme influence' over the Senate should be taken at face value – she still could not, as a woman, even set foot inside the chamber – they prove that the senators publicly played along with the *idea* at least that Livia could exercise such power, if she chose to.[82] The words 'great favours towards men of every rank' also offer tangible evidence of Livia's influence, underlining her ongoing role as a powerful networker and patron behind the scenes of imperial bureaucracy. And as a whole, the lines reinforce the ideal, of which the public had been reminded with the dedication to her of statues after her son Drusus's death, that Livia had provided 'service' to the state through having given birth to the *princeps*, in a way com-parable to the 'service' provided by great statesmen and generals. In short, they leave little room for doubt that Livia's political influence, even if to some extent only symbolic, was taken very seriously.

The *Tabula Siarensis* states that Livia along with Antonia, Agrippina Maior and Germanicus's younger sister Livilla – though they were not actually allowed in the Senate – were involved in the senatorial process of drawing up a short list of suitable funerary honours for Germanicus. Tiberius was given the final say and the Senate duly dispatched an announcement to all Roman colonies and municipal towns that three monumental arches were to be built in Germanicus's honour, one on the mountain in Syria where Germanicus had held his last command, one on the banks of the Rhine near the cenotaph erected to the memory of his father Drusus, and one in Rome itself, near the Portico of Octavia and the Theatre of Marcellus. Although to this date triumphal arches had been strictly all-male affairs in terms of who was allowed to appear on them, it was decreed that the Roman arch was to be topped by a statue of Germanicus in his victor's chariot and flanked by statues of eleven family members including both his parents, his wife Agrippina and all his sons and daughters, echoing the whole family's inclusion in Germanicus's joyous real-life triumph of 17. It also constitutes the first evidence of statues of women other than Livia and Octavia being included within the capital city itself.[83]

Despite the promise of such a revolution in the medium of public sculpture, the *SC* reminds us of the prohibitively and reassuringly bland manner in which the imperial women were generally still represented. In lauding his widow Agrippina, his mother Antonia and his sister Livilla for their restraint in bereavement, and paying tribute to Livia for schooling the deceased's sons in the same respect, a counter-example to Seneca's criticism of Octavia's over-emotional mourning for Marcellus, it recycles stock laudatory epithets – Agrippina the fecund wife, Antonia the chaste widow and Livilla the obedient daughter and granddaughter:

> ... the Senate expresses its great admiration: of Agrippina, whom the memory of the divine Augustus, by whom she was greatly esteemed, and of her husband Germanicus, with whom she lived in unique harmony, and the many children born of their most fortunate union ... and further the Senate expresses its great admiration of Antonia the mother of Germanicus Caesar, whose only marriage was to Drusus the father of Germ[anicus], and who, through the excellence of her moral character, proved herself to the divine Augustus worthy of so close a relationship; and of Livi[ll]a the sister of Germ[anicus] whom her grandmother and her father-in-law, who is also her uncle, our

Princeps, hold in the highest esteem – whose esteem, even if she did not belong to their family, she could deservedly vaunt and can do so all the more as she is a lady attached by such family ties: the senate greatly admires these ladies in equal measure for their most loyal grief and their moderation in that grief.[84]

However, between the lines of the Senate's po-faced encomium of these women's collective virtues, and behind the sculptural commissions promising family unity, many people realised that all was not as harmonious in the Julio-Claudian family household as Tiberius's regime would have liked them to think.

Tensions between Agrippina and her relatives over the suspicious death of her husband did not go away after the case against Piso and Plancina was settled. On the day of Germanicus's funeral itself, Tiberius was said to have been infuriated by the reception the people gave Agrippina whom they called 'the glory of her country . . . the only true descendant of Augustus'.[85] Lingering antipathy between the two grew steadily worse over the next few years. Their hostility was exacerbated by the machinations of the Iago of the piece, Lucius Aelius Sejanus. A veteran soldier of Julio-Claudian military campaigns in Germany and the east, Sejanus had been appointed by Tiberius in 14 to the post of praetorian prefect, the head of the emperor's personal guard, and from that position, began to wield increasing influence. After Germanicus's demise, Tiberius's biological son Drusus Minor became the de facto heir to the throne. But his death in 23, at the age of thirty-six – in circumstances which later drew a charge of poisoning on his wife Livilla, who was said to have been having an affair with Sejanus – tipped the balance of succession towards Germanicus's family again and hope now rested chiefly on the latter's three sons Nero Caesar, Drusus Caesar and Caligula.[86]

Ambitious for power, the wily Sejanus now used his opportunity to pick away at the scab of resentment between Livia and Agrippina, attempting to foment the empress's and her son's antagonism towards Germanicus's widow by trading on what Tacitus described as Agrippina's 'insubordination' and 'ill-concealed maternal ambitions'. He was aided in his endeavour by the *Augusta*'s circle of female confidantes, including a woman named Mutilia Prisca, said to have 'great influence over the old lady', and Livilla, Germanicus's sister.[87]

Meanwhile relations between Tiberius and his mother were no less rocky during the 20s than they had been the previous decade. Public iconography celebrating their accord is countered by rumours in the literary record of further private flare-ups and disagreements. On 23 April 22, her dedication of a statue to the deified Augustus near the Theatre of Marcellus provoked Tiberius's ire when she had her own name placed above his in the accompanying inscription. A surviving record of the inscription in a calendar of the period, the *Fasti Praenestini*, confirms that her name was indeed placed before Tiberius's.[88] Perhaps it was an unwelcome reminder to Tiberius of the Senate's earlier attempts to style him by the infantilising moniker of 'son of Livia'. The gap between official spin and public speculation was being exposed once again.

When Livia fell seriously ill shortly after this spat, any ill-feeling between mother and son was concealed from the public. In a display of filial duty, Tiberius rushed back to Rome from Campania, where he had been convalescing himself, to be at her side. In the event, the eighty-year-old empress survived the health scare, and amid the tributes to her recovery, a bronze *dupondius* coin was issued later that year from the Roman mint, featuring the slogan *Salus Augusta* beneath her portrait, a long-overdue coin debut for the longest-lived and most influential woman in the Julio-Claudian dynasty.[89] *Salus*, signifying health or well-being, alluded to Livia's personal recovery and also toasted the health of the empire of which she was the ceremonial mother-figure. In the same year, more bronze coins (*sestertii*) were minted with an image of a *carpentum*, a wheeled carriage harnessed to mules which had previously been reserved for the exclusive use of the Vestal Virgins. They were emblazoned with the inscription SPQR *Iuliae Augustae* – 'The Senate and the People of Rome to Julia Augusta' – the first time an imperial woman had actually been identified by name rather than context on official coinage.[90]

The appearance of the *carpentum* on her coins strongly indicates that Livia was now permitted to use this special form of transport. It set her apart from other aristocratic women who usually had to travel on foot or in sedan chairs, and later that year, Livia also earned the right to sit with the Vestals in the audience of the Roman theatre, rounding off her steady appropriation of the special privileges of these hallowed priestesses, which had begun with her husband's gift of freedom from male guardianship back in 35 BC.[91] Yet the stories of quarrelling between her and Tiberius continued. By 26, the year that Tiberius chose to retire from Rome and take up more permanent residence first in Campania and then on the island of Capri, a nadir was reached when Livia failed to persuade her son to add a provincial candidate of her choosing to the judges' roster. This provoked her to confront the emperor with some unwelcome home truths about his stepfather's real opinion of him.[92]

> Tiberius agreed . . . on one condition – that the entry should be marked 'forced upon the Emperor by his mother'. Livia lost her temper and produced from a strong-box some of Augustus's own letters to her commenting on Tiberius's sour and stubborn nature. Annoyance with her for hoarding these documents so long, and then spitefully confronting him with them, is said to have been his main reason for retirement to Capri.[93]

Meanwhile Agrippina was also continuing to prove a thorn in Tiberius's side. That same year, a row broke out when one of her cousins, Claudia Pulchra, was charged with immorality, witchcraft and conspiracy against the emperor. Agrippina regarded the persecution of Claudia and other female friends of hers as a personal attack, and is said to have furiously confronted her uncle while he was in the middle of a sacrifice to his predecessor:

> 'The man who offers victims to the deified Augustus', she said, 'ought not to persecute his descendants. It is not in mute statues that Augustus's divine spirit is lodged – I, born of his sacred blood, am its incarnation! I see my danger; and I wear mourning. Claudia Pulchra is an idle pretext. Her downfall, poor fool, is because she chooses Agrippina as friend!'[94]

In response to her outburst, a tightly wound Tiberius was quoted as replying, 'And if you are not queen, my dear, have I then done you wrong?'[95] Following Claudia's condemnation, Agrippina became ill, and broke down when visited by Tiberius, begging to be allowed to remarry: 'I am lonely', she said, according to the diaries of her eponymously named daughter Agrippina Minor, which Tacitus consulted during his research. 'Help me and give me a husband! I am still young enough, and marriage is the only respectable consolation. Rome contains men who would welcome Germanicus's wife and children.' But Tiberius feared the implied political threat in this plea and chose to ignore her.[96]

For all the precariousness of Agrippina's position, underlined by the fact that every movement she made was said to have been spied on by Sejanus's agents and that she refused to eat food handed to her by her uncle at the table, it seems that Germanicus's widow was not quite without protection. Despite the well-attested dislike between Livia and Agrippina, and Sejanus's attempts to foment discord between them, the fact remains that for as long as her stepgrandmother was alive, Agrippina came to no harm.[97]

But that protection could not last much longer. Livia was now very near the end of her life. In a society in which life-expectancy was below thirty for most people, even the well-born, and in which it is estimated that only 6 per cent of the population made it past sixty years of age, the fact that she had now lived more than eight decades was either a stunning feat of genetic durability or a tribute to the skills of her private physicians – she had at least five working for her at one time or another, according to the record of the *Monumentum Liviae*.[98] Like many age-defying record-breakers, she was said to have sworn by a daily dose of alcohol, in her case a glass of red wine from the Pucinum region of northern Italy, a prescription for the elderly later recommended by Galen, the court physician in Emperor Marcus Aurelius's day. If the rest of his advice were followed, this would have been supplemented by a diet that included the use of plums as a laxative while excluding cheese, snails, lentils, milk and water, and a regimen of massage, gentle exercise and tepid baths. Old age was a dispiriting time for Roman women, more so than for men. The pages of Roman satire were filled with negative stereotypes of old women as toothless, wrinkled crones addicted to sex, the bottle or futile attempts to reverse the ageing process by applying face packs and thick make-up. Deprived of their fertility and their beauty, old women lost their *raison d'être* in society, though for a few wealthy women, widowhood had its attractions, bringing with it a certain degree of financial and social independence from male authority.[99]

Livia eventually died in the year 29 at the age of eighty-six, after more than half a century surveying Roman society from the top of its female pyramid.[100] Sympathetic Roman historians reported that Tiberius's reaction to his mother's death was one of profound sorrow, though more hostile accounts claimed that the emperor made no attempt to visit his mother's deathbed, pleading that he had business to attend to, and then ordering the funeral to go ahead without him when Livia's body had decomposed so badly that the ceremony could not be put off any longer.[101] In the event, the eulogy was delivered by the *Augusta*'s seventeen-year-old great-grandson Caligula, the wag behind Livia's sobriquet '*Ulixes stolatus*'. The funeral itself was a modest affair, in keeping with the frugal principles laid down by Augustus, and Livia's ashes were deposited in her husband's mausoleum, probably in an alabaster cinerary urn of the type found for other female members of her family.[102]

In homage to Livia, the Senate once more proposed honours completely unprecedented for a woman, including a suggestion that she should be deified and worshipped as a goddess, and voting that an arch, a monument with a distinctly military flavour, should be built in her honour, on the grounds that 'she had saved the lives of not a few of them, had reared the children of many, and had helped many to pay their daughters' dowries'.[103] They also ordered that all the women of the empire should go into mourning for a year. But Tiberius insisted that business should continue as usual, vetoing the proposal to deify his mother and at the same time refusing to honour certain financial bequests made in her will. He did allow statues to mark her passing and acquiesced to the arch on condition that he was given personal financial responsibility for its construction. It was never built. Tiberius pleaded that in rejecting deification of Livia he was not being petty but simply doing what his mother wanted, and there may have been something in that. Public refusals of honours could then, as now, serve a propagandistic function every bit as useful as their acceptance, a lesson Augustus committed to heart in handing back powers offered him by the Senate when he first came to power. Even after the death of his beloved sister Octavia, Augustus had capped the honours initially voted her by the Senate. Yet few believed at the time that Tiberius had anything other than spite in mind towards the woman who had raised him and whose awe-inspiring authority over him he was widely thought to have resented.[104]

The portrait of Livia the iron lady of Rome, a cold, clever proponent of petticoat politics, is one of the most enduring of Roman imperial history and has won widespread acceptance in subsequent retellings, both fictional and non-fictional. But it both undersells Livia's role as a trailblazer for the role of imperial *materfamilias* and oversimplifies the complexity of her as a personality in Roman public life. All remaining emperors in the Julio-Claudian dynasty who followed in Augustus's footsteps were descended directly from Livia – only two could claim the same relationship to Augustus – and all clearly recognised Livia's importance to the legitimacy of their succession.[105] Consequently, portraits of her continued to be produced, and despite Tiberius blocking her deification, Livia did eventually go on to become the first Roman empress to be declared a goddess, although she would have to wait some years for that honour to be bestowed retrospectively by one of her descendants. In the intervening years, her acolytes in Rome's provincial communities such as Lepcis Magna jumped the gun by honouring her with cult statues that explicitly invited her worship as a divine figure.[106]

She lived on in other ways too. Marriage contracts for couples in Roman Egypt invoked her name, and calendars tell us her birthday was still being publicly celebrated during the time of the Emperor Trajan almost a century later.[107] Remarkably, it seems that even some of her clothes and jewels were kept either in storage or on display in the palace, which were ceremonially given as gifts to brides of the Roman imperial family as many as 400 years later. A tradition was thus inaugurated in Livia's name whereby one first lady would dip into the wardrobe of a predecessor, and thus acquire by association some of the majesty and authority that the garments had bestowed on their first wearer.[108]

Most importantly, long after her death, Livia's was still a powerful name to drop in Roman political circles, proof of which will emerge. Even Tacitus, one of her sternest critics, seems to betray a grudging admiration in his obituary for her that, despite all the crimes laid at her door, it is hard not to share:

> Her private life was of traditional strictness. But her graciousness exceeded old-fashioned standards. She was a compliant wife, but an overbearing mother. Neither her husband's diplomacy nor her son's insincerity could outmanoeuvre her.[109]

The principal and most immediate victim of Livia's death was Agrippina Maior. Soon after the *Augusta*'s demise, a letter from Tiberius on Capri was read out at Rome, denouncing his former stepdaughter for 'insubordinate language and disobedient spirit'.[110] The accusations were said to have come to light only now because Livia had suppressed the letter while she was alive. Besides demonstrating her clout, this may also have been evidence of the same pragmatic streak that had led Livia to advise her friend Salome to avoid creating a feud in her own family. As a result of the incriminating letter being read, and in

spite of protests outside the Senate by loyal crowds brandishing stat-
uettes of Germanicus's widow in support, Agrippina was eventually
sent into exile on Pandateria, the same tiny island where her mother
Julia had been banished in disgrace years before. After suffering cruel
treatment from her captors, including being beaten to the point of
losing an eye and force-fed when she tried to end her life through
starvation, Agrippina died there in her forties around the year 33. Her
eldest two sons, Nero Caesar and Drusus Caesar, were also impris-
oned and starved to death, the latter reportedly reduced to chewing
the stuffing of his bed in a desperate bid to survive.[III] Four surviving
children were left behind – daughters Drusilla, Julia Livilla and Agrippina Minor, and the youngest son, Caligula. The future of the Julio-
Claudian dynasty now rested in the hands of these four.

Agrippina Maior was one of the few Roman women of the imperial
period whose life story was held up in later centuries as an exemplar
of how to be a 'good' woman. Her emotional journey to Brundisium
caught the imagination of neo-classical painters in the eighteenth
century, including William Turner, Gavin Hamilton and Benjamin
West, whose famous painting *Agrippina Landing at Brundisium with the
Ashes of Germanicus* was commissioned by the then Archbishop of
York, Dr Robert Drummond. During a dinner-party discussion,
Drummond had read the relevant passage from Tacitus to an enthused
West, who then took it as his template for the painting, unveiled in
1768 to royal approval from King George III.[112] The sudden popularity
of the image of Agrippina grieving at Brundisium, previously an
obscure one in the history of art, arose in part out of a propaganda
war raging in British royal politics centred on the undue influence of
court favourite the Earl of Bute over Augusta, Dowager Princess of
Wales. In a damage-limitation exercise aimed at improving the public
image of the princess, paintings were commissioned of the scene at
Brundisium and analogies publicly drawn between the mother of King
George III, and this famous Roman mother and grieving widow.[113]
Thirty-two years later, in 1800, West was one of the guests at a
Christmas party given by the notoriously wealthy peer and dilettante
William Beckford at his Wiltshire estate of Fonthill Abbey, where the
glamorous guest list included Britain's greatest sea warrior Admiral
Nelson, his friend Sir William Hamilton and the latter's wife Lady
Emma – heavily pregnant at the time with Nelson's child. In coy
homage to West's painting, the company were treated one evening to
a special performance by Lady Emma, who had once been an artist's

model and now entered dressed to re-create Agrippina's famous landing, complete with gold urn. Her display was greeted with delight by her audience, well fortified with sweet confectionery and spiced wines, and described in a contributor's letter to the December 1800 edition of popular periodical *The Gentleman's Magazine* as conveying 'with truth and energy, every gesture, attitude and expression of countenance which could be conceived in Agrippina herself . . . the action of her head, of her hands and arms in the various positions of the urn, in her manner of presenting it before the Romans, or of holding it up to the gods in the act of supplication, was most classically graceful'.[114] The amusing irony of a notorious professional mistress who was at the time married to one of the onlookers and visibly pregnant with the child of another, acting the part of a Roman woman revered for her uxorious piety, was surely not lost on her audience.

Agrippina was not the last victim of Livia's death. Plancina did not last long either once her old friend was gone. She died at her own hand, we are told, after the deaths of both Agrippina and her patroness revived the old accusations against her.[115]

In a telling reflection of the sobering influence Livia was thought to have commanded over him, even Tacitus writes that until Livia's death, there was some good in Tiberius as well as evil.[116] But in the eight remaining years of Tiberius's reign after his mother's demise, Sejanus's influence continued to fester, and the period following the exile of Agrippina and the death of Livia was characterised by a series of witch-hunts and death trials against powerful members of the Senate. But Sejanus's own downfall was to prove as brutal and owed its conclusion to an unlikely agent. In 31, Antonia Minor received word that a conspiracy against Tiberius was being masterminded by Sejanus, ambitious to interrupt the Julio-Claudian succession and seize power for himself. Summoning her secretary and trusted freedwoman Caenis, she dictated a letter, warning her cousin of the plot, and entrusted it to another servant, Pallas, to be delivered to Tiberius on Capri, under cover of darkness. Subsequently, in October that year, Sejanus was executed, his body thrown to the mercy of a vicious mob and his children put to death as well.[117]

In a piece of tragic irony, one of the victims of the fallout from this affair was Antonia's own daughter Livilla, accused in the suicide note of Sejanus's wife, Apicata, of having conspired not just in this coup against the emperor but in a cover-up of the murder of her own husband Drusus eight years previously by her secret lover, Apicata's husband. The penalty for Livilla was death – a sentence, according to one account, carried out by her own mother.[118] That Antonia's rigid code of duty would induce her to starve her own daughter, as was claimed, seems brutal to us, but it cemented her reputation as a faithful guardian of the astringent moral legacy laid down by her grandfather Augustus, and immortalised her as the latest woman to save Rome from its enemies.

Livilla subsequently became the first woman in imperial history to suffer the indignity of what has become known as a *damnatio memoriae* – an order to destroy all statues of her across the empire, obliterating her name and face from public memory.[119] She was not to be the last. Her fate was an ominous prelude to the next chapter in the history of the women of the imperial house. If Agrippina Maior was the Roman matron to whom the great ladies of Emma Hamilton's generation wanted most to be compared, then the women who took over the imperial mantle next were the ones to whom comparison proved most embarrassing.

4

Witches of the Tiber: The Last Julio-Claudian Empresses[1]

I tried dissipation – never debauchery: that I hated, and hate. That was my Indian Messalina's attribute: rooted disgust at it and her restrained me much, even in pleasure.

> Edward Rochester on Bertha Mason, in Charlotte Brontë's
> *Jane Eyre* (1847)[2]

Let him kill me – provided he becomes emperor!

> Agrippina Minor, in Tacitus's *Annals*[3]

Two days' journey south of Rome, a reassuring distance from the increasingly sour and strained atmosphere of the imperial court during Tiberius's last years, lay the popular seaside spa resort of Baiae on the Bay of Naples, holiday home of the Roman jet set. The Bay of Naples was the Hamptons of the ancient Mediterranean, its salubrious climate, epicurean seafood delights and cosmopolitan clientele making it the getaway of choice for wealthy Romans who headed there in their droves once the city began to heat up in March and April. For hedonists, it offered evening boating picnics on pleasure-craft bobbing about the sparkling bay, beach parties, concerts and luxury shopping, while the health-conscious could try the various thermal spa cures on offer, including outdoor saunas heady with sulphurous vapours emanating from the volcanic soil.[4]

Anyone who was anyone in the imperial age had a summer place in or around Baiae, from Augustus himself, who had disapproved of the drunken antics of the rowdy local set his daughter Julia ran with and once even wrote a curt letter reproving a male admirer for visiting her there, to Antonia, senior matriarch of the imperial family now that Livia and Agrippina were dead.[5] Home for Antonia was a luxury villa in the small, exclusive enclave of Bauli (modern Bacoli), just south of Baiae. Formerly the possession of Republican grandee Hortensius – the same Hortensius from whose descendants Augustus had summarily appropriated the imperial house on the Palatine – Antonia's villa was a must-see on the local tourist trail thanks to its tenant's eccentric habit of keeping a lamprey, somehow adorned with gold earrings, in the ornate fishpond. With its beautiful gardens and stunning views from the colonnade across the bay towards Pompeii, this maritime mansion provided Antonia with a welcome retreat, not just from the searing summer heat of the city but from the internecine feuding on the Palatine during the dark days of Tiberius's reign, which had resulted in the deaths of two of her three children, Germanicus and Livilla.[6]

Two decades down the line and under new ownership, this same tranquil villa near Baiae was to be the scene of perhaps the most notorious and colourfully described assassination in Roman history after that of Julius Caesar. That the assassins' victim this time was a woman signifies how much bigger a political target women had become since the days of the republic. The years leading up to this bloody event were marked by the passing of three emperors and the accession of a fourth who would be the last of the dynasty founded by Augustus and Livia to wear the purple. If the names of these men came to stand, in the accounts of the moralising commentators of the next generation, for the worst that imperial rule could offer in the way of corruption, scandal and abuses of power, then their consorts proved highly satisfactory advertisements for the maxim that the health of the Roman Empire could always be gauged by the conduct of its first ladies.

Like the rest of her Julio-Claudian female relatives, few details survive of the early life of perhaps the most famous of this new generation of imperial women, Agrippina Minor, one of the six offspring of Germanicus and his admired wife Agrippina Maior. Born on 6 November 15 on her father's campaign trail in the German provincial city of Ara Ubiorum (Cologne) and taken to Rome as a baby to be raised on the Palatine with her siblings, little Agrippina had just turned four when news came through of Germanicus's death in Syria and she was taken by her uncle Claudius to meet her grieving mother's convoy from Brundisium on the Appian Way. From that time, all we know is that she, her two younger sisters and elder brother Caligula were apparently allowed to remain with their mother in her Palatine apartments. The next we hear of her is in 28, when at the age of thirteen, she was wedded at the instigation of her great-uncle Tiberius to an impeccably blue-blooded but rather shady grandson of Octavia, Gnaeus

Domitius Ahenobarbus, a man accused once of deliberately driving his carriage over a child playing with a doll on a village road.[7] The marriage eventually produced one son born at Antium on 15 December 37, Lucius Domitius Ahenobarbus, better known to history simply as 'Nero'.

Nero's birth came nine months after the death of Tiberius, who had breathed his last on 16 March at the age of seventy-eight, having spent his final years as a recluse at his hilltop villa on Capri, the remains of which still overlook the sparkling blue of the Mediterranean. He was not missed, his self-imposed seclusion having created an atmosphere of political stagnancy and suspicion at Rome, and his morose temperament and natural frugality having failed to endear him to a public afflicted by grain shortages, who are said to have gleefully shouted 'To the Tiber with Tiberius' on hearing of his death. Tales of cruelty and sexual orgies with little boys on Capri, his once burly physique reduced to gaunt, blotchy disfigurement, provided an ignominious finale to a biography that had once promised so much.[8]

After years of foot-dragging, the question of Tiberius's succession had finally been decided. Only three credible candidates were available. They were Germanicus's younger brother, Claudius, Caligula or Tiberius Gemellus – the son of the disgraced Livilla. Claudius was considered a non-starter on account of his handicaps, and his nephews Caligula and Gemellus were named joint heirs, but the former quickly had the emperor's will annulled, and Gemellus was forced to commit suicide later that year.[9] Twenty-four-year-old Caligula thus became Rome's third emperor, trusting, in the absence of any real political or military experience, the popular memory of his father Germanicus to win him public support.

Despite his reign lasting only four years, Caligula's name was to become synonymous with some of the grossest excesses of the Roman imperial age. An infamous story that he once tried to have a favourite racehorse named consul is just one of many preserved anecdotes illustrating his egotism, cruelty and profligacy. They include the charge that he had citizens thrown to wild beasts or sawn in half for minor offences such as criticising his shows; that he made parents attend their own sons' executions and had torture trials conducted in his presence during mealtimes; that he served golden meat and bread at his feasts, and drank pearls dissolved in vinegar – a narrative echo of the trick once played by Cleopatra, that other traducer of Roman values. An additional rumour that Caligula had in fact hastened the death of Tiberius, with whom he had been staying on Capri at the time, by smothering his adoptive grandfather with a pillow, became the blueprint for subsequent violent usurpations of imperial power.[10]

Nonetheless, Caligula's reign began auspiciously enough with a series of crowd-pleasing measures which included his making a personal pilgrimage across stormy seas to the island of Pandateria to recover the ashes of his mother Agrippina, which he carried back to Rome in his own hands and interred with great ceremony in the mausoleum of Augustus.[11] It was a poignant reverse of the journey he had made when just seven years old, when he accompanied his mother on her own voyage home from Brundisium, carrying the ashes of Caligula's father. Games were now inaugurated in honour of the new emperor's mother, at which an image of her was carried around the arena in a mule-drawn *carpentum*, and her rehabilitation was completed with the issue of a new bronze coin series featuring the notice 'The Senate and the People of Rome – To the Memory of Agrippina', backed on the other side by her portrait and titles.[12] Caligula thus drew a line in the sand between himself and the unpopular Tiberius, who had treated Agrippina so badly.

Caligula's living female relatives also came in for star treatment in the early days of his reign. He insisted that his three sisters, Drusilla, Julia Livilla and Agrippina Minor, should be given the same privileges as the Vestals, the best seats in the house at public games, and that their names be included alongside his own in the wording of public oaths. They also became the first living women to be pictured and explicitly identified on a coin of the imperial mint – a bronze *sestertius* produced in 37–8 which showed three tiny full-length images of the sisters, each captioned by name but depicted with the accoutrements of three female deities personifying abstract qualities crucial to Roman success: *Securitas* ('Security'), *Concordia* ('Harmony'), and *Fortuna* ('Fortune').[13]

Antonia, the emperor's grandmother and former guardian, was not forgotten. The Senate was persuaded to bestow on her at a single stroke all the honours ever won by Livia during her lifetime, which included the vacant position of priestess to the divine Augustus's cult, the travel privileges afforded the Vestal Virgins and the right to style herself *Augusta*, a title Antonia declined, just as her mother Octavia had once done. Caligula wed three women in quick succession during his time as emperor (he had married his first wife, Junia Claudilla, before coming to the throne) but not one of them was ever awarded that title, indicating that it was still seen very much as a dowager's privilege, and too sensitive a form of address for the wife of the emperor.[14]

With all of these honours, Caligula was acknowledging first the importance of his matrilineal connection to Augustus through his mother Agrippina and his grandmother Antonia. However the elevation of his sisters is crucial. Precious little of note is known about Caligula's four wives. His first, Junia Claudilla, died giving birth to a stillborn; his second was Livia Orestilla, whom – in a replay of Livia and Augustus's union – Caligula was said to have abducted from her husband Piso just hours after their wedding and then divorced only days later; in a similar scenario, his third wife, the wealthy Lollia Paulina, was summarily wrested from her husband, a provincial governor, apparently after Caligula heard his grandmother Antonia commenting on her beauty, though she too was soon discarded; finally, in around 39, he married his mistress Milonia Caesonia, described by the third-century historian Cassius Dio as 'neither young nor beautiful', but a woman who shared Caligula's extravagant and promiscuous characteristics, and whom he was said to have paraded naked in front of his friends. The four women had only one characteristic in common – none of them ever provided the emperor with a male heir. Only Caesonia successfully carried a pregnancy by Caligula to term, reportedly giving birth just after their wedding to a daughter named Julia Drusilla, of whose paternity Caligula was convinced when she tried to scratch out her playmates' eyes, thus proving she shared his own violent temper. The emperor lacking a son, his sisters would be vitally important in continuing the Julio-Claudian line.[15]

Ancient historians speculated darkly about Caligula's sexual preferences. It was whispered that he was incestuously involved with all three of his sisters, that Drusilla was his favourite and that Antonia had caught them in bed one day at her house. Given that virtually all of Rome's most infamous emperors were accused of incest at one stage or another, reflecting as it did unease about the overlap between family and government in a dynastic power system, we would probably be wise to take rumours of bed-hopping with his sisters with a pinch of salt.[16] Nevertheless, when Drusilla died in the summer of 38, she became the first Roman woman to be deified, leapfrogging Livia, whose prior claim had been vetoed by Tiberius. Although Drusilla did not receive a temple in her name, a statue of her was placed in the temple of Venus Genetrix, the only instance of a Roman woman's image being so venerated.[17]

Despite their auspicious debut, Caligula's grandmother and surviving sisters did not bask in the sunshine of his approval very long. Within six weeks of his taking up the reins of imperial office, the venerable Antonia was dead, the precise date of her death given as 1 May 37 by a calendar found in the Roman forum in 1916.[18] Some sources state it was suicide, though her grandson's disinterested conduct while observing her funeral from the comfort of his dining room added colour to reports that he had speeded up her death with a dose of poison – a murder weapon typically associated with a woman, thus reinforcing Caligula's reputation for effeminate perversity. The fate of Antonia's ashes is unknown, though they were in all likelihood placed in the family mausoleum.[19]

Two years later, as the increasingly volatile Caligula's reign descended into chaos, his sisters Agrippina Minor and Julia Livilla went from standard-bearers for womankind to public outcasts, accused in 39 by their brother of being accessories to a plot against him by Drusilla's ex-husband Marcus Lepidus. Their possessions were confiscated and they were expelled to the exile islands of Pandateria and Pontia, just as their mother and maternal grandmother had been before them. In a piece of mocking revenge theatre, Agrippina was given the urn carrying the remains of the executed Lepidus, alleged to have been her lover, and ordered to re-enact her mother's famous journey with the ashes of Germanicus. Another two years went by, during which Caligula undid much of the good work accomplished at the start of his reign, falling out badly with the Senate, many of whom were offended by his increasingly bizarre and despotic behaviour, which included his trying to have himself worshipped by his subjects as a living god. Eventually, Caligula was assassinated with the Senate's support by his own guardsmen on 24 January 41, during a lunch break in a performance of the Palatine games. His wife Caesonia and baby daughter Julia Drusilla were also murdered, the one stabbed – apparently offering up her own neck to the assassin's knife in a display of unnerving bravado – the latter smashed against a wall.[20]

The subsequent accession of Claudius as emperor, the runt of the imperial family, was a completely unexpected amendment to the

Julio-Claudian script. Caligula's failure to nominate an heir had left a vacuum which his fifty-year-old uncle, relatively untested in either military service or public office and the butt of jokes throughout his life on account of his physical handicaps, seemed ill-qualified to fill. But with no other obvious adult male candidates left in the imperial family and with the Senate still dithering over what should be their next move, members of the emperor's bodyguard who were said to have found Claudius hiding behind a curtain in the palace decided the matter by frogmarching him to the barracks of the praetorian guard and summarily declaring him emperor before the Senate could object.[21]

Despite the military's seal of approval, which he was careful to consolidate with big increases in their pay packet, Claudius faced hurdles from the start, the first being his lack of support from the senatorial classes who objected to his cavalier coronation. He remained estranged from them throughout his thirteen-year reign, relying instead on a powerful clique of freedmen who became the key power-brokers in the imperial court during this period.

The second obstacle was that, like Tiberius before him, Claudius could not claim the ultimate badge of legitimacy – direct descent from Augustus. His closest point of contact to the Julian family tree was his mother, Antonia, niece of Rome's first emperor. This made it all the more essential to exploit his connections to the Claudian half of the dynasty, headed up by his paternal grandmother Livia. He duly cashed in by ordering Livia's long overdue deification on 7 January 42, elevating her to the same divine status as Augustus, with whom her cult statue now shared temple room, and granting her the honour of sacrifices conducted under the auspices of the Vestals. Thus Claudius was at least able to claim his own divine ancestress, if not ancestor.[22]

To publicly demonstrate his link to the Julian side of the family, Claudius also bestowed the previously rejected title of *Augusta* on his recently deceased mother Antonia, and gold, silver and bronze coins featuring her face and title were introduced into Roman currency for the first time. Ironically, the boy whom Antonia and Livia reputedly castigated as a monster and a fool was now the one responsible for granting them their greatest honours. Finally, Claudius recalled his nieces Agrippina Minor and Julia Livilla from their island exile and restored to them the inheritance confiscated by Caligula, or what was left of it after Caligula had sold their jewels, furniture and slaves. It must have seemed to the emperor and his advisers that nothing but good could come from the reprieve of the daughters of Claudius's talismanic and still fondly remembered brother Germanicus.

Despite Agrippina Minor's future infamy as one of the most powerful and controversial woman in the annals of imperial history, her return to the family fold in 41 was followed almost immediately by another period of relative anonymity. Now around twenty-five years of age, she had already received a thorough grounding in the cut-throat world of Julio-Claudian politics that had resulted in the death or exile of so many of her relatives, including most of her immediate family. Widowed by the death of her husband Domitius Ahenobarbus shortly before Claudius's accession, though reunited with her four-year-old son Nero, who had been left in the care of Domitius Ahenobarbus's sister Domitia Lepida, she quickly formed a second union with Passienus Crispus, a wealthy socialite with a handsome estate across the Tiber, who had in fact previously been married to Domitia Lepida. Little more is heard from Agrippina over the next five years, an educated guess inviting us to presume she may have accompanied her new husband to his proconsulship in Asia in 42.[23]

In the meantime, it is a relative newcomer to the pantheon of imperial ladies who dominates the literary sources relating to the 40s. Prior to his elevation to the purple, Claudius had already been married and divorced twice, first to Plautia Urgulanilla, the granddaughter of Livia's old friend Plautia Urgulania, and then to a member of Sejanus's family, Aelia Paetina, with whom Claudius had had a daughter, Claudia Antonia.[24] His third marriage, formed shortly before his accession, was to Valeria Messalina. In an illustration of the highly convoluted nature of Julio-Claudian marital politics, Messalina was the teenaged daughter of another of Domitius Ahenobarbus's sisters, Domitia Lepida Minor, and a great-granddaughter of Octavia on both her father's and mother's side.[25] With such a sparkling pedigree, Messalina looked on paper to be the perfect dynastic helpmate to stabilise the Julio-Claudian succession following Caligula's brief, unhinged tenure, particularly when the timely proof of her fertility was taken into consideration – their only son was born three weeks after Claudius took the throne in February 41. The couple's other child, Claudia Octavia, had been born the year before.

Publicly at least, Messalina's early career followed the script written by her more august female predecessors. From his accession, Claudius devoted considerable energy to trying to win over the sceptics by beefing up his political and military CV, and in 43 he pulled off by far the biggest coup of his reign by doing what even Julius Caesar had been unable to do, namely conquer the island of Britain, which now became the new northern boundary of the empire. At the triumphal procession through the streets of Rome which followed in 44, Messalina was permitted to follow her husband's chariot in a mule-drawn *carpentum*, ahead of the victorious generals from the campaign, and the couple's son, hitherto known by the name of Tiberius Claudius Caesar Germanicus, received the new sobriquet 'Britannicus' in recognition of his father's great victory. Messalina meanwhile received most of the honours that by now had become a formality for Julio-Claudian women, including a grant of public statues, and she was also given the right to sit in the front seats of the theatre once occupied by Livia, the only woman who had hitherto enjoyed the status of being both wife to the reigning emperor and mother to the boy who would potentially succeed him one day.[26]

One honour that Livia had enjoyed eluded Messalina, however. Following the birth of her son Britannicus, the Senate offered her the title of *Augusta*. But, not for the first time, an emperor vetoed the Senate's offer.[27] Claudius's denial may have been part of an attempt to mollify members of the Senate still chafing at the autocratic nature of the new emperor's peremptory inauguration. But in later years his denial became a rallying point for a wave of saturnine mockery directed against Claudius's wife. Writing a few decades after Messalina's death and borrowing from republican-era poet Propertius's description of Rome's female *bête noire* Cleopatra as a *meretrix regina* – a 'harlot-queen' – the satirist Juvenal rechristened Messalina the *meretrix Augusta* ('her Highness the Whore') perverting the empire's most honorific title for a woman.[28]

Juvenal's joke encapsulates the abiding image of Messalina as a carnal prodigy whom no amount of triumphs or titles could turn into a respectable matron. As young as fifteen when she married Claudius, who was some thirty years her senior, Messalina's persona both in antiquity and subsequent folklore was of a Roman Lolita who ran rings around her gullible elder husband and had an appetite for sex so gluttonous and insatiable that she was given a listing in Alexandre Dumas' catalogue of the all-time great courtesans of history, became a pornographic icon to writers such as the Marquis de Sade – who wrote of one prostitute's performance that she 'went on for nearly two hours, flinging herself about like Messalina' – and was made the face of an anti-venereal disease campaign in France in the 1920s.[29] Juvenal himself held up the black-haired young empress as the satirical epitome of the unfaithful wife, claiming that she used to wait for the oblivious Claudius to fall asleep, then sallied forth to trade in disguise as a prostitute under a pseudonym:

> Preferring a mat to her bedroom in the Palace, she had the nerve to put on a nighttime hood, the whore-empress. Like that, with a blonde wig hiding her black hair, she went inside a brothel reeking of ancient blankets to an empty cubicle – her very own. Then she stood there, naked and for sale, with her nipples gilded, under the trade name of 'She-Wolf', putting on display the belly you came from, noble-born Britannicus. She welcomed her customers seductively as they came in and asked for their money. Later, when the pimp was already dismissing his girls, she left reluctantly, waiting till the last possible moment to shut her cubicle, still burning with her clitoris inflamed and stiff. She went away, exhausted by the men but not yet satisfied, and, a disgusting creature, with her cheeks filthy, dirty from the smoke of the lamp, she took back to the emperor's couch the stench of the brothel.[30]

Other sources claimed that Messalina compelled other noble women to follow her into adultery, forcing them to have sex in the palace while their husbands watched – a mirror of one of Caligula's favourite pastimes – and fobbing off the suspicions of Claudius by providing him with housemaids to sleep with.[31] So consuming was her own sex drive that she was said once to have challenged a professional prostitute to see which of them could last longest in a sex marathon, a contest the empress won after servicing her twenty-fifth client in non-stop succession, earning her a place in a recently compiled volume of 'world records' from the ancient world.[32]

Despite successes such as the conquest of Britain, the years following Claudius's peremptory and turbulent accession were characterised by an atmosphere of paranoia and suspicion in his court, stage-managed, it was alleged, by the empress herself. Witch-hunts and political trials against rivals were commonplace and a sense of competition for places was keenly felt among the imperial family itself. Both Messalina and her husband shared a similar Achilles heel, namely that there were others with potentially better claims to stand in their shoes. Direct descendants of Augustus and Germanicus still survived, like the recently recalled sisters Agrippina Minor and Julia Livilla, whose husbands might make plausible alternatives to Claudius as emperor while the women themselves could be seen as more attractive candidates for the role of empress.

Julia Livilla was particularly vulnerable in this equation. At the time of Caligula's death, some had considered her husband, the one-time consul Marcus Vinicius, to be a worthy pretender to the crown bestowed by the praetorians on Claudius, and despite the fanfare of her recall from exile, it was not long before she fell foul of her uncle's regime and was sent back to her island on charges which were generally agreed by later commentators to have been fabricated. The order for her banishment was credited to Claudius, but some claimed that Messalina's was the hand behind the move. Driven by jealousy of Julia Livilla's beauty and closeness to her uncle, Messalina was believed to have invented a charge of adultery with the wealthy intellectual Seneca, who was also sent into exile. Julia Livilla met her death through starvation, just like her grandmother Julia, putting an end to any hopes her husband might have had of usurping Claudius. Her ashes were later brought back to Rome – the alabaster funerary urn which contained them is now housed in the Vatican Museums.[33]

The downfall of Julia Livilla on unsubstantiated charges of sexual misconduct underlines how interchangeable transgressions of a sexual or political nature were in Roman societal discourse. Adultery was a convenient excuse to get rid of opponents. Meanwhile, the young empress's sexual jealousies were said to have led to the deaths of a long and illustrious list of other victims of the regime between 42 and 47. They included Julia Livilla's widowed husband Marcus Vinicius and Messalina's own stepfather and governor of eastern Spain, Appius Silanus – both of whom were condemned after rejecting the empress's advances; and a granddaughter of Antonia's named Julia, who, like her cousin Julia Livilla, was seen as a potential rival to the empress.[34]

While there was a chance of rehabilitation, in the eyes of the Julio-Claudian regime's ancient critics, for a husband whose wife or daughter was behaving badly, as long as he took the proper steps to punish her – as Augustus had done in banishing his own daughter Julia – Claudius did nothing to stop Messalina's charge-sheet of crimes from mounting up. This was a fundamental aspect of his characterisation in antiquity as a weak and emasculated ruler, the puppet of not just his profligate wife but his ex-slave advisers. Indeed, the clique of household freedmen who formed the nucleus of the Roman emperor's confidential inner circle and managed the reins of imperial bureaucracy were charged with aiding Messalina in her exploits. Within this close circle, there were three key players: Narcissus (secretary to the emperor), Pallas (treasurer) and Callistus (in charge of petitions). Their recognisably Greek names would have acted as a further signifier of untrustworthiness to a Roman audience.[35] Narcissus was the most powerful of the three, and, alongside the opportunistic public prosecutor Publius Suillius, regularly acted as the empress's partner-in-crime. Together, they used a foiled conspiracy against Claudius in the aftermath of Appius Silanus's death in 42 as an excuse to crack down viciously on their enemies, forcing slaves and freedmen to inform against their innocent masters and sending men and women to the scaffold, whilst pocketing bribes to spare the guilty.[36]

The fact that Messalina was seen acting hand-in-glove with a freedman was yet another important mark against both her and her husband. A society where the wife of the emperor hobnobbed with foreign ex-slaves and cavorted with a roll-call of lovers who included actors and other members of the lower social order, as Messalina is said to have done, was a society turned upside down, an imperial household in disorder.[37] In short, Claudius's wife was a lightning conductor for everything that was iniquitous about his regime in the eyes of his critics.

Agrippina Minor meanwhile had continued to remain in the shadows, managing to avoid the same fate as her sister perhaps simply by staying well out of sight, on her own or her husband Passienus's estates.[38] Then, in 47, five years after Julia Livilla's second exile, she made a prominent return to public life, putting in an appearance at the Saecular Games, last held in the capital during the era of Augustus. Traditionally, one of the most important events at this occasion was the parade of young Roman boys on horseback in an obscure equestrian drill known as the Troy Game, commemorating the legendary Trojan conflict which Romans saw as a pivotal part of their foundation story. Among those taking part this time were Claudius's now six-year-old son Britannicus and Agrippina's nine-year-old son Nero. The agreed feedback from the day was that of the two boys, the crowd had applauded young Nero the more warmly, a fact later touted as a prophecy of his future power but thought at the time to have been prompted both by goodwill towards his mother Agrippina as the daughter of the popular Germanicus and his much-pitied wife, and antipathy towards the current empress.[39]

Messalina now knew for certain that she faced a serious potential rival in the young Agrippina, the mother of another credible male heir and the possessor of the direct lineage from Augustus that Messalina lacked. The empress moreover had already made a series of fatal mistakes that year, beginning with the targeting of a provincial plutocrat named Valerius Asiaticus. A former brother-in-law of Caligula – Asiaticus's spouse Lollia Saturnina was the sister of Caligula's third wife, Lollia Paulina – as well as an accomplice in that emperor's assassination, Asiaticus was a well-connected man of immense wealth, who had been the first man from Gaul to attain the consulship. He had used some of his fortune to acquire and redevelop one of Rome's most magnificent private properties, the pleasure gardens of Lucullus, a famous general, politician and glutton of the first century BC.

The circumstances of Asiaticus's death in 47, as described by Tacitus, make for bizarre reading. Envious of his acquisition of the gardens which she had designs on for herself and jealous of his lover Poppaea Sabina, her rival for the attentions of the celebrated Greek actor Mnester, Messalina put her legal henchman Publius Suillius to work. Asiaticus was arrested while vacationing in Baiae and subjected to a private inquisition in Claudius's bedroom. Here, Messalina and Suillius accused him of adultery with Poppaea Sabina, of trying to corrupt the army and of being 'too soft', in other words, of being sexually effeminate – a deeply insulting attack on a Roman opponent's masculinity. Asiaticus's spirited defence seems to have produced a moment of teary-eyed vulnerability from Messalina, but having mastered herself she set another of her agents, Vitellius, to the task of persuading Claudius that death was the only punishment available to Asiaticus, though the condemned man should be allowed the dignity of administering it himself, an option which Asiaticus accepted and carried through, lamenting that his demise should come as a result of *fraus muliebris* – 'womanly trickery'. Poppaea Sabina was similarly pressured into committing suicide.[40]

Asiaticus's elimination was agreed to have been a costly error by Messalina. There was resentment against the bullyboy tactics employed by Publius Suillius, who was accumulating vast wealth by bringing a wave of lucrative prosecutions against powerful defendants, and the failure to grant ex-consul Asiaticus a fair trial in front of the Senate surely antagonised its members. The execution around the same time of the powerful freedman Polybius, one of Claudius's secretaries who was also named as one of Messalina's lovers, was said to have further weakened her position, alienating the other palace bureaucrats like Narcissus who had been such a key support to her, and in the end it was these freedmen allies who wrote Messalina's death warrant.

One autumn day in 48, while Claudius was away performing a public engagement at Ostia, 16 miles (over 25 kilometres) outside of the city, a strange rumour spread through Rome. The word on the street was that Messalina had publicly 'divorced' the emperor by going through a marriage ceremony with a consul-in-waiting named Gaius Silius, complete with bridal costume, witnesses and wedding break-fast near the modern Piazza del Popolo. The empress had conceived a love 'which bordered on madness' for Silius, the best-looking man in Rome, a passion so intense it had driven all possible schemes of revenge against Agrippina Minor out of her mind. Silius, having been forced by Messalina to divorce his wife Junia Silana, had reconciled himself to the agreeable life of a kept man as his mistress show-ered him with gifts and honours, and even moved some of her slaves, freedmen and furnishings from the imperial palace into his house. All the while Claudius, ever the gullible cuckold, remained unaware of his wife's affair.

As the wedding party drank and danced like bacchants, the freedmen who had once helped Messalina do her dirty work betrayed her. Disillusioned by her persecution of Polybius, and fearing for their own positions if her new alliance heralded a *coup d'état*, they sent a warning to Claudius who, it was said, could only repeat anxiously, 'Am I still emperor?' Learning of her exposure, a panicking Messalina left her new 'husband' and hitchhiked out of Rome on a garden waste disposal vehicle to try and intercept Claudius on his return journey, watched in amused mockery by clusters of her subjects. As soon as she came in sight of her husband's convoy, she began to shout for his forgiveness, reminding him that she was the mother of their children. Her freedmen accusers tried to drown her out, handing the emperor a list of her conquests. After hearing his wife in silence, Claudius eventually sent Messalina back home to the garden prop-erty she had stolen from Asiaticus, promising her an audience in the morning.

But there was to be no reckoning for Messalina. Her executioners came to call in the night, sent by her former collaborator Narcissus.

Having earlier failed to heed the pleas of her mother Domitia Lepida Minor, who had had little affection for her daughter during her life but now urged her to take the only honourable way out and kill herself, Messalina tried hopelessly to pluck up the courage to cut her own throat as her execution squad closed in on her. But she could not force herself to do it. Instead, she was slaughtered there in the luxury of the gardens she had once coveted so much.[41] Tacitus concludes his account of the affair:

> Claudius was still at table when news came that Messalina had died: whether by her own hand or another's was unspecified. Claudius did not inquire. He called for more wine, and went on with his party as usual.[42]

Even Tacitus, the most vociferous scourge of the Julio-Claudians, had to admit that elements of this melodramatic episode sounded too fantastical to be true, though he insisted he was just passing on what others had written before him.[43] Many have asked themselves the same questions – why on earth would Messalina have gone through with such an insane plan as to 'marry' another man? Was she simply thrill-seeking, as Tacitus himself would have it? Was the plan really a risky attempt at a *coup d'état* that banked on Silius's promise to adopt Britannicus to make his usurpation of Claudius palatable to a Roman audience? Was it a reaction to the arrival on the scene of Agrippina and her son Nero? All of these theories have been suggested, and are possible, though none is truly satisfactory. The only firm conclusion we can draw from her fall from grace was that it was indeed sudden and violent.[44]

For the deep scars left by Messalina's disgrace are still there for all to see. Like another woman to whom she has often been compared, the French queen Marie Antoinette, of whom it was said 'may her loathsome memory perish for ever', the very memory of Messalina was to come under attack.[45] After her death, Messalina became only the second woman after Livilla to be subjected by the Senate to a *damnatio memoriae*, which mandated the removal of all portraits and all inscriptions bearing her name from public and private spaces. Brutal traces of this attempt to wipe Messalina's memory from the face of history can be seen in the gaping lacunae left in stone inscriptions which originally testified to the presence of her sculptures. On a marble base discovered in Rome in the sixteenth century, once the support for a golden dedication to Claudius's family donated by a Roman prefect of Egypt, the section of the inscription that named Messalina as mother of the emperor's children has been obliterated by a deliberate gouge. The scars of similar surgical deletions can be seen on inscriptions from Verona in Italy, Lepcis Magna in North Africa, and Arneae in Turkey. Obedient subjects from south-western Turkey even had Messalina's name chiselled off their coin faces.[46]

The Senate's orders were carried out to the letter. No certain sculptural portrait of Messalina survives, a repeat of Julia's fate. However, three vandalised portraits from collections in Dresden, Paris and the Vatican of what looks to be the same rather baby-faced woman have recently been plausibly identified as her. The first shows a clearly important woman with a turret crown and laurel wreath perched over locks fashionably crimped into the pattern of soft waves and tight curls commonly sported by wealthy women of the 30s and 40s. On the face, a long scar snakes down from her scalp across the bridge of her nose and cuts across the left-hand corner of her full-lipped mouth, the fissure left by a heavy blow to her skull. No such blemish mars the complexion of the second, a life-sized statue of a similarly chubby-featured veiled woman supporting on her left hip a small boy, presumably her son Britannicus, who reaches out with his pudgy hand to the folds of drapery at her neck. But her torso was originally discovered smashed into heavy fragments which have since been pieced together. The elaborate crown of the third bust is similarly badly battered and chipped, as though with a chisel. None of this damage need of course automatically signify foul play, but the severity, similarity and pattern of the damage looks suspiciously deliberate, as though someone had taken violent revenge on all three.[47]

With only a few blurry reproductions of her profile available from provincial coins, the only clue otherwise left as to Messalina's physical appearance is the record of her black hair disappearing under her blonde wig in Juvenal's satirical poem about her nocturnal exploits. Graves's novel I, Claudius appropriates the detail in his description of Messalina as 'an extremely beautiful girl, slim and quick moving, with eyes as black as jet and masses of curly black hair'.[48] Unlike her Julio-Claudian predecessors Livia, Antonia and the elder Agrippina, no relatives came to Messalina's posthumous rescue with pledges, restoring her good name, producing new statues of her, or giving her a dignified burial. Instead, her obituary was written solely by the literary stalwarts of later dynasties who earned their stripes by lambasting the Julio-Claudian regimes of Claudius and his successor Nero, in infelicitous contrast to the rulers of their own day.

Not all ancient accounts of Messalina's downfall were completely unsympathetic. No more than twenty years after her demise, an anonymously authored tragedy called the *Octavia*, which focused on the outcome of the ill-fated marriage between Nero and Messalina's daughter Claudia Octavia, described its eponymous heroine blaming Venus, the goddess of love, for her mother's mad conduct in marrying Silius, and for stirring Claudius to a fury that resulted in the murder of his 'unhappy' wife: 'by her death she engulfed me in everlasting grief'.[49] Another contemporary work, the *Apocolocyntosis*, or 'Pumpkinification' – a satirical sketch which may have been circulated at the court of his successor and which imagined the scene of the buffoonish Claudius arriving amongst the gods seeking to have his deification ratified – reserves its vitriol not for Messalina but for the emperor, lampooning his forgetfulness on the subject of whether or not he had killed his young wife.[50] This perspective of Messalina as more hapless victim than villain has percolated through to some modern reimaginings of her, such as an 1876 play *Messalina* by Italian dramatist Pietro Cossa, which portrays its female protagonist as a vulgar vamp yet one who was also motivated by devotion to her son and who was tragically betrayed by the man she was foolish enough to fall in love with.[51]

These versions nonetheless all have one thing in common – they conceive of Messalina's promiscuity as central to her downfall. The picture of Claudius's teenaged third wife as the girl who just could not get enough served a darker purpose than mere titillation. In the Roman moral imagination, any sexually promiscuous woman whose body was available to all comers represented at the very least a temporary failure of control on the part of her husband or father. But if she, like Messalina or Augustus's daughter Julia before her, was also a member of the family who held the keys to the Roman Empire, the repercussions were even more serious. At stake was not just humiliation for her cuckolded husband, but the security of his regime, and of Rome itself. For if a man could not keep his own house in order, how could he ensure the inviolability of the empire whose political heart beat within that very household? This was a conundrum that would continue to obsess the Roman imperial establishment.

In the fallout from Messalina's death, a conundrum of another kind now occupied the imperial household: who should succeed her as

Claudius's wife? The question was settled, according to Tacitus, in a political beauty contest judged by a panel of Claudius's freedmen, a comic charade that served to underscore the emperor's impotency in the face of his own courtiers.[52] Petitions were heard in support of various candidates, including Narcissus's proposal of Claudius's former wife Aelia Paetina and Callistus's suggestion of Caligula's wealthy ex-wife Lollia Paulina, but the choice eventually fell upon Pallas's nomination of the thirty-two-year-old Agrippina Minor. Recently widowed by the death of Passienus Crispus, the daughter of the great Germanicus and the mother of Nero – who had recently been hailed with such enthusiasm by the audience at the Saecular Games – her credentials were impeccable, better even than Messalina's, and she was endowed with wealth and beauty to boot. There was just one problem. Agrippina was Claudius's niece, and Roman law clearly prohibited incestuous unions. Nevertheless, the marriage was seen as too good a chance to unify the family and the Senate was persuaded by Claudius's fixer Vitellius to waive the restrictions forbidding a man to marry his brother's child. On 1 January 48, less than three months after the death of Messalina, Agrippina became Claudius's fourth wife.[53]

Given the legal manoeuvring that had been required to sanction the marriage and the fact that even as the wedding took place, the name and portrait of Claudius's last wife were still being hastily scrubbed away from public view, careful thought went into the question of how to sell this new empress to the Roman public. As usual, coinage was the primary medium, and Agrippina became the latest imperial woman to set a new precedent here, with both hers and her husband's head featured together on the same coin.[54] Under her brother Caligula's aegis, Agrippina's coin images had been too small-scale to give any sense of her appearance but these new official issues allowed her profile to be seen in greater close-up. They showed a woman with the strong facial features that often characterised portraits of her Claudian relatives, including a slight overbite and heavy jaw, an orthodontic contour that might be connected with a rumour that she had an extra canine tooth on the right-hand side of her mouth, thought to be a sign of good luck.

Provincial mints in cities across the empire played along with the new mood, showing the newly married couple in 'jugate' or 'joined' pose, their overlapping profiles juxtaposed side by side. Claudius was wreathed in laurel as befitted the successful military ruler and Agrippina wore the corn-ear crown associated with the goddess of fecundity and maternal love, Ceres. As attributes seen previously on portraits of Augustus and Livia, the message was forced home that here were the inheritors of that perfect imperial partnership.[55] Other items donated by private patrons helped to reinforce the message of dynastic continuity and bountiful promise, seen to de luxe effect in a piece known as the Gemma Claudia, a sardonyx cameo about the size of an ostrich egg which is thought to have been a wedding gift to the couple. It shows the laurelled jugate heads of Claudius and Agrippina Minor facing mirror images of the bride's parents Germanicus and Agrippina Maior. Each pair of busts billows out from the opposite ends of two fruit-laden cornucopias, while an eagle carved in between stares up at the new figureheads of the Julio-Claudian dynasty.[56]

By giving Agrippina more honours than either his previous wife or any Roman woman before her had been afforded, Claudius and his acolytes had a clear strategy. They wanted to underline the idea that both this marriage and the regime were starting afresh – people's memories of Messalina's downfall could not be erased by *damnatio memoriae* alone. Yet elevating Agrippina in this way came with attendant risks. For in visual terms, it placed the emperor's wife on a form approaching equality with the emperor. As in Livia's case, the spectre of Agrippina sharing the spotlight with the ruling emperor was to become a particularly touchy subject over the next decade.

In providing a departure from the memory of Messalina at least, the strategy worked. From the very start, both supporters and enemies of Claudius's regime could agree on one thing, namely that Agrippina was a fundamentally different character to Messalina. Where Messalina was savage, passionate and profligate, Agrippina was hard-headed, analytical and, like her great-grandmother Livia, self-disciplined. No sooner was her marriage to Claudius consecrated than the seeds of her longing to exercise political power on her own behalf began to germinate:

> From this moment the country was transformed. Complete obedience was accorded to a woman – and not a woman like Messalina who toyed with national affairs to satisfy her appetites. This was a rigorous, almost masculine despotism. In public, Agrippina was austere and often arrogant. Her private life was chaste – unless power was to be gained. Her passion to acquire money was unbounded. She wanted it as a stepping-stone to supremacy.[57]

No one doubted that Agrippina was deeply ambitious for her adolescent son Nero from the start. Hers was the hand behind the recall from Corsica of her sister Julia Livilla's exiled paramour Seneca, who was promptly given the prestigious rank of *praetor* and placed in charge of the young Nero's education, a key role in the coaching set-up of any emperor-in-the-making and traditionally the appointment of the boy's mother. On 25 February 50, Agrippina's hopes were given a boost when Claudius adopted Nero as his own son and changed the boy's name from Lucius Domitius Ahenobarbus to the more Julio-Claudian denomination of Nero Claudius Drusus Germanicus Caesar. This effectively put the emperor's natural and adopted sons in head-to-head competition in the succession stakes and within three years of his mother's marriage, Nero had been fast-tracked ahead of his younger rival, depicted alongside his mother on imperial coins while Britannicus remained completely invisible in the dynastic portraiture of his father's principate. In 53, the marriage of fifteen-year-old Nero and the only other child of Claudius's ill-fated union with Messalina, thirteen-year-old Claudia Octavia, made his coronation look inevitable.

As Nero's star rose, so too did his mother's. She was endowed with the usual seating privileges at the theatre, the right to ride in her own mule-drawn carriage and other distinctions that had by now become fairly commonplace for leading imperial women, but the *coup de grâce* was the conferral upon her in 50 of Livia's old *cognomen Augusta*, the title that Claudius had vetoed for Messalina. Although Livia had been called *Augusta* after her husband's death and Antonia had been awarded the title posthumously, no woman before Agrippina had received it while she was the consort of the reigning emperor, and, for good measure, the mother of the likely emperor-in-waiting. It marked the start of a sea-change in how the title of *Augusta* would be awarded in future. Instead of its just being the honorific privilege of mature women whose husbands were dead and whose childbearing years were behind them, regimes increasingly bestowed it on younger women of the imperial family, sometimes not even the wives of the ruling emperor but those who nonetheless might be able to provide the dynasty with future heirs. In addition, it sent out a clear message that Britannicus's hopes of succeeding to the throne now were slim at best.[58]

That same year, all across the empire, the memory of her illustrious parents and the growing fame of her son earned Agrippina glowing endorsements from the provinces. A veterans' colony for retired soldiers was established in her name on the site of her birthplace in Germany and named Colonia Agrippinensis (now the city of Cologne). Its residents would henceforth call themselves *Agrippinenses*.[59] Like her role model Livia, she had political and personal ties to a number of other provincial client-cities. Their subjects could appeal to her as a benefactor, and preserved inscriptions prove that she gave her financial backing to games in the Asian provinces of Adalia and Mytilene.[60] Statues of her proliferated throughout the empire, portraying her with a strong facial likeness to her father Germanicus and with a curly hairstyle similar to her mother, though the younger Agrippina's locks were crimped closer around her head. All in all, it was an auspicious beginning.[61]

Yet some of Agrippina Minor's actions soon began to court controversy. In 51, at an audience to mark the public unveiling of a triumphal arch celebrating Claudius's victory over the Britons eight years previously, eyebrows were raised when the defeated and captured leader of the British resistance, Caratacus, was paraded with his family in front of Claudius and Agrippina and then led in chains to ask for mercy first of the emperor, and then his wife, seated on her own platform nearby. The sight of an empress sitting in state before the military standards of the Roman army and personally receiving the homage of foreign captives was a novelty, and Agrippina's habit of attending this and other public functions at Claudius's side was remarked on by some who saw it as proof of her desire to be an equal partner in the running of the empire.[62] It insidiously conjured up the controversial spectres of other women who had breached the cordon surrounding the male sphere of the military – Plancina, who had attended cavalry drills while her husband Piso was governor of Syria; Fulvia, who had marshalled troops on the plains of Perusia on her husband Antony's behalf; and Caesonia, whom Caligula was said to have taken with him when he rode out to inspect the troops, clothing her in a helmet, cloak and shield.[63] Even Agrippina's own respected mother had provoked the ire of Tiberius when she routed the German army at the bridge over the Rhine. For some ancient observers, such women epitomised an aberrant category of female described in Roman literature as a *dux femina* (a 'woman general'), an oxymoron of a title that implied an unnatural combination of male and female characteristics. Agrippina Minor's reception of Caratacus was just the first of many incidents that tarred her with the reputation of acting too much the man.[64]

Over the next three years, between 51 and 54, a haze of discontent settled over the metropolis and its outposts. For all the fanfare of the emperor's remarriage and the drawn-out celebrations of the victory over Britain, the streets of the capital were hit by demonstrations against corn shortages, and on one occasion Claudius himself was attacked in the forum by an angry bread-throwing mob. Rumours flew about a row within the imperial household between the two stepbrothers, sparked by Britannicus's provocative refusal to call Nero by his new Julio-Claudian name. Britannicus's future certainly looked bleak. Nero was getting much more positive publicity and Agrippina's manoeuvring even went as far as removing old household retainers and installing individuals who would be loyal to herself and her son. One such appointment was the new prefect of the praetorian guard Afranius Burrus, a one-time procurator on Livia's estates and a stolid individual who would have a key supporting role to play in events to come.[65]

Plunging on in the face of public disgruntlement, Claudius tried to claw back popular ground in 52 by staging a spectacular mock naval battle on the Fucine Lake 50 miles (80 km) outside Rome, to celebrate the eleven-year culmination of an ambitious public works project to dig a drainage tunnel that would prevent the surrounding region from flooding. The event attracted an audience of thousands from the city and the provinces and involved the participation of 19,000 player-combatants, navigating about the 12-mile-long (19-km-long) lake in two teams of fifty ships a side.[66] One of those present in the wooden viewing stands that day was the great Roman writer Pliny the Elder, who described the dazzling sight of Agrippina dressed in a golden *chlamys*, a Greek version of the Roman military cape that her husband was wearing. The *chlamys* was a foreign warrior's garment, hardly the typical uniform of a Roman woman, though tellingly it was the dress of Virgil's tragic heroine of the *Aeneid*, Queen Dido of Carthage, who like Agrippina had taken on traditionally male responsibilities, attempting to found a new kingdom for her people.[67]

Then, what should have been a spectacular public-relations coup for Claudius fizzled into a damp squib. The grand opening of the drainage tunnel failed to lower the level of the lake, an engineering blunder that reportedly provoked a behind-the-scenes spat between Agrippina and the agent of the works, Narcissus, drawing complaints from the disgruntled freedman about the *Augusta*'s 'dictatorial feminine excess of ambition'.[68] Narcissus, agent of Messalina's destruction, now found himself increasingly sidelined at court in favour of Pallas, the freedman who had championed Agrippina as Claudius's new bride and with whom, people whispered, the *Augusta* was sharing her bed.

Agrippina's use of sex was another of the key differences between Claudius's old wife and his new one, according to her ancient appraisers. Like Messalina, she was said to have used murderous force to eliminate her enemies and sexual favours to keep her supporters close. But if Messalina, portrayed as a born whore, had traded politics to gratify her love of sex, Agrippina traded sex to gratify her love of politics.[69] In other words, she had sex 'like a man', using it purely as a means to an end just as her great-grandfather Augustus was said to have done during his campaign against the profligate Antony, tapping up the wives of his enemies to secure information against them.

Like Messalina, Agrippina chalked up a long list of victims during Claudius's reign, but the latter's motives were usually seen to have been pragmatic rather than sexual. Those whose downfall was attributed to her included Caligula's former wife Lollia Paulina, once considered a candidate to replace Messalina as Claudius's bride, who was accused of involvement with magicians and astrologers; her vast fortune was confiscated and she was sent into exile, where according to one account she was forced to commit suicide, and in another, decapitated, her severed head later brought for inspection and identification to the *Augusta*.[70]

The influence accumulated over Nero by Domitia Lepida, the elder sister of Agrippina's first husband who had taken guardianship of the boy while Agrippina was in exile under Caligula, was also resented, and a death sentence was passed against Lepida for sedition and trying to curse the emperor's wife. In 53, Agrippina was accused of bringing about the false prosecution of the senator Statilius Taurus, on the grounds that she coveted his gardens. That this was exactly the same reason given for Messalina's decision to frame Valerius Asiaticus surely hints that at least some of the accusations against Agrippina Minor were just recycled fiction. Such duplications of plotline recur frequently throughout the history of Roman imperial women – and indeed men – reflecting a tendency to adopt a one-size-fits-all approach to the 'good' and 'bad' wives of 'good' and 'bad' emperors. Another of the ancient historian's favourite recurring characters was the emperor's wife who poisoned her husband to pave the way for her own choice of successor. In this respect, Agrippina was to prove herself the true successor to the historical legacy of her great-grandmother Livia.[71]

Accounts of Claudius's last years describe him as afflicted by poor health and a dissatisfaction with his choice of wife that saw him take to the bottle, reportedly slurring one day that it was his lot in life to marry outrageous wives and then punish them. This ominous remark, coupled with other dropped hints that he regretted having adopted Nero and now wanted Britannicus to succeed him after all, apparently spurred Agrippina to take action. Although most later reports were convinced that the sixty-three-year-old emperor met his death at his wife's hand, wildly differing accounts of how she managed it were in circulation. One line of thought had it that she had employed Claudius's official taster Halotus to slip a drug into his master's dinner at an official banquet. Another said that Agrippina herself had spiked Claudius's favourite dish of mushrooms at a family dinner, mimicking Livia's supposed trick with Augustus's snack of green figs. Yet another claimed that Agrippina had enlisted the services of notorious professional poisoner Locusta, but that when Claudius did not seem to be succumbing to his toxin-laced mushrooms as hoped, a panicking Agrippina threw caution to the wind and called in the family doctor Xenophon to baste Claudius's throat with the poison which eventually had the required effect.

Whichever version one chooses to accept, the end result was the same. On 13 October 54, Claudius's death was announced. In an almost identical replay of events involving Livia following the death of Augustus, news of the emperor's demise had been concealed until the Senate could be convened and all arrangements for a succession confirmed. Once Agrippina was satisfied that everything was in place, the doors of the imperial palace were flung open, and sixteen-year-old Nero emerged, flanked by his praetorian prefect Burrus, to be dutifully hailed by his troops as emperor.[72]

In 1979, archaeologists working on the eastern side of the ancient city centre of Aphrodisias in Roman Asia Minor, made a remarkable discovery. During the first century, Aphrodisias, a small but prosperous provincial city with a population of around 50,000, enjoyed a special relationship with the Roman imperial family, thanks in large part to the Julio-Claudian family's long-standing claim to be descendants of the city's patron goddess Aphrodite. In tribute to the connection, not long after Tiberius's accession, the people of Aphrodisias had spent several decades constructing an elaborate religious complex consisting of a 100-metre-long (330-foot-long) walkway flanked by three-storeyed porticoes of relief panels carved from single blocks of native white medium-grained marble, dedicating the monument to the worship of the Julio-Claudian emperors.

When the remains of this complex, known as a Sebasteion (after the Greek word *Sebastos*, meaning 'Augustus') were found, only around half of the original sculptural relief panels survived, but several preserved images of a stellar line-up of the key Julio-Claudian players, including one, pieced together from eleven fragments of varying size, showing Agrippina Minor standing next to Claudius whilst he was crowned with an oak wreath by a representative of either the Roman Senate or the people. In keeping with their semi-divine personae here, Claudius appears naked but for a military cloak hanging off his right shoulder, while Agrippina wears the flowing *chiton* gown typical of female deities, and, by the sheaf of corn-ears in her left hand, is clearly intended to be associated with Demeter, Greek patron goddess of the harvest. Husband and wife are shown clasping hands, a gesture that signified marital or political concord rather than affection in Roman portraiture, though it seems ironic now given the alleged nature of Claudius's demise.

But an even more startling sight met the excavators' eyes when they flipped over another heavy, almost perfectly preserved slab, 172 cm (67 inches) in height and 142.5 cm (56 inches) in width, found face-down in the north portico, where it originally would have hung. It was a larger-than-life sculptural relief of Agrippina, standing to the right of her son Nero, on whose head she almost casually places a laurel wreath. Once more, she is dressed in the regalia of Demeter, and in the crook of her left arm is balanced an overflowing cornucopia of pomegranates, apples and grapes. Nero wears military dress, and gazes off into the middle distance while Agrippina's stance is angled inwards, towards him, seemingly contemplating her son's profile as she rests the laurel over his carefully ordered locks. It is the first known visual representation of one member of the Roman imperial family crowning another, let alone of a mother stage-managing her son's coronation. Since Nero's dress proclaims him a military victor, Agrippina's appropriation of the role of master of ceremonies, rewarding him for his notional triumphs, is all the more startling, and contrasts sharply with her depiction as a dutiful hand-holding spouse at the side of Claudius. Not even Livia had been given so powerful a role in her son's iconography.[73]

From the day that her sixteen-year-old son stepped out of the imperial palace to be hailed by his troops as emperor, Agrippina was in fact given a standing in Roman public life closer to a man's than any woman before her had enjoyed. Gold and silver coins minted in 54 to mark Nero's accession featured the profiled heads of both the emperor and his mother facing each other nose-to-nose on the same side of the coin, inscribed underneath with the words *Agripp[ina] Aug[usta] divi Claud[ii] Neronis Caes[aris] mater*: 'Agrippina Augusta, mother of the divine Claudius Nero Caesar' – Agrippina's name, note, given precedence. No Roman mother had been previously given pride of place in an emperor's genealogy as opposed to his father – Tiberius of course had vetoed similar advertisements of the relationship between himself and Livia – while the head-on pose of these facing portraits appeared to give neither seniority.[74]

The effect of all these images was to make it very clear to whom Nero owed his authority as emperor. During that first year of his reign, Agrippina was promoted both publicly and privately as her son's running mate, a ubiquitous companion in the officially sanctioned artistic expression of his authority. She was also a perpetual presence at his side in the popular anecdotes of his principate that did the rounds of Roman society long after his downfall. It was said Nero's mother reclined next to him while they travelled about in his litter, wrote letters to foreign dignitaries on his behalf and generally managed the business of empire for him.[75] When, as was customary, the new commander-in-chief was asked by his personal bodyguard for a password to assist with security arrangements, Nero chose *optima mater* – 'best of mothers'.[76]

The Senate also contributed unusual honours to Agrippina, voting that she have the right to be accompanied by two public officials or *lictores* – going one better than Livia who had only been permitted a single lictor in her train – and decreeing that Agrippina become the official guardian of Claudius's divine cult, ironic given the clamorous insistence of the literary record that she had had a hand in his murder.[77] Agrippina was subsequently credited with striking foundations on the Caelian hill for a temple dedicated to her deified husband's worship. When finished, the structure would be one of the largest temple complexes in Rome, though it had a difficult route to completion: Nero had the building ripped down before it was later salvaged by future emperor Vespasian.[78]

The priesthood to their deified husbands was still the only official position women of the imperial household were permitted to hold, and it is not clear exactly what kind of public duties it required. But Agrippina's apparent ability to wade into the lion's den of Roman imperial power during the early days of her son's reign was without precedent, stressing how much Nero's claim to the throne depended on her. In part, this was an inevitable consequence of Nero being so young and needing advisers around him. His first speech in the Senate made an attempt at appeasement of its patrician members, offering assurances that from now on, the separation of imperial house and state would be respected, and the Palatine would not intervene in the jurisdiction of the Senate as had happened some- times under the previous incumbent. This promise was somewhat undermined, however, by the fact that meetings of the Senate were now often convened in the imperial palace, precisely so that Agrippina could eavesdrop on proceedings from a curtained-off vantage point at the rear of the room. One wonders whether she had a discreet way of making her feelings on matters known. She certainly tried to involve herself in their decisions, as evidenced by her attempt – and failure – to overturn an old policy of Claudius that aspiring *quaestors* should be required to finance gladiatorial shows from their own pockets.[79]

The fact that Agrippina was not allowed to be seen – or probably heard – at these meetings, does post an important reminder that the ban on women playing an official role in affairs of state remained firmly in place. There were tense moments when a certain amount of hasty diplomatic manoeuvring had to take place to avoid that line being crossed. One such incident took place at the end of 54, when a pro-Roman delegation from Armenia arrived for an audience with Nero concerning the crisis in their country. As Nero began to hear their representations, Agrippina approached the party. But instead of taking up a position on her own separate platform, as she had while receiving the entreaties of Caratacus as the consort of Claudius, she began to climb the steps of her son's dais, with the apparent inten- tion of taking a seat beside him. It took some quick thinking on the part of the ever-present Seneca to defuse a potentially awkward situ- ation, whispering to his young charge that he should go forward and greet his mother, and thereby smooth over what could have been an extremely provocative political gaffe.[80]

Tensions surrounding Agrippina's influence over imperial policy refused to go away, though. Rome's political elite voiced scepticism that an emperor, barely past seventeen and moreover, *qui a femina regeretur* – 'one who was ruled by a woman' – could possibly quell insurgencies throughout the empire.[81] It was one thing for a woman to undertake the proper supervision of her son's upbringing and education, as Cornelia, Antonia and Livia had done to great acclaim, and Agrippina took her duties in this regard seriously, with her arrangement of Seneca's appointment as her son's tutor, for example, and her personal steerage of him away from inappropriate areas of study such as philosophy, regarded as too idle a subject for an emperor-in-the-making. But it was quite another matter when she openly tried to interfere in politics.[82]

Just as Livia's and Tiberius's relationship was portrayed as increasingly strained after she achieved her heart's desire of smoothing her son's path to the throne, sources depict a cooling between Agrippina and Nero. The first official evidence of a chilling effect came with the sudden disappearance of Agrippina's portrait and titles from her son's coinage in 55, less than a year into his reign, leaving Nero to stare out from his coins alone. So abrupt an erasure is striking, in view of the fanfare with which Agrippina's face was initially blazoned across the official state currency and given a prominence equivalent to her son's. It may well be that with Nero now securely established on the throne, it was decided that it no longer presented a good image to show him tied to his mother's apron strings, and that it looked better for him to be seen standing on his own two feet, a ruler in his own right. But literary sources reinforce the point that Agrippina's power over her son had clearly begun to wane.[83]

In one account, the catalyst for their falling-out was Nero's affair with a freedwoman called Acte. Nero had never shown a drop of affection for his young wife Claudia Octavia. His trysts with Acte were arranged in the face of scolding protests from his mother, who was said to have objected to any female rival for her son's attentions. These outbursts only succeeded in alienating her son. According to one insider at the Julio-Claudian court, Cluvius Rufus, who wrote a history of this period which was later drawn on extensively by Tacitus as a research source, Agrippina was so desperate not to lose her hold over Nero that she resorted on several occasions to dolling herself up and trying to seduce her son after long alcohol-fuelled lunches – although another contemporary historian, Fabius Rusticus, countered that it was Nero who made the move on his mother. But Agrippina's wheedling failed to have the desired effect, and she lost her temper when Nero sent her a gift of a dress and jewels from the palace's collection of clothing worn by former imperial women, pointing out that his power to make such a gesture derived entirely from her.[84]

Consequently, Nero increasingly turned to his tutor Seneca and other court insiders for advice and support. Relations between Agrippina and her son's two closest mentors, Seneca and praetorian prefect Burrus, who both originally owed their position in Nero's circle to her favour, had reportedly grown frosty at an early stage as a result of their determination to curb the *Augusta*'s influence. Narcissus had already dropped out of the picture, an early casualty of the regime change from Claudius to Nero, though whether he had disappeared through suicide, illness or murder is unclear.[85] Competition for the young emperor's favour created tensions within the palace. The empress's lover Pallas was relieved of his imperial duties, an act which provoked Agrippina into taunting her son that Britannicus had a stronger claim to the throne than he did and, if she chose to do it, the power to reinstate Britannicus by confessing her own crimes, was in her hands. She reputedly threw one last challenge at him: 'It was I who made you emperor', the implication being that what she had given, she could also take away.[86]

Disturbed by his mother's threats, the now seventeen-year-old Nero resolved to bring about the death of his younger stepbrother, and enlisted the help of the same poisoner, Locusta, who had reportedly prepared the toxin that killed Claudius. After one aborted attempt, a successful assassination was carried out in February 55, at the family dinner table. Tacitus claims that an unsuspecting Britannicus was handed a drink which sent him into convulsions, depriving him first of speech, then breath. As his stepbrother was carried away to die in agony, Nero casually dismissed this odd turn as a symptom of epilepsy, a display of callousness that his neglected wife Claudia Octavia received without betraying a flicker of emotion, so adept had she become at keeping a close counsel in the face of Nero's cruelty. But the look on Agrippina's face, as she stared at her son in dawning horror and shock, told the assembled company that she had no prior knowledge of the scheme.[87]

Things went rapidly downhill from this point, and in stark contrast to public images highlighting family unity on early coins of Nero's reign, open warfare now reigned between mother and son. On one side, Agrippina declared herself a staunch ally of her downtrodden daughter-in-law Claudia Octavia. At the same time, she chaired secret meetings with friends, hosted audiences with tribunes and centurions and collected financial donations as if amassing a war chest for a political campaign. In retaliation, Nero gave commands for the *Augusta's* German bodyguard to be withdrawn and ordered that her belongings be moved out of his own house so that she could no longer host her supporters there. Instead she was relocated to her grandmother Antonia's old quarters on the Palatine. Nero seldom visited his mother, and only when accompanied by an intimidating squad of centurions. On occasions, she retreated to her country estates, but here her rural retirement was disturbed by yobbish gangs hired by Nero to harass her by whistling and cat-calling as they drove or sailed past. Agrippina's throng of admirers melted away, and she was left in political isolation, visited only occasionally by old friends such as Gaius Silius's former wife Junia Silana, whom he had divorced in order to pursue Messalina.[88]

Even this friendship proved fickle. For Silana apparently bore a secret grudge against Agrippina over the latter's role in scuppering her prospects of remarriage to a noble suitor, on the grounds that she did not want Silana to have a husband to bequeath her sizeable fortune to, having designs on it herself. This spurred Silana to entrust two of her personal clients, Iturius and Calvisius, with planting a charge of conspiracy against Agrippina, claiming that she was planning to set Rubellius Plautus, a great-great-grandson of Augustus, on the throne in her son's stead. An inebriated Nero, on hearing the accusation, was thrown into a panic, and hell-bent on having his mother executed. He was restrained by his sage counsellors Seneca and Burrus, who insisted, perhaps in silent acknowledgement that they owed their promotions originally to her, that the emperor's mother should be given a chance to respond to the charges. Both men proceeded to visit Agrippina at her house, whereupon she offered a fierce and scornful rebuttal of the prosecution, dismissing Silana as a childless woman who could not understand a mother's emotions towards her son, and pointing out the absurdity of her wanting him dead:

> If Britannicus had become emperor could I ever have survived? If Rubellius Plautus or another gained the throne and became my judge, there would be no lack of accusers![89]

Agrippina demanded that proof of her subterfuge be brought to bear, and riding roughshod over her startled but secretly impressed interlocutors' appeals for her to remain calm, insisted on an interview with her son. No details are given of what was said in that meeting, but the upshot was that, in an extraordinary turning of the tables, Agrippina's accusers, among them Junia Silana, Calvisius and Iturius, found themselves sent into exile. Meanwhile friends and supporters of the emperor's mother were appointed to a series of extremely prestigious imperial posts. It looked like a complete rout for Agrippina.[90]

Whether this reversal of fortune was a real wind change, signalling a reconciliation between mother and son, or a story designed by ancient commentators to reinforce her credentials as an overbearing mother and savvy political operator, Agrippina's victory did not signal a renewal of her images on Roman coins nor a new wave of public sculpture announcing her return to equal prominence at her son's side. On the contrary, she seems to have remained in the shadows of public life for the next three years.

We can deduce where she lived for at least part of that time. Like her great-grandmother Livia and her grandmother Antonia before her, Agrippina owned several estates of her own. She was not the only woman to whom Nero had made gifts of property. His freedwoman mistress Acte was the deed-holder of a sizeable amount of real estate in Egypt, Sardinia and Italy, which she could only have acquired through the largesse of the emperor. Agrippina had already been given Antonia's house in Rome, and it seems likely that she simultaneously inherited the full package of her grandmother's properties in Egypt and Italy, many of which Antonia in turn had been bequeathed by her father Mark Antony. One of the jewels in that real estate portfolio was Antonia's old summer villa at Bauli, with its luxury views of the sea and ornate garden fishpond.[91]

It was at this seaside villa at Bauli that matters between Agrippina and Nero reached their fatal, dramatic conclusion. The temporary détente established after Silana's failed plot collapsed in 58 when Nero began an affair with the married Poppaea Sabina, an eponymously named daughter of Messalina's one-time rival for Mnester's affections. This younger Poppaea was the famously beautiful wife of Salvius Otho, a friend and protégé of the emperor who had been dispatched to a foreign governorship to clear any obstacles to his wife's assignations with Nero.[92] Though born a Roman, Poppaea was described in antiquity in terms clearly intended to evoke comparison with Rome's most notorious foreign nemesis, Cleopatra. She was said to have kept her perfect complexion by bathing daily in the milk of 500 asses, and, like Cleopatra, was credited with a recipe for make-up – an oily concoction called *pinguia Poppaeana* – which was used by other women. The fact that, in a coincidence made in historiographical heaven, Cleopatra's and Poppaea's respective rivals were both called Octavia, also provided Roman writers with food for the imagination.[93]

Poppaea's extravagance and sex appeal were the trademark characteristics of all Roman femmes fatales.[94] According to both Tacitus and Cassius Dio, it was Poppaea who fanned the flames of Nero's murderous resentment towards his mother, although the historians also acknowledge that the emperor had long been plotting her end. Fearing that Nero would never divorce Claudia Octavia and marry her while Agrippina was still alive, Poppaea was said to have reproached the emperor for buckling to his mother's will, accusing him of being a lapdog. She claimed that the only reason he had not yet made an honest woman of her was because of Agrippina's opposition and her desire to prevent Poppaea's speaking out against the *Augusta*'s crimes. Her taunts persuaded Nero that his mother had to be put out of the way, and he began to ponder how best to achieve this goal. What followed, as relayed in the account of Tacitus, was an extraordinary piece of revenge theatre.[95]

In March 59, a conciliatory invitation was sent by Nero to his mother Agrippina, inviting her to an evening banquet in Baiae, where he was presiding over a festival in honour of the Roman goddess Minerva. He greeted her in person on the shore, seating her in the place of honour and conversing with her as though all enmity between them was forgotten and he had eyes only for her.

> The party went on a long time. They talked about various things; Nero was boyish and intimate – or confidentially serious. When she left, he saw her off, gazing into her eyes and clinging to her. This may have been a final piece of shamming – or perhaps even Nero's brutal heart was affected by his last sight of his mother, going to her death.[96]

Nero had considered and discarded various options for the disposal of his mother, including poison (which had to be ruled out as Agrippina had built up an immunity to such an ambush by regularly imbibing antidotes), and death by the sword. But in the end it was a strategy concocted by Anicetus, a former tutor of Nero's, that was adopted. Nero had provided a new luxury craft for his mother's return journey to her Bauli villa across the bay. But this was no ordinary boat. In accordance with Anicetus's instructions, it had been designed to collapse and break up during the crossing, crushing the *Augusta* and dumping her out to sea. Nero escorted his mother to the shore, saw her into the vessel, and watched as she set sail.

The sky was filled with stars as the convoy set out across the calm harbour. Accompanying Agrippina was her maid Acerronia, who was leaning over her mistress's couch, chatting with her about Nero's surprising conduct, and Crepereius Gallus, one of her household retainers, who had stationed himself near the tiller. At a given signal, the canopy over the empress's party, heavily weighted down by lead, suddenly caved in. Crepereius was instantly crushed to death, but the high sides of the couch on which they were sprawled protected Agrippina and Acerronia. In the ensuing confusion, the boat slowly ditched into the water. Acerronia panicked, trying to get rescuers' attention by shouting out that she was Agrippina. But her fatal error only drew the fire of the boat's crew, who clubbed her to death with their oars and pikes. Agrippina meanwhile kept her mouth shut and swam silently away into the gloom, escaping with only a glancing wound to her shoulder. She was picked up by one of a batch of small boats, which conveyed her back to her villa, where, applying dressings and ointments to her wound, she grimly surmised who was behind the attempt on her life.

When Nero heard that the plot had failed, he feared his mother's vengeance. In a panic, he summoned Seneca and Burrus. The latter advised him that the praetorian guard of which he was commander would never agree to harm the daughter of the great Germanicus. Instead, Anicetus should finish what he started. Nero agreed to the plan. When an envoy arrived from Agrippina, carrying a carefully worded letter which she had composed to try to buy herself time, hiding her suspicions of her son's involvement, Nero even went so far as to distract attention from his own scheme by claiming that the messenger was an assassin. As Anicetus's death squad neared the shores of Baiae, the beach and shallow waters near her house filled with crowds who had heard rumours of Agrippina's narrow escape, and wanted to offer congratulations on her safe return. But they scattered as the armed men stormed her property, muscling aside slaves who tried to stand in their path, until they reached the bedroom where she had taken up sanctuary.

In sharp contrast to Messalina's cringeing terror in the face of her own death, though in faint reminiscence of Caesonia's end, Agrippina's final moments were of eloquent defiance. In the dim light cast by one lamp, she looked into the faces of her assassins, led by Anicetus, and remarked that if this was a social call, they might take back news of her recovery, but if it was not, then she would never believe that her son had ordered her death. Yet as she was surrounded and the blows began to fall on her head, she summoned up the presence of mind to issue what must go down as one of the great last lines in history. Baring her belly to the centurion preparing to run her through with his sword, she cried out 'Strike here!', pointing to the womb that had spawned her treacherous son. Her executioners cut her down. For a woman so often accused of acting too much the man, it was an appropriately masculine sort of death – a violent assassination rather than the cold-blooded exile and starvation that had become the pattern for many of her ill-fated female predecessors.[97]

Apocryphal coda or faithfully recorded epitaph, Agrippina's famous last words resonated for a long time, inspiring the following rather grotesque reworking in the fourteenth century:

> Nero . . . ordered his mother to be brought before him, for he was living
> in concubinage with her, and he also sent for his doctors and ordered
> them to kill his mother, for the desire and the will had come to him to
> see the secrets of his mother's belly and how a child was formed in the
> womb . . . And when they opened her belly, the emperor looked at the
> inside of the womb and saw in it seven little compartments each adapted
> for a human form and prepared for a seventh child. Then he was filled
> with great indignation and said, 'I came out of such a place.' And he let
> down his breeches and relieved himself into the belly of his mother . . .[98]

Nero's actual behaviour in the aftermath of his mother's death was rather more muted. Some authorities had it that he went to examine his mother's corpse, commenting on its perfections and imperfections in between drinks to slake his parched throat, before ordering her cremation. Agrippina was burned while lying on a banqueting couch, in a nondescript funeral ceremony, and no grave marker was provided for her ashes. Retreating to Naples, Nero swiftly exculpated himself for ordering his mother's death by sending a letter to the Senate which accused Agrippina of plotting against him and reminded the public of her frequent attempts to usurp traditional male authority. The

Senate responded in placatory fashion, deciding that annual games should be held to accompany the festival of the goddess Minerva in specific recognition of the foiled plot against the emperor's life. Agrippina's birthday, formerly included on the calendar as a day of celebration, was reclassified as a day of ill-omen.[99]

Verse graffiti on city walls at the time nevertheless responded impudently to the emperor's self-justifying rhetoric, showing that not everyone was willing to swallow the party line. The first example given here rhymes Nero with two characters in Greek myth who committed matricide; the second explains a formula whereby the numerical equivalent of the letters that spelled Nero's name in Greek was the same as for the phrase that described his crime:

> Alcmaeon, Orestes, and Nero are brothers,
> Why? Because all of them murdered their mothers.

> Count the numerical values
> Of the letters in Nero's name,
> And in 'murdered his own mother':
> You will find their sum is the same.[100]

At the same time as these lampoons did the rounds, persistent rumours circulated that Nero was afflicted with guilt. Such was his jittery preoccupation with the magnitude of his crime that he had even convinced himself that his mother's ghost had returned to haunt him.[101] This was an image that evidently caught the popular imagination, as illustrated in the doom-laden tragic play the *Octavia*, set three years after Agrippina's death, in 62, and probably written no more than a decade later. In the play's third act, the ghostly shade of Agrippina herself makes a melodramatic entrance, confessing her own crimes to the audience, ruing aloud her own shipwrecked fate and predicting a violent end for Nero and Poppaea:

> . . . there will come a day and time when he will pay for his crimes with his guilty spirit and pay his enemies with his throat, deserted and thrown down and utterly destitute. Oh, how far my labours and prayers have fallen! . . . I wish that before I brought you into the light as a tiny baby and suckled you, wild beasts had ripped apart my womb! . . . why am I slow to hide my fate in Tartarus, I who blight my kin as a stepmother, wife and mother?[102]

Until recently, the *Octavia* was actually suspected to be the work of Nero's most trusted but later disillusioned aide and counsellor, Seneca, who appears as a character in the play and whose admiration by poets and playwrights in medieval Europe – and especially those of the Renaissance – made the *Octavia* extremely popular in that era, inspiring Monteverdi's opera *L'incoronazione di Poppea* (1642), and many other works. Though it is now thought that Seneca – who was implicated in an unsuccessful conspiracy against Nero in 65, and committed suicide as a result, three years before the end of Nero's reign – was probably not the author, whoever wrote the play left behind an extremely valuable clue of the mood at court in the weeks and months following Agrippina's assassination. During her soliloquy in the play's fourth act, Agrippina's blood-stained wraith recalls that after her death, her son 'throws down the statues and inscriptions that bear my memory throughout the world – the world that my ill-starred love gave him as a boy to rule, to my own harm'.[103]

Archaeological evidence uncovered in recent years validates the *Octavia*'s suggestion that, like Livilla's and Messalina's before her, a purge of Agrippina's images was carried out following her death. During the 1990s, an excavated area between the Arch of Constantine and the Colosseum disclosed the remnants of a first-century monument that had once carried a statue of the emperor's mother alongside other members of her family. Signs remained that not long after Agrippina's demise, her statue had been removed from her position next to Claudius on the monument's plinth, and the other figures reshuffled to cover up her absence.[104]

However, whereas no certain replica of the disgraced Messalina's portrait has been identified from antiquity, sculptures of Agrippina do survive in respectable numbers, despite Nero's prohibition. Dedicatory inscriptions to her have also turned up unscathed, and although Agrippina's preserved sculptural legacy cannot match Livia's in terms of numbers, at least thirty-five portraits of her have managed to squeeze through the bottleneck of history, depicting her at various stages of her life – as first sister, wife and then mother to successive Roman emperors.[105] In one of the most recent discoveries, scholars from the Ny Carlsberg Glyptotek in Copenhagen established in 1994 that a dark green basalt head of Agrippina, acquired by the museum from a Lithuanian count in the late nineteenth century, was the missing partner of a hitherto anonymous female torso in a storeroom of the Capitoline Museum in Rome.

The torso itself had been found during the construction of a military hospital in 1885, split into large pieces and used as building material in a foundation wall probably cemented in the medieval period, when many classical sculptures were broken up and recycled for scrap.[106]

As with other imperial women before her, making sense of Agrippina's life is in itself an attempt to fit fragmented pieces together like a jigsaw. She did not attract the same attention as a Messalina or a Poppaea among writers and artists post-antiquity looking for a Pygmalion-esque mannequin of intoxicating sexual allure, but the fascination she has exerted has been just as enduring. As the historical epitome of conniving female kingmaker and overbearing mother, she has almost no equal, a guise in which she appeared with increasing frequency in later culture, in works including Handel's four-hour opera *Agrippina*, first performed on 26 November 1709, with a libretto by diplomat and cardinal Vincenzo Grimani.[107]

Handel's and Grimani's reworked portrait of Agrippina as a devious but comical character, who confesses to her sins but pleads that she did it all for Rome, may not qualify as an attempt at rehabilitation. But her incarnation as a remorseful if self-pitying ghost in the anonymously written *Octavia*, coupled with evidence that sculptures of her were erected in public building works commissioned by later emperors such as Trajan, suggests that Agrippina was remembered with at least some degree of respect and pity by her subjects.[108] This is acknowledged even by Tacitus, who reports that after her gruesome murder, some of her household staff clubbed together to build her a memorial near Bauli, with views over the bay. It seems that there were some who did indeed mourn Agrippina.[109] It is an impression also articulated by the infuriated response of one of the architects of the French Revolution, Maximilien Robespierre, to the flawed strategy of journalist Jacques Hébert at the trial of the French queen Marie Antoinette. When Hébert's false claim that the queen had committed incest with her son was successfully refuted, Robespierre was scathing in his exasperation:

That blockhead Hébert! – as if it were not enough that she was really a Messalina, he must make her an Agrippina also, and furnish her with the triumph of exciting the sympathy of the public in her last moments.[110]

* * *

There is one last reason for the endurance of Agrippina's memory long after her death. For this enigma of a woman attempted to leave behind something more tangible and personal than rumour or sculpture for posterity to remember her by. She wrote and published a set of memoirs, an accomplishment now expected almost as a matter of form from modern first ladies, but which no other Roman woman is known to have emulated. Their one-time existence is testified to by Pliny the Elder and Tacitus, authors of the first and second centuries respectively, each of whom cites Agrippina's own writings as one of his research sources.[III]

The date of the memoirs' composition and the original contents are both unclear, though Tacitus describes them as taking the form of 'commentarii', a factual, plain-prose genre of writing that emerged during the republican era and was exclusively dominated by men wanting to publish accounts of their political careers – Agrippina's Julio-Claudian male forebears Augustus, Tiberius and Claudius all produced such documents. Since Tacitus tells us that he used Agrippina's memoirs to piece together his account of the argument between her mother and Tiberius over the elder Agrippina's desire to remarry, it has been suggested that they were more like a gossipy diary than the kind of dignified commentarii expected of career politicians. But as a woman's, Agrippina's 'career' of course revolved around different concerns to a man's. Her public role was defined in terms of being a wife and mother, and the fact that the only other snippet of the memoirs' contents we have is Agrippina's testimony that Nero was born feet first, in a breech birth, may indicate that she intended her own commentarii to be a female take on this very male literary genre.[112]

Like her tomb, no copy of Agrippina's writings has ever been found, and, barring a papyrological miracle, it is now lost for ever. The fascination that this document nevertheless exerts over the imagination is eloquently expressed in a poem by the American William Wetmore Story – the author of a separate drama, The Tragedy of Nero, written in 1875:

> Stern Agrippina's diary and life
> Writ by herself, recording all her thoughts
> Deeds, passions, – all the doings of old Rome
>
> swarming around her, rife with scandals,
> crimes, joys, struggles, triumphs –
> all the portraits sharp of men and women

> as they lived, talked, loved – Not as in History's limbo
> they appear, mere names and ghostlike shadows,
> but alive, fierce, restless, human – what a book to find! [113]

Agrippina's career had triggered the most anxious soul-searching yet within the Roman elite about the encroachment of women on to the political field. It may be no coincidence that over the course of the next century and a half, the women of empire seem to become almost invisible.

5

Little Cleopatra: A Jewish Princess and the First Ladies of the Flavian Dynasty[1]

Oh Rome! Oh Berenice! Wretched me!
Must I be emperor, and love?

The Emperor Titus, in Jean Racine's *Bérénice*[2]

On 21 November 1670, at the company of the Hôtel de Bourgogne on the rue Mauconseil in Paris, French playwright Jean Racine awaited the premiere of his latest tragedy, *Bérénice*, in some trepidation. In precisely one week's time at the rival company of the Palais-Royal on the rue Montpensier, Pierre Corneille, the doyen of French tragic theatre, would unveil his own work, *Tite et Bérénice*, on exactly the same subject matter, the doomed first-century love affair between Julia Berenice, a daughter of the Herodian royal family of Judaea, and the Roman emperor-in-waiting Titus, a scion of the Flavian dynasty that succeeded the Julio-Claudians in the year 69.

This tale of Titus and Berenice, two star-crossed lovers forced to part reluctantly in deference to a sense of patriotic duty inspired a number of revisitations during the seventeenth century both in Britain and in France, where the history of Rome was a much-mined source of characters and situations perceived as relevant case studies for the moral and political progression of the age.[3] The circumstances under which Racine and Corneille both came to stage new productions based on precisely the same material within one week of each other are nonetheless murky. According to Voltaire, their competitive efforts were responses to a commission by Henrietta, Duchess of Orléans, who was moved by the echoes she perceived between Titus's and Berenice's doomed passion and her own noble renunciation of her love affair with her brother-in-law the Sun King Louis XIV, though others have found a closer parallel with Louis' severance of his relationship with Marie Mancini. At any rate, much pride was riding on this dramatic head-to-head, though in the end Racine need not have worried. It was his play that achieved a triumphant run while Corneille's effort was a relative flop.[4]

While Berenice's story captivated seventeenth-century dramatists, it is even more intriguing for the historian of the Roman first ladies. Though the mistress, not the wife, of an emperor-in-waiting, and a member of the Jewish rather than the Roman ruling family, she is an important link in the chain connecting Rome's imperial consorts. She entered the scene at a time when, thanks to the choice of Titus's father Vespasian – and later Titus himself – the emperor would rule without an empress. This was a decision that theoretically promised a cessation of the accusations that had all too frequently attached themselves to the Flavians' Julio-Claudian predecessors, namely of being 'petticoat governments', infiltrated by females. Yet, as Berenice's story and others demonstrate, women still loomed large in the orbit of the Flavian emperors, women who in different ways both abetted and threatened to derail the Flavians' project to present themselves as revolutionaries who would sweep aside the tainted memory of Messalina, Agrippina Minor, and the rest of the *ancien régime*.

Julia Berenice was born in 28 into the family of the Herods who governed the Roman provincial outpost of Judaea, in a year when Livia's son Tiberius still ruled at Rome, and a supposed carpenter's son from Nazareth was causing the local governing elite some inconvenience. The great-granddaughter of King Herod the Great and his beautiful wife Mariamme, her father was Marcus Julius Agrippa – named in tribute to his ancestors' long-standing friendship with the family of Julius Caesar. Like several others of the Herodian royal clan, Julius Agrippa had lived in the Palatine household at Rome from the age of four or five right through until his thirties, receiving the same education afforded to Claudius's and Tiberius's heir Drusus Minor and acquiring a reputation as a happy-go-lucky urban playboy whose spend-thrift tendencies were held in check only by his mother Berenice, who doled out his allowance with a watchful eye. After her death, his ruinous spending habits left him heavily in debt, and the death of his friend Drusus in 23, allegedly at the hands of Livilla and her lover Sejanus, led him to flee his creditors and sail to his Judaean home-land. In around 27, a son, Agrippa II, was born to himself and his wife Cypros, and the following year, a daughter, named Julia Berenice after her paternal grandmother.

After spending several years moving his young family between Judaea and Syria and falling out with successive relatives and friends in his failed bids to resurrect his fortunes, in 36 Julius Agrippa decided his only option was to leave his wife and children in Judaea and return to Rome to try and ingratiate himself with the imperial family once more. Once in Italy, his debts caught up with him again, and he was only rescued from his predicament by Antonia Minor, who out of regard for her old friend Berenice, and Julius Agrippa's friendship with her son Claudius, lent him the 300,000 drachmas he owed to the Roman treasury. This kept Julius Agrippa's enemies at bay for a time longer, and he used his connections with Antonia to strike up a friendship with her grandson Caligula, a friendship which would later pay dividends. Its more immediate side-effect, however, was to land him in prison later that summer when he was allegedly overheard expressing a hope that Tiberius might abdicate soon in favour of Caligula. His stay in captivity was ameliorated a little by the continued care of Antonia, who obtained a promise from the prefect of the praetorian guard, Macro, that Julius Agrippa should be allowed daily bathing rights and visits from friends who brought him clothes and some of his favourite foods.

Then in 37, Julius Agrippa suddenly experienced a remarkable reversal of fortune. The death of Tiberius duly saw the accession of Caligula, who summoned his ally from prison and appointed him tetrarch of territories including the area north-east of the Sea of Galilee, which had previously been the kingdom of Julius Agrippa's deceased uncle Philip. Later, he also received the territory of Galilee and Peraea, confiscated by Caligula from Agrippa's brother-in-law Herod Antipas. In the summer of 38, he returned to take possession of his new kingdom, where he was reunited with Cypros, Agrippa II and ten-year-old Berenice.[5]

Having spent this first decade of her life being towed around Palestine, Syria and Judaea in the wake of her father's ambitious schemes for recouping his wealth, the elevation of her father to a kingship resulted in a complete change in Berenice's circumstances and prospects. While her brother Agrippa II was dispatched to Rome just as his father had once been to receive an education in the imperial household, a suitable marriage was arranged for Berenice with Marcus Julius Alexander, the son of an old family friend named Alexander the Alabarch, whose family was one of the wealthiest in Alexandria. The marriage took place in 41, when she was thirteen years old.[6]

That year also witnessed the murder of Caligula and his succession by Claudius, Julius Agrippa's old friend from his childhood on the Palatine. Caligula's reign had been characterised by a number of tense flare-ups between Rome and its Jewish subjects, notably when Caligula

1. Livia supervising the making of clothes for her family, in a drawing by the French artist André Castaigne. Wool-working was the archetypal pastime of the Roman matron.

2. The actress Siân Phillips gives a famously malevolent performance in the role of Livia, in the BBC's adaptation of Robert Graves's novel *I, Claudius*.

3. The lush gardenscapes from the summer dining room of Livia's villa at Prima Porta are among the most magnificent Roman paintings ever recovered.

4. Jean Auguste Dominique Ingres, detail from *Virgil Reading the Aeneid to Livia, Octavia and Augustus* (1819). Octavia swoons at hearing the name of her son Marcellus, watched by Livia, who was suspected of involvement in the young man's death.

5. This portrait bust of Octavia was found at Velletri, just south-east of Rome, her family's home town. It has strong facial similarities to portraits of her brother. Like Livia, Octavia wears her hair in a *nodus* style.

6. Mark Antony (*right*) courted controversy by featuring not just his own profile but that of his lover Cleopatra on coins issued by eastern Roman mints under his control.

7. The miniature image of Augustus's daughter Julia on the reverse of this issue of 13–12 BC is flanked by the heads of her two infant boys, Gaius and Lucius.

8. This marble bust of Antonia Minor is known as the 'Wilton House Antonia', named after the residence of its one-time owner, the eighth Earl of Pembroke and Montgomery.

9. The American painter Benjamin West's canvas *Agrippina Landing at Brundisium with the Ashes of Germanicus* was unveiled in 1768, and earned him the patronage of King George III.

10. In Federico Fellini's 1972 film *Roma*, a young boy at the cinema pictures the local pharmacist's wife, described as 'worse than Messalina', greeting customers queuing for sex outside her car, and then gyrating on top of the vehicle in Roman costume.

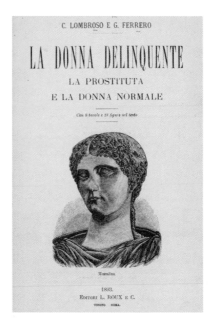

C. LOMBROSO E G. FERRERO

LA DONNA DELINQUENTE

LA PROSTITUTA
E LA DONNA NORMALE

Con 8 tavole e 18 figure nel testo

Messalina.

1893.

EDITORI L. ROUX E C.

TORINO   ROMA.

11. By using a line drawing of a Roman bust thought to depict Messalina as the title-page illustration for their landmark publication on female criminology, *La Donna Delinquente* (1893) Cesare Lombroso and Guglielmo Ferrero implied that one could read the empress's propensity for misdemeanour on her face.

12. The Gemma Claudia, possibly a wedding present to Claudius and Agrippina Minor. The jugate heads of Claudius and Agrippina Minor (*left*) are shown facing the bride's popular parents, the deceased Germanicus and Agrippina Maior.

13. This relief of Agrippina Minor crowning her son Nero was discovered in 1979 at Aphrodisias, in Roman Asia Minor. She carries a cornucopia of fruit in her left arm, thus associating her with Demeter, Greek patron goddess of the harvest.

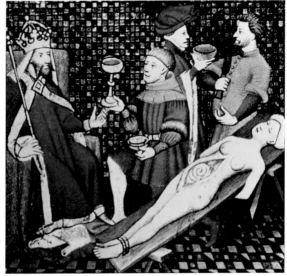

14. A story that Nero had his mother Agrippina's belly cut open after her death, so that he could see where he had come from, gained popularity in the medieval period. This illumination is from a fifteenth-century manuscript of the *De casibus virorum illustrium* (*On the Fates of Famous Men*) by Giovanni Boccaccio.

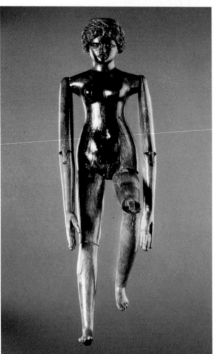

15. A second-century terracotta tomb relief from Ostia showing a Roman midwife preparing to deliver a baby while another woman stands behind the birthing chair, supporting the labouring mother. Such chairs had crescent-shaped holes in the seat through which the baby could be received.

16. A jointed ivory doll found in the grave of a girl named Crepereia Tryphaena who lived in the second century. Notice the adult proportions of the doll, with its wide child-bearing hips, and the hair styled in a fashion made popular by imperial women of the time, such as Marcus Aurelius's wife Faustina.

17. Roman necklace with amethyst, garnet and topaz elements, dating to the second or third century. The question of how much jewellery a woman should wear was a fraught subject in the Roman imagination. Too much could imply a frivolous and greedy nature, too little could reflect poorly on her husband or father's status.

18. This painted mummy-portrait of a richly jewelled woman from the Fayum district in Egypt makes a colourful contrast to official portraits of imperial women.

19. An ivory comb from a woman's grave dating to the third or fourth century. It appears to be engraved with the woman's name, Modestina. Many such items from Roman women's dressing tables have been recovered, including scent bottles, make-up boxes and even a *calamistrum* (curling iron).

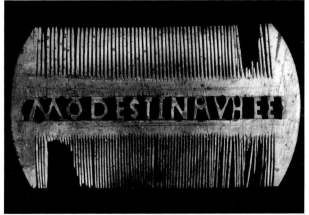

20. A portrait bust of Livia, with her hair fashioned in the austere *nodus* style commonly worn by Roman matrons of the first century BC.

21. The luxurious arrangement of precisely drilled waves and curls sported by Agrippina Maior formed a stark contrast to the rigidly plain *nodus* worn by her predecessors.

22. This portrait, commonly thought to be of Domitia, shows off to excellent effect the flamboyant style of hairdressing that became popular under the Flavians, during the second half of the first century.

23. The stiff, rigid coiffure of Trajan's wife Plotina does not seem to have set a fashion among women of the second century.

24. The plaited bun hairstyle of this woman, thought to be Julia Mamaea, was a precursor of similar styles worn by women in the later third and fourth centuries.

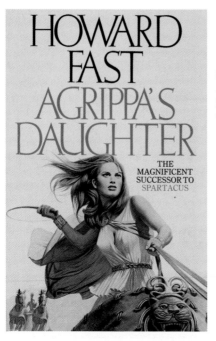

HOWARD
FAST
AGRIPPA'S
DAUGHTER

THE
MAGNIFICENT
SUCCESSOR TO
SPARTACUS

25. Howard Fast's novel *Agrippa's Daughter* (1964) casts Berenice as a plucky – and beautiful – flame-haired champion of her people.

26. This image from the Vatican Museums of second-century emperor Antoninus Pius and his wife Annia Galeria Faustina, being borne upwards to the heavens in conjugal unity, represented the first joint imperial apotheosis portrayed in Roman art.

27. The Berlin tondo of Septimius Severus, his wife Julia Domna and their two sons, Caracalla and Geta, is the only painted portrait of an imperial family to survive from antiquity. The obliteration of Geta's face was executed on the orders of his brother.

28. In Paolo Veronese's *The Dream of St Helena* (c. 1570), two angels carrying the True Cross appear to Constantine's mother as she sleeps, inspiring her to seek out its hiding place.

29. The moment of Helena's discovery of the True Cross, on which Jesus was crucified. She is accompanied by a female attendant to her left, and Judas Cyriacus to her right. The Judas Cyriacus version of the Cross's discovery was immensely popular in the Middle Ages.

30. The vast porphyry sarcophagus of Helena, mother of Constantine. It was originally placed in a mausoleum near her estate in Rome, but was removed in the twelfth century to serve as a tomb for Pope Anastasius IV. Its militaristic decoration scheme suggests it may originally have been intended for a male member of Constantine's family.

31. The Vandal-born general Stilicho, with his wife Serena
and their son Eucherius.

32. Pulcheria was a prominent figure at her brother Theodosius II's court in
Constantinople. Coins depict her with the elaborately jewelled coiffure typical
of imperial female portraits of the fifth century; on the reverse, an image of
the goddess Victory painting the Christian chi-rho symbol onto a shield.

33. The empress Galla Placidia, caught with her children, Honoria and Valentinian III, in a storm that threatened to capsize their boat, utters her prayer to St John the Evangelist.

34. Though Galla Placidia's remains are almost certainly entombed in the imperial mausoleum beneath St Peter's in Rome, her body was once thought to lie in a sarcophagus in the so-called Mausoleum of Galla Placidia in Ravenna. The building is famous for its exquisite blue mosaic interior, rich in Christian symbolism.

had attempted to have a statue of himself set up in the most holy of all Jewish shrines, the Temple of Jerusalem. As satellite kings appointed by the Romans, the Herods tended to side with their Roman mentors in such disputes, but Julius Agrippa used his personal connections with Caligula to persuade the emperor against such an antagonistic action. Indeed, Julius Agrippa's influence at the Roman court was such that he is said to have assisted behind the scenes in Claudius's hastily engin-eered accession to power, earning his reward when the new emperor extended the territory over which Agrippa ruled to include Judaea and Samaria.[7]

Berenice's brief marriage to Marcus Julius Alexander was abruptly cut short in 44 by her husband's death, and a second marriage was quickly arranged for the fifteen-year-old princess with her uncle Herod, Julius Agrippa's brother, to whom Claudius duly awarded the tiny kingdom of Chalcis, north of Judaea.[8] Not long afterwards, Berenice's father died of a dramatic collapse while attending games in Caesarea, temporarily ending the rule of the Herods in Judaea, as their impe-rial masters chose to pass control of the territory to a succession of procurators appointed from Rome. The death of her elderly uncle-husband Herod four years later in 48 left Berenice a widow for the second time at the age of twenty and she now became a resident in the house of her elder brother, who in 50 was given the deceased Herod's kingdom of Chalcis to rule.[9] Since their peripatetic childhood at the heels of their father, this was the first time Agrippa II and Berenice had shared a permanent abode. For the next fifteen years and more, she remained under her brother's roof, a living arrange-ment that would in hindsight draw scandalised accusations of incest upon their heads from commentators in Rome. According to the historian Josephus, a Jewish insider at the courts of Vespasian and Titus, the incest rumours shamed Berenice into moving out of the palace in 65 at the age of thirty-seven, and embarking on her third marriage with Polemo, the king of Cilicia, who even agreed to be circumcised and convert to her faith. But Berenice soon requested a divorce, and returned to live under the protection of her brother.[10]

These are the known facts of Berenice's life to this point. By the mid-60s, she was evidently a woman of some public standing in the eastern Mediterranean landscape. Like the consorts of Roman emperors, she had established herself as a benefactress and public patron of good works. An inscription referring to her as 'queen' or *basilissa* survives from Athens, originally accompanied by an honorific statue (now lost), and in the 1920s another inscription featuring her name was found in Beirut, recording the gift by Berenice and Agrippa II to the citizens there of marble and columns to restore a theatre first built by the pair's ancestor King Herod.[11] She herself had amassed a great deal of personal wealth, thanks to her acquisition of corn granaries and marriage settlements, and was also to demonstrate the 'good' Roman woman's knack of exerting a pacifying influence on her ruling relations – credited, for example, with persuading her brother not to execute Justus, a Jewish insurgent against Roman rule. Earlier, she made a notable appearance in 60 as a silent witness at the famous audience with St Paul when the latter defended his Christian faith before Festus, the Roman procurator of Judaea, and her brother Agrippa II, an event described in the Bible.[12]

Yet there was still little in her biography thus far to predict the flurry of interest she was to attract in the seventeenth century.

The events of 66 changed all of that. It was the year in which the First Jewish Revolt began, an uprising by Jewish factions against Roman rule in the province – whose leaders included the aforementioned Justus – lasting four years. Within that time-frame, Agrippina's son Nero met his death, and no fewer than three emperors came and went in the space of eighteen months before a fourth – Vespasian – restored stability to the empire. Agrippa II and his sister were key players at the heart of these tumultuous political events which in turn set Berenice on a collision course with Titus and her posthumous incarnation as a doomed heroine in dozens of dramas, operas and novels from the seventeenth century onwards.

The troubles of 66 were precipitated by Gessius Florus, the brutal new Roman procurator of Judaea whom Poppaea, the woman for whom Nero had finally exiled and executed Claudia Octavia and murdered his mother, had recommended for the post in 65. In a highly provocative gesture, Gessius Florus sent soldiers into the Temple of Jerusalem to retrieve taxes he claimed were owed to the Roman purse, and a violent stand-off between Roman troops and Jewish protesters followed. Berenice happened to be in Jerusalem at the time and, according to the first-hand account of Jewish historian Josephus, she was so shocked at the brutality of the Roman soldiers, whose actions she was privy to from the vantage point of her palace overlooking the Temple, that she proceeded to dispatch several senior members of her household staff and personal bodyguard to Florus, petitioning him to stop the slaughter. When all her envoys were rebuffed, she went to see him herself, standing barefoot before his tribunal, but was treated disrespectfully and protected from harm only by her bodyguards.[13]

Undeterred, Berenice now wrote a letter to Cestius Gallus, the Roman governor of Syria, asking him to restrain Florus. Her request was eventually answered when Gallus sent a fact-finding envoy who arrived in Jerusalem at the same time as the hastily returning Agrippa II, who had been on a diplomatic mission to Alexandria. In a bid to calm tensions, Agrippa called a mass meeting and appealed to the more militant rebels not to start a war with the Romans, placing his sister on the roof of the Hasmonean Palace, where she could be seen by all those at the meeting below. But his impassioned appeal fell on deaf ears, and despite historic precedents whereby women such as Octavia and Agrippina Maior had defused potentially violent situations by virtue of their calm diplomacy and nobility of bearing, Berenice's appearance failed to appease the insurgents. Agrippa II and his sister had no choice but to flee the dangerous atmosphere of the city.[14]

Over the next year, the Jewish rebels inflicted a series of embarrassing defeats on the Roman legions sent to crush them. Then in 67, Nero chose the semi-retired fifty-seven-year-old general Vespasian to head up the Roman response to the rebellion. Vespasian, a highly successful veteran of the British campaigns under Claudius, was grateful for the opportunity, having disgraced himself by falling asleep during one of Nero's self-promoting poetry readings a year earlier. He was also an old friend of Berenice's father, their connection stretching back to the days of the elder Agrippa's sojourn in Antonia's court, and on being appointed to his command, Vespasian set out for Antioch in Syria, to meet up with a delegation including the Herodian princess and her brother. Just before leaving for Syria, he issued orders to his twenty-six-year-old son Titus, whom he had chosen to act as his deputy in the campaign, instructing him to round up the rest of the legions from Alexandria, and meet his father in Ptolemais.[15]

The precise time and setting of Titus's and Berenice's first meeting are nowhere recorded. They may have encountered each other at Ptolemais as Titus and his father prepared for their campaign against the Jewish rebels, or it could just as easily have been later in the summer of that year, when he and Vespasian spent several weeks as guests of Agrippa II's at Caesarea Philippi, the city 25 miles (40 km) north of the Sea of Galilee where Berenice's brother had a magnificent palace.[16] The blank canvas at the beginning of their relationship has been filled by a great deal of colourful romantic speculation. *Agrippa's Daughter* (1964), a follow-up by the novelist Howard Fast to his bestseller *Spartacus* – which went on to be famously adapted for film – conjures up an opening encounter worthy of Mills & Boon:

> She remembered the first time she saw him, not tall – so few of the Italians were tall – but well formed, like a Greek athlete, short, straight nose, deep brown eyes, a wide sensuous mouth, black, curly hair, close-cropped – twenty-eight years old and so strangely without arrogance, two vertical lines between his heavy, dark brows marking him with a sort of patient despair, as if all his days were destined to be spent in hopelessness. He stood and looked at her, stared at her – until, provoked and embarrassed, she turned on her heel and left the room. Afterward, her brother Agrippa said to her, 'He's in love with you – hopelessly, idiotically in love with you'.[17]

In another, much-loved novel of the twentieth century, Lion Feuchtwanger's *The Jew of Rome* (1935), Titus looks back on his first meeting with Berenice, and recalls her 'long fine face', her 'golden-brown eyes', and how 'there was always just a touch of huskiness in her voice. At first I actually disliked it.'[18]

Alluring though such reconstructions are, the only concrete historical reference to this developing relationship over the next four years comes in a brief comment in Tacitus's *Histories*, where the historian notes that Titus's reluctance to return to Rome at the height of the campaign in 68 was thought by some to be influenced by his desire not to leave Berenice behind:

> Some believed that he turned back because of his passionate longing to see again Queen Berenice; and the young man's heart was not insensible to Berenice . . .[19]

However, the death of Nero in June 68 and the ensuing confusion – because the emperor had left no heir – was the more plausible reason for Titus's dilemma. The decade since the murder of Agrippina had seen Nero's reign lunge from one crisis to another; from the revolt in Britain led by the legendary Queen Boudicca in 60 and the great fire that devastated Rome in 64 – for which some blamed Nero himself –

to a sequence of alleged conspiracies against the increasingly mega-lomaniacal young emperor between 65 and 68 which resulted in the vengeful executions or enforced suicides of numerous eminent members of the elite accused of having masterminded them, including the once trusted Seneca. Poppaea, too, was dead, her embalmed, spice-scented body interred in the mausoleum of Augustus with full state honours – a fusion of eastern and Roman burial traditions which were surely in part the invention of a literary tradition determined to cast her as a reincarnation of Cleopatra.[20] Ostensibly, her death provoked great grief in Nero, who gave her funeral eulogy, though several sources report that it was in fact he who had caused her death in the summer of 65, by kicking her violently in the belly, while she was pregnant with their child.[21]

In 66, Nero had made a third marriage, to a noblewoman named Statilia Messalina – no relation to Claudius's infamous third bride – who kept a low profile, and managed to survive Nero's brutal demise. This came after a series of breakaway declarations by provincial gover-nors offering a challenge to the emperor's authority led to his being declared a public enemy by the Senate on 9 June 68. In a panic, Nero fled the city to the sanctuary of a villa owned by one of his freedmen, where he stabbed himself to death at the age of thirty-one, his arm guided by one of his secretaries.[22]

Into the breach left by Nero's exit stepped Galba, an elderly governor of the province of Spain who had secured the support of the prae-torian guard and the Senate, kick-starting the chaotic period between the summer of 68 and the winter of 69 commonly known as the Year of Four Emperors. Galba's brief six-month tenure on the Palatine finally severed the umbilical cord that had previously tied all of Augustus's successors to Livia. The new emperor nonetheless took care to flash around his connections to Rome's first empress, in whose household he had grown up and in whose will he had been named as a beneficiary. He included her on his brief regime's coins in a gesture demonstrating all too clearly that Livia's support, even from beyond the grave, was still seen to carry a powerful cachet.[23]

It was not enough, however, to secure Galba's acceptance as emperor. The legions on the Rhine refused to swear allegiance to him, and on 2 January 69, they instead gave their public backing to Vitellius, the governor of Germania and an old ally of the Julio-Claudians. At the same time, Galba faced a challenge on another front from Marcus Salvius Otho, the governor of Lusitania (Portugal), ex-husband of Poppaea and the man at whose seaside villa the fateful dinner party that precipitated Agrippina Minor's assassination had taken place. Otho himself also had links to Livia through his grandfather, who like Galba had been brought up in her household, and one protégé of Rome's first empress soon replaced another, when Galba was murdered on 15 January by the praetorian guard, and Otho was duly recognised as emperor in his place. Yet he in turn lasted barely three months, racking up debts and ordering unpopular executions before a major defeat at the hands of Vitellius's forces in northern Italy persuaded him to commit suicide on 16 April. The Senate duly recognised Vitellius as emperor in his place.[24]

Then a new twist. On 1 July, the Roman legions stationed on the eastern frontiers of Rome's empire, in Egypt, Syria and on the Danube, declared Vespasian their choice for emperor and gave him their full military backing. Suddenly the unthinkable was possible for the modestly born Vespasian, a man with no ties whatsoever to Livia or any branch of the Julio-Claudian dynasty. The names of an influential circle of eastern-based supporters were attached to this attempted *putsch*, headed by Mucianus the governor of Syria, but also including Agrippa II and Berenice, who was said by Tacitus to have been a favourite of Vespasian's for her 'youthful beauty'.[25] Some, in a typecast of Berenice as the marital opportunist, have surmised that her actions betrayed her deep-seated ambitions to be empress at Rome, but it seems also reasonable to suppose that the young Herodian royals had understandable domestic political motives for wanting to attach themselves to a winning ticket.[26]

Leaving command of the Judaean campaign in the hands of Titus, Vespasian headed west and after defeating Vitellius, who was caught and killed in the act of preparing to flee the city, he was acknowledged by the Senate as emperor on 21 December 69, inaugurating the era of the Flavian dynasty which would rule Rome for the next quarter of a century. The following year Titus secured victory over the Jewish rebels by sacking their stronghold in Jerusalem and destroying their holy Temple. The victory helped legitimise Vespasian's seizure of power, and was followed by a triumphal procession through the streets of Rome in 71, a triumph still memorialised in eternal, painful relief on the Roman forum's Arch of Titus, which shows the menorah and other sacred treasures of the Temple being carried aloft through the streets of Rome.

After almost a century, the Julio-Claudian dynasty had finally lost its grip on power. Those fond of omens and portents noted that the laurel grove at Livia's old villa at Prima Porta had also withered and died.[27]

Like Augustus a century earlier, who had also come to power at the tail end of a civil war, the immediate challenge for Vespasian and his sons was to justify their seizure of power in the absence of any links to the previous regime. Just as Augustus had used the treasure of Cleopatra's Egypt to finance his sculpting of the city's landscape in a way that glorified his own deeds, Vespasian set about using the profits of his plunder of Judaea to legitimise his newly won power by stamping his mark on Rome, rebranding it with the cultural insignia of his new dynasty while commissioning buildings that, in contrast to Nero's personal pleasure domes, would benefit the whole community, buildings such as the mighty Flavian Amphitheatre, better known today as the Colosseum. Taking another leaf out of Augustus's book, Vespasian also elected to shun Nero's grotesquely extravagant palace – the *Domus Aurea*, or Golden House, built after the fire of 64, whose grounds sprawled over an area approximately 1 mile (1.6 km) square between the Palatine and Esquiline hills – and made it free to the public. Instead, he chose a mansion in the beautiful Gardens of Sallust as his chief residence, where he made a virtue of being accessible to his subjects, and earned a reputation for himself as an unassuming, generous, down-to-earth *princeps*, fond of a dirty joke and a game at the ball-courts.[28]

The Flavians were nonetheless an entirely different breed from their Julio-Claudian predecessors, scions not of a great aristocratic clan but of an Italian middle-class one. Their arrival in Palatine politics was a watershed on several fronts. Vespasian spurned attempts to whitewash over his humble origins and his key legacy was the creation of a new Roman ruling class, a political elite that for the first time was not principally chosen from a narrow clique of Roman aristocratic families. It was from this new political class that not just the next generation of emperors would be chosen but, by extension, the next generation of empresses.[29]

Little splash had been made by the wives of the men who occupied the throne so fleetingly in the year between Nero's death and the Flavians' successful coup. Galba was a widower and Otho had not remarried since his divorce from Poppaea, though he apparently thought of marrying Nero's widow Statilia Messalina before suicide cut short his reign.[30] Vitellius, on arriving in Rome from Germany, had staged an emotional reunion with his mother Sextilia on the steps of the Capitoline Hill and had her endowed with the title *Augusta*. But there is no mention of a similar honour for his wife Galeria Fundana – who in a rare exception to the historiographical rule that corrupt emperors had corrupt wives, was said to have been a woman of 'exemplary virtue', who had not participated in her husband's crimes. Fundana was spared, along with her daughter Vitellia, in the aftermath of Vitellius's death, while Sextilia died shortly before.[31]

When Vespasian himself became emperor at the age of sixty, he like Galba was a widower, having buried a wife and daughter in the years prior to his accession, and he now became the first emperor since Tiberius to remain unmarried throughout his time in office. As the father of two adult sons, Titus and Domitian, who were already grown-up, he had no need of a wife to provide him with an heir, and seems to have preferred to rule without one. His decision may have been motivated by practical considerations, such as the desire to minimise the break-up of his estate amongst more posthumous inheritors than necessary, but also shrewd political caution, given the drama and scandal that had attended the consorts of the previous dynasty.

Nonetheless, there was a first lady of sorts during the first half of Vespasian's ten-year reign, a woman cut from a very different cloth to her high-born predecessors – Antonia Caenis, a freedwoman who had once served in the household of Claudius's mother Antonia, the very same Caenis to whom that venerable matron had dictated the fateful letter in 31 that warned Tiberius of Sejanus's plot against his life. After her mistress's death in 37, she became the lover of the rising Vespasian, in circumstances for which sadly we have no more detail. A formally recognised relationship, however, was out of the question. Although Vespasian was not a member of a high-ranking Roman family, the *leges Juliae* passed by Augustus had decreed that marriage between an equestrian and a freedwoman was forbidden. Instead Vespasian went on to marry a clerk's daughter named Flavia Domitilla. After her death, which occurred prior to his accession, Vespasian renewed his connection with Caenis, who now moved in with him as his concubine. Marriage was still not an option. Yet even when he became emperor, this former slave-woman remained under his roof, and ancient report claimed that he made her his empress in all but name.[32]

Caenis is a fascinating and rare surviving example of a woman from outside the inner imperial family circle who evidently was able to acquire a certain amount of prestige, personal wealth and access to the political process, even if such privileges made only a few faint cracks in the glass ceiling for women in Roman political life. Like her married female predecessors, her proximity to the emperor gave her opportunities to acquire influence, and she was said to have pocketed vast sums of money in return for recommending individuals for governorships and generalships to Vespasian. There were certainly precedents for freedwomen and female slaves bettering their financial prospects on the back of their association with the emperor. Records of the estate-holdings of Nero's own freedwoman concubine, Claudia Acte, show that she acquired a large number of slaves and property holdings in Italy and Sardinia during her lifetime, which she can only have come by through the gift of her imperial lover.[33]

Caenis did not survive Vespasian's full term as emperor, dying in the mid-70s, but her funerary inscription survives on a large, heavily decorated marble altar discovered close to the Porta Pia in Rome, on a site now the home of the Italian Ministry of Transport. She is thought to have owned a private estate here, and baths were later established bearing her name.[34] Her epitaph was the gift of Aglaus, one of the freedmen in her employ, and was simply dedicated from himself and his children:

> To the spirits of the departed,
> Antonia Caenis
> Freedwoman of the Augusta.
> Excellent patroness.
> Aglaus [her] freedman with Aglaus
> and Glene and Aglais
> his children[35]

As with the story of Berenice's and Titus's affair, interpreters in more recent years have been drawn to the attractive romantic template of the story of the enduring relationship between Vespasian and Caenis, two individuals unable to marry due to social convention but who, despite temporary separation, happily reunited in their late middle age. The writer Lindsey Davis, author of a 1997 novel based on the relationship, calls Caenis's story the 'archetypal Secretary-to-Boardroom plot'.[36] Yet despite the dramatic potential of her rags-to-riches promotion, and the intrigue of her influence behind the scenes as imperial consort-in-chief, Caenis did not occupy a position of any equivalence to that of imperial women such as her former mistress Antonia. She could never be awarded the special privileges of an empress or the title of *Augusta* and the incongruity of her position is underlined by Suetonius's story that Vespasian's younger son, Domitian, refused to allow her a stepmother's privilege of kissing him but would only shake her hand.[37] No portraits of her were commissioned, no titles conferred upon her, no images stamped on coins.

Nor, in fact, do any securely identified images survive of Vespasian's former wife, Flavia Domitilla, mother of Titus and Domitian. This absence of official portraits of living female members of the ruling imperial family represents a significant break with the tradition established by the Julio-Claudians. A distinctive Flavian female portrait tradition did eventually emerge, centred around the figures of Domitian's wife Domitia Longina, and Titus's daughter Julia Flavia. But it was not until the advent of the Flavians' successors, at the beginning of the second century, that images of women came to be utilised so visibly once more as mastheads for traditional Roman virtues.[38]

Vespasian's ten-year reign was thus very much a judiciously sifted mixture of something old, something new, representing a departure from his predecessors, while at the same time copying their more popular and successful traits. His discreet relationship with Caenis did nothing to upset senatorial traditionalists, still jittery from the heyday of Messalina and Agrippina Minor, leaving him free to emulate the best of the Julio-Claudian traditions of power originating with Augustus. Yet there was one echo of Augustus's rise to power that Vespasian probably would rather not have emulated – namely the disturbing presence of a foreign queen. Enter Berenice.

By the end of the Flavians' first year in power, Vespasian's somewhat ramshackle younger son Domitian, who was said to have had a misspent youth seducing married women, had cleaned up his act by marrying Domitia Longina, the daughter of the great general Corbulo. It was a shrewd choice of bride, though it had come at the expense of Domitia's former husband Lucius Aelius Lamia, who was forced to give his wife up much as Tiberius Claudius Nero had been induced to relinquish Livia to Octavian for the latter's political benefit. In Domitian's and Domitia's case, an alliance between an emperor's son and the daughter of Corbulo, the greatest military leader of recent times, who had, moreover, been forced to commit suicide by Nero, could only help the new dynasty stake out a position as champions of the heroic victims of the previous emperor's tyranny. It also provided the provincial Flavians with a valuable tie to an old and respected Roman family of unimpeachable lineage.[39]

The love life of Domitian's elder brother on the other hand was causing his father more of a problem. Prior to Vespasian's meteoric rise to the purple, Titus had already been married twice, first to Arrecina Tertulla, daughter of a one-time commander of the praetorian guard, and then, after her death, to the well-connected Marcia Furnilla, whom he divorced after she had given birth to a daughter, Julia Flavia, born in around 65. A family nurse named Phyllis was given charge of the infant, and it is generally assumed that Julia Flavia was later taken to live in the household of her uncle Domitian on his marriage to Domitia Longina in 71, Caenis being deemed unsuitable to act the role of duenna in the way Antonia and Livia had once done for the children of the Julio-Claudians.[40] When Titus eventually reappeared in Rome in 71 to play his part in the great triumph held to celebrate victory in Judaea, he returned unaccompanied. But by the year 75, Berenice had also arrived to take up residence in the city, chaperoned by her brother Agrippa II. Her sojourn in the capital, which seems to have lasted for the next four years, was to prove a public relations minefield for the Flavian dynasty.[41]

Only glimpses of Berenice's and Titus's life together in Rome survive, but they are enough to give a flavour of the mixture of tabloidesque excitement, satirical mockery and rumbling discontent that greeted her installation in the Flavian family tableau. On her arrival, she and Titus followed the example of Vespasian and Caenis by living together as if they were married. But while the emperor and his mistress cohabited in relatively discreet seclusion in the Gardens of Sallust, Berenice and Titus moved into the imperial palace on the Palatine, an ostentatious gesture that raised hackles in certain quarters. The verdict of some was that Titus's foreign mistress 'was already behaving in every respect as if she were his wife', echoing Cicero's violent condemnation of Cleopatra's presence in Caesar's home.[42]

Titus did not commit Antony's solecism of commissioning Roman statues or coins featuring his foreign lover. In fact no portraits of Berenice survive from antiquity at all, as one might expect of a princess of the Jewish faith, which prohibited artistic representation of individuals. The only clue we have to her appearance is the mention of a jewel that she used to wear. Writing shortly after the death of the

Flavian dynasty, the satirist Juvenal mockingly referred in the course of a diatribe against women's obsession with jewellery to a 'legendary diamond' once worn by Berenice, which he said was much coveted by other women. He listed the diamond as a gift from 'the barbarian Agrippa to his incestuous sister', dredging up the rumour of their sexual liaison.[43]

By drawing attention to Berenice's diamond, Juvenal was gleefully encouraging old-fashioned members of his audience to suck in their cheeks in self-satisfied disapproval.[44] Such ostentatious personal adornment formed a stark contrast to the frugal example set by jewel-free paragons of Roman womanhood such as Cornelia, and a group of Roman matrons who had sacrificed their trinkets to pay a ransom to invading Gauls in the fourth century BC. This latter story was one of Rome's favourite feminine morality tales. The potency it held over the Roman imagination had first been demonstrated more than two centuries before Berenice's lifetime, during a notorious debate in 195 BC over the repeal of the oppressive Oppian Law, originally passed during a crisis point in the Punic Wars with Hannibal twenty years earlier. It had aimed to restrict women's extravagance in order to stop vital funds being siphoned away from the war effort, forbidding them from possessing more than half an ounce (14 grammes) of gold, from wearing clothing dyed with expensive coloured pigments – particularly purple – and from riding in horse-drawn carriages within the city precincts. However, when it looked as though there was a chance the law might not be repealed, some Roman matrons reportedly entered the forum to demonstrate in protest. After a furious debate, during which the redoubtable consul Cato spoke in favour of keeping the law, the motion was carried for the other side, and women were allowed to put on their purple once more.[45]

The furore over the Oppian Law reveals a great deal about Roman attitudes to female consumption and adornment, within whose currents Berenice and her female counterparts found themselves caught up. On the one hand there was a view, advocated by Cato's opponents during the debate, that a woman's clothing and jewels were to her what triumphs and badges of office were to a man, allowing her to show off her wealth and status, and complement that of her husband and father in the process. Painted, privately commissioned funerary portraits of women discovered around the empire at sites such as Fayum in Egypt, show them dripping with jewels. Fashionable gemstones included pearls, sapphires, rubies, citrines, garnets, aquamarines, emeralds or uncut diamonds like Berenice's, set into finger-rings, earrings, bracelets or necklaces, which could be wound in double or triple strands around the neck. Some very wealthy houses had their own jewellery-makers. As the finds from the *Monumentum Liviae* prove, Livia herself had someone to set her pearls for her.[46]

Yet look at portraits of Livia, and you will look in vain for these pearls. In fact, a glance at almost any marble bust of the women of the imperial family before late antiquity reveals only bare necks, wrists, fingers and earlobes. This lack of adornment, in stark contrast to the visual evidence from art and archaeological finds that women – including Livia herself – obviously wore jewellery in 'real life', reflects the anxieties about displays of luxury on a woman's body.[47] Juvenal was not the only writer to satirise women's magpie-ish love of sparkly baubles and trinkets, nor was Berenice the only woman to be singled out for disapproval. Caligula's fabulously wealthy third wife Lollia Paulina was criticised for attending a simple betrothal banquet smoth-ered in forty million sesterces' worth of emeralds and pearls, while Lollia's ancestor Antony had famously cavorted with a woman so profligate that she thought nothing of dissolving a priceless pearl in a glass of wine to win a bet. The point was also made that jewellery cost Roman men a fortune to import from India, Egypt and Arabia. In short, Berenice's diamond cast her as a reincarnation of Cleopatra, come to make trouble and spread her alien, unprincipled foreign ways.

The statement of one of her modern biographers that Berenice turned the Palatine into an eastern court is a better reflection of these suspicions about 'un-Roman' influences than it is of any literal trans-formation of the Palatine on the Flavians' watch.[48] However, that Titus's lover did indeed find herself in controversial political territory is borne out by a cryptic comment by the contemporary Roman advocate Quintilian, who, in his famous guidebook to the training of a successful orator, remarked that he once argued a case in front of 'Queen Berenice', at which she was also the defendant.[49] Why Berenice had been summoned, we are not told. It is possible that in fact Quintilian was not referring to a criminal trial, but to a meeting of the imperial advisory council, and that Berenice had been invited – perhaps even by Vespasian himself – to give testimony or advice on some issue in which she had expertise, such as the management of Judaea.[50] Nonetheless, it was a provocative scenario, and it is clear from other sources that the Herodian princess's residence in Rome was doing Titus's image no favours. Opposition to her continued presence in the city is attested by the protests of two Cynic philosophers, Diogenes and Heras, who were punished for their public protests against Titus's immoral relationship. Diogenes was flogged for entering a theatre and delivering a lengthy and bitter tirade denouncing Berenice's and Titus's affair, while Heras suffered more harshly for his public condemnation of the pair and was subsequently beheaded.[51]

Titus's passion for Berenice was seen as part and parcel of a list of vices for which he acquired an unflattering reputation during his father's reign. Allegations of debauchery with eunuchs and accepting bribes in return for swinging the outcome of court cases were bandied about. The suicide of two senators, Caecina and Marcellus, after Titus pronounced them guilty of conspiracy in 79, provoked hostility from other senators towards the emperor's eldest son. Suggestions that the Roman people faced the prospect of another Nero on the throne, should he succeed to his father's dignities, were publicly voiced. The stench of corruption lingered over the Flavian household and something needed to be done about it if they were not to be lumped together with the worst of the Julio-Claudians.[52]

On 24 June 79, Vespasian died after ten years in power, and was succeeded by his eldest son. Almost overnight, so we are told by his ancient biographer Suetonius, Titus's reputation was transformed from dissolute merchant of vice to wise and beloved emperor, his raucous drinking parties reinvented as elegant, decorous symposia, his harem of dancing boys sent back to the stage and his undesirable troupe of friends replaced with a circle of sage political advisers. He was generous to his public, staging lavish gladiatorial entertainments of their choice and sometimes even bathing with them at the public baths, and reportedly considered a day wasted if he had not granted a boon to at least one of the many petitioners whom he always made time to see. But the most powerful proclamation of this image overhaul was the dismissal of his lover Berenice from the capital.[53]

Even critical Roman writers characterised the decision to separate as a difficult one for both parties. Suetonius gave a succinct digest of the parting moment between the Roman emperor and his Herodian lover as – *demisit invitus invitam*: 'he sent her away though he was unwilling and so was she.' This was to become the catalyst for the reinterpretation by Racine and others of this poignant tale of two divided lovers.[54] Titus bowed to public opinion nonetheless, and Berenice received her *congé*. One ancient report claims she later returned to the city but that there was no moving the newly obdurate Titus, and Berenice disappeared once more.[55]

No more was heard from the Jewish queen and one can only presume she returned to live out her days in Judaea.[56] The fascination of her unknown fate is perfectly captured in a scene from George Eliot's 1876 novel *Daniel Deronda*, which, in part, tells the story of a young man who in the process of uncovering his Jewish roots falls in love with a mysterious Jewess named Mirah. Arriving one day at the house of his friend and rival for Mirah's affections, the artist Hans Meyrick, Deronda learns that Hans has conceived a plan to paint a 'Berenice series' of five movements from the heroine's life, with Mirah as the model: Berenice clasping the knees of Gessius Florus in Jerusalem; Berenice alongside her brother Agrippa as he appeals to his fellow countrymen for peace; Berenice exulting in the prospect of being empress of Rome; Berenice being sent away from Rome by Titus, 'both reluctant, both sad – *invitus invitam*, as Suetonius hath it'; and Berenice 'seated lonely on the ruins of Jerusalem' – an ending which Meyrick admits is a figment of his imagination: 'That is what ought to have been – perhaps was ... nobody knows what became of her.'[57]

As in the case of her Egyptian alter ego Cleopatra, it is the very qualities that render Berenice so seductive a subject for a modern audience that made her an object of suspicion and revilement among a number of Roman observers. Her reputed beauty, her exoticism, her otherness, the fascination she exerted over the emperor, were all the hallmarks of several of the straw women who had troubled the Roman imagination, from Cleopatra to Poppaea. Berenice's entanglement with Titus provided ammunition for those who argued that allowing women to get too close to the machinery of government would always prove the downfall of Roman dynasties. Within only a few years of the Herodian queen's departure from Rome, those concerns would be recentred on Domitia, the wife of Titus's brother and successor.

Titus's rule as emperor lasted only two years. He faced a number of difficult challenges during that short period, most notably the eruption of Mount Vesuvius in the autumn of 79 which buried the towns of Pompeii and Herculaneum in a solid sea of volcanic ash and left thousands dead or homeless. The following year, a serious fire swept through Rome, destroying Octavia's old portico alongside other major building works, and the city's tragedies were compounded by an outbreak of plague. Titus's personal contribution to the disaster relief efforts in the aftermath of all these events nevertheless won him a great deal of popular goodwill which was boosted still further when the Colosseum was finally officially opened in 80 and one hundred days of spectacular games were held in celebration. But the honeymoon period was cut short by his death from fever at the age of forty-one on 13 September 81, paving the way for a rash of conspiracy theories over the likely meaning of his cryptic final words, 'I have but one regret'. Some at the time took this to be a reference either to his refusal to share power with Domitian, or to an alleged – though strenuously denied – liaison with his brother's wife Domitia, though others since have chosen to interpret the line more romantically as a lament for his loss of Berenice.[58]

Into Titus's shoes stepped twenty-nine-year-old Domitian, the younger of Vespasian's two sons. At fifteen years, his reign was the longest of the three Flavian emperors and would be remembered as, on the one hand, a period of rich cultural production, but, on the other, an age of tyranny and cruel repression that undid much of the public relations legwork put in by his father and elder brother – a trend that eventually earned this bald, fastidious and idiosyncratic individual the punishment of *damnatio memoriae* from the Senate.

Unlike his family predecessors, Domitian was already married when he took the throne on 14 September 81. Domitia Longina thus became the first – and, as it would turn out, the only – official 'first lady' of the Flavian dynasty, and also the first wife of a Roman emperor since Poppaea in 65 to be anointed *Augusta*.[59] She was moreover granted the title within two weeks of Domitian's accession, an unusually quick bestowal of the accolade.[60] The cachet offered by the title of *Augusta* had clearly changed since the days when it was only awarded cautiously to elderly matrons like Livia and Antonia, who no longer had the biological capacity to affect the succession. Now that the principle of imperial rule was well embedded, emperors these days no longer had to be so coy about honouring their women.[61]

Domitia and Domitian, both in their late twenties, were in fact still childless. A son born to the couple before Domitian became emperor died in infancy and had been posthumously deified, a gesture accompanied by the issue of coins honouring Domitia as *Mater Divi Caesaris* – 'Mother of the Divine Caesar'. No other Roman empress is thought to have received the tribute of being called the mother of a 'god' during her lifetime, and there must have been great hope that Domitia could still capitalise on the accolade by providing an heir for the Flavian dynasty, in the absence of any born to Titus.[62] Unlike Augustus's and Livia's densely branched family tree, which regularly offered several options for the provision of a Julio-Claudian heir, the hopes of the Flavians rested heavily on Domitia, although there was an alternative source of future heirs in Titus's teenaged daughter Julia Flavia, on whom the accolade of *Augusta* had also been bestowed, despite her being so young.

Like his father before him, Domitian set about trying to portray himself in the early years of his reign as a political heir of Augustus, embarking on a stunningly ambitious architectural overhaul of the city, expanding the empire's borders and making moral reform a centre-piece of his agenda. In this vein, he followed Augustus's suit in publicly promoting wool-working as the ideal pastime for women by giving pride of place on the temple of Minerva in his new forum to a scene of Roman matrons weaving under the aegis of the goddess. He also announced a reintroduction of the first emperor's legislation on sexual mores, a policy whose sting was, as before, felt most keenly by elite women. The old *Lex Iulia* against adultery – which had not been rigor-ously enforced in the decades since Augustus's reign – was revived and the death penalty reinstated for Vestal Virgins who were found to have broken their vow of chastity. One of those who fell foul of this legislation, the chief Vestal Cornelia, was apparently subjected to the archaic punishment of live burial, while her alleged lovers were stoned to death.[63]

Meanwhile, the *Lex Voconia* of 169 BC, which had limited women's rights of inheritance, was also resurrected in a bid to curb the growth of a small but significant group of Roman women benefiting from liberal property rights laws. These laws were allowing certain elite women to amass large personal fortunes from will bequests and divorce settlements, women such as Ummidia Quadratilla, an immensely wealthy matriarch who was reported to have lived a life of such inde-pendent leisure that she could fund her own troupe of mime actors to perform for herself and her community's amusement.[64] Women may have remained as shut out from the institutions of political power as ever, but Domitian's attempts to reinvigorate the old Augustan laws on adultery and property inheritance make it apparent that an old debate raged on, and that there were renewed calls for women's increasing financial and social freedom to be curbed.[65]

Domitian himself, however, showed no inclination to emulate his father's man-of-the-people stance by choosing modest living quarters. Instead, he joined the otherwise unbroken line of emperors from Augustus onwards who had set up their own establishments on the Palatine. It was a hundred years since Hortensius's modest stone house had been requisitioned to serve as the home of Rome's first emperor, and the swathe of hill where Augustus's and Livia's old home still stood like a historic museum was now completely unrecognisable. Each of their descendants had taken his turn extending and adding to the imperial residence, and Domitian's own plans to create a palace complex in his family's name were so ambitious that they transformed the entire hill. Masterminded by his architect Rabirius, the new 'Domus Flavia' took shape on the very peak of the Palatine, a brick palace covering around 40,000 square metres (47,850 square yards) and incorporating a dazzling public area adorned with polychrome marble walls and columns designed for the reception and entertainment of guests, a hippodrome, and a cordoned-off private zone reserved for the sole use of the emperor and his family, built around colonnaded garden peristyles whose fountains and flower beds provided a respite from the hubbub of the public audience rooms. Ancient authors fell over themselves to praise the overall effect, one poet calling it 'one of the most beautiful things in the world'.[66]

Domitian's love of virtuosity in his aesthetic surroundings was mirrored by a flamboyant transformation of the portrait traditions of women under the Flavians, as modelled by Domitia and Julia Flavia. From Livia's modest *nodus* at the end of the first century BC to the more elaborate, adventurous arrangements of curls and ringlets sported by the Agrippinas in the first half of the first century AD, the Julio-Claudian era had witnessed a gradual trend for women to let their hair down, so to speak. But under the Flavians, hairdressers achieved new flights of frothy fantasy with the birth of the so-called *Toupetfrisur*, a style characterised by a high beehive of closely woven curls, whose honeycombed façades have also been compared to sea sponges and tortellini pasta.[67]

To achieve this new style, rows of minuscule curls as many as eight tiers high ascended to form a small pointed peak. So high was the hair piled on top of the heads of Domitia, Julia Flavia and their counterparts in these portraits that wire frames are thought to have been used as a kind of scaffolding around which to mould the locks.[68] Dyes and pomades were used to give tint, sheen and hold, the effect of which is now lost to us since ancient marble portraits have long since been stripped of any layers of paint that might have given us an idea of the colours used. Eye-watering ingredients were recommended for these hair dyes, from leeches soaked in red wine to dye one's tresses black, to an alkaline mixture of goat's fat and beechwood ash known as *sapo* to lighten them. These had to be used with care, as testified by one of Ovid's poems in which he gleefully admonishes a woman who had attempted her own home-dye job:

'I *told* you to stop using rinses – and now just look at you!
No hair worth mentioning left to dye ... If your hair's fallen out, it's not
Any envious tongue that's to blame. You applied that concoction
Yourself. It was you that did it. *All your fault.*'[69]

Elaborate, towering styles like the *Toupetfrisur* must have taken hours to achieve, using teams of *ornatrices* and styling implements such as the *calamistrum* (curling iron) or ivory comb, examples of which have been recovered in excavation.[70] The *ornatrix* who failed to satisfy her mistress or customer faced harsh punishment, if the portrait of the Roman satirists is anything to go by: 'Why is this curl sticking up?' a woman demands of her hapless hairdresser in one such scenario, before venting her rage with a bullwhip.[71] We even know the names of one of Domitia's own *ornatrices*, thanks to a marble plaque put up in her memory by her husband, which tells us her name was Telesphoris and she died at the age of twenty-five.[72]

A female audience, milling about the public places where portraits of Domitia and Julia Flavia appeared, would have recognised that, unlike the achievable *nodus*, such styles as the Flavian emperors' female relatives sported were the preserve of the very wealthy only, who could afford to devote so much leisure time and slave labour on the creation of these elaborate concoctions. Still, some aristocratic women evidently did emulate the new trends. Juvenal mocked the vanity of a female who 'weighs down her head with tiers upon tiers and piles her head high with storeys upon storeys', so that even though she might look short from the back she would suddenly look unnaturally tall from the front.[73]

However, like any other organic matter, few samples of real hair survive to us from antiquity, obscuring the relationship between formal portraits and everyday styles, although some pieces have been found in sites such as Britain, Gaul and Judaea, ranging in shades from blonde to black. Mummy portraits from the province of Egypt feature women with hairstyles just like those modelled on sculpted portraits from the imperial capital at Rome, but this still does not mean that the women featured went through the elaborate ritual of having their hair styled like this on a day-to-day basis.[74]

We might well wonder why the socially conservative Flavians, who in many respects sought to disassociate themselves from the extravagant excesses of the previous regime under Nero, would adopt what looks to our eyes so frivolous a hairstyle as the *Toupetfrisur* as the signature look for public portraits of female family members. In fact, these rigorously and laboriously styled coiffures bespoke a message of carefully tamed, cultivated, civilised order which chimed perfectly with their husbands' and fathers' broader political agenda. From the age of adolescence, a respectable Roman woman never wore her hair loose in public. Untamed locks were the signature style of sexually unchaste or barbarian women like the British warrior queen Boudicca, or women in mourning whose show of unkemptness was appropriate in the context of their grief, or else the special preserve of goddesses, who were exempt from the usual civic norms. For the Flavians, the impressive technical feat represented by the *Toupetfrisur* echoed the dynasty's ambitions to impose morality, control and order on the empire.[75]

Another politically relevant reform of the portrait tradition for both men and women of the Flavian era was the flirtation with the 'realistic' style which had last found favour in the republican era. Throughout the Julio-Claudian period, portraits both of the men and the women of the imperial family had generally presented a youthful, airbrushed appearance to the world, even when the subject had reached old age. But beneath the new heavy and ostentatious hairstyles adopted by their Flavian successors, women's faces began to show their age again. One marble bust of a middle-aged woman widely thought to be Domitia in later life, now located in the San Antonio Museum of Art in Texas, illustrates this new phenomenon.[76] Her hair is painstakingly coiled into four domed rows of precision-drilled curls, a tour de force exhibition of the *ornatrix*'s art, but instead of the taut, youthful contours of the typical Julio-Claudian visage, she has a heavy-set countenance, her brow sinking frowningly over heavy-lidded eyes, and with the indents of her naso-labial lines clearly visible against her puffy cheeks.[77]

In steering portraiture back in the direction of the 'realistic' style sported by male portrait statues in the republican period, the Flavians presumably hoped to appeal to nostalgic memories of that era inhabited by paragons of female virtue women such as Cornelia, long before Agrippina Minor and Poppaea blotted the Roman first ladies' copybook.[78] But behind the dazzling palace façade and the magnificent moral fashions, Domitian's and Domitia's marriage was in fact showing depressing signs of sliding into the worst habits of the Julio-Claudians.

In around 83, two years after her husband's accession, Domitia was accused of adultery with a celebrated pantomime actor who went by the name of Paris, apt given the mythical Paris's crime of running off with Helen of Troy, herself the wife of a king. While the thespian Paris was publicly executed and his grieving fans who tried to mark the spot of his murder with flowers were threatened with the same fate, Domitia and the emperor were divorced.[79]

Domitia was not the first woman of the imperial house to be indicted for getting involved with someone in show business. Amongst the accusations levelled at Augustus's daughter Julia had been the charge of cavorting with an actor called Demosthenes, while Nero's first wife Claudia Octavia had been framed for adultery with an Egyptian fluteplayer, to justify her execution in exile. The ubiquity of such cases underlines that accusations of sexual impropriety, particularly with actors or other servile lovers, were a classic excuse to get rid of women for more political purposes.[80] If, however, there was an explicit political motive for giving Domitia her marching orders, it does not emerge clearly from our sources, though her failure to produce an heir is a plausible theory.[81] Since the penalty for adultery was deportation, we can presume that like other disgraced Roman wives, Domitia was banished from the city, although there is no indication of whether she was destined, like Julia, Agrippina Maior and other imperial women, for exile on Pandateria.

For the time being, Domitia's position as leading lady of the empire was usurped by the emperor's niece Julia Flavia. Now aged around eighteen, she had some experience of the public spotlight already. Since her father Titus had remained unwed after Berenice's departure from Rome, she had served as the face of his coinage, depicted in association with the goddess Ceres, the most popular role model for imperial women. Despite surviving sculptures that show her sporting the lavish spiralling head of curls worn by other fashionable ladies of her generation, her official coin portraits show her with a far more modest chignon reminiscent of some of Livia's later profiles, a nod to the Flavians' admiration for Rome's first empress, though in an abrupt departure from Livia's portrait tradition, both Julia Flavia and her aunt Domitia are sometimes shown wearing what looks to be a crescent-shaped diadem in their hair. Such queenly insignia had not been seen on an imperial woman's head before.[82]

On coming of age, Julia Flavia had been made the bride of her cousin, Flavius Sabinus, but the match was not, if Suetonius's account is correct, her father's first choice.[83] When she was still a young girl, Titus had urged his younger brother to throw over Domitia and take Julia Flavia as a wife instead in a bid to strengthen the Flavian dynasty, a suggestion Domitian violently repudiated, supposedly due to his passion for Domitia, though the unhappy precedent set by Claudius's marriage to his niece Agrippina Minor would also have justified his refusal.[84][5] Following the departure of Domitia in 83, Julia Flavia's assumption of the role of companion to her uncle proceeded to generate just the kind of gossip that Domitian would have wished to avoid. Details are sketchy and contradictory, but it appears that tongues began to wag as the pair were seen living, in the words of one commentator, 'as husband with wife, making little effort at conceal-ment'.[85] Julia Flavia's husband Flavius Sabinus was executed by the emperor for treason, and the rumours intensified with suggestions that Julia now exercised a special political influence over her uncle, persuading him to raise to the consulship an ex-prefect of Egypt named Ursus, who had only recently been under threat of execution for showing insufficient deference to the emperor.[86]

But within as little as a year, the saga of the emperor's personal life took yet another twist. Domitia staged a comeback. Crowds are reported to have gathered in the streets and demanded the empress's return, an echo of public protests that demanded the recall of Julia in 2 BC, and of Claudia Octavia following the false charges laid against her by Nero in 62. In contrast to those two sad cases, the result this time was that Domitian, said by some to have been regretting the separation – though conceivably also seeking to quash the rumours about himself and his niece – was reconciled with his wife. Julia Flavia remained on the Palatine, but subsequently died in around 87 or 88 at the approximate age of twenty-two in what was whispered to be a failed abortion attempt, imposed on her by the father of her child – Domitian.[87]

This confusing picture of incest and betrayal sits oddly with the subsequent deification of Julia Flavia ordered by Domitian after her death when coins were emblazoned with images showing her being

carried to the heavens on the back of a peacock.[88] The stigma that
had once made emperors like Augustus and Tiberius so cautious about
deifying their women had clearly fallen by the wayside – Vespasian's
daughter Domitilla, who did not live to see her father become emperor,
was also honoured as a goddess on his coinage.[89] But the story that
Julia Flavia had aborted her uncle's child refused to go away. Juvenal,
writing obliquely about the affair only a few years later, critiqued the
hypocrisy of those who preached morality while behaving in the
opposite manner – the 'adulterer' here being Domitian and the 'bitter
laws' a reference to his revival of Augustus's moral legislation:

> Exactly so was the adulterer of more recent times, defiled by a union
> worthy of tragedy, who tried to revive bitter laws to terrify everyone,
> even Venus and Mars, at the very moment when his Julia was unsealing
> her fertile womb with numerous abortion-inducers and pouring out
> lumps which resembled her uncle.[90]

Amid the obfuscation, one clear fact emerges. Julia Flavia's fate was
eloquent proof that, despite the ease with which the honour of deification was now bestowed on a woman of the imperial family, divine
honours were less of a personal tribute than a routine benefit intended
more for the glorification of her ruling emperor than the recipient.
They jarred, moreover, with her own fragile mortal lot. However
important a prop she might be at one time to the emperor's public
profile, she was both disposable and replaceable – a bit-player in a
narrative bigger than her own, a narrative which would always threaten
to swallow her up.

The final decade of Domitian's reign was a tumultuous one, marred
by repeated clashes with the Senate, who chafed at the emperor's autocratic style of government and insistence on being addressed as 'Lord
and God', and the execution of numerous of his opponents. Among
those who were eliminated was the consul of 95, Flavius Clemens,
the husband of Domitian's own niece Flavia Domitilla, on a charge
of atheism. Flavia Domitilla herself was added to the long line of
imperial women who had been exiled to Pandateria, where she died,
though she was later claimed as an adherent of Christianity by the
Greek Orthodox Church and the Roman Catholic Church, and made
a saint.[91]
So great was Domitian's paranoia in the face of perceived threats

that it was said to have led him to install mirrored walls in his palace so that he could see his enemies coming. But a genuine plot to dispatch him was eventually hatched by his own courtiers, a plot that it was universally assumed the emperor's wife Domitia was privy to. One source claims specifically that the empress had come to fear for her own life, and, when she chanced to find a 'death list' scribbled by her husband of those whom he planned to do away with next, she informed the intended victims, who brought forward their plans for assassination. The emperor was stabbed to death in his bedroom on 18 September 96.[92]

Domitian was the last of the Flavians. He and Domitia never did have children to continue the family line. After his death, his body was given to the care of the family's old nurse Phyllis, who had him cremated in her garden on the Via Latina and smuggled his ashes into the temple of the Flavian *gens*, which Domitian had established as the family mausoleum on the site of his birth home in Rome's 'Pomegranate Street', on the Quirinal hill. Phyllis chose to mix his ashes in with those of his niece Julia Flavia, whom she had also raised from infancy.[93] A later version of Domitian's obituary had it that Domitia had requested her husband's body, which had been hacked into pieces, and commissioned a sculptor to model a statue from its reassembled form, a statue which then appeared in the Capitol in Rome. This sixth-century account was perhaps invented to explain cracks in the statue in question, cracks which may have been the partially healed scars of the *damnatio memoriae* against Domitian.[94] An eye-witness description of the unbridled and savage pleasure with which Domitian's portraits were vandalised by his subjects after his death affords us an idea of the kind of scenes that must have greeted similar mandates to destroy sculptures of damned women such as Messalina.

> It was a delight to smash those arrogant faces to pieces in the dust, to threaten them with the sword, and savagely attack them with axes, as if blood and pain would follow every single blow. No one controlled their joy and long awaited happiness, when vengeance was taken in beholding his likenesses, hacked into mutilated limbs and pieces, and above all, in seeing his savage and hideous portraits hurled into the flames and burned up, in order that they might be transformed from things of such terror and menace into something useful and pleasing.[95]

Unlike Messalina's and Domitian's defaced portraits, however, Domitia's remained pointedly intact. Two bronze coins from Asia Minor featuring the facing heads of the emperor and his empress, show signs of deliberate damage to his profile, while hers remains untouched. Portraits of Domitia survive which can be dated to this twilight period of her life, indicating that Domitian's successors saw some value in promoting her image. It may well be that they perceived the political capital of venerating the wife who was suspected of having a hand in his downfall, thus ridding the Roman public of an unpopular ruler.[96] In this respect, Domitia was able to carve a reputation for herself independently of her husband, defying the historical convention whereby a wife's fate and reputation was irredeemably tied to that of her spouse.

Like Livia, the only previous *Augusta* to have survived her husband, Domitia retained a respectable foothold in society in widowhood. Though, in contrast to Rome's first empress, she receives no mention in literary sources after her husband's assassination, there are indications that she maintained an independent source of cash flow in widowhood deriving from brick factories. The year of her death is unknown, though the date stamped on surviving bricks from her factories indicates that not only did she outlive her husband by at least thirty years, she saw two more emperors come and go after him. This would have made her around eighty years old at her death. An inscription on a marble tablet found at the ancient city of Gabii, just outside Rome, records the dedication in 140 of a temple to the memory of 'Domitia Augusta', on a plot of land donated by the local town council and financed by one of the empress's freedmen and his wife, Polycarpus and Europe. They also set up a fund to allow the town to celebrate Domitia's birthday (11 February) every year with distributions of food, a benefaction that was advertised on a bronze tablet and posted in public for locals to read.[97]

The Flavian dynasty marks a caesura in the history of Roman first ladies. In contrast to the first decades of imperial rule, when politics had been the preserve of one family, the circumstances of the Flavians' rise had resulted in the outsourcing of the throne to a wider circle for the first time, signifying a sea-change in Roman political circles. A new *arriviste* elite now lined the corridors of Roman power, men who had been given a leg-up by Vespasian and his sons, and it was from this pool of talent that Rome's next generation of emperors and empresses would be chosen. Berenice, Caenis, Julia Flavia and Domitia, though very different women who stood in very different relationships to the emperor, seemed in some ways to represent a final echo of the old guard: Berenice with her resemblance to Augustus's old enemy Cleopatra; Caenis with her close links to the Julio-Claudian household; Julia Flavia, another imperial woman tarred by allegations of incestuous influence over her uncle; and Domitia, accused of having conspired in the murder of her husband, like so many of her predecessors.

Yet this diverse group of women also pointed the way to new models of Rome's first lady. As the second half of its imperial history unfurled, the city's consorts began to be drawn from a far more disparate circle of candidates – from families without a long political pedigree; from origins as humble as the peasantry; from provinces as far afield as Syria. No longer would the right to be a member of this elite female club be the exclusive preserve of one family, one class, or one native region.

6

Good Empresses: The First Ladies of the Second Century

> The body was burned on the shore, not long after my arrival, as prelim-
> inary to the triumphant rites which would be solemnised in Rome.
> Almost no one was present at the very simple ceremony, which took
> place at dawn and was only a last episode in the prolonged dramatic
> service rendered by the women to the person of Trajan. Matidia wept
> unrestrainedly; Plotina's features seemed blurred in the wavering air
> round the heat of the funeral pyre. Calm, detached, slightly hollow
> from fever, she remained, as always, coolly impenetrable.
>
> *Memoirs of Hadrian*, by Marguerite Yourcenar (1951)[1]

One dawn morning in November 130, some three decades after the
Flavian dynasty had ended, a group of high-profile Roman sightseers
assembled together at the feet of one of Egypt's most popular visitor
attractions. The party included the ruling emperor Hadrian, his wife
Sabina, and an amateur poet and member of the provincial royal house
of Commagene named Julia Balbilla. The object of the tourists' awe
was the 'singing' Colossus of Memnon, a 60-feet-high (18-metres-high)
seated statue erected as one of a pair at Thebes *c.*1400 BC to honour
the pharaoh Amenophis. It had acquired its tuneful sobriquet thanks
to a high-pitched squeal akin to a snapping lyre-string which seemed
to originate in the statue's larynx, though this was probably just the
sound caused by overnight moisture evaporating from its sandstone
joints as they buckled under the rising desert heat. Nonetheless, several
among the hundreds of tourists who made the pilgrimage to the seated
mammoth every year had scratched verses on its legs to commemorate
the miraculous experience of hearing the statue speak.[2]

The atmosphere among the visiting VIPs that November morning
was perhaps a little subdued. Just a few weeks previously, Hadrian's
beloved boy companion Antinous, who should have formed one of
the party, had freakishly drowned in the Nile. The emperor's party
had already made one pilgrimage to the Colossus the previous day
but the statue had remained silent, and the local officials who managed

the site could be forgiven for being nervous lest their charge should once again fail to perform its famous party trick for this illustrious audience. But this time, thankfully, as the sun came up and warmed the monument's craggy stone contours, the trademark wail was finally heard. In tribute, four poems recording the visit of the imperial party were composed by Julia Balbilla and etched on the Colossus's left leg and foot, alongside the other honorary literary offerings already left there, each a rather more elegant and formal version of an 'I woz 'ere' graffito:

> I, Balbilla, when the rock spoke, heard the voice of the divine Memnon
> or Phamenoth. I came here with the lovely Empress Sabina. The course
> of the sun was in its first hour, in the fifteenth year of Hadrian's reign,
> on the twenty-fourth day of the month Hathor. [I wrote this] on the
> twenty-fifth day of the month Hathor.[3]

Seventy years after Hadrian's and Sabina's visit, another emperor, Septimius Severus, made his own family trip to the statue, and in a well-intentioned gesture, ordered that the damage caused to it by an earthquake in 27 BC should be repaired. The unforeseen consequence was that the 'singing' stopped, and the stream of tourists dried up. Today, the Colossus of Memnon remains silent, and the poems etched by Julia Balbilla are barely visible, scrubbed away by the swirling sand of the desert.[4] Just as these poems have faded, so too has much of our picture of Sabina and her fellow imperial Roman women of the second century.

Although the Flavian dynasty was succeeded in 96 by an imperial hall of fame, a period famously christened by Renaissance philosopher Niccolò Machiavelli as an age of five 'good' emperors, the women of that era remain relative unknowns. Nerva (96–8), Trajan (98–117), Hadrian (117–38), Antoninus Pius (138–61) and Marcus Aurelius (161–80) presided over a period of relative political stability, free of assassinations and civil war, which saw Rome unfurl its wings to their utmost territorial limit.[5] Yet the women these new emperors chose as their consorts receive little attention both in contemporary accounts of the period and in the works of later artists and dramatists who pounced on the trials and tribulations of their more disreputable and glamorous first-century sisters with such glee.

The anonymity of Plotina and Sabina, when viewed in a line-up of suspects that includes Messalina and Agrippina Minor, could be read

as an indication that the emperors had now managed to get their relatives to conform to their ideals of quiet domesticity and strict morality.
Perhaps, in keeping their wives and daughters out of the limelight,
Trajan, Hadrian and the other 'good' emperors of the second century
succeeded where their Julio-Claudian, and to some extent their Flavian,
predecessors failed. In part, though, this impression comes courtesy
of the new literary terrain in which we now find ourselves. Tacitus
and Suetonius, the chief executors of the historiographical fate of
Livia and her Julio-Claudian descendants, wrote their histories as
insiders in the courts of Trajan and Hadrian, and served these emperors'
interests in commentating on the depravity of previous regimes in
felicitous, antidotal contrast to the rulers of their own day. Neither of
their accounts extends beyond the reign of Domitian, leaving us to
rely on other, less satisfactory written sources for most of our information about second-century imperial history and the place of women
within it, such as the late, anonymously authored and notoriously
unreliable *Historia Augusta*, which is riddled with obvious fabrications
and invented citations.[6]

However, there is another important reason for this apparent
anonymity. With the advent of the dynasties that ruled Rome in the
second century, a woman's reproductive capacities were removed as
the link in the chain that determined the transfer of power from one
emperor to another. Between the accession of Nerva in 96 and Marcus
Aurelius's bequest of the throne to his son Commodus in 180, each
successful candidate for emperor would be head-hunted and officially
adopted as a son by his predecessor, to whom he bore little or no
blood relation. In part, this was a policy forced on the imperial family
by the fact that the marriages of Trajan, Hadrian and Antoninus Pius
all failed to produce sons. But it was spun by loyalists of their regimes
as a positive outcome that ensured emperors would be chosen on
merit and that Rome would not be saddled with another dynastic
disaster like Nero.[7]

Yet while ancient literary sources preserve a mostly tight-lipped
silence on the activities of Plotina and her second-century cohort,
archaeological investigation reveals that official portraits of second-
century imperial women on coins and statuary were just as ubiquitous
across the Roman Empire as those of their more notorious predecessors.[8] Moreover, the suffocating veil drawn over the lives of the
second-century empresses in the biographical mainstream is belied by
the evidence of more quixotic sources, including private letters and

fortuitously preserved inscriptions, which afford us brief but colourful glimpses of the wives of Trajan, Hadrian and company, making their own vital mark on the legacies of their husbands.

The power vacuum in the wake of Domitian's murder in 96 was temporarily filled by Marcus Cocceius Nerva, a distinguished ex-consul who was the reluctant choice of Domitian's assassins in the absence of other candidates. It proved more of a caretaker role for the elderly and childless Nerva, who was compelled to placate disgruntled elements in the army by adopting the popular, hard-drinking governor of Upper Germany, Marcus Ulpius Traianus ('Trajan') and anointing him as his successor, thus guarding against another period of instability. Upon Nerva's death on 28 January 98, Trajan stepped smoothly into his adoptive father's shoes. His nineteen-year rule established him as one of Rome's most successful military supremos, whose achievements included increasing the empire's holdings to encompass Arabia, Armenia and Mesopotamia, defeating Rome's old enemy Parthia, and winning a great victory across the Danube in the Dacian Wars, commemorated in painstaking detail on his eponymous column erected in the heart of Rome.

Born in around 53 in the province of Baetica in southern Spain, Trajan was the first Roman emperor to come from outside Italy. His accession represented a breakthrough for the new political class of provincial elites who had been promoted under the Flavians, including men such as Trajan's own father who had successfully commanded the tenth legion under Vespasian during the defeat of the Jewish revolt and been rewarded with a consulship for his efforts. If Trajan's accession represented a quantum leap for this *arriviste* set, the same can be said for the new breed of women who took up the mantle of empress.

Pompeia Plotina was the first of this new wave. Little is known of her background, but she is thought to have come from Nemausus (the French city of Nîmes) in Gaul and to have been born in around 70, just as Vespasian became emperor.[9] That she was chosen as a bride for Trajan, the up-and-coming scion of the Ulpian clan, indicates at least that her family, of whom no information survives, came from similarly well-connected senatorial stock. The marriage between this son and daughter of new elite families, heralding from areas hundreds of miles from the empire's capital, reflected the diverse social make-up of the dominant new political class at Rome.

Plotina was almost thirty years old and had been married to Trajan for at least ten years before he became emperor. But prior to that day when she set foot in Domitian's old palace as Rome's newest first lady, not a trace of her life-story survives. This was in part a reflection of the usual indifference to a woman's upbringing in contrast to that of her husband. But it is also related to the fact that, as a childless woman, Plotina was not even a supporting player in the formative years of a future emperor as Livia was, denying us the kind of anecdotal gems that enrich Livia's biography, such as the latter's escape from a Spartan forest fire with her baby son Tiberius in her arms.[10]

However, when Plotina eventually made her debut in the historical record, she did so with a flourish worthy of Rome's first empress. Having ascended the flight of steps and crossed the threshold of her new Palatine home for the first time, she is said to have turned slowly to address the sea of faces watching her and grandly uttered the following line:

I enter here the kind of woman I would like to be when I depart.[11]

It was an appropriate pledge for the female figurehead of a new dynasty determined to wash away the unpleasant taste left by the domestic civil wars of Domitian's household, just as the Flavians had tried to put as much distance as possible between themselves and the worst excesses of the Julio-Claudians. For Plotina, the chance to follow in the footsteps of Domitia was something of a mixed blessing. Commonly credited as one of the architects of her husband's downfall, Domitia was now living in luxurious retirement, enjoying the fruits of the income from her brickwork factories, and continuing to receive deferential honours right up until her death. But the memory of the damage done to the Flavian legacy by Domitian and Domitia's marital flare-ups, the scandal of their separation and Julia Flavia's abortion, had not faded. Gossip about the warring couple was still doing the rounds, and Plotina thus found herself in a position where she could provide a refreshing moral contrast, but at the same time she had to negotiate the sinister shadow her predecessor had cast over the role of first lady.[12]

From day 1 of Trajan's reign, care was therefore taken to craft an unexceptionable image for Plotina that ran no risk of similarity to Domitia or any of her more disreputable female forebears. After spending his first two years in power on an inspection tour of his armies, Trajan appeared in Rome in 100 for the first time since his accession, and had his arrival trumpeted in a speech of praise by Pliny the Younger, delivered by the author to an audience of the emperor and the Senate.[13] Much of it was given over to praising Trajan for his good behaviour in explicit contrast to his tyrannical predecessor Domitian, but Pliny also took care to praise the new emperor's choice of wife, observing that while 'many distinguished men of history' (Pliny did not need to spell out the allusion to previous emperors) had suffered irreparable damage thanks to their ill-considered choice of a wife, Trajan had chosen in Plotina a woman of old-fashioned virtue, modest personal style and approachable demeanour who did him nothing but credit:

> From your position she claims nothing for herself but the pleasure it gives her, unswerving in her devotion not to your power but to your-self. You are just the same to each other as you have always been, and your mutual appreciation is unchanged; success has brought you nothing but a new understanding of your joint ability to live in its shadow. How modest she is in her attire, how moderate the number of her attendants, how unassuming when she walks abroad! This is the work of her husband who has fashioned and formed her habits; there is glory enough for a wife in obedience.[14]

Pliny never once mentioned Plotina by name in his speech. This was quite deliberate, for his encomium of her modest demeanour and devotion to her husband was less about her as an individual than a tribute to Trajan's schooling of her. Whereas previous emperors had struggled to stand up to the close scrutiny of their private lives that went hand-in-hand with holding high office, Pliny's paean praised Trajan for ensuring that his whole household fell into line with the spotless standard of moral conduct which he himself maintained. The common thesis remained: a ruler who kept his domestic affairs in order was bound to keep the empire in good order too. The deflection of the credit for Plotina's conduct to her husband may in part have been down to the inherent traits of panegyric as a genre, but it also advertised the new place of women in this new regime – several steps back, safe in the emperor's shadow.[15]

This picture of meek family unity in the house that served as the headquarters of Roman government was reinforced by Pliny's praise for the harmonious relationship between Plotina and Trajan's widowed elder sister Ulpia Marciana. Like her sister-in-law, Marciana is an enigmatic figure in the annals of history, her persona utterly subsumed to that of the emperor, and the only morsel of evidence we have as to her character is Pliny's tribute to a woman who favoured the same 'frank sincerity and candour' as her brother. Once again, though, Pliny was less interested in helping out Marciana's future biographers than in ostentatiously drawing attention both to the concord between brother and sister, and between the two sisters-in-law, in implied contrast to the catfights and rivalries of former female residents of the Palatine such as arch-nemeses Livia and Agrippina Maior, or Agrippina Minor and Poppaea:

> Nothing leads to dissension so readily, especially between women, as the rivalry which is most likely to arise from close proximity, to be fed on similarity of status and inflamed by jealousy until it ends in open hatred; all the more remarkable then must it appear when two women in the same position can share a home without a sign of envy or rivalry. Their respect and consideration for each other is mutual, and as each loves you with all her heart, they think it makes no difference which of them stands first in your affection. United as they are in the purpose of their daily life, nothing can be shown to divide them; their one aim is to model themselves on your example, and consequently their habits are the same, being formed after yours.[16]

From the allusion to their close proximity and based on precedent, we can probably take it that Marciana accompanied Plotina and Trajan to their new residence on the Palatine. Unlike in the days of Livia and the Julio-Claudians, however, the imperial palace of the early second century no longer echoed to the sounds of children running up and down through the corridors and playing in the gardens. Plotina's union with Trajan remained barren while his widowed sister Marciana had only one child, a grown-up daughter named Salonia Matidia. Salonia Matidia had two daughters of her own, Matidia Minor and Vibia Sabina, but the discovery in the 1950s of a lead water-pipe bearing Salonia Matidia's name, near the Piazza Vittorio Emanuele, raises the possibility that she and her daughters kept to their own property and did not accompany her mother, uncle and aunt to the palace.[17]

Trajan did not immediately scramble to advertise the existence of his female relations either in state-approved architecture or on his official currency, again in stark contrast to his Julio-Claudian fore-bears. This reticence was in part a consequence of his mission to monopolise the spotlight as the undisputed strong man of Roman politics. It was also a recognition that for the first time in Roman imperial history, the sitting emperor owed neither his right of accession nor his ability to provide an heir to a female member of his own family. Therefore it was not until 112, fourteen years into his reign, that Plotina was granted a look-in on her husband's coins. Many of these issues affiliated her with the goddess Vesta, the guardian of Rome's sacred flame, and Minerva, goddess of warfare and wisdom. Another set publicised her dedication of a new shrine called the *Ara Pudicitia* – the Altar of Chastity. Plotina was the first woman to be associated with the legend 'chastity' on her coins, and neither Vesta nor Minerva, virgin goddesses both, had previously been affiliated with imperial women. There was little point associating Plotina with a goddess of fertility like Ceres, given her lack of children.[18]

Though Trajan's female relatives made a late debut on state currency, statues of them appeared just as frequently around the empire as those of their predecessors.[19] However, in contrast to previous imperial consorts, whose images often evolved over a period of years, Plotina's official portrait underwent little change during her lifetime. After the extravagant designs of Flavian women's hairstyles, Plotina's coiffure was by comparison modest and controlled, characterised by a rigid visor of stiffly coiled hair arching above a band of tightly packed comma-shaped curls along her hairline, a throwback to Livia's demure *nodus*. It dovetailed neatly with Pliny's description of her as a deferential and modestly dressed spouse, and was mimicked in the hairstyle of her niece Salonia Matidia's portraits, though the fashion seems not to have found favour with other elite Roman women who showed no signs of adopting it.[20] More popular among female social climbers was the arrangement favoured by Plotina's sister-in-law Marciana, whose locks were strictly sculpted by her *ornatrices* into a two-tier fan arrangement of overlapping segments shaped like mussel shells. While a more audacious design, the architectural precision of Marciana's style still served as a metaphor for the discipline her brother was determined to impose on both his household and his empire.[21]

Trajanic imperial sculpture continued the Flavian trend of opting not to airbrush every wrinkle and blemish out of the sitter's face in homage to the realism of republican portraiture. To residents of the empire chancing to look up as they wandered through town streets and forums or visited the temples and baths, the sight of Plotina's, Marciana's and Salonia Matidia's realistic, rigid, matronly faces glaring back with pursed lips and frowning severity under their carefully primped tresses offered a reassuring reminder to the empire's subjects that this dynasty would be stable and scandal-free.

Most of Trajan's nineteen years on the throne were spent away from the city, in pursuit of military campaigns across the Danube and in the east. In 112, his sister Marciana died, aged in her sixties.[22] That same year, dreaming of emulating his all-conquering hero Alexander the Great, Trajan departed for the east in preparation for hostilities with Parthia, taking Plotina and Salonia Matidia with him, the latter now the most senior surviving female member of the emperor's blood family. No signs of the criticism that was once levelled at the elder Agrippina's presence on Germanicus's foreign tours of duty attended Trajan's wife and niece on their trip. But their return journey was to carry powerful and tragic echoes of that of Germanicus's ill-fated wife. After capturing the Parthian capital Ctesiphon (just south of Baghdad) in 115 and annexing Mesopotamia, Trajan was forced to withdraw his forces from the east under pressure from insurrections behind his front lines by the Jewish populations of Egypt, Palestine and other border territories. Heading back towards Italy in the summer of 117, he fell seriously ill off the coast of southern Turkey, was forced to draw into harbour at Selinus on the south-west coast of Sicily, and died there on 8 August at the approximate age of sixty-four. The grieving pair of Plotina and Matidia carried the fallen warrior's ashes in a golden urn back to Rome, for interment in the pedestal base of Trajan's Column.

But there was a twist in the tale of Trajan's death. On his deathbed, he sent a bulletin to the Senate naming his second cousin Publius Aelius Hadrianus (Hadrian), the forty-one-year-old governor of Syria, as his adopted son and heir. Suspicions were raised in some quarters by the fact that the letter bore not the emperor's signature, but Plotina's. It may simply have been that Trajan was too weak to write himself and delegated the task to his wife. But some observers of the time were unhappy, and concluded that the empress's signature was the imprimatur of a wider plot to hijack the succession. The principal author of this conspiracy theory was Cassius Apronianus, the historian Cassius Dio's father. He conducted an investigation into Trajan's death some decades later while he was a governor in Sicily, and eventually deduced that Trajan's death had been concealed for several days in order to allow the adoption of the empress's favoured choice of successor, Hadrian, to be arranged and announced to the Senate. An embellished version of the story even put it about that Plotina had hired a decoy to lie in Trajan's darkened bedroom and imitate the emperor's weakened voice, in order to prolong the charade that the emperor still lived.[23] Plotina, the silent spouse of the second century, thus joined Livia, Agrippina Minor and Domitia in the gallery of Roman imperial women accused of covering up or conspiring in their husbands' deaths.[24]

As in the case of the almost identical charges laid against Livia, one could make the rebuttal that such concealments actually fulfilled a valuable function in ensuring a smooth hand-over from one emperor to another and became part of the political furniture of many monarchical regimes. But two modern parallels provide further food for thought. In 1919, Edith Wilson, the second wife of President Woodrow Wilson, was charged with forging his signature on White House documents after a stroke rendered him incapacitated, leading to outraged accusations of her running a 'petticoat government'. Four years later, when President Warren Harding died from what his doctor said was a bout of food poisoning, some, seeking to discredit this explanation, claimed that his wife Florence was the real culprit, and a bestselling – though obviously mischievous – book was published on the subject in 1930.[25] Given the regularity with which such episodes recur in both ancient and later historiography, and with such convenient similarities, the case for treating them with caution would seem particularly strong.

Despite the suspicious nature of his inauguration, the new emperor, Hadrian was well qualified to succeed his second cousin. Born in the late 70s in the same region of Spain as his predecessor, he had passed into the guardianship of Trajan following his father's death when he was no more than nine years old. Under his cousin's aegis he had enjoyed a meteoric rise, appointed three times to a military tribuneship before the age of twenty-one, and was later given a legionary command during the Dacian Wars before being made governor of the key province of Syria shortly before Trajan's death in 117. In further recognition of the special relationship between himself and the emperor, Hadrian had married Salonia Matidia's younger daughter Sabina in 100, a union allegedly orchestrated by the girl's aunt, Plotina.[26]

Plotina's hand in bringing Hadrian together with his wife was the overture to a close relationship between her and the new emperor, who spent his first year in power undoing some of Trajan's military policy decisions and facing down bitter teething problems with a Senate angered by his peremptory promotion. In 118, Hadrian returned to Rome and launched a public-relations offensive. Crowd-pleasing measures including a tax rebate, generous handouts both for plebeians and cash-strapped senators, and the establishment of charitable foundations to provide food for children did much to restore goodwill towards him. Moreover, a lavish building programme which included the renovation of the Pantheon, promised to beautify the city. In 121, he left on a four-year inspection tour of his empire, the same year in which an exchange of letters took place between himself and Plotina, letters which were later copied out in marble facsimile and displayed for public viewing in Athens. They offer a rare and remarkable window into communications between Hadrian and his adoptive mother, as well as providing us with the closest approximation we have to a record of her own voice.

Their correspondence revolved around who should be chosen as the new head of the Epicurean school of philosophy in Athens. Taking the side of Popillius Theotimus, the acting head of the school, Plotina's opening gambit petitioned Hadrian for a change in the current law which would extend eligibility for the post to non-Roman citizens, and would allow the school's regulations pertaining to the succession to be written in Greek, instead of Latin.

> How much I am interested in the School of Epicurus, you know very well, *domine*. Your help is needed in the matter of its succession; for in view of the ineligibility of all but Roman citizens as successors, the range of choice is narrow. I ask therefore in the name of Popillius Theotimus, the present successor at Athens, to allow him to write in Greek that part of his disposition which deals with regulating the succession and grant him the power of filling his place by a successor of peregrine status, should personal considerations make it advisable; and let the future successors of the School of Epicurus henceforth enjoy the same right as you grant to Theotimus; all the more since the practice is that each time the testator has made a mistake in the choice of his successor, the disciples of the above school after a general deliberation put in his place the best man, a result that will be more easily attained if he is selected from a larger group.[27]

Hadrian's affirmatory response was then reproduced in a brief subscript, and the inscription concluded with Plotina's congratulatory letter, written in Greek, to the Epicureans: 'Plotina Augusta to all the Friends, greeting. We have now what we were so eager to obtain.'[28]

In stark contrast to her passive anonymity in the literary record, this inscription from Athens recasts Plotina as a highly educated woman, active on behalf of causes close to her heart and with the kind of access to the emperor once enjoyed by Livia. Augustus's letter declining the Samians' request for independence a century earlier had publicly acknowledged Livia's efforts on the islanders' behalf, but this dedication at Athens is the only preserved example of such a petition which gives pride of place to an empress's own letter on behalf of the applicants.[29]

Plotina's role as patroness of a philosophical role is interesting, as a great deal of satire was composed during this period lampooning a certain breed of rich women who fancied themselves as intellectuals and hired philosophical gurus. One such piece described a venerable Stoic philosopher named Thesmopolis having to look after his mistress's Maltese dog during a journey to her country villa, and suffering the indignity of having it lick his beard and wee on his cloak.[30] Such satire would have carried no sting if it did not chime with recognisable currents of complaint about female behaviour at the time. Women's burgeoning interest in philosophy, and Plotina's own patronage of the subject, may in part have reflected second-century Roman society's blossoming love affair with Greek culture, of which Hadrian himself had been a keen aficionado since childhood. Plotina was not the first imperial woman to have shown interest in the subject – Livia had been consoled by a philosopher named Areus after the death of her son Drusus – but she was the first to set herself up publicly as a champion of it, a guise in which she was later emulated to powerful effect by one of her successors.[31]

Age and social status were the measuring sticks by which philosophy seems to have been judged an acceptable subject for women to engage in. Women who read philosophy without censure tended to be wealthy widows. Widowhood granted breathing space to a lucky few Roman women, those who had produced the three children required by law to free themselves from male guardianship and had personal fortunes of their own to fall back on. Plotina's own twilight years, which were more peaceful and prosperous than those enjoyed by virtually all her predecessors on the Palatine, placed her firmly in this relatively emancipated category. Bricks stamped with her name have been found scattered around Rome, proving that, like Domitia

Longina, she owned factories from which she could enjoy an inde-pendent source of income in her old age, while coins demonstrate that Hadrian was meticulous about paying his adoptive mother due honours, depicting her under the new legend, 'Plotina, *Augusta* of the Divine Trajan'.[32]

Plotina died six years into Hadrian's reign, in 123 – her age and the manner of her death are unknown, but she must by now have been well past her fiftieth birthday. The emperor went into black mourning clothes for nine days and had the magnificent temple built for his predecessor Trajan rededicated to become the temple of Divine Trajan and Divine Plotina, in acknowledgement of her consecration as a goddess. Her ashes joined those of her husband in the base of the Column of Trajan nearby. Hadrian was later heard to pay the following tribute to her: 'Though she asked much of me, she was never refused anything.' This may not sound the most fulsome elegy, but according to Cassius Dio, Hadrian simply meant by this that 'Her requests were of such a character that they neither burdened me or afforded me any justification for opposing them'.[33]

Plotina's death was preceded by that of Salonia Matidia in 119 – again, the circumstances are unknown. Salonia's eulogy was delivered by her son-in-law Hadrian, who also ordered her consecration and commissioned a vast Corinthian temple devoted solely to her in the prestigious locale of the Campus Martius near the Pantheon, making her the first deified woman to be honoured with her own temple inside the city limits of Rome.[34] Hadrian's motives for showering such honours on the woman who linked him through marriage to Trajan are not difficult to read. On the one hand, lavish funeral celebrations gave emperors a useful excuse to throw a public wake and court popu-larity with their subjects. Salonia Matidia's consecration was observed on 23 December 119 with a handout of 2 pounds (0.9 kilogramme) of perfume and 50 pounds (22.6 kilogrammes) of incense to the local population and other reports suggest gladiatorial games were held too.[35] But Hadrian was also savvy to the fact that by treating Salonia Matidia and Plotina with kid gloves, offering them the same public homage due to an emperor's own blood relatives, he could engender an image of dynastic continuity within the new system of adoptive succession. Furthermore, by deifying them, he was ensuring that the Spaniards of the Trajanic-Hadrianic dynasty would be well represented in the corridors of heaven, an exercise in one-upmanship over the Julio-Claudian and Flavian clans.[36]

With Plotina and Salonia Matidia now gone, the latter's daughters Matidia Minor and Sabina became the new senior women of Trajan's family. Matidia Minor, who would outlive both her sister and her brother-in-law Hadrian, proved to be the dynasty's very own maiden aunt, and, as will emerge, a valued and beloved member of the clan who succeeded her brother-in-law. No evidence survives that she ever married, which would make her an extremely curious female in pre-Christian Rome. She was also more than unusually wealthy by male or female standards, possessed of a staggering portfolio of real estate at locations in Italy, North Africa and Asia Minor, while money she and her mother gave to a foundation for imperial statues in the northern Italian city of Vicetia was still yielding funds for the city as late as 242. A prolific philanthropist, she spent millions of sesterces on community projects such as the foundation of a public library at Suessa Aurunca in Campania, the building of a road and the endowment of a charitable foundation for boys and girls.[37]

The legacy of her younger sister Sabina was a less happy one.

In the absence of a rich literary tradition, we have to sift through fragmentary epigraphic remains for most details of Sabina's early life. From such piecemeal clues, we can deduce that she was the daughter of Salonia Matidia's marriage to a senator named L. Vibius Sabinus, thus giving her the full name of Vibia Sabina, and that she probably married her cousin Hadrian at the typical age for an imperial bride of fourteen or fifteen, giving her a date of birth of around 86, and making her around thirty years old when she became empress.[38] Described as 'irritable' and 'ill-tempered' in comments attributed to her husband, rumours of friction dogged the marriage between herself and Hadrian, to the point that one source claims Sabina took precautions not to become pregnant by her husband, a piece of gossip most likely invented to account for the couple's childlessness.[39]

Unlike her aunt Plotina, no surviving documentation offers proof of Sabina exercising any influence over the emperor. Nor is there any substantial evidence of her lending her protection or patronage either to individuals or public buildings in the manner of many of her predecessors, although one inscription discovered in Trajan's forum records that she oversaw the building of some kind of structure for the matrons of Rome, which one of her third-century successors, Julia Domna, later restored.[40] A glance through Sabina's financial affairs does at least provide a glimpse of a more enfranchised woman than her nondescript literary and artistic profile would suggest. Like her sister, she had inherited a great deal of family wealth. As well as a property in Rome, she continued the recent tradition of owning brickyards around the city, and kept a large retinue of freedmen. She is surely also the same Vibia Sabina who around the time of her marriage, is on record as having donated the huge sum of 100,000 sesterces, to a local charitable foundation, or *alimentum*, in Velleia.[41]

Much of Sabina's time as empress was spent on the road, establishing a pattern that was continued by women in future administrations. Hadrian passed more than half of his twenty-one-year reign as emperor on foreign tours, a practice necessitated by the demands of policing an increasingly restless empire. For the first of his long absences in 121, he headed for an inspection of his forces in the Rhineland and then made a rare appearance by a Roman emperor in the northern backwater province of Britain in 122, with Sabina in tow. There, he set to work building his famous Wall, which marked out the empire's northern border in turf and stone.

The legacy of this visit to Britain was marred by reports of an embarrassing personal incident involving Sabina which led to the dismissal of two key aides. Few details of the episode are given, but it centred on an alleged indiscretion by the praetorian prefect Septicius Clarus and Suetonius Tranquillus – the very same Suetonius whose biographies of the Caesars give us so much of our portrait of the Julio-Claudian and Flavian emperors, and who at this time worked as Hadrian's private secretary. Both Septicius and Suetonius were apparently dismissed from their posts on the grounds of behaving in too informal a manner with the emperor's wife, and only a sense of uxorial duty to his position stopped Hadrian from sending Sabina into exile. [42]

Although the original source of this report is the heavily fictionalised *Historia Augusta*, this incident in Britain has inspired fevered speculation among modern historians, who have entered into the spirit by imagining that Septicius and Suetonius somehow forgot themselves with the empress at the equivalent of a 'wild office party'. By contrast, other modern verdicts on Sabina describe her in more sombre tones, claiming that she had a 'sour expression', 'grim hairdo' and a 'tight button of a mouth' on the evidence of her sculptural appearance, though in actual fact, Sabina's surviving portraits mimic the bland passivity of all her other female counterparts.[43] A hairstyle was gradually evolved for her that broke with the fussy curls and rigid tiered beehives favoured by the Flavian and Trajanic ladies, and instead showed her with thick wavy hair brushed back from a centre parting and wrapped into a loose nest at the back of her head, a style inspired by the goddesses of Greek myth. The second century was a period in which, more than ever, there was a great premium placed on Greek culture within the Roman Empire, and the style of Sabina's later portraits certainly chimed with these tastes.[44] Hadrian himself was well known for being a passionate Graecophile, right down to the beard he sported in contrast to previous clean-shaven emperors.

On his return to the west, and after taking a three-year sabbatical at Rome in the mid-120s, Hadrian and his entourage resumed their hectic travelling schedule, and the years between 128 to 132 were spent zig-zagging between Africa, Greece, Syria and Judaea. There, the emperor's provocative order to build a Temple to the Roman god Jupiter Capitolinus on the sacred site of the Jewish temple destroyed by Titus and Vespasian, together with an attempt to refound Jerusalem as a new colony named after Hadrian's family, elicited a bitter backlash from the Jewish population. In 130, the emperor headed for Egypt with a travelling entourage estimated to have included as many as 5,000 aides and hangers-on. Among the convoy was Sabina, the poet Julia Balbilla, and a beautiful young man named Antinous, who originally came from Bithynia, in north-western Turkey, and whom literary sources tell us was Hadrian's lover.[45]

For a Roman emperor to have male as well as female sexual partners was not unheard of, nor did it automatically lead to his vili-fication. Roman sexual mores dictated that as long as the penetrated party in a sexual relationship was the man's inferior in terms of age, gender or social rank, a man's masculinity need not be compromised – although in the case of Caligula and Nero, their own lovers' corrupting foreign origins and their shameless public vaunting of their passion, figured as proof of their own depravity.[46] Hadrian's and Antinous's relationship divided opinion among writers of antiquity, some of whom portray Hadrian's passion for the boy as too overt. But thanks to the startlingly large number of sculptures that survive of this beautiful Greek boy, images that inspired fevered adoration among art collectors of the eighteenth century, Antinous is fêted today as a gay icon. It is unquestionably his idolisation that has fuelled much of the modern backlash against Sabina as a sour termagant from whose reproaches Hadrian gratefully escaped into the arms of his golden-limbed boy-god.[47] In counterpoint, Sabina's travelling companion Julia Balbilla is nowadays sometimes cast as the empress's Sapphic consolation prize, a piece of role play lent authenticity by the fact that Balbilla wrote in the same Greek dialect used by the famous poetess of Lesbos.[48]

Much of the year 130 was spent by the emperor's travelling party based in Alexandria, venturing out for hunting excursions in the scorching desert, visits to the pyramids and the Valley of the Kings and to pay homage before the tombs of the emperor's heroes Pompey and Alexander the Great. Then a pleasure-seeking cruise up the River Nile one day ended in a tragedy worthy of the pages of an Agatha Christie novel when Antinous was mysteriously drowned – in circumstances said variously to be an accident, a suicide or a case of human sacrifice designed to assist in a spell to make Hadrian live longer.[49] Hadrian's devotion to Antinous's memory became legendary. After his death, supposedly on the order of the emperor, the entire Roman world from coast to coast was flooded with images of this obscure boy from Bithynia while the foundation stone for a city called Antinoopolis was laid on 30 October at the edge of the Nile, next to where he met his fate. Temples heralded the creation of a new cult in his honour, a gesture that drew mockery from a few who pointed out that the emperor had not gone to so much trouble for his own sister when she died.[50] Not long afterwards, the imperial party arrived at the Colossus of Memnon where the four poems composed by Balbilla preserve a record of their visit between 19 and 21 November.[51]

The presence of an otherwise unknown female poet laureate from Commagene (near the modern Turkish border with Syria) in the entourage of the empress of Rome is intriguing. Female poets had certainly been a fixture in Roman society since the days of the republic, though the only Latin poetry written by a woman that still survives came from the *stilus* of Sulpicia, an aristocratic contemporary of Augustus's daughter Julia. Sulpicia's elegiac compositions on her love affair with a man named Cerinthus were preserved among the writings of her uncle Messala's protégé Tibullus.[52] Love poetry was seen as a suspect occupation for a woman, however. It was presented as a mark against vilified republican matron Sempronia that she was a skilled versifier, and society ladies of the early empire who dabbled in the fashion for composing witty epigrams risked mockery from the satirists, who dubbed them 'magpie poetesses' and sneered at them for trying to compete with the great Sappho.[53] Balbilla, the royally connected sister of a friend of Hadrian's, was herself a disciple of Sappho, as shown by her choice of poetic metre. She would surely have come in for similar criticism. The forty-five poorly preserved lines that make up her poetic tribute to Sabina and Hadrian, all that remain of her *oeuvre*, have certainly garnered poor reviews, one modern critic dismissing them as 'atrocious'.[54] But they are nonetheless precious fragments of an all too rare category of evidence from antiquity – writing by a woman – of which the Colossus of Memnon is a surprisingly rich repository. Three more women, Damo, Dionysia and Caecilia Trebulla, also signed themselves the authors of lines engraved on the statue's legs.[55] Just beneath the last of Balbilla's four offerings, a short postscript acknowledging the Colossus's performance was even added by Sabina herself.[56] In the silence left by the women of antiquity, such crackles from the past, when just for a moment a female voice can be faintly heard, cannot help but strike a chord of longing, particularly in the light of Sabina's own murky and contradictory historical persona.

By May 134, Hadrian's and Sabina's travels ended with their arrival back in Italy, where an exhausted Hadrian now remained for the last three years of his life, dealing *in absentia* with a serious insurrection that had earlier broken out in Judaea under the leadership of Simon bar Kokhba, during the suppression of which over half a million Jewish insurgents would be brutally slaughtered. From the tranquil vantage point of his magnificent imperial playground at Tivoli, Hadrian began to ponder the choice of who should succeed him as emperor. His health was poor, and ongoing construction work on the mausoleum in which he would be buried overlooking the Tiber, could only remind him of his own mortality. Like the marriage of Plotina and Trajan, his union with Sabina had remained childless, so he could not deviate from the recent precedent of selecting an artificial 'son and heir' from outside his own family. In 136, he decided to plump for one of that year's consuls, Aelius Caesar. But the death of Aelius two years later forced Hadrian to think again. Close to death himself, the emperor now offered to hand the baton to the well-regarded fifty-one-year-old ex-consul Aurelius Antoninus, on the condition that Antoninus agreed to adopt both his wife Annia Galeria Faustina's nephew Marcus Annius Verus – a young favourite of Hadrian's – *and* Aelius Caesar's young son Lucius Ceionius Commodus as his reserve successors, a suggestion to which Antoninus in due course acquiesced.

Before Aelius Caesar's death had upset Hadrian's plans, Sabina herself died, close to her fiftieth birthday. Hadrian's stone elegy for his wife, which visitors to Rome's Museo del Palazzo dei Conservatori will find embedded high in the wall of the main staircase, acted like a cool, silent reproof to the kind of lurid claims later made in the *Historia Augusta* that the emperor had poisoned his wife or even driven her to suicide.[57] An exquisite, though now heavily restored, marble relief, its composition shows a recumbent Sabina suspended above the flames of her funeral pyre, her eyes tilted contemplatively into the distance as she is serenely transported on a diagonal flight path into the heavens, borne side-saddle on the back of a female messenger with eagle-wings, who brandishes a flaming torch like a broomstick. In the foreground, feet planted on *terra firma*, sits Hadrian who crooks his finger up towards the stars, as though pointing the way for his wife.[58]

The scene depicts the apotheosis, or divine ascent, of Sabina in accordance with her posthumous deification on the order of Hadrian. Coins struck at the same time and featuring Sabina being carried up to heaven on the back of an eagle, with the legend *consecratio* stamped beneath, formed companion pieces to the relief.[59] Although emperors such as Titus had appeared in such a guise before, never before had an imperial woman's apotheosis been portrayed in art. Like other such 'firsts' for imperial women, though, it was less an encomium of Sabina in her own right than a gesture intended to reflect glory on to Hadrian's own family legacy.

Hadrian survived his wife by barely a year. He died at Baiae on 10 July 138, at the age of sixty-two, possibly of coronary heart disease.[60] In 139, his remains were dug up from their temporary resting-place in the gardens of Domitia and reinterred in his just-completed 50-metres-high mausoleum overlooking the River Tiber, alongside those of Sabina. Two bronze peacocks preserved from the tomb's remains probably stood guard over Sabina, since peacocks were the traditional vehicle for female apotheosis, while eagles performed the same service for new male deities.[61] Reinvented by subsequent generations as a medieval fortress, a prison and a safe house for the pope during times of political unrest, today Hadrian's and Sabina's tomb has been swallowed up into the cylindrical drum of the Castel Sant'Angelo which looms like a fat sentinel over the approach to the Vatican. Hadrian and Sabina did not live a peaceful coexistence in death. When a horde of angry Goths sacked the city of Rome in August 410, they are said to have despoiled the mausoleum of the urns that contained the couple's ashes.[62]

Probably the least high-profile in the modern consciousness of the 'good emperors' of the second century, Hadrian's successor Antoninus governed the empire for twenty-three relatively peaceful years, the longest reign of any emperor since Tiberius. The fact that he had barely set foot outside Italy and possessed no military credentials to speak of before taking office did not prove a bar. Wealthy and popular, but down-to-earth enough to get his feet dirty with regular folk in the annual grape harvest, he was welcomed with open arms by the majority of the Senate and in tribute to his piety in successfully pressing that reluctant body to deify Hadrian, he was given the official title Antoninus Pius – 'Antoninus the Righteous'.[63]

Part of Antoninus's appeal as a plausible successor to Hadrian had been his connections to the powerful Annii family, acquired through his marriage to Annia Galeria Faustina, daughter of olive-oil baron Annius Verus and his wife Rupilia Faustina.[64] Annia Galeria Faustina's elder brother Verus had married a woman named Domitia Lucilla, the wealthy heiress to a huge family brick-factory fortune, and it was from this union that Annia Galeria Faustina's nephew Marcus Annius Verus, who would grow up to become the emperor Marcus Aurelius, was born in April 121.

Although the Annii originally hailed, like Trajan's and Hadrian's families, from the province of Baetica in southern Spain, the young Marcus Aurelius was brought up in his family's mansion in the wealthy and fashionable district of the Caelian hill in Rome. The early death of his father had seen Marcus being taken under the wing of a series of male mentors and tutors, including Hadrian himself, who apparently took a shine to this scholarly young lad. On Antoninus Pius's succession in 138, the new emperor honoured the promise he had made to Hadrian to adopt the now seventeen-year-old Marcus, and Aelius Caesar's eight-year-old son Lucius Ceionius Commodus, as his joint-heirs. Amalgamating their new sire's names into their own, Marcus now became known as Marcus Aurelius Verus Caesar, while Lucius's name changed to Lucius Aurelius Commodus – though he is better known now as Lucius Verus. In a further tacit acknowledgement of Marcus's seniority, a prior betrothal between Antoninus Pius's daughter Faustina and Lucius was nullified, and Faustina rebetrothed to Marcus.[65]

Much to Marcus's frequently expressed reluctance, he was now obliged to take up residence in the imperial house on the Palatine. Over the next two decades, the task of grooming him for the top job of emperor was entrusted to a number of advisers and educationalists, chief amongst whom in his late teens and early twenties was a doughty, gout-riddled rhetoric instructor named Cornelius Fronto. A long correspondence between the two was maintained over the next twenty years and preserved in an edited collection of Fronto's papers but no traces of it survived the literary clear-out of late antiquity when most classical literature was lost at the hands of Christian censors. Then, more than a thousand years later, between 1815 and 1819, a cardinal called Angelo Mai, who was head librarian at first the Ambrosian library in Milan, and then the Vatican library in Rome, miraculously turned up extracts from the correspondence hidden for centuries beneath the overwritten copy of a Christian text.[66]

Though still little-studied, these letters not only constitute a priceless record of the friendship between a young prince and his educational mentor, they also provide us with precious first-hand glimpses of life on the Palatine, and of a young emperor-in-the-making's affectionate relationships with the women around him – chief among whom was his mother Domitia Lucilla. In his reports to his tutor, Marcus often writes of his closeness to his mother, who he says used to sit on his bed chatting to him before the gong went for dinner – a meal characterised as an informal affair, eaten on one occasion in the villa's olive-oil-press room, where the chatter of the 'yokels' gave the imperial family much amusement.[67] Day-to-day domestic crises are also described, such as the traumatic week in which Marcus's sister Annia Cornificia was seized with agonising 'pain in the privy parts' (probably a reference to menstrual cramps) and Domitia Lucilla 'in the flurry of the moment, inadvertently ran her side against a corner of the wall, causing us as well as herself great pain by the accident'.[68] We are also given a hint that unlike Livia and other upper-class Roman mothers, Domitia Lucilla followed the great Cornelia's example by breast-feeding her son when he was an infant – although this may have been a piece of throwaway rhetoric on Marcus's part designed to cast his mother in the most flattering light.[69]

Another trait shared with Cornelia was Domitia Lucilla's linguistic expertise, which emerges as one of the most powerful themes of Marcus's and Fronto's correspondence. Fronto offers gushing tribute to her intelligence, paying her the compliment of writing letters to her in Greek – a language in which Roman men who wished to show off their learning wrote to each other – and strewing them with literary quotations from Homer and the like. He expresses anxiety at her finding grammatical mistakes in his letters to her, for fear that she should 'look down on me as a goth'.[70] And he also defers to the role she clearly played as superintendent of Marcus's studies: 'very likely you have heard [this] from your mother', he writes, when passing on one of his gems of wisdom to his young charge.[71]

Some of this was doubtless flattery from a man who knew that he owed his recommendation for the post of tutor to his pupil's mother. As firmly established in successive imperial households, such tutorial appointments were commonly the preserve of the lady of the house, and consequently Fronto's letters to Marcus almost always sign off with a message of good wishes to Domitia Lucilla rather than to the boy's male guardian Antoninus Pius, a doffing of the metaphorical cap of deference to his benefactress.[72] Yet the compliments on intelligence within these letters provide rare, first-hand confirmation of something that was usually only referred to obliquely and hypothetically in ancient sources – the necessity of a woman's being educated enough to oversee the education of her sons. Elsewhere, Domitia Lucilla receives an even rarer tribute. Among all the women whose lives intersected with the Caesars, she has the distinction of being publicly thanked in writing by her son for her role in his life. Beginning his famous philosophical treatise the *Meditations* with a list of the people to whom he owed his most important life-lessons, Marcus ranked Domitia Lucilla at number three, behind only his grandfather and father, leaving Fronto and the rest of his tutors trailing in her wake:

> From my mother [I learned] piety and bountifulness, to keep myself not only from doing evil but even from dwelling on evil thoughts, simplicity too in diet and to be far removed from the ways of the rich.[73]

As the years went by, however, and the boy grew into a man, Domitia Lucilla's name disappeared from Fronto's and Marcus Aurelius's correspondence, to be replaced by another leading lady. In April 145, after a seven-year engagement, the royal wedding between himself and Faustina, the teenage daughter of Antoninus Pius, finally took place. It was celebrated with the striking of coins bearing the heads of the young couple and a handout of money to the army. The birth of

Marcus's and Faustina's first child, a daughter, was recorded on 30 November 147, resulting in Faustina being immediately granted the name *Augusta*, and over the next twenty-three years, as many as fourteen children were born to the imperial couple. Each birth and illness was cooed and commiserated over by a doting Fronto: 'I have seen your little chicks, and a more welcome sight I shall never in my life see, so like in features to you that nothing can be more like than the likeness', he writes after seeing Marcus's twin boys Antoninus and Commodus, born on 31 August 161.[74]

One woman who makes little appearance in the correspondence with Fronto and was not present at the wedding of her daughter to Marcus, was the girl's mother, Annia Galeria. Antoninus Pius's wife of twenty years survived just the first two years of his reign before dying in the winter of 140. Her husband's celebration of her memory went beyond almost anything a Roman emperor had previously done for his wife and ensured that she remained a strongly felt presence in the city. Silver and gold statues were placed around the capital, and a charitable foundation was set up in her name to help destitute girls, advertised on coins showing her portrait on one side and the grateful orphans – now known as *puellae faustinianae*, or 'Faustina's girls' – on the other.[75] On top of that, a hail of coins was minted by the emperor associating her with the full range of traditional goddesses representing family values, including Juno, Ceres and Vesta, as well as personified themes such as *Aeternitas* (eternity), *Pietas* (piety) and *Concordia* (marital harmony). They showed Annia Galeria being carried to the heavens on the back of an eagle or winged female messenger just as Sabina had been on her marble relief, while a cult was established in her name, its focal point being a temple in the Roman forum itself.[76] The temple's colonnaded remains now enclose the seventeenth-century church of S. Lorenzo in Miranda but the inscription on the façade still bears the empress's name.

Antoninus Pius and Annia Galeria were held up as an example of the perfect married couple, in life and in death. Under new marriage protocols introduced by Antoninus, young betrothed couples were obliged to approach the altar of the deified empress and her still-living husband and pray that they too should live up to such an example of *concordia* in their own marriages. Annia Galeria was thus cast as a patroness of marriage just as Livia had been, and in one of his few preserved letters to Fronto, Antoninus Pius wrote to thank his adopted son's tutor for a recent speech in which he had praised the empress:

'By heaven, I would sooner live with her in Gyara [a place of exile] than in the palace without her.'[77]

Antoninus himself never remarried, contenting himself, as Vespasian had once done with Caenis, by taking one of his wife's former slaves as a mistress. However, his new companion seems to have exercised little of the good influence over the emperor's diet with which Marcus credited his mother Domitia Lucilla in the *Meditations*. Indeed, Antoninus's eventual demise on 7 March 161, at the age of seventy-four, was attributed in part to his partaking too freely of some Alpine cheese. One of the first actions of his successors, Marcus and Lucius, was to honour their adoptive parents with a joint monument of apotheosis, even though Annia Galeria had been dead for twenty years. The Column of Antoninus Pius, as it is now known, was a technically glorious riposte to Trajan's own eponymous erection, comprising a 50-feet-high (15-metres-high) pink granite cenotaph topped with a bronze statue of the emperor, the whole structure set on top of an 8-feet-high (2.4-metres-high) illustrated marble base. Its remains were dug with some difficulty out of a hillside in the Monte Citorio area in the eighteenth century and since 1787 the white marble base has been preserved in the Vatican Museums, where it currently sits in a courtyard outside the Pinacoteca, framed by a backdrop of umbrella pines and Michelangelo's mighty dome. Three of the pedestal's sides are given over to the traditional decoration scheme of an apotheosis relief, while the composition of the fourth panel depicts the startling sight of Antoninus and Annia Galeria being chauffeured to heaven together, the divine cargo of a nude angel or 'genius' whose broad wingspan unfurls across the entire central width of the pedestal's marble face.

Everything about this image was geared towards the reinforcement of the idea that this couple, the dynastic figureheads of the next generation of Roman emperors, were inseparable, joined at the hip and hand, even in death. Never before had two figures been shown hitching a ride on the same 'genius' in Roman art, and nothing in the picture hints that this husband and wife died twenty years apart. Intriguingly, the composition may have borrowed inspiration from the funerary art of the freedmen classes of Rome, which commonly affirmed the durability of the marital bond even in death.[78]

Following Antoninus's death, the Roman Empire now obeyed two masters, for the first time since Octavian toppled Antony. Although Lucius Verus had always played second fiddle to him in the succession stakes, at the first meeting of the Senate following Antoninus's demise in 161, Marcus Aurelius insisted that his adoptive brother and fellow consul for that year should be made his co-emperor. The only asymmetry in their positions was signalled by Marcus's ordination as Rome's chief priest (*Pontifex Maximus*). Marcus now took Antoninus's name and became Marcus Aurelius Antoninus, while Lucius appropriated his brother's cognomen, and was known as Lucius Aurelius Verus, the first joint Augustus in imperial history. Lucius had remained a bachelor ever since Faustina had been summarily reassigned away from him when he was eight years old, and now Marcus's eleven-year-old daughter Lucilla was lined up to marry her adoptive uncle as soon as she came of age, uniting the two family branches.

Faustina meanwhile became the first Roman woman to succeed her mother as empress. Now in her thirties, she had already given birth to nine children. Her remarkable powers of reproduction, reminiscent of the elder Agrippina's and a stark contrast to her childless predecessors Plotina and Sabina, provided the impetus behind an extraordinary nine distinct portrait types for her, more than for any other Roman empress, indicating that every delivery of a child was celebrated with a new portrait of her.[79] At the time of Marcus's inauguration, she was three months pregnant with the hopes of the dynasty, her twin boys Commodus and Antoninus, who were born on 31 August 161. The birth announcement was celebrated with the issue of coins, showing Faustina's profile on one side, framed by the legend *Faustina Augusta*, and on the reverse, two baby boys facing each other in a richly draped crib, beneath the proclamation *Saeculi Felicitas* – 'The Fruitfulness of the Age'![80] It seemed an auspicious start and made Faustina the first empress since Poppaea, a century earlier, to have given birth while her husband was in power, a remarkable statistic that highlights the shift in women's dynastic function over that period. Despite the fact that at least half of her babies did not survive childhood, Faustina's prodigious fertility now rendered surplus to requirements the adoptive system of succession that had chosen Rome's emperors since Nerva's death.

But the new regime's honeymoon period was over almost before it had started. Although the Roman Empire under Antoninus Pius had remained superficially peaceful, Marcus Aurelius and Lucius Verus faced several troubling crises almost immediately. Disturbances in Britain and Upper Germany had to be suppressed, while war with Rome's old enemy Parthia had become inevitable in the face of growing aggression from King Vologaeses IV. When Vologaeses sent his armies into the Roman province of Syria, Marcus and Lucius realised one of them must take personal charge of the war effort. Thus, Lucius, the more youthful and physically robust of the two brothers, was dispatched to oversee the Roman response while Marcus held the fort back in Rome.[81]

With Lucius away on the eastern frontier, Marcus grappled with various domestic problems including the fallout from the Tiber bursting its banks in the spring of 162 and the destructive trail of famine that followed. The birth of yet another child for Marcus and Faustina, a son born at the end of that year, gave the imperial house something to celebrate. But letters exchanged between Marcus and Fronto around this time hint at some of the stresses and strains that Marcus was under, increased by the periodic illnesses of his wife and children. It was fortunate the family had a very old and redoubtable kinswoman living nearby to take some of the load off their hands. Just down the road, now aged around eighty years old, lived Matidia Minor, the surviving sister of Sabina and honorary great-aunt of Marcus through Hadrian's adoption of Antoninus Pius. Correspondence from Marcus to Fronto just after his succession reveals that the emperor's infant daughters, Cornificia and Fadilla, sometimes went to stay with Matidia at her house in the city.[82]

Over in Syria, meanwhile, the Parthians were proving stubborn opponents. Thanks, however, to the efforts of talented young generals such as Avidius Cassius, by 165 the Parthian front line had been pushed back into Medea (modern Iran), the Parthian capital Ctesiphon sacked and Vologaeses forced into flight. Lucius himself could not claim much personal credit for the victory. He had lent his name and authority to the mission but spent most of his time behind the front line at a resort near Antioch, earning himself a reputation as a playboy prince. During that time, his prospective bride Lucilla reached marriageable age, and Marcus himself chaperoned his thirteen-year-old daughter, the eldest of his surviving children, as far as Brundisium and put her on a boat to Ephesus. She was met there by Lucius who had taken time out from his not very arduous military duties to marry her. After the wedding in 164, Lucilla became known as *Augusta*, just like Faustina, sisters-in-law and joint empresses now, as well as mother and daughter. By 166, Lucius's presence in the east was no longer required and he returned to celebrate a joint triumph with Marcus in Rome on 12 October.[83]

Plague dragged back to the city by the eastern armies soured the victory, however, causing the deaths of millions across the empire and delaying the start of a new military mission to reinforce the Danube frontier. In 168, the German campaign against the Marcomanni and Quadi tribes finally got under way, but in January 169, the further spread of plague forced Marcus and Lucius, whose joint presence at the front was now deemed necessary, to abandon their winter camp at Aquileia. Two days into the journey back to Rome, Lucius suffered a stroke and died just short of his fortieth birthday. Under pressure to return to the Danubian campaign, Marcus quickly betrothed the widowed Lucilla to one of his generals, the Syrian-born Claudius Pompeianus, a marriage which both Lucilla and her mother were said to have protested against on the grounds of Pompeianus's advanced age, though their complaints fell on deaf ears.[84]

All of Marcus's attentions were now focused on the war effort. In the winter of 169–70, in preparation for the delayed offensive against the Germans, he based himself at Sirmium (in Serbia), and was accompanied there by Faustina and their youngest child, three-year-old Aurelia Sabina. A heavy financial deficit had forced Marcus to raise funds for his expedition by auctioning off some personal possessions including silk robes and jewellery belonging to Faustina. It was the prelude to the bestowal on the emperor's wife in 174 of the unprecedented title 'mater castrorum' – 'Mother of the Camp'. In Livia's or Agrippina's day, this epithet would have been an unthinkable honour for an empress, an inappropriate and unnatural trespass into the most masculine sphere, but its award bore witness to the greater military pressures now faced by the empire. It configured Faustina as a female figurehead who would keep the home fires burning, and act as a kind of forces sweetheart, albeit of a maternal mien.[85]

The Marcomanni and Quadi invaders were eventually pegged back but Marcus had his hands full with rebel groups in the Balkans and Spain as well, and spent the next few years pacifying these various elements. By 174, Marcus was once more at Sirmium, preparing for a new phase of his war, this time against the dangerous Sarmatian tribe, the Iazyges, based on the Hungarian plain. The news that former ally Avidius Cassius had been proclaimed emperor in Syria, Egypt and other parts of the east was an unwelcome distraction, but the disorganised coup soon fizzled out. In July 175, Marcus left Sirmium and taking Faustina and his son Commodus with him, embarked on a tour of the east. That same winter, Faustina died suddenly in the village of Halala in Cappadocia, aged in her mid-forties.[86]

Two traditions survive of how Faustina met her death. The first ascribed her demise to gout. This explanation would fit with the evidence of Fronto's and Marcus Aurelius's correspondence, which often referred to Faustina's malaises. The other version, infinitely more damaging to Marcus Aurelius, claimed that Faustina had reluctantly joined the doomed conspiracy of Avidius Cassius out of anxiety for her children in the event of Marcus Aurelius's death, adding for good measure that she was an adulteress whose son Commodus had been fathered by a gladiator, and a murderess who had fed Lucius Verus poisoned oysters to stop him exposing her crimes. According to this account, she had then committed suicide when Cassius's plot failed.[87]

The latter theory of course repeated sinister narrative templates already familiar from Livia's and the younger Agrippina's biographies – the women's use of poison, for example – and relies heavily on the much-fictionalised *Historia Augusta*. It was also undermined by Marcus Aurelius's publicly grief-stricken reaction to his wife's death. The village of Halala was renamed Faustinopolis in the empress's memory, and the order was given that a gold statue of Faustina should sit in her old seat at the games in the amphitheatre, whenever Marcus Aurelius himself was present. An alimentary fund for underprivileged girls equivalent to the one set up after the death of Faustina's mother was instituted. Finally, an extensive and unprecedented range of coins was issued from the Roman mint, celebrating both her consecration as a goddess, her role as a patron saint of the army, and her apotheosis into the stars, driving a chariot, like the hunter goddess Diana.[88]

Marcus Aurelius himself died five years after Faustina, on 17 March 180, at the age of fifty-eight. His nineteen-year-old son Commodus subsequently became the first emperor since Domitian almost a century earlier to succeed to the dignities of his biological father. But his reign only served to confirm the opinion alluded to in Pliny's panegyric for Trajan, that the principle of hereditary succession risked lumbering the empire with a bad ruler. Commodus's twelve-year reign was remembered as a nightmarish, megalomaniacal re-hash of the bad old days of Caligula and Nero, a farcical, bloody roller-coaster ride that, amongst other indignities, witnessed the bizarre sight of the emperor of Rome sporting his canvas in the arena and trying to reinvent himself through his dress and nomenclature as a modern-day Hercules.

The end of a golden age for the Roman Empire, following the glory days of his Antonine predecessors, Commodus's arrival also went hand-in-hand with a revival of the old idea of women as the destructive agents in the downfall of dynasties. This was witnessed by the indictment, exile and eventual execution of both Commodus's sister Lucilla – who was allegedly involved in a conspiracy to overthrow him in 182 – and his wife Bruttia Crispina, whom he had married in 178 and who was put to death, in her case on a charge of adultery.[89] In Crispina's place, Commodus took a mistress named Marcia, who, in a replay of the exploits of Agrippina the younger and Domitia, was later said to have conspired in his murder. For all the pains taken during the second century to present a flattering image of the ruling dynasty through the careful public representation of its women and the selection of new privileges bestowed upon them, Commodus's accession demonstrated just how easily such efforts could be forgotten.

7

The Philosopher Empress: Julia Domna and the 'Syrian Matriarchy'[1]

Mother that didst bear me, mother that didst bear me, help! I am being murdered.

Cassius Dio, *Roman History*[2]

Tucked into the shadow of the pretty seventh-century basilica of San Giorgio in Velabro, a popular wedding venue just off Rome's Piazza della Bocca della Verità, nestles a small marble arch. It dates to the year 204, but despite a near miss during a bomb attack in 1993, its richly decorated grey and white surface is well preserved, and on the opposite faces of its inner bay, two relief panels survive, marble stills of the ruling Roman imperial dynasty of the early third century in action. In the right-hand frame, a serene-looking woman clad in a veil and moon-shaped diadem stands next to her toga-hooded husband, whose right arm is frozen in the act of pouring a libation over a small altar piled up with pine cones. In the left-hand panel of the arch, the couple's young bearded son mimics his father's action. The overall scene is of a religious sacrifice, and the identity of the three suppliants confirmed by an inscription recording that the arch was commissioned by a group of businessmen in honour of the ruling emperor Septimius Severus, his wife Julia Domna and their son Caracalla. Theirs were the faces of the new Roman family dynasty which rose to power in the aftermath of Commodus's demise and ruled the Roman Empire for almost the entire first half of the third century.

Today, the Arch of the Argentarii ('Arch of the Money-men') is ring-fenced for its own protection, preventing too close an inspection of the rich decoration scheme. But to a critically minded viewer, pressing the face up between the spiked metal railings for a closer look at the arch's workmanship, it might appear that the empress Julia Domna's awkwardly crooked left arm is rather poorly carved. Adjacent to this flaw, the right-hand margin of the panel is curiously blank, its vacancy made glaringly obvious by the fact that the disembodied head of a caduceus staff, once held by the empress, seems to be floating in mid-air above her shoulder. Following the direction of Julia Domna's gaze, across to the arch's left-hand panel, one notices that there is also a yawning gap to the young Caracalla's right, where the surface of the marble is raised and roughly textured, as if one or more figures had once stood there, and been laboriously scrubbed away.[3]

These lacunae are in fact the scars of a violent exorcism that took place barely a decade after the arch's celebratory unveiling, which saw this scene of family togetherness viciously slashed through and several original members of the tableau unceremoniously obliterated. Like a conjuring trick gone badly wrong, the cracks in this illusory façade of a family united could not be more starkly exposed. And to this family, newcomers to the imperial scene in uncertain times, the preservation of a united front mattered more than most.

The rise of the Severan dynasty spearheaded by Septimius Severus and Julia Domna is one of the more remarkable chapters in Roman imperial history. The beneficiaries of the bloody fallout from Commodus's ill-starred reign, their tenure on the Palatine witnessed the accession of Rome's first African emperor in Severus himself, and its first empress from the east, in the person of Julia Domna. Two people whose distant provincial birthplaces would have had them labelled as barbarian parvenus by the elite political classes of the Roman west in Livia's and Augustus's day now held the reins of empire. With Severus's imperial legacy depending on the Syrian-born Domna's side of the family, whose members ensured the dynasty's survival for forty-two years, it also marked a return to a principle of matrilineal succession not seen since the accession of Agrippina Minor's son Nero.

So powerful has the political influence of Julia Domna and her female relatives appeared to many modern historians, that the Severan dynasty has often been painted as a matriarchy, in which first Domna herself, then her sister Julia Maesa and great-nieces Julia Soaemis and Julia Mamaea held the apron-strings of their baby-faced progeny as they succeeded in turn to the dignities of Severus. Julia Domna in particular attracted attention from scholars of the nineteenth and early twentieth centuries, thanks to her association with a prominent Athenian sophist named Philostratus, who dubbed her 'the philosopher'.[4] Domna's devotion to philosophical pursuits, her sponsorship of Philostratus and her patronage of a controversial 'circle' of the leading literary, philosophical and scientific thinkers of the day, mean that she is fêted as perhaps the most intellectual woman ever to wear the mantle of Roman empress.

These qualities have not always won her admirers. Born in Syria, Domna was accused in the nineteenth century of turning Rome into a bastion of 'orientalism' by introducing the worship of foreign goddesses into Roman state religion (and inviting comparison between these deities and herself). The great eighteenth-century historian Edward Gibbon believed that the Severan dynasty was responsible for setting the Roman Empire's feet on a path to decline, though Gibbon himself reserved his own criticism especially for the 'pride and avarice' of the Syrian women who succeeded Domna as *Augusta*; by contrast he praised her as a woman who 'deserved all that the stars could promise her'.[5] More recently, Domna's 'political caprice' coupled with her 'intellectualism' incurred her description as an unflattering hybrid of Catherine de' Medici, Christina of Sweden and Julio-Claudian bad girl Messalina.[6]

Yet by comparison at least to her Julio-Claudian predecessors Livia and Agrippina Minor, the only other two women previously to have served as first wife to one emperor and then mother to another, Domna received a relatively good press from contemporary observers in antiquity, earning plaudits for the quality of her advice to her son Caracalla when he eventually ascended the throne, and winning sympathy for her hostile treatment at the hands of her husband's power-hungry aide Plautianus, whose persecution drove her to seek refuge in a world of literature and learning. This complimentary portrait survives even though Julia Domna occupied a more promi-nent and arguably more powerful role in the administrations of her husband and her son, than any other empress before her. Strikingly, she seems to have been received into these roles without protest from any surviving source that a woman from the east should be installed as Roman empress, a contrast to the vitriol once levelled at Berenice's and Cleopatra's incursions on to the imperial scene.

Such circumspection was in part a reflection of the shifting sands of the Roman political landscape. Julia Domna and Septimius Severus were role models for a new-look cosmopolitan Roman elite of the third century, for whom Latin was often no longer one's automatic first language and obscure birth no longer a disqualification from the highest office. The cultural and political hegemony of Rome itself was weakening – Septimius Severus was to be the first emperor to celebrate his provincial origins in public building projects. The Roman

Empire itself was tilting uncertainly on its axis, still clinging to its inherited cultural and religious traditions, yet continuing to be buffeted by challenges to that orthodoxy, from artistic influences to eastern mystery cults such as Christianity. Marcus Aurelius's tenure as emperor during the final half of the second century had also coincided with increasing difficulties in the policing of a bloated empire. The military pressures of securing thousands of miles of accumulated territory had escalated sharply. Rome, the capital of empire, was separated from its most far-flung frontier of Syria, Julia Domna's homeland, by over 1,500 miles (2,400 km). War with Rome's old eastern rival Parthia, unrest from Teutonic tribes in Europe, spasmodic internal rebellions against the emperor and widespread plague all combined to place the machinery of empire under increasing strain.

More than ever, the defence of empire called for strong military leadership. But the promotion of such army strong men, so critical to the empire's security, had the potential to backfire if any of them decided to stake a claim to the biggest job of all – the emperor's own. This conundrum was one of the problems that would beset the empire for the rest of its lifetime. It also had repercussions for the role played in each new administration by the emperor's wife and family, whose positions became ever more precarious in the face of multiple, and often life-threatening, challenges to their legitimacy.

Septimius Severus, born on 11 April 145, was a native of the northern African colony of Lepcis Magna in Tripolitania (Libya), the scion of a provincial family whose heads had risen to senatorial rank under the aegis of Trajan. With his family's sponsorship, Severus himself embarked on a senatorial career and rose steadily through the ranks under Marcus Aurelius. Along the way, he acquired a wife, a fellow countrywoman named Paccia Marciana, and at the age of thirty-five, shortly after the death of Marcus Aurelius in March 180, he received a posting to the Roman province of Syria, as commander of the prestigious legion IV Scythica. It was during this tour of duty that Severus first crossed the path of the young Julia Domna.

She hailed from the city of Emesa (modern Homs), located in the fertile valley of the River Orontes in central Syria. Once the principal seat of an Arab kingdom, it was later annexed by the Roman Empire and ruled by a series of client kings, who, like their close allies the Herods down in Judaea, provided diplomatic and military support to their Roman superiors in times of crisis such as the Jewish Revolt of

66–70. Not long afterwards, as the Flavian dynasty consolidated their grip on power and the last of the Emesene kings died out, the territory was smoothly incorporated into the Roman province of Syria.[7]

Thanks to its rich, volcanic soil which nourished well-watered crops of wheat, fruit and olives, and its location on the Orontes trade route ferrying goods from east to west, Emesa was a wealthy city, though an obscure one in political terms. Best known as the home of the cult of the Emesene sun-god Elagabal, Emesa drew pilgrims journeying to worship a cult object in the form of a large conical black stone. The guardian priests of the sun-god's cult, who clad themselves in the working costume of a long gold and purple tunic topped by a crown of precious stones, were the descendants of the client-kings who had ruled Emesa in the first half of the first century. When Septimius Severus visited in 180, perhaps drawn by visitor accounts of the vast and famous temple of Elagabal, the hereditary incumbent of the guardian post was Julia Domna's father Julius Bassianus. He had another young daughter, Julia Maesa, and the family's Roman-sounding nomenclature reflected their former privileged status as satellite rulers of the Roman Empire, although the girls' *cognomina*, Domna and Maesa, were Semitic in origin. Domna came from the Arabic *Dumayna*, an offshoot of the word for 'black', and Maesa's name is thought to be taken from the Arabic *masa*, meaning to 'walk with a swinging gait'.[8] Domna's and her sister's birth years are unknown, though at the time of Severus's visit in 180, they had probably not yet reached their teens.[9]

As with the first meetings of other emperors and their consorts, such as Titus and Berenice or Livia and Augustus, we do not know when or where Domna met her future husband, who was still married to Paccia Marciana at the time of his visit to Emesa. A good guess is that Severus and Bassianus had some kind of acquaintance, and that the latter introduced this promising Roman general to his daughters. Following his departure from Syria, Severus's career stalled for a few years. In the absence of further assignments, he spent some time engaged in private study in Athens before his services were called on again in 185 by Commodus, when he was dispatched to the province of Gallia Lugdunensis to take up his first governorship. Not long after his arrival there, Paccia Marciana died (of natural causes, to the best of our knowledge), and the still-childless Severus's sights swivelled back in the direction of Emesa, to Bassianus's daughter Domna. A marriage proposal soon made its way from Severus's headquarters in Gaul to Bassianus's residence in Syria, and was duly accepted.[10]

Years later, it was said that Severus had chosen Domna as a bride after meeting her on his Syria trip, because her horoscope had made the prediction that she would marry a king, and this seemed a good omen for an ambitious man such as himself. Severus would also of course not have been blind to the more prosaic advantages of an alliance with a girl who, if she was the same Julia Domna mentioned in a legal text of this period, was the great-niece of a senator and ex-consul named Julius Agrippa (no relation to Berenice's father), to whose sizeable fortune she was in part heir.[11] The horoscope story was probably invented and disseminated many years later after Severus's accession, to make the new emperor's curriculum vitae look more impressive. In the summer of 187, the wedding between forty-two-year-old Severus and his young Syrian bride took place. Severus's talent for being visited by portentous omens led him to declare later that he had a dream in which a marriage bed for himself and his betrothed was prepared for them by Marcus Aurelius's wife Faustina, in the temple of Venus and Rome near the imperial palace.[12]

Domna's and Severus's union was quickly blessed by the birth of two sons. Their first, born in Gaul on 4 April 188, was named Bassianus after his maternal grandfather from Emesa, while the second, born at Rome on 7 March 189, was named Geta, a name shared by Severus's father and brother. Fatherhood coincided with an improvement in Severus's career prospects. In 190, after he and his young family had spent a year in Sicily, he attained the coveted rank of consul at the age of forty-five. The promotion ensured them a place at the apex of Roman society, and gave the young Domna a taste of life as a political consort and hostess at their town house in the city. Conversations at the dinner parties and entertainments attended by the consul and his wife were pregnant with speculation and tension.[13] Severus's year of office was served out against the bloody background of Commodus's twilight years, during which the emperor's behavior became so erratic that he was said to have taken to entering the gladiatorial arena and slashing the heads off the competition, which might have been more impressive if his opponents hadn't been ostriches. The historian Cassius Dio, a beneficiary of the Severans' eventual rise to power, described how he and his fellow senators were forced to stifle their giggles at the sight of this bird-fighting spectacle in order to avoid their emperor's ire.[14]

There was of course a serious side to the unravelling of Commodus's reign. The months before the start of Severus's consulship saw the fall of the unpopular and unscrupulous Cleander, a freedman chamberlain who had pulled the emperor's strings since the death of the previous court favourite Perennis in 185. Accusations of conspiracy against the emperor flew around the city, and a wave of senatorial executions followed, including that of an Emesene kinsman of Domna's named Julius Alexander. Severus was surely glad to put some distance between himself and the hothouse atmosphere of the city in 191, when he was dispatched to a governorship in Upper Pannonia, on the recommendation of Laetus, the head of the praetorian guard. Finally, Commodus's increasingly unpredictable and violent behaviour convinced Laetus and his new imperial chamberlain Eclectus to act. On 31 December 192, with the connivance of the emperor's mistress Marcia, Commodus was first poisoned and then strangled in his bath after twelve erratic, childless years of rule. Marcia's reported role in the affair was a convoluted rehash of the part played by Agrippina Minor and Domitia in the deaths of their husbands – it was claimed she warned Laetus and Eclectus of the existence of a proscription list, on which their names were included, and then mixed poison into Commodus's evening glass of wine, which only caused him to vomit copiously, forcing the conspirators to hire a professional wrestler to finish their victim off.[15]

Publius Helvidius Pertinax, the son of an ex-slave, was a distinguished military and civil servant under Marcus Aurelius and Commodus, and had already been installed by the conspirators as emperor by the time word of Commodus's murder reached Severus, 683 miles (1,009 km) away in the Pannonian capital of Carnuntum.[16] According to the contemporary civil servant Herodian, who wrote a history of the empire from 180 to 238, Severus dreamed that night of a horse unseating Pertinax and taking himself up in his stead as he passed through a gauntlet of cheering supporters, convincing Severus that the fulfilment of a cherished ambition was just around the corner. Though Pertinax himself was so determined not to be accused of despotism that he sought to emulate Augustus by styling himself *princeps senatus* and declining to accept for his wife, Flavia Titiana, the title of *Augusta*, his administration lacked the funds to keep the praetorian guard in the style to which they had become accustomed under Commodus.[17] When the domino effect started, and Pertinax was brutally usurped by a former consul named Didius Julianus in March 193, Severus was ready, despite a rival claim to the purple from Pescennius Niger, the governor of Syria. Carried along by the acclamation of his own and neighbouring legions, Severus marched on Rome to make his bid for power, though not before ensuring that his sons and Julia Domna were spirited to his side to ensure their safety.

Less chivalry was shown towards the wife and children of his rivals. Having arrived on the outskirts of Rome, and convinced the Senate to condemn Julianus on 1 June, Severus was accepted as emperor and his entourage admitted to Rome on 9 June to a dutifully rapturous reception from its citizens, dressed in white and lining flower-decked streets. One of the new emperor's first actions was to order his right-hand man Plautianus to find and hold hostage the children of Niger, who was declared an enemy of the state. Niger was eventually defeated in battle at Antioch in April 194, his severed head exhibited at Rome, and his wife and children executed. The threat from another rival for the throne, Clodius Albinus, the governor of Britain, was at first negated by Severus in a less ruthless manner, with the offer to his rival of the deputy rank of Caesar. However, when Clodius decided a couple of years later that this was not good enough for him after all, he too was defeated – this time in Gaul – and his abused body thrown into the Rhône along with those of his wife and sons. Their fate was a stark reminder of what had been at stake in defeat for Domna and her own children.[18]

During the 1930s, the National Museums in Berlin acquired a fragile portrait from a Parisian art dealer. It depicted the newly enthroned Septimius Severus and Julia Domna standing like proud parents behind their two young sons.[19] A homespun artwork, daubed in egg-yolk tempera paint on a circular panel of wood, it was the work of an Egyptian artist, and it perhaps commemorates a trip by the emperor and empress to Africa in around 200. The 'Berlin tondo', as it is known, is not only the most famous portrait of Julia Domna and her husband, it is the only painted portrait of members of the Roman imperial family that survives from antiquity, affording us for the first time a unique and precious chance to look on the faces of the new incumbents of the Palatine in 'colour'. With his silvery curls and beard, Severus's appearance fits with descriptions of him in Roman literary sources, while his skin tone against the gold stripes of his toga is several shades darker than his wife's, a counterpoint to his official marble portraits whose material hue depicted him as white as any other emperor before him and an important piece of evidence in support of the theory that Severus was Rome's first black emperor.[20]

Domna's creamy-skinned oval face on the other hand is characterised by wide-set eyes, thick straight eyebrows and full lips. Fat white
pearls the size of gobstoppers circle her neck and drip from her ears,
a departure from the minimalist approach to women's jewellery
adopted by imperial Roman sculptors and further proof of the gulf
between ideal and reality in women's adornment.[21] Her dark, thickly
crimped locks, however, are entirely in keeping with sculptural images
of her. Of all the Roman empresses, Julia Domna's hairstyle was the
most distinctive, a rippling, centre-parted, helmet-like coiffure which
is thought to have been created with the aid of a wig. It has been
suggested that she even introduced the Syrian practice of wearing
wigs to the women of Rome, although several detachable marble
hairpieces belonging to female sculptures from the early and mid-
second century have been found of late, some with traces of a plaster
adhesive called gesso which was presumably used to stick the marble
'wig' to the head. This suggests that some of Domna's imperial predecessors may have already been familiar with the practice of wearing
them in real life.[22]

Domna's baptism into the role of Roman first lady was anything
but the staid affair this Quakerish hairstyle might suggest. Less than
a month after her husband's proclamation as *Augustus* and her own
as *Augusta*, she and Severus were on their way east to deal with the
threat from Niger and to square up to the Parthian territories which
had sided with his enemy. After settling both scores, Severus doubled
back to Gaul and crushed the last of his rivals, Clodius, in February
197. Throughout these hard-fought campaigns, Domna was at her
husband's side, enduring the same dry, thirsty desert conditions as he
and his troops, and unlike certain of her female forebears, receiving
nothing but praise for her role as army mascot. Following in the
footsteps of Marcus Aurelius's wife Faustina, another lauded camp-
follower, she was rewarded with the title *mater castrorum* ('Mother of
the Camp') on 14 April 195. A statue of her in this guise was set up
along Rome's Sacred Way, near the temple of Antoninus and Faustina.[23]

As well as setting up Domna as the reassuring guardian of Roman
stability, both domestic and military, there was another agenda behind
the bestowal on Domna of a title first awarded to Faustina. When
and wherever possible, Severus strove to link himself to Rome's last
'good' emperor, Marcus Aurelius, even to the extent of wearing the
same Greek-style beard as his and getting Marcus's physician Galen
to prescribe him the same cassia-based medicine he had administered

to his former patient. The military, economic and political uncertainties of the third century had made it even more important for Septimius Severus than it had been for his predecessors to establish strong roots for his dynasty in the solid traditions of a stable past. From the portraiture commissioned and churned out in vast quantities by the empire's master sculptors, cameo-makers and painters, to the insignia and slogans chosen for his family's appearances on Roman coinage, Severus not only modelled himself on his most successful Antonine predecessor but claimed to be that dynasty's natural heir. The same year that Domna was linked to Faustina with the title *mater castrorum*, Severus adopted himself into the Antonine clan, declaring himself the son of Marcus Aurelius. Riskily, this also meant accepting kinship with Commodus, so the bluntly pragmatic decision was taken to deify the former emperor, thus sweetening the pill and legitimising Severus's seizure of power.[24] The elder of Severus's and Domna's sons, Bassianus, was meanwhile renamed Marcus Aurelius Antoninus after his newly acquired ancestor, though like Caligula, an emperor to whom he was unfortunately later compared, it is by his nickname – 'Caracalla', a reference to the hooded cloak that he habitually wore – that he is far better known.

Unsurprisingly, this charade did not pass without a wry comment or two from Severus's public. One wag commented on the emperor's newly arranged family tree by quipping that it was nice that he had finally found himself a father.[25] Severus's artificial 'self-adoption' was certainly a piece of remarkable chutzpah. Yet in doing it, he was showing himself a keen student of previous emperors, such as Augustus and Vespasian, who had shored up their own legitimacy quotient by emphasising – and sometimes embellishing – their ties to admired former leaders. Another profitable stratagem, as we have already seen, was to stress one's connections to former emperors' wives – a tactic adopted, for example, by Galba and Otho in relation to Livia, and by Hadrian in tribute to Plotina. Severus himself could boast of no such personal friendships or family ties to famous empresses. So, instead, he improvised. By mapping the deified Faustina's image on to Domna's, even though she, like him, had no ties, blood or otherwise, to the Antonines, Severus fostered an illusion that his dynasty came with divine approval. The story that he had dreamed of Faustina preparing the wedding couch for himself and Domna shortly before his marriage, was just one component of such propaganda, whose urgent purpose was to provide a reassuring sense of continuity and stability, glossing over the war-ridden interlude of the early 190s, while also distracting attention from the interloper status of the new first family.[26]

As a consequence, all corners of the Roman Empire were bombarded with images of the Severans as a family unit during their first few years in power. Every imperial house since the Julio-Claudians had seen itself celebrated in group portraits, but none had included the emperor's wife and children with such regularity. On almost every public monument featuring Severus, Domna and their boys were beside him, heavily underlining her symbolic importance as the maternal guarantor of the Severan dynasty's future. Coinage issues reinforced the message – gold *aurei* issued from 202 featured a portrait bust of Domna framed on either side by the profiles of her sons. The accompanying slogan *felicitas saeculi* ('The Fruitfulness of the Age') deliberately echoed the message of a similar coin featuring Faustina and her boys.[27]

But these compositions, with their statement of togetherness, were to have their message tainted. Soon the image of one family member would be obliterated.

The army of slaves, freedmen and civil servants who had run the imperial household on the Palatine since the days of Augustus and Livia saw little of its new occupants for the first decade of Septimius Severus's reign.[28] Refurbishments to the palace were commissioned, such as the addition of a new imperial audience box from which Severus and his family could enjoy a bird's-eye view of the races in the Circus Maximus down below, but there was little initial opportunity to enjoy this luxurious facility. Having criss-crossed the empire eliminating internal rivals for the throne, the new emperor returned by sea to the east in 197 to take on the external threat posed by the Parthian Empire and did not set foot in Rome again for the next five years. Domna and his sons continued to accompany Severus on this odyssey, as well as his closest adviser and fellow African, the newly appointed praetorian prefect Fulvius Plautianus.

For Domna, the trip meant a welcome return to her native land, Syria, and perhaps a reunion with members of her Emesene family. To have a locally born wife could only have done Severus's approval ratings in the region good, and during these changing and uncertain times in which the empire's centre of gravity was gradually shifting outwards from Rome to its peripheries, it was politically useful to have eyes and ears so close to Rome's easternmost borders in the form of Domna's relatives. Several of her Emesene kinsmen in fact rose to prominent positions within the emperor's circle, perhaps with the help of lobbying from Domna herself if the example of Livia and Plotina was anything to go by. Most notable among those promoted included Domna's brother-in-law Julius Avitus Alexianus, a former equestrian officer who was brought into the Senate at the beginning of Severus's reign and later awarded the consulship. Alexianus was the husband of Domna's sister Maesa, who had come to live with Domna when she became empress, giving her an insider's view of palace politics that would come in useful later in her own career.[29]

By January 198, Severus was celebrating the emulation of Trajan's achievement in the capturing of the Parthian capital Ctesiphon. He now chose to bestow on Caracalla the imperial title of 'Augustus' – which had never been shared by a father with his son in order to delineate the latter as heir – and gave Geta the more junior title of 'Caesar'. Domna could now claim to be the first imperial woman to be simultaneously wife and mother to two Augusti. After an aborted attempt to lay siege to the Arab fortress of Hatra, Severus and his entourage went on an extended tour of Egypt in 199, echoing the trip up the Nile taken by Hadrian and Sabina. The new first family visited the same cultural monuments as their Antonine predecessors, including the Colossus of Memnon, where Domna was able to walk up and read the verses composed by Balbilla to commemorate the visit of Sabina. It was on this same trip that Severus issued his unfortunate order to 'fix' the singing statue, silencing it for ever more.

In contrast to Hadrian's and Sabina's reputedly stilted relationship, there are no reports of disharmony in the union between Severus and his Syrian-born wife. In truth, little is said about their relationship at all, although the amusing piece of information that Severus spoke Latin with an accent thick enough to make him pronounce his own name as 'Sheptimius Sheverus' leads one to assume they most likely conversed in Greek, a language that Domna herself would have spoken growing up in Emesa.[30] The only discordant note about their marriage appears in the Historia Augusta, which claims that the emperor refused to divorce Domna even though 'she was notorious for her adulteries, and also guilty of plotting against him'.[31] This story more probably had its roots either in the kind of pre-ordained narrative traditions established for the careers of previous imperial wives, or alternatively in a smear campaign against her by another member of her husband's circle – Fulvius Plautianus, the head of the praetorian guard.[32] A fellow native of Lepcis Magna, Plautianus had enjoyed a flourishing career under Domna's husband, but was said to dislike the empress intensely, for reasons that will soon emerge.

In 202, the imperial family finally arrived back in Rome to great fanfare, and Plautianus's position as the emperor's most powerful and trusted aide was strengthened still further. In an echo of the attempts of Tiberius's ruthless praetorian prefect Sejanus to ingratiate himself into the imperial family, Plautianus saw his daughter Plautilla married to Caracalla, making him father-in-law to the future Augustus. The wedding took place in April as part of the celebrations marking the tenth anniversary of Severus's rule and was described by Cassius Dio, one of the wedding guests, as a lavish affair at which the gifts were paraded through the forum and up to the palace, and the guests were served both refined dishes of cooked meat yet also 'live, raw meat' such as barbarians would eat.[33]

Both this detail and the observation that the dowry Plautianus provided for his daughter would have covered the dowry costs of fifty women of royal rank, reflected Cassius Dio's distaste for the father of the bride, whom he described as a sensual glutton who would eat and drink so much at banquets that he vomited at the table, and whose lust for boys and girls stood at odds with his puritanical treatment of Plautilla, whom he kept in purdah and refused all visitors.[34] The fourteen-year-old groom Caracalla in turn detested Plautianus and treated his new bride Plautilla with vicious contempt.[35] Domna's own sentiments towards her new daughter-in-law, who became her equal in rank with the award of the title *Augusta* and whose coiffure, at least in her early portraits, was styled to resemble her own, are not recorded.[36] But if the testimony of Cassius Dio is correct, she had reason to fear the intrusion into her family of Plautianus; ever since his arrival on the scene, he had made it his mission to discredit the Syrian empress, even torturing her friends to get information on her that he could pour into Severus's ear:

> So greatly did Plautianus have mastery in every way over the emperor, that he often treated even Julia Augusta in an outrageous manner; for he cordially detested her and was always abusing her violently to Severus. He used to conduct investigations into her conduct as well as gather evidence against her by torturing women of the nobility. For this reason she began to study philosophy and passed her days in the company with sophists.[37]

Cassius Dio's affidavit that Julia Domna retreated into a private world of study and philosophic conversation in the face of Plautianus's persecution has been the driving force behind the archetypal image of her, distinguishing her term as first lady of Rome from all of her predecessors as one of real intellectual engagement. It complements famous remarks made by one of the leading literary figures of the day, a Greek sophist and crony of the imperial court named Philostratus, who noted in the prologue to his most important work *Apollonius of Tyana* (a biography of a neo-Pythagorean philosopher of the first century) that he had been aided in his research for the work by its commissioner, Julia Domna herself, of whose 'circle' he was a member: 'for she admired and encouraged all rhetorical discourse – she set me to transcribe these works . . . and to take care over their style'.[38]

Julia Domna's 'circle' has long been the subject of passionate disagreement and debate. On one side it has been much compared to the 'salons' presided over by educated female hostesses of eighteenth- and nineteenth-century Europe, and described as being populated by the cream of Severan academic society, not just sophists like Philostratus, but well-known mathematicians, lawyers, historians, poets and doctors.[39] The evidence against the existence either of a formal 'salon' or one with so long and illustrious a list of attendants is that Philostratus, the only ancient source to mention any such circle in the first place, in fact names only one other member – a sophist and rhetorician named Philiscus of Thessaly who 'attached himself closely to Julia's circle of mathematicians and philosophers, and obtained from her with the emperor's consent the chair of rhetoric at Athens'.[40] As important research has proven, the identity of many other supposed members of Domna's circle, including Cassius Dio and medical writer Galen, has in fact been presumed on the sole testimony of a historian of the nineteenth century, who came up with the list off the top of his head but whose speculations were subsequently quoted by other scholars as if fact.[41]

Although we draw a blank on membership of Domna's circle, and indeed the question whether she hosted soirées in the manner of society hostesses such as the eighteenth century's Madame du Deffand or the seventeenth century's Madeleine de Scudéry, this should not be allowed to obscure the fact that the Syrian empress was clearly an intellectual sponsor of considerable influence. Moreover, she had personal interests in a wide range of studies that no other imperial woman is known to have shared. Of course, her services to Philostratus and Philiscus were entirely in keeping with the role of patron that we have already seen performed by other imperial women such as Octavia, to whom Vitruvius paid tribute for inspiring *On Architecture*, and Plotina, who herself helped parachute a candidate of her choosing into the chair of the Epicurean school at Athens. But more than that, Domna herself appears to have engaged in conversations not just about philosophy, but also about rhetoric, two subjects that were otherwise presented by most Roman literary sources as the educational preserve of men. An opaquely expressed letter survives, addressed by Philostratus to Julia Domna and seemingly a continuation of an ongoing dialogue between them, in which the former tries to persuade his patroness of the merits of the florid rhetorical style of the sophists, and urges her to refute attacks on them, 'in your wisdom and knowledge'.[42]

Julia Domna was the first woman of the imperial age to have her interest and proficiency in both of the 'male' subjects of rhetoric and philosophy held up for public approbation.[43] But the question of what should constitute a woman's education was still as much of a contested issue as it was in the day of Domna's Augustan namesake Julia. One parodist of the second century bemoaned the trend for fashionable women, influenced by Rome's burgeoning love affair with Greek culture, to hire rhetoricians, grammarians and philosophers from Greece to trot at their heels. Some ladies were even said to have received instruction from their gurus while they were in mid-toilet, if there was no time to go to their lectures themselves.[44] Other writers, rather than lamenting women's frivolity, complained more bluntly that an education in rhetoric turned a woman into an erection killer: 'You ask me why I don't want to marry you, Galla? You are so literate. My cock often commits a solecism.'[45]

Undoubtedly, some elite men felt disgruntled about women's attempts to enter into certain areas of study. A Roman woman's job was to steer her son away from philosophy, not engage with it herself; to preside over her son's oratorical education, not make speeches on her own behalf. Having said that, there were voices, Seneca's being one, Plutarch's being another, who supported subjects like philosophy and mathematics as suitable studies for a woman, on the grounds that a fuller education would make her a wiser, better wife and household manager. While it may be that Domna's example was seen as an eccentricity permitted in the empress because of her exalted and separate status, it could also signify that, at least among the women of the privileged classes, private study in these intellectual spheres was not as taboo nor as rare as our more vitriolic sources may lead us to believe.

Despite the political witch-hunt being conducted against Domna by Plautianus, a public front of dynastic unity was preserved among the Severans for the time being. Shortly after his ten-year anniversary celebrations had concluded in 202, Severus took the whole family, new members Plautianus and Plautilla included, on a tour of Africa. Included on the itinerary was a visit to his home town of Lepcis Magna. It was Domna's first trip to the region. Lepcis, which is today one of the best preserved Roman cities in the Mediterranean, was transformed during the reign of its most famous son, with Severus spending massive sums to turn the city into a show-ground for the Roman imperial brand in Africa. When the family arrived in 202, construction was about to get under way on a vast new forum while a colonnaded avenue running from the public baths down to the brand-new harbour was being completed. Everywhere they went, the visitors were met by the gratifying sight of newly completed statues of themselves – Severus, Domna, their sons, new recruits Plautianus and Plautilla, and even the emperor's dead first wife Paccia Marciana, a fellow native of the city.[46]

One of the jewels on the city's magnificent new skyline was a four-way triumphal arch stretching across the junction of the city's two main roads. Unusually for a triumphal monument, its decorative scheme was as much a celebration of Severus's achievements on the domestic front as on the military field, showing a bearded Septimius and an adult Caracalla grasping right hands in a gesture of solidarity in addition to a scene of religious sacrifice.[47] In both of these panels, the figure of Julia Domna with her distinctive helmet of hair is easily recognisable amid the otherwise male line-up. Her watchful presence both at the ceremony between her husband and her son, and at the sacrifice – a highly unusual artistic depiction for an empress to this point – was a reminder of her symbolically significant role in holding her family together, at a time when strong military leadership was required from her male relatives. Her images incidentally also provide us with a preview of an emerging female clothing trend of the third century that would become increasingly popular over the coming decades. In one panel, Domna wears the gap-sleeved tunic that had been traditionally worn by Roman matrons up until now. In the other, her shoulders are completely covered, the gaps in the sleeves sewn up – a hint towards greater concealment and modesty in women's dress that would become increasingly common into the next century.[48]

After several months in Africa, the family returned to Rome once more, where preparations were under way for the great public occasion of the Saecular Games – a festival held every 110 years to mark the beginning of a new era in Roman history, last held during the reign of Domitian. Domna became the first imperial woman to play a star role on this occasion, hosting 109 married women in sacred banquets on the Capitol in honour of the goddesses Juno and Diana.[49] Severus's increasing determination to portray himself as a natural successor not just to his Antonine predecessors, but to Rome's first emperor, had already led him to announce a new revival of the strict adultery laws introduced by Augustus – with the amendment that provincial women should be allowed to share in the same legal rights enjoyed by Roman women.[50] Similar image considerations were in part behind Domna's sponsorship of the restoration of the venerable and ancient temple of Womanly Fortune, the same temple whose preservation had once been the pet project of Livia.[51] Even the two women's names were assimilated – Domna was known as Julia Augusta on her coinage, the same nomenclature granted to Livia after her husband's death.[52]

Domna's *bête noire* Plautianus and her daughter-in-law Plautilla, meanwhile, were also now firmly established members of the Severan tableau. Vast numbers of portrait types of Plautilla had been rushed into production in the immediate aftermath of her marriage to the emperor's eldest son, some of the later ones depicting her with a previously unknown hairstyle, dubbed the 'skull-braid coiffure' on account of its tight plaits arranged up the back of her head, a style which became popular among elite women for many years afterwards.[53] The faces of her and her father had been included both on the arch at Lepcis Magna and on the Arch of the Argentarii, which was dedicated shortly before the Saecular Games. Yet Severus, if report is to be believed, was growing suspicious of his aide. He was unhappy at the number of statues in Lepcis that he had found set up to honour Plautianus and moreover had been warned by his brother, the elder Geta, who died in 204, to beware his increasingly ambitious praetorian prefect.[54] Though the rift over the statues was patched up, the hatred of one member of the family towards Plautianus, it seems, had not cooled.

Proof of this was brought to bear in violent fashion by the events of 22 January 205. According to the detailed account of Cassius Dio, the imperial family had just gone into dinner that evening, when three centurions arrived at the palace in possession of a letter apparently containing a warrant to kill Severus and Caracalla. Instead, the centurions loyally passed the letter to the emperor, who immediately sent a summons to Plautianus, on the pretext of needing to consult him about some other business. On arriving at the palace, and having been ordered to leave his companions outside, a wary Plautianus entered Severus's presence alone and was quietly interrogated by the emperor. But as soon as the prefect began to repudiate the charges against him, Caracalla, who was hovering nearby, launched himself at his father-in-law and on being dragged off by Severus, hurled a command at one of the attendants, to slay Plautianus. The attendant duly obliged. Someone – presumably Caracalla himself, though it is left unsaid – proceeded to pluck a handful of hairs from Plautianus's head, strode into the next room, and triumphantly showed them to Domna and Plautilla, who had been left outside, presumably still waiting for dinner to start. 'Behold your Plautianus', came the cruel remark, provoking grief in Plautilla and quiet satisfaction in Domna.[55]

From the planting of the letter to the enlistment of the centurions, the whole episode had in fact been stage-managed by Caracalla, according to the account of Cassius Dio. Severus's son now finally rid himself of his unwanted wife Plautilla by having her banished to the island of Lipari, where she was later put to death. Images of her and her father were desecrated. It was their figures who originally occupied the blank space alongside Caracalla on the Arch of the Argentarii, and the inscription on the arch was also doctored to eliminate their names. Domna was the eventual beneficiary of this excision, since it made room on the arch for extra lettering to be added after she was awarded a new title in 211 – mater senatus et patriae ('Mother of the Senate and of the Fatherland'). Some of Plautilla's statues even show signs of having been physically attacked and mutilated, the young Augusta's eyes gouged out, as though reflecting the vengeful Caracalla's desire to wreak the same punishment on his wife's own person.[56]

Despite the removal of Plautianus, Caracalla was evidently still an angry young man. The focus of his antipathy now switched to another target – his younger brother Geta, with whom he became co-consul in 205. The two boys were now aged sixteen and fifteen respectively, and the death of Plautianus spurred a simmering rivalry which saw them vie on the field of sexual conquest and sporting competition, even challenging each other to a neck-or-nothing chariot race, which was so aggressively fought that Caracalla fell from his two-wheeled chariot and broke his leg.[57] Their father meanwhile had become increasingly restless since his return to Rome in 204, irritated by political trials and petty outbreaks of brigandage in Italy. The delinquent behaviour of his sons had not escaped his attention either. When a letter arrived from the governor of Britain in 208, pleading for help with rebellious barbarians there, Severus snatched at the opportunity to introduce Caracalla and Geta to some much-needed discipline while flexing his soldiering muscles one last time.[58]

Severus duly packed up his whole household, his wife and sons, and all the bureaucratic machinery of government, and headed for the 'desolate and swampy' northern climes of Britain.[59] The emperor was now sixty-three and sorely plagued by pains in his legs and feet (possibly due to gout or arthritis) which required the old soldier to be carried in a litter for most of the way and were probably not helped by Britain's colder climate. For Domna, it was the completion of a journey from one margin of the empire to the other, from Syria in the east to Britain in the west. On arrival, the imperial entourage, which included Domna's brother-in-law Alexianus, took up residence at Eboracum (York), from where Severus and his eldest son Caracalla led military attempts to subdue northern Scotland while Geta remained with his mother Domna in Eboracum, delegated the task of supervising the administrative affairs of the empire.[60]

Domna's activities during the family's three-year sojourn in Britain go mostly unrecorded with the exception of a bizarre encounter with the wife of a British clansman. After a treaty had been agreed between the Romans and the British rebels, Domna and the wife of one of the Caledonian delegates, Argentocoxus, were apparently standing around chatting about the difference between the sexual behaviour of Roman women and British women. Domna is said to have made a joking remark about British women's free-and-easy approach to sex with their men. Her companion snapped: 'We fulfil the demands of nature in a much better way than do you Roman women; for we consort openly with the best men, whereas you let yourselves be debauched in secret by the vilest.'[61] The line, which appears in Cassius Dio's account in the context of a discussion of Severus's revival of the Augustan adultery laws, is an amusing subversion of the typical Roman prejudice against 'barbarian' sexuality – here the tables are turned on Roman women, discomfiting Domna, many of whose imperial predecessors of course were the worst offenders. Though most probably a fictitious piece of reportage, it does nonetheless add to the body of evidence that suggests part of a Roman empress's job on tours abroad was, like her modern counterparts, to socialise with the wives and other female dignitaries.

Meanwhile, inscriptions prove that Domna received a new addition to her roster of honorary titles during the stay in Britain – *mater Augustorum* or 'Mother of the *Augusti*'. This advertised the promotion of Geta to the rank of Augustus alongside his brother. The imperial mint, still churning out new coin designs despite the family's absence from the capital, issued celebratory gold *aurei* depicting all four family members, Septimius and Domna on one side, and Caracalla and Geta on the other, bearded to advertise their transition from boys to men. But the accompanying legend *Perpetua Concordia* – 'Everlasting Harmony' – was a red herring.[62] Caracalla's and Geta's rivalry had reached new heights of vindictiveness, and stories abounded that Caracalla's increasingly murderous intentions towards his younger brother had begun to veer towards his ailing father too. Despite these alleged threats on his life, which included an attempt by Caracalla to run his father through with a sword while they were out riding together, Severus was said to have spared Caracalla punishment, allowing 'his love for his offspring to outweigh his love for his country; and yet in doing so he betrayed his other son, for he well knew what would happen'.[63] That ominous prediction was indeed soon fulfilled.

On 4 February 211, Severus died aged sixty-six at Eboracum, officially carried off by his ailments, though Caracalla's hand was suspected in some quarters.[64] The emperor's death immediately intensified the already volatile feud between his two sons, to whom Severus had bequeathed co-command, causing great alarm to Domna, and to the council of advisers who had been appointed to guide the footsteps of the young *Augusti*. The situation was made even more perilous by the temporary location of the imperial family in Britain, far removed from the central authority of the Senate in Rome, who alone could ratify the succession. Caracalla, a popular figure with the army, initially tried to persuade them to pledge him their sole support, but his failure, combined with the pleas of Domna and the council of advisers, persuaded him to accept an uneasy truce with Geta for the time being.

Severus's cremated remains were accompanied back to Rome in a purple urn, which a grieving Domna perhaps carried herself in an echo of the similar journeys made by previous imperial wives.[65]

The public funeral in the capital, at which a wax model of the deified emperor was flanked by a black-clad Senate on one side and a delegation of noble matrons dressed in plain white on the other, was barely over before the feud between the two new young co-emperors was reopened. The metaphorical dividing lines between them were drawn literally. Not only was the vast imperial palace split up between them, with separate entrances and separate quarters established, but according to one account, the brothers even began to negotiate a two-way division of the empire itself.[66] This was apparently more than Domna, who had been summoned to a meeting of the brothers along with their council of advisers, could stand, and according to the account of Herodian, she appealed to her boys to come to terms, emulating the example of female peacemakers like Octavia and the Sabine women as she did so:

> ... Julia [Domna] cried out: 'My sons, you have found a method of partitioning land and the sea ... but what about your mother? How do you propose to partition her? How am I supposed to divide and carve up this unhappy body of mine? Very well, kill me first and each of you take a part of my torn body to your territory and bury it there. In this way I can be shared out between you along with the land and the sea.' With these words she began weeping and crying out. Then she threw her arms around them both and drew them into an embrace, trying to reconcile them.[67]

For a time, Domna's intervention worked. Her two sons ruled together and Domna's honours and privileges only increased under the joint reign. In 211, the captions *Pia* ('Pious') and *Felix* ('Fortunate') were appended to her nomenclature on coins, titles which had for the most part been the exclusive privilege of emperors. Coin types issued in conjunction with the official announcement of Severus's deification also gave her the extra title *mater patriae*: 'Mother of the Fatherland'.[68] The latter was of course the title that Tiberius had vetoed when it was offered by the Senate to Livia, and made clear that Domna was now outstripping that former great matriarch of empire – after all, even Livia could not claim uxorial and maternal ties to no less than three *Augusti*.

Yet before the outwardly harmonious power-sharing agreement

between Domna's sons was two years old, it was ruthlessly torn up. On 26 December 212, Caracalla invited Geta to their mother's quarters on the pretext of effecting a fuller reconciliation, whereupon he gave an order to his centurions to have his twenty-three-year-old younger brother brutally stabbed. Cassius Dio's account of the affair describes how Geta clung to his mother, who had been as deceived about Caracalla's intentions as he, and cried out to her as his assassins moved in, before breathing his last in a helpless, blood-soaked Domna's arms. So gory was the scene that a shell-shocked Domna did not notice that she had also received a cut to her hand.[69]

A ruthless cull of Geta's portraits was immediately ordered, resulting in the barely disguised defacement of monuments such as the arch at Lepcis Magna and the Arch of the Argentarii, where the inscription honouring Domna as 'Mother of the *Augusti*' was cynically edited to read 'Mother of *Augustus*' – just the one now.[70] Coins featuring Geta's image were melted down in every corner of the empire and it became a capital offence to speak or write the name of Caracalla's younger brother. Geta's memory was not only the victim of effacement – there were also gestures of degradation. The crude faceless void left by the erasure of his portrait on the Berlin tondo, for example, shows signs of having been smeared with excrement for good measure.[71]

A few of Geta's images, preserved mostly on privately owned curios such as gems and seals, did slip through the net. A story that Caracalla used to burst into tears at the sight of his dead brother's portrait has been interpreted as constituting evidence that the images in question were private keepsakes preserved by Geta's grieving mother, Domna.[72] But if the empress indeed sought a mourning period for her youngest son, no opportunity was given her:

> . . . she was not permitted to mourn or weep for her son, though he had met so miserable an end before his time (he was only twenty-two years and nine months old), but, on the contrary, she was compelled to rejoice and laugh as though at some great good fortune; so closely were all her words, gestures, and changes of colour observed. Thus she alone, the Augusta, wife of the emperor and mother of the emperors, was not permitted to shed tears even in private over so great a sorrow.[73]

So strict was Caracalla's dictat on this score that a female relic of the last dynasty, Cornificia – daughter of Marcus Aurelius and Faustina, and the sister of Commodus – was put to death on the charge that she had wept with Domna over the death of Geta.[74]

For all Domna's acknowledged impotence in the face of the personal tragedy of her eldest son's violent seizure of power, Caracalla's five-year turn at the head of the Severan dynasty ironically ushered in the era in which she was credited with her most direct influence in the imperial set-up. In the absence of a consort for the new emperor, following Plautilla's execution in exile on Lipari, Domna was left to play the part of Rome's de facto 'queen mother' which first Livia and then Agrippina Minor had fulfilled for their own sons. In stark contrast to those two matriarchs, mind, Domna's promotion was acknowledged to have been forced on her unwillingly through the murder of her son, rather than the suspicious death of her husband.

Since Caracalla, like several of his predecessors, nurtured fantasies of apeing that great folk hero Alexander the Great, in 214, after a period of campaigning on the Danube, the imperial court was uprooted eastwards to Antioch, in Domna's homeland of Syria. Here, in a tribute to her superior education, she was assigned responsibility for handling Caracalla's Greek and Latin correspondence and dealing with the daily round of petitions that arrived for the young emperor from various parts of the empire. Such duties would normally have been the remit of an *ab epistulis* (a freedman secretary) and although previous empresses, such as Livia and Plotina, had previously written and received letters from petitioners to the emperor, there is no sign that any woman had previously been given such a formalised role in the imperial administration. Not only that, but Domna, despite her much-reported dislike of him, was said to have given Caracalla well-regarded advice on numerous matters, rebuking him on one occasion, for example, for his lavish spending on his soldiers, to which Caracalla replied with insouciance, 'Be of good cheer, Mother: for as long as we have this' (showing her his sword), 'we shall not run short of money.'[75]

Such accounts, plus the testimony that Domna hosted public receptions for the most prominent men just as the emperor himself did and was given her own security detail of the praetorian guard, have led some modern historians to conclude, over-optimistically, that Domna was effectively her son's co-regent – in other words that she had a level of executive authority far beyond the incidental influence gained through proximity that had been wielded by Livia and Agrippina. The *Historia Augusta* even reports a titilating tradition that Caracalla had married the 'very beautiful' Domna (erroneously referring to her as his stepmother), who had tempted him by revealing her beautiful form to him, and thus added incest to his list of depravities which already included fratricide. Herodian meanwhile claims that a number of mocking caricatures of Caracalla did the rounds while he and his mother were staying in Alexandria, referring to his murder of Geta and nicknaming Domna as 'Jocasta', after Oedipus's mother who unwittingly married her patricidal son, unaware of his identity.[76]

While the similarities between Agrippina's allegedly incestuous relationship with her son and reports of Domna's attempts to seduce her own should be ascribed to the source's intent to paint Caracalla as a second Nero, one must wonder at the atmosphere in the royal house and the relationship between Domna and Caracalla, after the latter's brutal murder of his brother.[77] Did Domna pragmatically make the best of her situation in acting as an ambassador for her surviving son or was she forced to conduct her role under a mask hiding her profound grief for her younger son and her husband, in the face of the tyrannical Caracalla's oppression? Did her decision not to rock the boat include thoughts of Agrippina Minor's fate at the hands of Nero? – we cannot know. But both she and Caracalla would at least have recognised her worth to him as the only available source of maternal and domestic symbolic authority for his regime to exploit. Plautilla was dead, and Julia Maesa, being Domna's sister rather than Severus's or Caracalla's, did not fit the traditional description of a dynastic female figurehead.

Caracalla's reign lasted five years in total, and did contain one important historical milestone, namely the edict issued in 212 which granted Roman citizenship to all freeborn inhabitants of the empire. This seemingly libertarian gesture was in fact aimed at raking in more tax revenue to boost the imperial war chest, which was being steadily emptied by Caracalla's ambitious military campaigns first against the ever persistent Germanic tribes, and then against the Parthians. He made frequent and concerted bids during his reign to curry favour both with the Roman populace and with the army, and his portraits styled him as a tough military general, reminding one of the sartorial attempts of some modern political leaders to convince their electorate of their own battlefield credentials. But he was eventually murdered by his own soldiers on campaign while relieving himself on the road near Carrhae (in modern Turkey) on 8 April 217. Into his shoes stepped his praetorian prefect, Opellius Macrinus, whose coup would have been foiled, according to Cassius Dio, if a letter warning Caracalla of it had not been sent on a lengthy detour to Antioch for sorting by Domna, who of course was in charge of dealing with all the correspondence he did not want to be bothered with.[78]

When Domna heard of Caracalla's death, which was shortly followed by the delivery of his ashes in an urn, the news apparently caused her deep consternation:

> . . . at the first information of her son's death she was so affected that she dealt herself a violent blow and tried to starve herself to death. Thus she mourned, now that he was dead, the very man whom she had hated while he lived; yet it was not because she wished he were alive, but because she was vexed at having to return to private life.[79]

Slightly varied accounts survive of her next actions. Cassius Dio reports that her inner turmoil gave way to wild thoughts of attempting to seize power herself before she resorted to her original plan of starving herself. Her death was after all already assured thanks to a cancerous lump in her breast which she had aggravated by the blow she dealt to her chest on hearing of Caracalla's death. Herodian agrees that she committed suicide, but hints she may possibly have been given little choice but to do so by the new emperor Macrinus, though in public at least the usurper seems to have shown due deference to Septimius Severus's widow, permitting her to keep her bodyguard and sending her a placatory message as an olive branch. However, it seems that now her husband and sons were dead, the men under whose aegis she had, for better or worse, acquired her public role and sense of purpose in life, Domna saw nothing left for herself in a future administration. Rather like another imperial matriarch, Antonia Minor, she chose – or at least accepted – to take the way out offered by suicide, a mode of death on which respectability had been conferred by the example set in the face of adversity by Roman heroines such as Lucretia.[80]

Following her death, Domna's remains were brought back to Rome by her sister and companion, Julia Maesa, and deposited, for reasons obscure, in the mausoleum of Augustus, although later they were removed to join those of her husband in the mausoleum of Hadrian.[81] Not long afterwards, Domna's deification was ordered, perhaps even at the direct intervention of Macrinus. He may well have seen political mileage in leading the tributes to Caracalla's mother, if her personal dislike of her unpopular son was indeed common knowledge. Domna thus became Diva Julia, joining the pantheon of imperial-women-turned-goddesses before her.[82]

With the death of its ruling emperor and queen mother, and the accession of Macrinus – the first Roman emperor without a senatorial background – the brutally snapped thread of Severan succession looked beyond repair. Caracalla had never remarried after Plautilla's banishment and death, and left no children to challenge his usurper. As she prepared to end her life, Julia Domna might well have expected to be remembered as the first and last of the Severan empresses.

But this failed to take into the reckoning the enterprising determination and opportunism of her Emesene family.

After her sister Domna's death, the recently widowed Julia Maesa, whose family had enjoyed twenty-five years as privileged house-guests in the imperial palace, was left out in the cold. Having joined Domna on the journey east when Caracalla uprooted the Severan court to Antioch, she was now ordered by Macrinus to settle on her family estates in Emesa, the senior matriarch of a family that included her two daughters Julia Soaemias and Julia Mamaea, and two teenage grandsons, Soaemias's son Avitus and Mamaea's son Bassianus. Since there was no precedent for the Roman imperial succession passing to the offspring of an empress's sister, it might seem there was no reason for Macrinus to fear any challenge from these Syrian boys. But Macrinus struggled to keep the Roman army in the style to which it had become accustomed under the free-spending Caracalla and his disgruntled soldiers began to look for a new source of compensation.[83]

Who first thought of the idea is unclear – both Herodian and the *Historia Augusta* state it was Maesa herself, since she was wealthy enough to offer the legions the financial incentive to desert Macrinus. Cassius Dio, though, gives her no credit, claiming it was all the brainchild of a pair of Emesene family friends called Eutychianus and Gannys. Either way, in May of 218, a year into Macrinus's rule, an audacious plan was hatched to have Soaemias's son Avitus – who apparently bore a conveniently strong resemblance to his cousin Caracalla – pronounced emperor. Having been smuggled one night into the camp of the legion III Gallica stationed at Raphaneae near Emesa, along with his mother Soaemias and grandmother Maesa, fourteen-year-old Avitus was paraded before the troops at dawn the next day, who duly hailed the boy as Caracalla's rightful successor, no doubt tempted by the promise of a handsome reward for their switch of allegiance.[84]

In retaliation, Macrinus declared war not just on Avitus and his cousin Bassianus, 'but also against their mothers and their grandmother', reportedly marvelling at their audacity but wasting no time in sending his prefect out with orders to kill Maesa's daughter and son-in-law before launching an attack on the rebels. A month of fighting ensued, from which one battle legend was born that Maesa and Soaemis had prevented a rout of their army by leaping from their chariots and pleading with the men to hold their ground. On 8 June, Macrinus was defeated at Antioch, and subsequently killed, his portraits condemned to destruction. The Severan dynasty, or perhaps we should say the Emesene dynasty, was back in business.[85]

Avitus was to become better known by the sobriquet Elagabalus, borrowed from the Emesene divinity whose cult he and his family presided over. Like his cousin Caracalla, his reign was to last five years and, amid its many controversies, was notable for the astonishingly visible role played in his administration by his mother and grandmother. Elagabalus went through three wives while emperor, among them Annia Faustina, a descendant of Marcus Aurelius, but all three played second fiddle to Soaemias and Maesa, who were both given the title of *Augusta*. So powerful were this pair perceived to be that they are the only two women on record to have ever been invited to attend meetings of the Senate, going one better than Agrippina listening from behind her curtain. A special 'Senate of Ladies' was even said to have been established, whose meetings on the Quirinal hill were chaired by Soaemias.[86]

This putative female senate, however, was no groundbreaking women's forum. Its agenda seems to have consisted entirely of the establishment of a pedantic roster of feminine etiquette, dictating matters such as who might wear gold or jewels on her shoes, who might be carried in a litter and what material it should be made out of, and who should make the first move in kisses of social greeting. The ancient literary tradition which claimed the body's existence in fact had no interest in flattering Elagabalus's mother, a fact that was not lost on later inheritors of this tradition such as Erasmus. His tract of 1529, *Senatulus* ('Little Senate'), was one of several medieval and Renaissance works which invoked Elagabalus's and Soaemias's 'Senate of Ladies' specifically to satirise the ludicrous idea of a women's parliament, as well as what he saw as a trivial obsession in his own day with standards of dress.[87]

Like previous Roman first ladies, Soaemias's and Maesa's reputations are better understood as reflections on the emperors they were associated with, than reliable mirrors of their own achievements. When the anonymous chronicler of the *Historia Augusta* wrote that Elagabalus was 'wholly under the control of his mother [Soaemias], so much so, in fact, that he did no public business without her consent, although she lived like a harlot and practised all manner of lewdness in the palace' such a portrait was less of a swipe at Soaemias than it was against the reviled Elagabalus, whose reign rivalled that of Nero and Commodus as one of the most licentious in Roman history.[88] On top of appointing menials such as a mule-driver, a cook and a locksmith to positions of high office, wearing make-up in public and maintaining a harem of male and female whores whose depilation, both facial and pubic, he maintained himself, the most provocative charge against Elagabalus was that he tried to introduce the worship of his eponymous Emesene god Elagabal as the chief deity in the Roman pantheon. His dress was also problematic. His grandmother Maesa tried to warn him before he entered Rome for the first time that his rich purple and gold priest's costume would not go down well with his public, who despite the influx of easterners into the elite still had a suspicion of 'womanish' foreign behaviour. But Elagabalus paid no attention.[89]

However, on 26 June 221, forced to heed Maesa's warnings of the precariousness of his position, sixteen-year-old Elagabalus did agree to adopt his twelve-year-old cousin Severus Alexander, son of Julia Mamaea, giving him the title of *Augustus* and naming him as his heir. Thus two camps and two rival *Augustae* were created in the imperial household, with Soaemias on one side and her sister Mamaea on the other. Mamaea played her cards shrewdly, we are told, keeping her son well away from his disreputable cousin's sphere of influence and fulfilling the Roman mother's traditional duty of overseeing his educational curriculum. When Elagabalus's jealousy of his young cousin's popularity became obvious, Mamaea ensured that only her own most trusted servants were allowed to prepare and serve Alexander's food. Meanwhile, she began to slip money to the praetorian guard to further ensure her son's protection, abetted by her mother, Maesa, with whom Elagabalus had never been a favourite, and whose years in Domna's inner circle had given her a thorough education in palace politics.[90]

The tension in the family finally came to a head when Elagabalus's attempt to have Alexander murdered rebounded on him, and on 12 March 222, Elagabalus and Soaemias were themselves brutally assassinated. Cassius Dio's account of their deaths paints a horrific scene, in which the struggling eighteen-year-old Elagabalus was dragged from his hiding-place, Soaemias clinging to her son. Their heads were cut off, their bodies stripped of their clothes and their naked corpses dragged around the streets of Rome before Soaemias's body was discarded and Elagabalus's thrown in the Tiber. Although other Roman first ladies had been brutally treated in death, this desecration of Soaemias's remains was the first and only time an imperial woman's dead body had been subject to such abuse.[91] It was a reflection, not just of the hatred and bitterness that had festered between the two wings of the family, but of the increased visibility of women in public life, that it should be necessary to make their execution and humiliation so public an event.

Fourteen-year-old Severus Alexander thus became the second Syrian emperor of the fledgling dynasty hatched by Julia Maesa, and Julia Mamaea now took her sister Soaemias's place as Roman imperial matriarch. Both she and her son attracted far less vitriol from ancient historians than their immediate predecessors, though like Elagabalus, the new emperor was said to be very much under the thumb of his mother: 'she took over the direction of affairs and gathered wise men about her son, in order that his habits might be correctly formed by them; she also chose the best men in the Senate as advisers, informing them of all that had to be done.'[92] Such filial meekness earned Alexander the appellation in literary sources of 'Alexander Mameae' – 'Alexander son of Mamaea' – a reversal of the usual convention whereby a Roman man would be recognised by the name of his father. Tiberius had of course angrily repudiated a similar title identifying him as 'son of Livia' when he assumed the throne. The fact that Alexander's matronymic was used on official inscriptions, referring to him as *Iuliae Mamaeae Aug[ustae] filio Iuliae Maesae Aug[ustae] nepote* – 'Son of the *Augusta* Julia Mamaea and grandson of the *Augusta* Julia Maesa' – proves that in her case the title was not just a piece of mockery cooked up by later commentators, but proof of the highly visible and enshrined role of the emperor's mother and grandmother in the new regime's public image.[93]

Alexander won early praise for his sober conduct, judicious handling of the Senate and several well-received political appointments. Cassius Dio himself was delighted to be awarded his second consulship, the reward of which concluded his history of the period. The provocation of allowing women into the chamber of the Senate was not repeated, and a resolution was passed condemning anyone who let one in again, confirming that the political access once afforded Soaemias and Maesa did not reflect any real shift in deeply entrenched Roman attitudes towards the prospect of women in government.[94] Despite the united opinion of ancient commentators that his mother and grandmother manipulated Alexander as a puppet, choosing his advisers and selecting his friends for him, no extravagant or exceptional honours were publicly paid to either Mamaea or Maesa, certainly not in the first years of his reign. Instead, they contented themselves with the titles that had already been paid to previous *Augustae*, while Mamaea's reported preference for a frugal lifestyle constituted a shrewd appropriation of Livia's and Plotina's example.[95]

With her mother Maesa's death (and subsequent deification) in around 223, Mamaea assumed the senior female role in the family, a position she did not relinquish even when her son married in 225 and another woman once more shared the title of *Augusta* with her – Sallustia Orbiana, daughter of the powerful senator Sallustius. Swiftly, the machinery of government set to work stressing a message of family '*concordia*' via the imperial mint. Orbiana was Mamaea's personal choice for her son, and coins struck to celebrate the royal wedding featured Orbiana and Alexander on one side and the bride's new mother-in-law on the other. But in 227, after just two years of marriage, when Sallustius was executed on a charge of conspiracy, Orbiana was in turn banished to Libya, the victim, it was said, of Mamaea's jealousy of her title, even though inscriptions and coins suggest Mamaea was given top billing anyway.[96]

Unlike Caracalla, Alexander was reputed to have loved his wife Orbiana, but fear of his mother prevented him speaking out against her fate. This presentation of Alexander as a cowed mummy's boy and Mamaea as a ruthless dominatrix was diluted by more favourable historical accounts of Alexander as a devoted son who built his mother a palace and pool near Baiae and Mamaea as a righteous woman who gave her son sage counsel. The portrait of devoted motherhood caught the imagination of later Christian writers who recruited Mamaea as a potential convert, claiming she once summoned the theologian Origen to give her religious instruction.[97]

Eight years of Alexander's reign remained, during which the choice of slogans and patron deities on his and Mamaea's coinage acknowledged the growing military threat from the east. In 224, the Persian ruler Ardashir had killed the last king of the Parthian Empire, Artabanus, the prelude to his foundation of the mighty Sassanid dynasty which would rule that region for the next 400 years. After attempts at diplomacy with Rome's new rival failed, in 231, Alexander declared war and coins were issued in which Alexander was styled as the great soldier and Mamaea was associated with *Venus Victrix* – 'Victorious Venus'.[98] Largesse was distributed to the soldiers in the name of both the emperor and his mother, aimed at stiffening their backbone for the fight and guaranteeing their loyalty. But several scrappy and unsuccessful encounters later, discontent had infected the army, and blame was targeted at Mamaea, castigated for the 'female timidity' which reinforced the old adage that a woman had no place on the field of battle.[99]

Unrest on the northern frontiers of empire began to simmer too, and in the winter of 235, Alexander and Mamaea both made for the Rhineland to deal with the threat from German tribes. Their decision to try diplomacy once more did not go down well with troops eager for war and the spoils that went with it. On 22 March 235, in a repeat of the fate of Elagabalus and Soaemias, twenty-seven-year-old Alexander and his mother Julia Mamaea were set upon by soldiers under the command of an officer named Maximinus Thrax. Just as Elagabalus and Soaemias were said to have clung together as the death-blows were struck, Alexander reportedly died hiding behind his mother, blaming her for his misfortune as they were both hacked to death.[100]

Alexander was the last Severan emperor, and Mamaea its last empress. Their dynasty had lasted a relatively impressive forty-two years, including the brief interval in which Macrinus temporarily assumed control, but their downfall ushered in a mini dark ages in Roman imperial history. This was reflected both in terms of the meagre historical sources available to record it, and in the bewildering roll-call of emperors who lined up and fell like dominos over the next fifty years. As a consequence, no Roman woman makes more than the faintest impression on the history of the period.

When a semblance of stability was eventually restored, the political landscape looked very different. Caracalla's uprooting of his court from Rome to Antioch in 214 foreshadowed the creation of new capital cities across the empire during the late third and fourth centuries, necessitated by the strategic needs of different emperors. The dynastic set-up itself was under revision, with multiple rulers often sharing power between themselves. Most significantly of all, and in counterpoint to

Elagabalus's failed attempts to introduce an Emesene god into the state pantheon, a dominant new religious force was on the verge of revolutionising the political, social and cultural agenda of the empire for good. It was a development that was also to transform the face of imperial womanhood.

8

The First Christian Empress: Women in the Age of Constantine

> It is reported (and I, for one, believe it) that some few years ago a lady prominent for her hostility to the Church returned from a visit to Palestine in a state of exultation. 'I got the real low-down at last', she told her friends. 'The whole story of the crucifixion was made up by a British woman named Ellen. Why, the guide showed me the very place where it happened. Even the priests admit it. They call their chapel 'the Invention of the Cross.'
>
> Author's preface to
> Evelyn Waugh's novel *Helena* (1950)

In 1945, shortly after the publication of his novel *Brideshead Revisited*, Evelyn Waugh embarked on a new writing project with the working title, 'The Quest of the Empress Dowager'. Over the next five years leading up to the book's appearance in print in 1950, it was a project that alternately enthused and deeply frustrated him, and one that he rightly anticipated would bring him some of the worst reviews of his career. Yet Waugh regarded this now little-read work as his 'great masterpiece'. According to his daughter Harriet it was the only one of his books that he liked to read aloud to his family. Its subject, one highly personal to Catholic convert Waugh, was the life and times of Helena, mother of Rome's first Christian emperor and a woman whom Waugh later accurately described as 'at a time, literally, the most important woman in the world. Yet', he added, 'we know next to nothing about her.'[1]

Thin on the ground though biographical details about her life are, the footprint left on history by Constantine's mother goes deeper than that of Livia, Messalina, Julia Domna and the rest of Rome's cohort of imperial women combined. From her canonisation as a Christian saint to her name's appearance on numerous sites on the global map, including the island where Napoleon spent his final days, Helena's historiographical and fictional credits are truly astounding.[2] All in tribute to an obscure woman of unknown parentage and humble upbringing who, thanks to a series of erratic turns taken by the Roman imperial juggernaut in the late third and early fourth centuries, rose in her old age to the rank of *Augusta*.

The impact on western civilisation of her son Constantine's decision to champion the hitherto minority cult of Christianity when he became Roman emperor in 306 is almost impossible to overestimate, utterly transforming as it did the social, political and religious landscape of antiquity and bequeathing a legacy that shaped history through the Middle Ages and beyond. It also had profound repercussions for the lives of Roman women from the fourth century onwards. Where Livia had once laid the groundwork for how the role of Roman first lady was conceived, Helena now became the beacon and role model for a new kind of empress – the Christian helpmate – the pathfinder for the generation of Roman and Byzantine empresses who followed in her wake. To those she inspired, the honour of being dubbed a 'new Helena' became the ultimate accolade.

Following the murder of Severus Alexander and his mother Julia Mamaea in the spring of 235, something akin to a dark age descended on Roman imperial history, both in terms of the lack of documentation that survives for it and the political and military chaos that are the hallmark of that era. Pressure from the revitalised Persians in the east, incursions by German tribes such as the Goths on the Roman Empire's northern frontier and a serious cash-flow problem incurred thanks to the heavy costs of repelling military threats on so many fronts, and of keeping the army's pockets well-lined enough to ensure the soldiers' loyalty to the ruling house, combined to create a combustible atmosphere at the heart of government. More than ever, third-century emperors were required to be soldiers as well as sovereigns, increasing the chances of their dying in battle or being murdered by disgruntled troops. Poor man-management of their officials and general economic discontent could create further resentment at court. No fewer than fifty-one legitimate and illegitimate claimants to the purple were declared emperor between 235 and 284.[3]

The rot was temporarily halted in 270 by the arrival in power of Aurelian, who during his briefly successful bid to re-establish some stability, repudiated the depredations on Roman territory by the best-known woman of the period, Syrian queen Zenobia of Palmyra. Zenobia had acted as regent for her young son Valballathus since the death of her husband Odenathus in 268, and had reputedly claimed ancestry from Cleopatra in seizing possession of Egypt and other eastern territories. As part of her bid to put her son in a strong position from which to bargain for accommodation with the Romans, she even had herself and Valballathus declared *Augusta* and *Augustus*. Yet she was defeated by Aurelian on Julia Domna's old home turf of Emesa in 272, and he brought her in humiliated triumph to Rome, whereupon she was freed to live out her days respectably at a Roman villa in Tivoli. Aurelian himself was murdered in 275, and the usual chaotic service in Roman politics was soon resumed. Little is known about the wives of these short-lived emperors of the mid-third century, and none had time to do much to influence the trajectory of the Roman first lady.[4]

Around the same time that Zenobia and the Roman Empire were locking horns for control of the eastern provinces, one of Aurelian's bodyguards, a young Illyrian-born army officer named Constantius – who was later destined to become emperor of Rome – found himself, if popular report is to be believed, passing through the marsh-sodden seaside village of Drepanum in Bithynia (Asia Minor). Pausing to rest overnight in this provincial backwater, his eye was caught by an attractive young stable-maid, Helena, with whom he would satisfy his lusts and sire a son, Constantine.[5]

Despite a medieval tradition which tried to claim her as a royal native of Britain, Bishop Ambrose's late fourth-century description of Helena as a *stabularia* – a stable-girl, or perhaps a serving girl at an inn – was accepted without demur in late antiquity. Indeed such lineage suited those hostile to Constantine, who less charitably referred to her as a common harlot, but also a Christian tradition rich in stories of prostitutes and low-born women who found redemption through faith.[6] Based on the obituary composed by her son's most vociferous champion, Eusebius of Caesarea, who stated that she was eighty years of age at the time of her death in 328 or 329, we can place her date of birth around 250, making her perhaps twenty years old when she became involved with travelling soldier Constantius. From this moment on, Helena's early biography assumes all the idiosyncrasies of a fairy-tale or parable. Medieval chroniclers, enabled by the uncertainty of her origins, wove uninhibited narratives around this unlikely romance. In one of the most fanciful, Constantius seduced the innkeeper's virginal daughter while on his way back from a diplomatic mission. The next morning, convinced by a vision from the sun-god Apollo that he had made Helena pregnant, he gave her a purple chiton and a gold necklace, and told her father to look after her. Some years later, when a group of Roman travellers staying at the inn mocked the young boy Constantine for claiming to be the son of an emperor, Helena proved her son's claim by producing the purple chiton, its colour the exclusive hallmark of the emperor, and report of the extraordinary tale back in Rome led to father and son being eventually reunited.[7]

Despite Helena's and her son's importance in the historical traditions of Christianity, even details such as Constantine's year of birth are hard to pin down. His birthplace at least was firmly established as Naissus (Nis, in Serbia), but how Helena came to give birth to him there is a detail unexplained by those who place Helena's meeting with Constantius at Drepanum, though it is plausibly assumed she must have accompanied him there as he continued to carry out his tour of duty.[8] Whether or not Helena and Constantius were married before or after Constantine was born is yet another bone of contention. While Christian panegyricists such as Eusebius wrote that Constantine was the 'lawful' son of Constantius and referred to Helena as the latter's *uxor* ('wife'), other, less partisan sources described Helena as a *concubina*.[9]

There was nothing clandestine about the practice of concubinage in the Roman Empire. If this were the nature of his relationship with Helena, Constantius would have found himself in good company. As we have already seen, Nero, Vespasian and Commodus all chose to live with concubines during their tenures as emperor. Moreover, *concubina* did not have the sense of a casual mistress or prostitute, but of a monogamous, and long-term, union.[10] However, it was one thing for an emperor to live with his concubine, it was quite another thing for that concubine to be accepted as the prospective ancestress of his future family line and for any offspring he fathered with her to succeed him. While a number of surviving inscriptions from her son's reign refer to Helena as the *uxor* or *coniunx* (another word for 'wife') of Constantius, the advertisement of any other kind of relationship would have been unprecedented and unthinkable. As many of his predecessors had discovered, the onus on Constantine to prove his legitimacy, his right to rule, was to hover urgently over his reign as emperor. The vacuum of evidence for his mother's origins, the muddying of the waters over her relationship with Constantius, provided a smokescreen highly convenient for Constantine's ambitions, one that he perhaps deliberately encouraged. It also created a blank canvas on which later writers, whether favourably inclined to his legacy – or otherwise – could create the Helena of their imagination.[11]

Having made a fleeting entry into the history books, Helena quickly faded out again. In November 284, a humbly born staff officer named Diocletian, continuing the trend of recent years for emperors to hail from obscure origins, assumed the reins of empire and put a stop to the revolving-door syndrome that had seen dozens of emperors ejected in the past fifty years. On 1 March 293, to enable more effective policing and administration of the empire's increasingly vulnerable borders, Diocletian established the tetrarchy, a radical new ruling arrangement whereby power was divided up between a college of four ruling emperors. This would consist of two senior colleagues, both sharing the title of *Augustus*, and two junior emperors or 'Caesars', who would shadow them. Diocletian, who retained overall executive authority, and his colleague Maximian took the senior roles, while as their deputies they appointed a proven military talent named Galerius, and Helena's seducer Constantius – later nicknamed *Chlorus* meaning 'the Pale'.[12]

The four tetrarchs would rarely be in the same place at the same time. Though none was confined to a single diocese, each gravitated towards certain cities and areas more than others. Diocletian and Galerius spent most of their time in the east, and Maximian and Constantius policed the western provinces. The threads that bound the four together were nonetheless strengthened by adoption and marriage. Galerius, who was adopted and mentored by Diocletian, was the husband of the latter's daughter Valeria. Constantius, meanwhile, put aside Helena for Maximian's daughter Theodora. The date of these marriages is unclear, thus we cannot be sure whether Diocletian and Maximian simply chose to promote the men who were already their sons-in-law, or whether the weddings were planned specifically to cement Galerius's and Constantius's places in the tetrarchy.[13] In either case, Constantius must have recognised from the start that Helena, the barmaid from Bithynia, was no politician's wife. No more is heard of her or her whereabouts for the next fifteen years.

With the advent of the tetrarchy, not one, or even two, but *four* women shared the duties of empress. Very little is known about either Valeria or Theodora, or indeed Diocletian's wife Prisca and Maximian's wife Eutropia, despite their symbolic role in binding the tetrarchs together as a family. There was no indication at this stage that Diocletian intended any of the tetrarchs' own biological sons to be part of future succession plans, and thus there was no advertisement of their wives as maternal guarantors of a dynastic inheritance. But it is clear that their experience as female figureheads of empire was quite different to that of Livia or even a more recent empress such as Julia Domna.

Rome, which had seen less and less of the emperor and his family since military pressures on the empire's frontiers demanded the second-century emperors' attention elsewhere, was no longer the bustling, buzzing hub of empire. It remained the home of the Senate and retained a symbolic cachet as the empire's ancestral capital, but the city was now sidelined as a political headquarters, and the old Palatine residence, principal home of the Roman *princeps* and his family since the days of Augustus and Livia, was left virtually unoccupied, the cinnabar-and-saffron-painted halls which had once echoed to the sounds of Julia's laughter and witnessed the bloody assassinations of Caligula and Geta, reduced to a dust-gathering second home for occasional imperial visitors.[14] Palaces in the new tetrarchic strongholds of Trier, Milan, Aquileia, Serdica, Sirmium, Thessalonica, Antioch and Nicomedia now assumed primary importance.

This was not the only departure from the days of Augustus and Livia. The pains to which the first emperor and his family had gone to affect the personal lifestyle of a 'normal' family in their style of living and dress were nowhere to be seen now. Instead head tetrarch Diocletian sought to enhance the dignity of the imperial office by adopting the glittering trappings more usually associated with an eastern court. These included eunuch chamberlains whose social and physical handicaps stopped them from being a threat to the emperor's own position, but who controlled access to him and offered him counsel. A requirement was also introduced that those admitted to his closely guarded inner sanctum prostrate themselves before him, kissing the hem of his robes if permitted, as if he were superior to ordinary mortals.[15]

The artistic tradition of idealised family portraits of the emperor standing alongside his wife and children was also gradually disappearing in favour of an iconography of the tetrarchs in discrete, jewelled isolation, set apart from ordinary mortals.[16] Valeria, Theodora and the faces of the other tetrarchic wives still appeared on coins and individual portraits, their hair styled in the mode of the day, a kind of braided bun, diamond-patterned like a hairnet and in the shape of a cobra's head, held in place with jewelled pins.[17] But group portraits of the whole imperial family in marble and stone of the kind that had dominated town squares and streets between the first and third centuries began to be phased out in favour of bullish, bearded, crew-cut portraits of the tetrarchs in military or ceremonial dress, the homogenised similarity of their features helping to present a united front. The most famous preserved example is the porphyry group of Diocletian, Maximian, Galerius and Constantius 'hugging', which can now be seen on the south-west corner of the Basilica di San Marco in Venice. No room for any wives here. Running the empire was unequivocally a man's job.

Although each of the tetrarchs spent most of his time on the road with his vast cortège comprising thousands of advisers, secretaries and personal armies, all four established ties to certain cities more than others. Diocletian's palace complex in Nicomedia, which reputedly covered over 7 acres (208 hectares) and was a little city in itself, contained a 'house' apiece for his wife and daughter.[18] For Constantius and his wife Theodora, 'home' was the strategically well-placed city of Trier on the River Moselle, in Gaul, a prosperous city renowned for its wine production. Divergences in the policies of the eastern and western tetrarchs could already be discerned. In February 303, Diocletian, a vigorous promoter of traditional Roman religion, declared a war of persecution on the empire's Christian population. Although the edict demanded measures such as the burning of scriptures and even the torture and execution of the most stubborn recusants, Constantius showed little inclination to follow the prescription to the letter in the west, restricting himself to the demolition of churches. Much of the traditional hostility from Roman authorities towards Christianity stemmed from the fact that as a monotheistic religion, it demanded allegiance to one god and forbade worship of deified emperors. Yet the very characteristics of dogmatic devotion to a single deity that invited such suspicion would later be harnessed to spectacularly powerful political effect by Constantine. Within twenty years, this persecuted minority cult, whose adherents at the time made up no more than a tenth of the population at most, would be heavily promoted as the officially favoured religion of empire.

Helena's whereabouts during this period are unknown.[19] Her son Constantine had been receiving his education at Diocletian's court in Nicomedia, presumably under Prisca's aegis though no surviving sources give her credit for it, and on the military campaigns of Galerius, also in the east. This reinvented the tradition of princes of eastern royal houses being brought up on the Palatine, ostensibly as guests under the supervision of imperial ladies such as Antonia, but also as security in return for their families' loyalty. Whether Helena accompanied Constantine to Nicomedia is unclear. But there is certainly no evidence of any contact between them. However, whatever the case, a reunion was not far around the corner. On 1 May, 305, the elderly and physically ailing Diocletian persuaded his reluctant co-*Augustus* Maximian to abdicate with him, and Constantius and Galerius were jointly elevated to senior honours. Their replacements as Caesar were named as Severus, another military insider, and Galerius's nephew Maximinus Daia. Although Constantius's three children with Helena's successor Theodora were too young to rule, Constantine, now over thirty, might have seemed an obvious choice to fill one of the junior spots. The omission was said to have reflected concerted lobbying by Galerius to sideline Constantius, and on the evidence that Constantine was later mocked as the 'son of a harlot' by his future tetrarchic rival Maxentius, tacit allusions to Constantine's dubious legitimacy may have been used in the argument, harking back to the days when Octavian and Antony had exchanged insults about each other's peccadilloes.[20]

But then in 306, the symmetry of the tetrarchy was thrown completely out of kilter when Constantius died at Eboracum (York) in Britain, and Constantine, who had ridden to be by his side, was proclaimed his successor by his father's armies on 25 July. Despite the fury of the other tetrarchs at this unauthorised rewriting of their script, they were forced to accept this new member into the imperial college, though they only allowed him to come in at the junior rank of Caesar, and elevated Severus to become *Augustus* instead. Constantine duly took up the reins at his father's main headquarters in Trier. It was in this city that some of the strongest legendary traditions about Helena took root, from which it is assumed that Constantine, now aged in his mid-thirties, invited his mother to join his court. Numerous clues in favour of this theory that Trier became Helena's home have been cited, some archaeological, some based on references in literature. In the ninth century, for example, Altmann of Hautvillers wrote a *Life* of Helena, which claimed that she was born in Trier, to a wealthy, noble family, and that she had donated a palace to the bishop of Trier to be reused as the city's cathedral, a story much repeated elsewhere.[21]

During excavations begun underneath Trier's cathedral in 1945–6, aimed at repairing bomb damage, the tiny fragmentary remnants of a painted ceiling fresco were uncovered 3 metres (3.2 yards) below the modern floor of the church, in the remains of a Roman house built in the early fourth century. It took almost forty years for all of the delicate plaster fragments to be retrieved and painstakingly pieced together, but when the jigsaw was complete, it was seen to consist of fifteen *trompe-l'oeil*-framed square portrait panels, laid out in a chequerboard pattern, each containing an image of a different figure. Four of the portraits were of women richly gowned and dripping with heavy jewels, in various poses – one with a lyre, one extracting a string of pearls from a jewel-box, another holding a mirror, and the last a silver *kantharos*, or drinking vessel – and all surrounded by a nimbus, a precursor of the Christian halo.[22]

The lavish nature of the decoration scheme, with its heavy use of the colour purple, the most expensive and exclusive pigment in the ancient palette, has convinced many that the ceiling and the room in which it was found were part of Constantine's imperial palace in Trier; more controversially, that the four women depicted were members of Constantine's family, one of them Helena – though no one can agree on which one. But the theory that this expensively appointed building formed part of the imperial complex is much more persuasive. The styling of the women in these frescoes, which reproduces a trend during the later empire for bigger, bolder jewellery, also demonstrates that luxury, pleasure and rich personal adornment were all still very much part of the elite Roman woman's vocabulary of aspiration in Helena's day, though that notion would come under a challenge after the rise to power of Helena's son.[23]

One of the other women identified on the Trier ceiling fresco was Fausta, the daughter of tetrarchy founding member Maximian and sister of Constantius's widow Theodora. In 307, the teenaged Fausta was married to Helena's son Constantine, a case of history repeating itself, in that it required Constantine to cast off his previous companion Minervina, with whom he had had a son, Crispus. Constantine's marriage to Fausta cemented a long-standing alliance between himself and ex-tetrarch Maximian, who had chafed against the abdication imposed on him in 305, and had recently emerged from retirement. The wedding was celebrated in a panegyric of 307 addressed to both the groom and his new father-in-law. Its anonymous author did his level best to imply that the engagement was of long standing, even though this was demonstrably untrue, claiming it had been predicted by a painted portrait in the imperial palace at Aquileia, which showed

Fausta as a child, 'adorable for her divine beauty', offering an engagement gift of a plumed helmet to her youthful swain.[24]

Fausta's and Constantine's marriage was a double celebration,
marking Constantine's promotion to the rank of *Augustus*. It also
coincided with a ratcheting up of tensions within the tetrarchy. In
Rome, Maximian's ambitious son Maxentius, determined not to let
his new brother-in-law Constantine steal a march on him, had bribed
the imperial guard to acclaim him emperor on 28 October 306. He
established the old capital city as his stronghold, giving the Palatine
a permanent tenant again, and repudiated all attempts to shift him.
Despite lending his son initial support, Maximian soon became
estranged from him, and Maxentius also began to lose the support of
Rome's inhabitants, their tempers frayed by famine. An appalled
Diocletian attempted to reassert his old authority, convening a meeting
with Galerius and Maximian in 308 to promote a new tetrarch, Licinius,
as a replacement for Severus – who was forced to abdicate for failing
to suppress Maxentius's rebellion – and condemning Maxentius himself
as a usurper. But then Maximian's stubborn attempts to claw back
some of his old power resulted in his arrest and suicide in 310; Galerius
died of bowel cancer in 311 and Diocletian once more retired bitterly
to his great palace in Split where he ended his days either from illness
or suicide. His wife Prisca and widowed daughter Valeria met with a
more brutal fate, according to the hostile account of Christian contemporary Lactantius. Valeria was cast out from the protection of
Maximinus Daia after she refused his offer of marriage, and condemned
to a year of poverty-stricken exile before she and Prisca were later
beheaded and their bodies cast into the sea.[25]

Four tetrarchs now vyed for supremacy: Maxentius, Constantine,
Licinius and Maximinus Daia. In 312, Constantine met Maxentius just
outside Rome at the battle of Milvian Bridge to decide who would
emerge triumphant in the struggle for the western half of the empire.
The occasion would be remembered partly for the farcical way in
which Maxentius was defeated, hoisted by his own petard when the
collapsing bridge he had rigged up to ambush Constantine's armies
rebounded on his own troops, sending them plunging into the Tiber;
but also for the moment the night before battle, when Constantine
claimed to have witnessed a vision in the sky, a vision that became
the defining moment of his life and a pivotal touchstone in the history
of Christianity. Accounts of the episode are wildly contradictory, and
have spawned a number of enterprising, if far-fetched, theories

attempting to rationalise what Constantine might have seen, from an atmospheric phenomenon known as the halo effect to a comet shooting across the heavens. But the key part of the story was that, either in a dream or waking state, Constantine saw a cross-shaped symbol in the sky – not a cruciform cross, but the chi-rho, a monogram symbol comprised of the first two letters of Christ's name as written in Greek – and was urged by a voice to send his troops into battle with this sign of God marked on their armour.[26]

Constantine complied, and from 312 onward, as he assumed control of the western empire comprising Gaul, Britain, Spain, Italy and North Africa, and formed an alliance with his eastern opposite number Licinius, who defeated Maximinus Daia for control of the eastern territories, the fortunes of Christianity took a turn for the better. In 313, echoing Octavian's and Antony's peace accord at Brundisium, Constantine and Licinius met in Milan to formalise their pact, which was sealed with the latter's marriage to Constantine's half-sister Constantia. A declaration was issued in both emperors' names, stating an end to the persecution of Christians.

However, the next decade then saw the uneasy concord between Constantine and Licinius disintegrate into all-out war for outright control. One of the key battlegrounds between the two was for the religious soul of the empire. Though not following so suicidal a path as to throw over Rome's traditional gods and alienate the empire's non-Christian population, Constantine devoted an increasing amount of time and imperial resources to the Christian Church, styling himself as its champion against Licinius's increasingly intolerant treatment of its followers in the east. In 324, Constantine defeated Licinius under a Christian battle standard, and reunified the empire. Despite Constantia's attempts to extract a plea-bargain for her husband, Licinius was murdered a year later, and Constantia returned to the household of her brother, now Rome's sole emperor. Helena, now almost in her eighties, was in due course proclaimed *Augusta*, a title she shared with her daughter-in-law Fausta.[27]

The next generation of Roman empresses would take their cue directly from Constantine's mother.

The Christianisation of the Roman Empire that followed Constantine's victory in 324 had a lasting impact on the role of women, not just those who played the part of *Augusta* from now until the end of Roman rule in the west in the late fifth century, but also for females from different walks of life across the empire. It carried social and legal impli-cations for issues affecting them such as marriage, divorce, childbirth, health, sexual ethics and financial inheritance, while also providing women with opportunities to play various kinds of minor leadership role within the new religion, whereas previously they had been all but excluded from the administrative hierarchy of traditional Roman cults (the Vestal Virgins representing the notable exception). This may explain why, before Constantine came along, more women than men of the Roman upper classes seem to have been drawn to membership of the faith. Some Christians even cultivated a theology with a built-in female principle, with the worship of the Virgin Mary (dubbed the *Theotokos*) alongside the Son and the Father. A new breed of female role model also emerged in the literary and historical sources of the period – the Christian heroine or martyr – whose virginal ideals evoked comparisons with one of Rome's most long-standing paragons of chastity, Lucretia.[28]

There was, however, an important difference between Lucretia and her Christian sisters. Whereas Lucretia had once represented the consummate Roman matron, who heroically sacrificed her life rather than allow the dishonour of her rape to tarnish her marriage, the fourth century witnessed the development of a new ideal for women – that of forgoing marriage, preserving one's virginity and living an ascetic life. This new template of virtue was pitched into competition with traditional Roman civic values of marriage which had always cast women in the role of wives and as symbols of fertility and pro-creation. The contradiction became a crux of serious division between different wings of the newly empowered faith, which was already riven with theological disputes and schisms over the official definition of what it was to be Christian.

The contest between champions of asceticism and marriage was not simply, as one might expect, split along lines of Christian versus non-Christian. For mainstream Christians, marriage retained its tradi-tional importance and Constantine directed many of his legal reforms at strengthening that institution. Inviting comparison with Augustus, Constantine's agenda in the area of family law included the intro-duction of draconian penalties for sexual misdemeanour within marriage, with the burden of proof stacked heavily against the female party. Women could only divorce husbands who were murderers, sorcerers or desecraters of tombs, and a false accusation would result in a woman's deportation. While a man was also required to produce equivalent grounds for divorce, he was still permitted to commit adultery with impunity unless he seduced a married woman. Women who committed similar indiscretions were subject to the death penalty. Slave women who aided and abetted their mistresses in sexual misdemeanour faced having boiling lead poured down their throats. Constantine even argued that a girl who had been raped should face punishment for not having saved herself by screaming for help.[29]

One of the most precious archaeological discoveries from the fourth century – a 2-feet-long (0.6-metre-long) solid silver casket donated as a wedding gift to a young Christian heiress named Proiecta in around 380, part of the treasure trove found by workmen digging at the base of the Esquiline hill in 1793 – testifies eloquently to the meeting between Christian and non-Christian ideology in late antiquity. While the casket's dedicatory inscription to the bride and groom read, 'Secundus and Proiecta, live in Christ!', its imagery, featuring scenes of both the goddess Venus and a wealthy woman attending to their respective toilets with the aid of servants – scenes which probably attest to the actual function of the casket as a luxurious vanity case – proclaimed that a woman could live a Christian life without giving up the exterior trappings of wealth and beauty.[30]

Such a message, however, sat uncomfortably with the criticism of Christian writers such as Jerome who took regular aim in the later fourth century at the rich, well-dressed Roman lady who preened herself in silks and jewels.[31] Jerome was no Juvenal. Like a number of other church fathers, he made a virtue of counting a number of women among his closest intimates. But what these female friends of his shared was their decision to tread a new path in life, a path of celibacy and ascetic simplicity.[32] Because for the first time, with the aid of the Constantinian revolution, women had the option of rejecting traditional duties to the family. No longer were they irrevocably obliged to marry and have children. Spinsterhood was a rarity prior to the fourth century. Marriage was what had always given women respectability, and although a few Roman women like Antonia had carved out a niche for themselves as *univirae* (women who did not remarry after the death of their first husbands) remaining single, unless one was a Vestal Virgin, rendered women of Antonia's class at least liable for higher taxes.[33] But in 320, prior to his defeat of Licinius and in keeping with his new religious sympathies, Constantine abolished those penalties on celibacy that had been on Rome's statute books since the reign of Augustus. The old laws that forbade women from acting for themselves in law or business were also dropped and prohib-itions against women's inheritance were relaxed.[34]

As a result, a small but prominent class of women emerged in the fourth century, wealthy, independent and educated, and fêted in Chris-tian literature as 'brides of Christ', who had swapped fidelity to any one man for fidelity to God. They studied the Scriptures, learnt Hebrew (a rare accomplishment even for a man at the time), trekked to the Holy Land in the east where they founded monasteries for the benefit of fellow-minded ascetics, and, in the case of a woman from Gaul named Egeria, wrote diaries of their travels. Some were even admitted to the church hierarchy, appointed as deaconesses who could assist with the private instruction of female worshippers.[35]

Did all of this represent 'progress' for women of the Roman Empire? Some would say yes, that Constantine's legislation and the ascetic movement combined were liberating for Christian women, freeing them from the bonds of marriage, the dangers of childbirth and domestic tyranny, and granting them opportunities for travel, study and platonic friendships with men that would have been denied them before.[36] Others would point out that such arguments played into the church fathers' propaganda, and that the ascetic life was still highly restrictive. Stereotypes of women as daughters of Eve – vain, frivolous and dangerous – prevailed, and women who won praise from the increasingly powerful ascetic wing of Christianity were those perceived to have risen above the weakness of their sex. They included women such as the early third-century Christian Vibia Perpetua, a victim of her church's persecution by Septimius Severus, who shortly before her martyrdom in the amphitheatre of Carthage, wrote of a vision she had had in which she turned into a man and handed defeat to her opponent the Devil; and the fourth-century ascetic pilgrim Egeria, who according to admirer Jerome, conquered the Egyptian desert with 'manly courage'. Whereas first-century wives like Fulvia, Agrippina Maior and Agrippina Minor had been routinely castigated for acting mannishly, Christianity now encour-aged their faithful counterparts to shrug off the temperamental shackles that limited their sex. This set ascetic woman on a collision course with the traditional Roman *matrona*, who still represented the moral majority, yet who, as the fourth century drifted into the fifth and beyond, found herself increasingly excluded from member-ship of Rome's moral elite.[37]

*   *   *

Despite these fourth-century challenges to traditional family dynamics, the importance of dynastic continuity remained a preoccupation of imperial and aristocratic houses, and the image of the emperor and his family, on coins, statues and paintings, in public and private art and architecture, remained as omnipresent as ever under Constantine and his successors.[38] The elevation of Helena and Fausta from the status of *nobilissimae feminae* ('noblest of women') to the rank of *Augusta*, following Constantine's victory over Licinius in 324, was an honour proclaimed on widely disseminated coins, in keeping with the treatment of previous imperial women. Helena's coinage displayed her captioned bust crowned with a jewelled headband, while an allegorical female figure standing with a child in arms under the legend SECURITAS REIPUBLICE ('Security of the republic') occupied the reverse face.[39] Fausta's coins were similarly styled, and showed her in company with the young male members of her alliteratively named brood – Constantine II, Constantius II and Constans. In total, Fausta and Constantine had five children – three sons and two daughters (named Constantina and Helena) born between 316 and the early 320s.[40]

Some of the less official tributes that were produced in honour of the new emperor and his family in the provinces had all the kitsch value of modern coronation paraphernalia. For example, the discovery in November 1992 in the Suffolk village of Hoxne of a silver cache buried in the fifth century, unearthed an extraordinary novelty item in the shape of a hollow silver pepper-pot, complete with a rotating disc for grinding this expensive imported Indian spice, and moulded to represent an empress – possibly even Constantine's mother Helena herself.[41] There was nonetheless a serious and particular political urgency about Constantine's ennoblement of his mother. Following her proclamation as *Augusta*, inscriptions appeared around Rome and other parts of the empire, registering her under her new title and reminding viewers of her status as both 'wife' and 'spouse' to the deceased Constantius Chlorus, and mother and grandmother to Constantine and his offspring. Those local dignitaries who sponsored such inscriptions, usually the accompaniment to honorific statues or routine tributes, thus showed themselves willing to act as co-conspirators in Constantine's bid to prove himself the legitimate heir to the empire, and fend off potential rival claims from his half-brothers by Constantius's marriage to Theodora.[42]

Contemporaneous sculptural or painted portraits of Helena and her daughter-in-law Fausta are hard to identity, despite attempts to match them with the women from the painted ceiling panels in Trier. In Helena's case, inscriptions survive from that time, which, along with later literary evidence, prove such sculptures once existed, in the forum of her son's new capital city Constantinople, for example.[43] But they have been separated from those statues, and thus no securely identified image of her can be agreed on, not even the most famous one commonly said to depict her, the head of a seated statue in the Capitoline Museum which was once so admired it became the model for great Italian sculptor Canova's famous early nineteenth-century portrait of Napoleon's mother Letizia Bonaparte in the collection of Chatsworth House in Derbyshire. At the time, though, the sculpture was thought to be of one of the Agrippinas – an infelicitous choice of model for Napoleon's mother if it had turned out to be the younger version – and it was only tentatively recategorised as Helena in the 1960s.[44] Undoubtedly the coiffure of the Capitoline Helena, with its thick plait wound around the head, accords far better with the snood-like hairstyle that was to become popular among fourth-century ladies than with the ringleted clusters sported by Agrippina Maior and her daughter. Such uncertainty of identification is a common complaint about the female portraiture of late antiquity which even more than its early imperial predecessors, focused far less on a distinct, individualised physical likeness than on a generalised expression of virtue.[45]

There are nonetheless more durable reminders of Helena's impact on the landscape of Constantine's empire. These include her son's renaming of her reputed birthplace of Drepanum as Helenopolis, mirroring Marcus Aurelius's gesture to his wife Faustina when the city of Halala was dubbed Faustinopolis after her death there.[46] Drepanum was identified as the modern Turkish village of Hersek by the British topographer Colonel William Leake in the early nineteenth century. Strong traces of Helena's links with the city of Rome also survive in the south-eastern corner of the city, enough to suggest that this area, which formed part of the wealthy district of the Caelian hill, became her principal residence during her son's reign, despite the marginalisation of Rome as the empire's political epicentre under the tetrarchy. Some time after her son's defeat of Maxentius at the Milvian Bridge in 312, Helena acquired a large estate here, the *fundus Laurentus*, the revenue from which provided funds for the Church. This area became a focal point for the new imperial family's avowal of itself as a Christian household, and provides the majority of our evidence outside the Holy Land for Helena's activities as a patron of buildings both Christian and non-Christian. One of Rome's first churches, named for Saints Marcellinus and Peter, was built on her estate. An inscription discovered near the local Basilica di Santa Croce in Gerusalemme also preserves the information that Helena restored baths nearby which had been destroyed by fire, and which are referred to as the *Thermae Helenae* ('Baths of Helen') in tribute.[47]

The basilica itself, one of Rome's most famous Christian shrines, is today a rich repository for relics of Helena's life-story. It stands in the footprint of a building complex known as the Sessorian Palace, a private imperial residence adjoining the *fundus Laurentus* which, on top of the restored 'Baths of Helen', once boasted amenities including a circus, a small amphitheatre and gardens. The Sessorian Palace is widely thought to have been given over to Helena's use and to have served as her Roman home. Only a few remains of its original shell survive, but during Constantine's reign, probably in the late 320s, one of the rooms in the palace was reinvented as a chapel, known variously in its early years as the *basilica Hierusalem* (the basilica of Jerusalem) or the *basilica Heleniana* (Helena's basilica). The Basilica di Santa Croce in Gerusalemme ('the Basilica of the Holy Cross in Jerusalem') is its modern incarnation, and is home to several statues and paintings eulogising Constantine's mother. Both the theme of these artworks, and the different names given to the building over the years, reflect the famous legend attached to the chapel's construction – that it was built to house a relic of the True Cross, salvaged by Helena from Jerusalem. That most famous chapter of Helena's life was about to begin. But not before family tragedy plunged her son's fledgling dynasty into new and damaging controversy.

In 326, two years into his reign as sole emperor, Constantine made a rare visit to Rome, to celebrate his *vicennalia* – the twenty-year anniversary of his acclamation as emperor following his father Constantius's demise in 306. That same year, he introduced his reforms of the marriage laws, with their harsh penalties for sexual offences. Constantine's draconian moral agenda did not endear him to certain sections of the Roman public already smarting at plans to found a 'new Rome' in the shape of the glittering, grandiose new city of Constantinople. The beautification of Constantinople, which loomed like an albatross over the narrow sea peninsula separating Europe and Asia on the site of the old city of Byzantium and the modern city of Istanbul, was eventually to come at the expense of Rome's non-Christian artistic heritage, which was liberally plundered to fill the new city's blank show-spaces. Constantine courted further antagonism with Roman traditionalists during the *vicennalia* by electing not to climb the steps of the Capitoline temple of Jupiter and make the usual imperial sacrifice to Rome's guardian deity, the first time he had so blatantly snubbed Rome's old religious pantheon.[48]

The year 326 was an *annus horribilis* for Constantine on a domestic front too. The bizarre deaths of both his eldest son Crispus and his wife Fausta cast a shadow over his emperorship and fuelled denigration of him in later years by anti-Christian authors, who also implicated Helena in their accusations of foul play. The product of Constantine's relationship with the obscure Minervina, Crispus had enjoyed an auspicious career in his father's court, elevated to the junior rank of Caesar in 317 when he was still in his teens, and earning plaudits for his key role in commanding the fleet that destroyed Licinius's naval capacity. In 321 or 322, he married a woman named, by bizarre coincidence, Helena, and there is one school of thought that would have it that the palace in Trier was in fact *their* marital abode and that the Helena myth that sprang up in Trier had confused the two women. Despite Crispus's mooted illegitimacy, he was trumpeted repeatedly on official coinage and contemporary panegyric literature as the empire's mascot and his father's right-hand man:

> Employing God, the universal king, and the son of God, the saviour of all men, as their guide and ally, the father and the son, both together ... readily gained the victory [over Licinius].[49]

Eusebius, Constantine's most partisan biographer, wrote these words in 324 or shortly afterwards, in the wake of the victory in question. But in a later edit of the work, this gushing encomium was cut, and no more mention was made of Constantine's eldest boy.[50] Some time in the spring or summer of 326, Crispus was put to death, and his name, as Eusebius's sudden clamming-up implies, subjected to *damnatio memoriae*. Subsequent attestations as to the manner of his demise are confused and contradictory. But all reports agree that Constantine's was the hand behind Crispus's death warrant, one adding the detail that the execution took place at Pola, on the western coast of Croatia. Shortly afterwards, Fausta, Constantine's wife of almost twenty years, was also put to death, in gruesome circumstances, scalded or suffocated to death in a deliberately overheated bath.[51]

The reasons behind these brutal eliminations were contested for centuries afterwards. One of the earliest surviving accounts, written at the end of the fourth century, made a much-repeated claim that Crispus had rejected the sexual advances of his stepmother, and that a vengeful Fausta had then accused him of rape. After having his son executed, Constantine was then stricken with remorse and, egged on by his outraged mother Helena, he ordered Fausta to be forced into her boiling grave. Though details of the story varied according to different accounts, this tale of seduction and betrayal evidently provided much food for gossip during the fourth and fifth centuries, despite being dismissed as slander by Constantine's literary supporters. But it bears too much resemblance to a plot from Greek tragedy, or a biblical scenario such as the attempted seduction of Joseph by Potiphar's wife, for us to be able to take it at face value.[52]

Alternative arguments have more recently been put forward to account for Fausta's death, including the theory that it was accidental, the result of a botched attempt to induce an abortion in the hot steam of the bath.[53] Among many abortion methods recommended by Roman medical practitioners – including heavy exercise, bleeding, and vaginal suppositories made of cardamom, myrrh, brimstone and absinthium – long hot baths, scented with linseed, fenugreek, mallow and wormwood, were indeed regarded as essential preparations for the detachment of the embryo.[54] But the tell-tale scars of *damnatio memoriae*, including one example in Sorrento where an inscription originally dedicated to Fausta has obviously been doctored and re-inscribed to Helena instead, are proof enough that there was a damaging scandal of some sort, perhaps relating to political tensions between Crispus and the offspring of Fausta. It was a subject that one of Constantine's nephews and successors, the stubbornly non-Christian Julian the Apostate, would taunt him with, claiming that he had turned to Christianity in a bid to seek atonement for his sins.[55]

It was against the backdrop of this sorry affair that Helena embarked on the journey which has come to define her life, a journey undertaken when she was approaching eighty years of age and just a couple of years away from her own death. As the dust settled on Fausta's and Crispus's deaths, the emperor's elderly mother departed in around 327 on a 'pilgrimage' to the Holy Land, accompanied only by her own entourage. The aim, according to Eusebius, was to trace the footsteps of Jesus Christ, and 'to inspect with imperial concern the eastern provinces with their communities and peoples'. He went on to record the highlights of the trip, which included her dedication of churches on the sites of important episodes in Christian history, including the cave of the nativity in Bethlehem and the point on the Mount of Olives where Jesus was said to have ascended to heaven. Besides the Church of the Nativity and the Church of the Ascension, she supervised the construction of a large number of other churches in the region, all in the name of her son. As the *Augusta*'s impressive cavalcade passed through each new town, crowds of townsfolk gathered to see her go by, hoping to benefit from the generous cash and clothing handouts she doled out to the poor, courtesy of the imperial treasury on which Constantine had given Helena permission to draw. Others such as soldiers and mine-workers also profited from her largesse:

> ... she showered countless gifts upon the citizen bodies of every city, and privately to each of those who approached her; and she made countless distributions also to the ranks of the soldiery with magnificent hand. She made innumerable gifts to the unclothed and unsupported poor, to some making gifts of money, to others abundantly supplying what was needed to cover the body. Others she set free from prison and from mines where they laboured in harsh conditions, she released the victims of fraud, and yet others she recalled from exile.[56]

Eusebius was adamant that Helena's journey was motivated by personal Christian piety, but acknowledged too the demands of imperial duty that required her attention. The timing of the trip has inevitably fostered the suspicion that Helena's departure was connected to the deaths of Faustus and Crispus, that it was a stunt designed to distract attention from the unpleasant aftertaste of the murders, as well as to appease discontent in the eastern provinces, so recently won from Licinius. The reported presence among the party of Fausta's mother Eutropia adds fat to the fire, intimating that the latter had perhaps been co-opted into a demonstration of Constantinian family unity.[57]

As with the question of whether Constantine's 'conversion' to Christianity was genuine, Helena's own personal religious faith has been the subject of close scrutiny. In his obituary for her, Eusebius declared that Constantine had 'made her Godfearing, though she had not been such before'. This version of events was both embellished and subverted by Christian writers of late antiquity and their medieval counterparts, who claimed that Helena was a follower of Judaism, and that she had written to Constantine from her home town of Drepanum, trying to persuade her son towards that faith too. But Pope Sylvester, popularly known in art and literature as the man who baptised Constantine after curing him of leprosy, had triumphed in a public theological debate with twelve rabbis, and through his miraculous resuscitation of a dead bull, stunned Helena into switching sides, and converting to Christianity. Meanwhile, other chroniclers insisted that it was Helena who converted Constantine, not the other way around.[58]

Although women had indeed played a significant role in proselytising on behalf of Christianity, long before Constantine came along, the question of whether Helena came to Christianity before or after Constantine, and how fervent was her conviction in her adopted faith, can never be known. The sight of an *Augusta* touring the empire's holdings, making charitable handouts and dedicating new building projects, was of course by no means a novelty. Livia, Agrippina Maior, Sabina and Julia Domna had all spent long periods on the road as companions to their husbands, doing just that, and the familiarity of such foreign tours provides a counterweight to conspiracy theories which insist Helena's journey must have been a hastily orchestrated gesture aimed at smoothing the waters after Fausta's and Crispus's deaths. Nor did Helena invent the concept of pilgrimage to the Holy Land – other Christian wayfarers had gone before her.

But Helena was the first pilgrim about whom detailed information survives, and crucially, what makes her different from Sabina, Domna and her counterparts is that Helena was the first imperial woman to make such a journey alone – in other words, without her husband or son accompanying her – and under a banner of personal religious conviction. In doing so, not only did she popularise pilgrimage to the Holy Land, she became the trailblazer for a generation of imperial and elite women who followed in her footsteps. These women included Paula, a close intimate of Jerome, who wrote an epitaph recording her journey of the 380s; Egeria, travelling in the same decade, who wrote her own account of her travels; and the two Melanias – Melania the Elder, an ascetic member of the senatorial elite who founded monasteries in Jerusalem, and her granddaughter Melania the Younger. The latter was a friend of Aelia Eudocia, wife of fifth-century emperor Theodosius II, and inspired the empress to make the trip to the Holy Land not once, but twice.[59]

For Aelia Eudocia and her fellow fourth- and fifth-century female travellers, including her sister-in-law Pulcheria and granddaughter Eudocia – whose stories will round off our gallery of Roman women – Helena was the figurehead. It was she who prescribed the model for the philanthropic behaviour they would emulate and who established the itinerary for the holy sites they and other Christian pilgrims would visit. One of these of course was Jerusalem, where Helena had been entrusted by Constantine with monitoring building works in the city. Shortly before his mother's departure, Constantine had written to the Bishop of Jerusalem, Macarius, commissioning a magnificent church to be built over a recently excavated area near the crucifixion site of Golgotha, where what was believed to be the tomb of Jesus had been discovered.[60] Although a few later writers assumed that the resulting Church of the Holy Sepulchre was the personal commission of Constantine's mother – and the pilgrim Egeria wrote in her travel diary of 381–4 that Helena had personally overseen her son's decoration of the building – it is virtually certain that the church and the excavations which attended its construction could only have been initiated on the say-so of Constantine. Still, despite the fact that no commentator during her lifetime referred to the revelation, it was during her activities in Jerusalem that history credited Helena with the personal discovery of the hiding place of the True Cross, the cross on which Jesus had been crucified and the most revered symbol in Christianity.[61]

That an object considered to be the True Cross was indeed discovered in the first half of the fourth century, perhaps in the excavations beneath the Church of the Holy Sepulchre, is very plausible. Certainly a profusion of highly coveted 'relics' from it appeared during that period in churches as far afield as North Africa. In around 350, Bishop Cyril of Jerusalem referred to the dispersal of these wood fragments of the cross all around the Mediterranean and in a letter to the ruling emperor of that time, Constantius II, even spoke of the 'saving wood of the Cross' being found in Jerusalem during the reign of that ruler's father, Constantine.[62] But the earliest surviving account of Helena's personal role in its discovery dates some sixty years after her death, when Bishop Ambrose of Milan delivered his obituary for the emperor Theodosius I on 25 February 395. Recalling the mother of the Christian dynasty whose mantle Theodosius had inherited, Ambrose described how Helena resolved to search for the wood of the cross at Golgotha, and how she identified the True Cross from a jumble of rival candidates:

And so she opens the ground; she casts off the dust. She finds three forked-shaped gibbets thrown together, which the debris had covered; which the enemy had hidden ... she hesitates, as a woman, but the Holy Spirit inspires a careful investigation, with the thought that two robbers had been crucified with the Lord. Therefore, she seeks the middle wood, but it could have happened that the debris mixed up the crosses one with another, and chance interchanged them. She returned to the text of Gospel, and found that on the middle gibbet a title had been displayed 'Jesus of Nazareth, King of the Jews'.[63]

Ambrose's Helena proceeded to scrabble around for the nails with which Christ had been crucified, and on discovering them, had one worked into a bridle and the other into a jewelled crown, both of which she sent to her son. These most Christian of symbols thus came into the guardianship of the Constantinian dynasty, and effectively become part of the Roman crown jewels – a useful epitaph to a sermon aimed at glorifying one of Constantine's Christian heirs.

Ambrose did not invent the story of Helena's discovery himself. It can be traced at least as far back as an author named Gelasius of Caesarea, who published a version (now lost but reconstructed thanks to fragments) of the finding of the cross a few years earlier in around 390. His account, in which Helena was able to identify the True Cross when its application against the body of a seriously ill woman cured her, spawned a number of fifth-century imitations.[64] Scholars to this day remain locked in debate over the question of whether Helena's really could have been the hand behind the cross's discovery. The most convincing argument against her having found the cross, its authenticity notwithstanding, is that Eusebius, Constantine's hagiographer and contemporaneous author of the only account we have of Helena's journey to the Holy Land, makes absolutely no reference to it. Why would Eusebius have missed the opportunity to publicise such an enormous coup for Constantine and his mother?[65]

Despite Eusebius's omission, it would be impossible to overstate the popularity and scope that the legend of Helena's discovery enjoyed in the literature and art of late antiquity right through to the present era. Several splinter versions of Ambrose's main narrative developed in the fifth century, including a Syrian account which ignored Helena altogether and instead claimed that a fictional wife of the Emperor Claudius named Protonike discovered the cross. The most famous and influential narrative, however, was the so-called

Judas Cyriacus version, also originating in Syria, which had it that a recalcitrant Jew named Judas reluctantly led Helena to the burial place of the three crosses whereupon she proved which was the True Cross by using it to revive a dead man. Convinced by this miracle, Judas was converted and baptised under the new Christian pseudonym of Cyriacus ('the Lord's own'), and the story concludes with Helena ordering that all the Jews should be banished from Judaea. In the Middle Ages, this version was a particular favourite, no doubt thanks to its anti-Semitic sentiment, surviving in over 200 manuscript accounts from the sixth century onwards, and used as source material for early English poems such as Cynewulf's ninth-century *Elene* and for Jacob of Voragine's thirteenth-century compilation of saints' legends, the *Legenda Aurea*, one of the most widely read and translated books in western Europe.[66]

Art, as well as literature, adopted Helena's popular association with the True Cross in myriad forms. Paolo Veronese's *The Dream of St Helena* in the National Gallery in London, shows a young Helena propped up by her elbow against the frame of an open window, dreaming as a cross supported by two cherubs appears in the sky above.[67] A standard iconographical type of Helena and Constantine standing on either side of the cross developed from the late fourth century onwards in Byzantine art, an interpretation of which can be seen today on a small gilt-silver altar in the collection of New York's Pierpoint Morgan Library, known as the Stavelot Triptych. This exquisite object, thought to have been brought from Constantinople to the west in around 1155, features various scenes from Helena's life alongside Constantine's, including her discovery and verification of the cross, while in the centre panel, Helena and Constantine are portrayed on either side of what is said to be a reliquary of the True Cross.[68] An estimated 1,150 separate relics of the cross have been counted in total from the available sources since the fourth century. Today, in churches all over Europe which boast relics of the True Cross among their collections, one can be almost certain of finding a fresco or stained-glass window depicting Helena too, be it in the cathedral of Cologne, or Rome's Basilica di Santa Croce in Gerusalemme.[69]

Helena returned to Rome from the Holy Land in 328 or 329, and died not long afterwards. The exact date and place of her death are unknown, but since coins featuring her image ceased to be produced after the spring of 329, it can be inferred that she did not live beyond that date. According to Eusebius, she carefully put her affairs in order as her end approached, drawing up her will in favour of Constantine and her grandchildren and dividing up her estate and possessions between them. Her son was with her when she died, 'ministering and holding her hands . . . her very soul was thus reconstituted into an incorruptible and angelic essence as she was taken up to her Saviour'.[70]

The fate of Helena's remains, like so much of her life, is full of plot twists. According to Eusebius, a military escort accompanied her as 'she was carried up to the imperial city, and there laid in the imperial tombs'. Since the imperial city in question almost certainly referred to Rome, the implication is that she was not in that city when she died, and since Constantine seems to have been in Trier campaigning against German tribes in the autumn of 328, it may well have been here that Helena breathed her last.[71] But a writer in the fifth century, Socrates Scholasticus, took the imperial city to mean Constantinople, where Helena's son was entombed, thus giving birth to a medieval tourist industry in which travellers came to marvel at the tomb of 'Constantine and Helena'. An alternative claim was peddled that after the fall of Constaninople in 1204, Helena's relics were moved to Venice.[72]

It is virtually certain, however, that Helena's real resting-place was a vaulted mausoleum which Constantine built on her *fundus Laurentus* estate, adjoining the basilica dedicated to Marcellinus and Peter.[73] It is known today as the Tor Pignattara, and medieval guidebooks to the area recognised this spacious, single-roomed structure's claim to be Helena's tomb. A list of the opulent gifts Constantine was said to have left in his mother's mausoleum, including four 12-feet-high (3.6-metres-high) silver candelabra weighing 200 pounds (90 kg) each and a chandelier decorated with 120 dolphins, records that an enormous silver altar stood before the great porphyry tomb. In the mid-twelfth century, Pope Anastasius IV decided that the sarcophagus should serve as his own tomb and instructed that it be relocated to the Lateran basilica, and eventually, under the aegis of Pope Pius VI, it found its way to the Vatican, where, by now heavily damaged, it was restored. It has remained there ever since, a vast, curiously militaristic affair, indicating that it was once intended for the remains of a male member of the imperial family, perhaps even Helena's son himself.[74]

When Anastasius appropriated Helena's sarcophagus for his own funeral, it was, however, almost certainly empty. A ninth-century source reported that in 840, during evening prayers, a monk named Theogisus stole some of Helena's treasured remains and carried them back to the Benedictine abbey of Hautvillers, near Reims. Three centuries later, to prevent further depredations on the tomb, Pope Innocentius II (1130–43) ordered what was left of Helena's corpse, including her head, to be moved for safe keeping to the church of Santa Maria in Aracoeli, in the centre of Rome. Today, visitors to this church, situated on the old Capitoline hill, will find a porphyry urn whose inscription bears the claim that it holds the remains of St Helena.[75]

Santa Maria in Aracoeli is one of many churches and monasteries across Europe which have claimed ownership of relics of Helena's body at one time or another, from Trier Cathedral to Echternach in Luxembourg. Given the roaring trade in relics in the Middle Ages, which led to her 'tomb' at Hautvillers being raided repeatedly between the eleventh and seventeenth centuries, there is every reason to believe medieval reports that Helena's tomb was a prime target for grave-robbers, even if many relic-merchants were inevitably trading in fakes.[76] Everyone wanted a piece of Helena, whose sainthood was a generally recognised fact in both the west and the east by the eleventh century, and from her death to the present day, rival cities and churches have keenly contested the right to claim true ownership of her story.[77]

In consequence, Helena's afterlife is a richly colourful tapestry woven of claim and counter-claim, fact and fiction, history and myth. Among those who have claimed her most passionately for their own is the English town of Colchester, which still names Helena as its patron saint. In the twelfth century, Geoffrey of Monmouth's influential and doggedly nationalistic *Historia Regum Britanniae* was greatly responsible for popularising the belief that Helena was no humble stable-girl from Asia Minor but actually a native of Britain and, furthermore, a daughter of Colchester's own King Coel ('old King Cole' of the nursery rhyme). These legends were in part preoccupied with the canonised Helena who had discovered the True Cross, and whose feast day in the western church calendar was celebrated at least from the ninth century onwards on 18 August, but also with the *Augusta* Helena – the imperial Roman woman who could provide a link between Britain and the Roman emperor who was claimed as an ancestor by British monarchs including Henry VIII.[78]

That Britain, the cold northernmost corner of the Roman Empire's territorial portfolio, should have one of the richest Helena traditions may seem odd, but it is rooted in the strong links between Constantine's father and the province which later enabled Henry

VIII's claims – Constantius Chlorus died at York, and Constantine was proclaimed emperor there in July 306. One glance at a map of that region reveals countless testimonies to Helena's popularity there – the city of St Helens on Merseyside, and thirty-four churches named after her in Yorkshire alone.[79] Henry of Huntingdon's *Historia Anglorum* was one of the twelfth-century British histories which suggested that Constantius had signed a peace treaty with Coel and then married the British king's virtuous daughter Helena.[80] It was this Helena whom Evelyn Waugh used as his model for the creation of the eponymous heroine in his finished novel, which he ended up naming *Helena* rather than the original 'Quest of the Empress Dowager'. Waugh also claimed in correspondence with his friend John Betjeman to have been inspired by the poet's wife Penelope, which may in part account for the grating tendency of this 1940s Helena to use expressions such as 'bosh' and 'beastly'.[81]

Despite the occasional swipe at her from anti-Christian commentators such as Julian, who called her the 'wicked stepmother' of his father Julius Constantius (the son of Constantius's second wife Theodora), it was Eusebius's analogous portrait of Helena as Mary to Constantine's Christ that won the day. Perhaps precisely because of the pliability of her image, Helena became the role model for the empresses who followed her.[82] Her example of pilgrimage to the Holy Land, her associations with the True Cross, were all encouraged in the wives of the emperors who assumed control of the empire at the end of the fourth century, and whose descendants would go down with the ship of the western Roman Empire, as it sailed into its twilight years.

9

Brides of Christ, Daughters of Eve: The First Ladies of the Last Roman Dynasty

> Even on the occasion of my first visit to Ravenna in 1913, the tomb of
> Galla Placidia seemed to me significant and unusually fascinating. The
> second time, twenty years later, I had the same feeling. Once more
> I fell into a strange mood in the tomb of Galla Placidia; once more I
> was deeply stirred . . . I had often wondered how it must have been
> for this highly cultivated, fastidious woman to live at the side of a
> barbarian prince. Her tomb seemed to me a final legacy through which
> I might reach her personality.
>
> Carl Jung, *Memories, Dreams, Reflections* (1963), 265–7

The city of Ravenna in the north-east of Italy has attracted a steady
stream of notorious visitors since the seventeenth century, when it
formed one of the stop-off points on the Grand Tour. A place of
pilgrimage for worshippers of Dante, who died there in 1321 and is
entombed in the city centre, the city was also the temporary residence
of Lord Byron between 1819 and 1821 whilst he conducted an affair
with a married local noblewoman, and was the subject of a prize-
winning poem in 1878 by the student Oscar Wilde. More importantly,
the fragmentary remains of Ravenna's sumptuous Byzantine architecture recall its glory days from the beginning of the fifth century,
when it was chosen to displace Milan as the western capital of the
Roman Empire.

Not all early tourists were as impressed as Wilde by Ravenna's
charms. Thomas Nugent's definitive handbook to the Grand Tour,
faithfully carried by every gentleman who undertook the trip, described
the water-bound city disparagingly as 'marshy and unwholesome'.[1]
But the guide did single out one landmark at least as a must-see.
Behind the cathedral of San Vitale lies the so-called Mausoleum of
Galla Placidia, a tiny cruciform chapel of soft pink brick famous for
its breathtaking interior wall mosaics and domed indigo ceilings
spangled with glittering stars, described by one poet as a 'blue night
sparkled with gold'. The effect is claimed to have inspired songwriter

Cole Porter, honeymooning in the city in the 1920s, to pen one of his most famous popular hits, 'Night and Day', and some have found parallels in the ceiling's decoration with the description of angels in Dante's *Divine Comedy*, part of which he composed while in exile in Ravenna.[2]

If one had visited the chapel between the fourteenth and sixteenth centuries, one might have been directed by those in the know to spy through a hole in the front of one of the great sarcophagi there. Through it, it was reported that the embalmed body of a female could be seen, richly dressed and seated in a chair of cypress wood. The body was thought to be that of the woman for whom the building was named, Galla Placidia, one of the last empresses of the Roman Empire. But hopeful visitors today will find no such peephole. If we are to believe medieval report, this is because in 1577, some children playing near the sarcophagus were trying to get a better view of the occupant by squeezing a lighted taper through the opening, and accidentally set fire to the body, reducing it to ash.[3]

The colourful life-story of Galla Placidia, daughter of one emperor, sister to another, wife to a third and finally mother to a fourth, is one tightly entangled with the tale of how the western half of the Roman Empire sank into its famous 'decline' over the course of the fifth century, leaving its eastern half to soldier on under the umbrella of the Byzantine emperors. She lived through an era of massive religious, political and social upheaval, defined by three central frontiers of tension – the ever-increasing pressure on Rome's territory by invading barbarian forces; the metamorphosing face of imperial power which saw a succession of youthful and inexperienced emperors dominated by a ruthlessly competitive cabal of advisers, officials and military leaders; and the repeated clashes between rival factions within the newly dominant religion of Christianity over the orthodox definition of their faith.

Against this precarious backdrop, a new generation of Roman first ladies attempted to establish themselves as the true inheritors of their role model Helena, the first Christian *Augusta*. Galla Placidia and her niece Pulcheria – the leading lady of the eastern Roman court of Constantinople for much of the first half of the fifth century – were the most successful imitators. But the ways in which these women approached that goal were quite different. Pulcheria, enabled by the religious and political transformation of empire brought about by Christianity's rise, forged a path unlike that of any previous Roman empress, paving the way for the Byzantine empresses and early medieval queens who would follow in her wake. Galla Placidia's journey, on the other hand, from coveted matrimonial prize to emperor's wife, mother and widow, was in many ways a pastiche of her predecessors', stretching all the way back to Livia. As such, their stories are an apt conclusion to this history of Rome's first ladies.[4]

To reach the heyday of Placidia and Pulcheria, our final port on this odyssey through the lives of the imperial women of Rome's empire, we must first navigate the choppy waters of the second half of the fourth century, during which the first shoots of their family tree took root. The years following Helena's death at the end of the 320s had seen her son Constantine grappling with many religious and military disputes across his uneasily unified empire. Having finally dedicated his new capital of Constantinople on the site of the old city of Byzantium in 330, he spent much of his last seven years in power there before dying in an imperial villa in Nicomedia on 22 May 337, shortly after being officially baptised into the Christian faith he had championed to such powerful effect.

Following his demise, a power-sharing arrangement was agreed between his three sons – Constantius II, Constantine II and Constans – all children of his marriage to Fausta. But fraternal infighting and an attempted coup by a usurper named Magnus Magnentius left only the eldest son Constantius II still *in situ* by 350. Magnus Magnentius, who was of Frankish descent, was one of a new generation of barbarian-born Roman officials whose families had been allowed to settle within the empire and who had swiftly risen to high command in the service of its army. This development was symptomatic not just of the manpower problems faced by the overstretched Roman military machine, but of an increasing dilemma faced by fourth-century emperors – namely, how to reach accommodation with the vast numbers of migrant barbarian tribe peoples, such as the Franks, the Alamanni and the Goths, who were now seeking a foothold within the empire's borders.

Although Constantius II had once been given the blame for an order to the Roman army in the wake of his father Constantine's death, to execute the male descendants of his grandfather Constantius Chlorus's marriage to Theodora, ensuring they could pose no threat to the succession of Helena's grandsons, he nonetheless enlisted one of the survivors of that purge, his cousin Gallus, to serve as his imperial representative in the east while he personally avenged the usurpation by Magnentius and brought the empire under his control once more in 351. Gallus, who was named Caesar and given his senior partner's sister Constantina as a bride, was soon accused of exceeding his mandate in the east, and executed on Constantius II's orders in October 354. But in another conciliatory gesture towards the descendants of Theodora, Gallus's half-brother Julian was named as his replacement, and it was twenty-nine-year-old Julian who succeeded Constantius II when the latter died of fever on 3 November 361.

Julian's two-year reign is best known for his attempts to turn the Roman Empire back towards paganism, which earned him the epithet Julian the Apostate. He was, however, to be Rome's last non-Christian emperor, and also the last emperor to try to govern the empire single-handed. His death in June 363 was followed up by six months of care-taker rule by the obscure Jovian. Then, following Jovian's death from suspected asphyxiation in 364, a Pannonian officer named Valentinian took up the baton, installing his court at Trier, and appointing his brother Valens to head up operations in the east from Constantinople. On 24 August 367, Valentinian publicly hailed his son Gratian – by his first wife Marina Severa – as his successor, dubbing him *Augustus* at the tender age of eight and thus setting a precedent for the inauguration of a generation of child-emperors which would have an enormous impact on the way government was run in the late fourth and fifth centuries.

Having policed the empire against barbarian incursions on its north-western frontier for just over a decade, Valentinian died of a stroke on 17 November 375, leaving sixteen-year-old Gratian as joint ruler with his uncle Valens. A rival claimant to power immediately emerged, however, in the person of Gratian's half-brother Valentinian II, the four-year-old-son of Valentinian's second wife Justina. Valentinian II's elevation was masterminded by two ambitious generals who held the threat of an army backlash over Gratian's and Valens's heads if they did not allow the boy to become a member of their imperial college. A deal was thus reached whereby the half-brothers and their uncle would share power, testimony to the clout of the generalissimos who would come to dominate Roman politics in the fifth century. A catas-trophic defeat at the hands of the Goths for Valens and his army at the battle of Adrianople on 9 August 378 then created a job opening for a new *Augustus* in the east, which was duly filled on 19 January 379 by recently appointed *magister militum* (field-army general) Theodosius, the Spanish-born founder of the Theodosian dynasty which presided over the twilight period of the Roman Empire.

During the unsettled transition between the house of Constantine and the house of Valentinian, few empresses had the time or the opportunity to make more than a cursory impact on the annals of history. Gallus's wife Constantina, one of two daughters born to Constantine and Fausta, died in Bithynia on her way to try and seek clemency for her husband with her brother Constantius II. The pubescent Gratian forged a useful family connection by marrying Constantius II's daughter Constantia, but she died just after her twenty-first birthday and makes only fleeting appearances in the literary and material record, though her Valentinian in-laws did not neglect to exploit the link she provided them to Constantine and Helena.[5] Eusebia, the second wife of Constantius II, also deserves mention for her role in acting as advocate for the young Julian in the mid-350s, persuading her husband to invite his teenaged relative to the imperial court in Milan and to agree to his attending university in Athens. She was said to have nurtured the young man's intellectual passions by giving him a collection of books, and to have encouraged his promotion to Caesar on 6 November 355. In recognition of his debt, Julian himself wrote a 'Speech of Thanks' to her, praising her virtue and noble deeds, a remarkable document given that it is the earliest example of an official speech of praise directed exclusively at an imperial woman.[6]

In a familiar paradox, the Eusebia who emerges from Julian's speech and other sources as a pious, kindly benefactress was painted elsewhere as a schemer with an eye to her own interests, whose kindly attitude towards Julian masked an icy determination to eliminate more effective rivals to her husband. She was accused of secretly poisoning Julian's wife Helena – the other daughter of Constantine and Fausta – to induce repeated miscarriages, ensuring that her own childlessness would not put her at a disadvantage. However, such deviousness, reminiscent of Livia's and Agrippina Minor's combined reputations for poisoning inconvenient rivals, was nothing compared to the portrait painted of Valentinian's second wife, Justina. The well-connected daughter of a provincial governor, Justina had been the widow of the usurper Magnus Magnentius before she married Valentinian. One account had it that the latter's first wife, Marina Severa, had befriended Justina and used to bathe with her, and that Valentinian was so smitten by his wife's description of Justina's naked form that in his determination to wed her, he connived at a change in the law to permit him to have two wives – a law, incidentally, of which there is no mention in ancient legal sources, clearly demonstrating that the story has little basis in fact.[7] Justina bore Valentinian four children before the emperor's death in 375 – a son, the boy-emperor Valentinian II, and three daughters, one of whom, Galla, would go on to marry emperor Theodosius and give birth to Galla Placidia. When her stepson Gratian became emperor, it was Justina who was summoned to the Danube frontier by the ambitious generals who wanted to put four-year-old Valentinian II on the throne, and as of then, she stopped at nothing to secure the interests of her own son.

Justina epitomises a certain abiding image of the empresses of this period – ambitious women who acted as de facto regents for their child-emperor sons and who created as many enemies as they did allies. But unlike previous 'queen mothers' such as Agrippina Minor or even the Severan empresses Julia Maesa and Julia Mamaea – all women who supervised the reigns of their very young offspring – Justina's and her cohort's historical reputations pivot largely on their religious behaviour. Christian asceticism continued to strengthen its challenge to traditional Roman social structures in the late fourth and early fifth centuries, creating an alternative template for ideal female conduct which some women of the fifth-century imperial court, as we shall see, took to heart.[8] But while this might have earned these women plaudits from some Christian moralists, other chroniclers of late antiquity and the medieval period, who did not subscribe to such newfangled doctrines, used their conduct as grounds for criticism and suspicion.

Meanwhile, doctrinal controversy raged within the Christian Church, centring principally on a long-simmering debate over the true nature of Jesus Christ. While the orthodox view, established by Constantine's Council of Nicaea in 325 and memorialised today by the Nicene Creed, affirmed that the Son was 'of the same substance' as the Father, believers who followed the teachings of the heretic Arius insisted that the Father and the Son were similar, but distinct, entities. Both Eusebia and Justina were followers of Arianism, which fomented suspicion against them in orthodox Christian quarters. Many held Eusebia responsible for her husband Constantius II's strong sympathy with these unorthodox beliefs, while Justina's Arianism brought her into conflict with church fathers such as Ambrose of Milan, whose biographer Paulinus accused her of having once sent an assassin to try and kill the bishop in his bedroom.[9]

Clashes between women of the imperial family and powerful men of the Church were to be a recurring theme for Eusebia's and Justina's successors, earning for several the condemnation by Christian writers as Eves and Jezebels. Such conflicts have fuelled the image of this generation of empresses as powerful regents dominating their feeble, coddled sons and brothers and presiding over their own courts, making executive decision independent of the emperor. But they are also a reflection of the battle for the ownership of the empire's soul that was taking place between the Roman emperors and the Christian Church during this period, a battle in which the women of the imperial family were beginning to play an increasingly significant role as foot-soldiers not of their husbands' and fathers' divine cults, but of God's.[10]

When Spanish-born Theodosius picked up the reins of power at the eastern capital of Constantinople in January 379, his wife Aelia Flac-cilla became the first empress of the Theodosian dynasty, the last house to reign before the rule of the Roman emperors was ended in the west in 476. Like founding matriarchs of previous years, Aelia Flaccilla laid down a behavioural benchmark for the women of her dynasty. She was of Spanish lineage, and her name *Aelia* would hence-forth be adopted as an honorific title on the coins of Theodosian empresses.[11] She had married Theodosius, the son of a once celebrated but later disgraced war hero, in around 376. In contrast to her western counterparts Eusebia and Justina, Aelia Flaccilla espoused the same Nicene Orthodox faith as her husband, and was credited on one occasion with persuading Theodosius not to grant an interview to the radical outcast Arian bishop Eunomius of Cyzicus, lest the emperor should prove susceptible to the bishop's powers of persuasion.[12] Such vigilance for her husband's religious health cast Aelia Flaccilla as the antithesis to Eusebia and other Arian empresses who tried to turn their husbands towards heresy, and earned the Spanish empress a reputation for piety among the Christian writers who monopolise the historiography of the period.

Aelia Flaccilla was famed for her philanthropy and charity work, particularly towards the disabled, and praised by one church historian for her bestowal of 'every kind of attention on the maimed and the mutilated, declining all aid from her household and her guards, herself visiting the houses where the sufferers lodged, and providing every one with what he required'. The same historian added reverently that the empress 'also went about the guest chambers of the churches and ministered to the wants of the sick, herself handling pots and pans, and tasting broth, now bringing in a dish and breaking bread and offering morsels, and washing out a cup and going through all the other duties which are supposed to be proper to servants and maids'.[13] The distribution of charity was hardly a novel act for an empress – the elder and younger Faustinas had, for example, established alimentary funds for girl orphans in the second century. Now though, such munificence was painted as the act of a good Christian lady, helpfully evoking comparison to another benefactress of recent memory: Helena, who had also tended the sick and needy.[14]

Aelia Flaccilla's status as heiress to the legacy of Helena and role model to future empresses was cemented when, in around 383, she was awarded Livia's old title of *Augusta*, an accolade withheld from Eusebia, Justina and every other empress since the death of Helena over sixty years previously. The honour coincided with the promotion of her eldest son Arcadius to the rank of *Augustus* alongside his father and western imperial partners Gratian and Valentinian II. In the process, Aelia Flaccilla also became the first empress since Helena to have a coin minted in her name. It is worth noting that after her death, empresses of the eastern court in Constantinople continued to receive the title *Augusta* on their coins, whereas the mints of the western territories of empire lagged behind. Indeed, no western empress of this era received a coin in her own name before 425, starkly highlighting the different attitudes to the role of the empress between the western and eastern courts, differences which would indeed later provoke recriminations between the camps.[15]

Flaccilla's coins introduced significant alterations to the typical empress format. Though retaining the braided hairstyle and jewelled headwear worn by Helena, the overall effect of Flaccilla's appearance was much richer, with rosettes of precious stones swathing her temples in such profusion that her coiffure, secured with pearl-headed pins, is almost obscured. She aslo wears a diadem, accessorised by a large jewel adorning the forehead, and clacking strands of jewels hanging down the nape of her neck. Such grandeur reflected the unashamed autocratic aesthetic that now prevailed in the imperial court of the late Roman Empire, a far cry from the minimalist modesty of Livia's day when the restoration of the republic was still a rallying cry. Flaccilla's costume is also an eloquent reminder of the time and distance travelled since the days of the earliest Roman first ladies. Instead of the usual tunic and *palla*, the conventional dress of women of antiquity, she is shown wearing a purple mantle known as the *paludamentum*. This is secured at her shoulder with a fibula brooch whose appearance is closely paralleled in archaeological finds that have been made around Europe of onyx and sardonyx brooches hung with delicate teardrop-shaped gems of emerald, glass and gold.[16]

The *paludamentum*, a military style of garment reminiscent of the *chlamys* which Agrippina Minor had once scandalously worn in public, had previously been reserved for the wardrobe of emperors. This hint of androgyny in Flaccilla's portrait styling is repeated with the inclusion of Victory on the reverse, the first time this goddess had ever appeared on a coin minted for an empress.[17] By being styled in the clothes and insignia of the emperor, a delicately reimagined role for the empress was being implied – a closing of ranks between *Augustus* and *Augusta*, a more open permission for her to be seen as a figurehead for the political decisions made by her husband's regime. The message was not lost on the citizens of Antioch, who while rioting against imperial taxes in the spring of 387, directed their ire at Aelia Flaccilla's statue as well as those of her husband and sons, tearing it down and destroying it.[18]

The presence of the Christian chi-rho symbol on Aelia Flaccilla's coins was also critical to this newly envisioned role. For it proclaimed the religious faith of Theodosius's wife, her status as the heiress of Helena's legacy, and the guarantor of imperial victory through her piety, updating the paradigm that a good and faithful imperial wife served as a symbol of political, as well as domestic, harmony at the heart of imperial power. Now, it was not just Aelia Flaccilla's marital fidelity but her Christian faith that promised to bring stability to the empire.

Aelia Flaccilla died in 387, eight years into her husband's reign, and was buried in Constantinople. By this point, Theodosius's opposite numbers in the western capitals of Trier and Milan were in a state of disarray. Gratian, co-emperor since 367, was assassinated in 383, leaving his twelve-year-old half-brother Valentinian II hanging onto the west by himself. A usurper named Magnus Maximus had had himself declared *Augustus* with the backing of forces under him in Britain and Gaul. Initially, Maximus made overtures of co-operation to young Valentinian II, and over in the east, Theodosius agreed to recognise the newcomer, probably out of reluctance to risk his own position against an opponent with so excellent a military reputation. But the situation changed in 387 when Maximus's invasion of Italy across the Alps forced Valentinian II into flight from his court in Milan.

According to the account of the fiercely anti-Christian Zosimus, who displayed the ancient historian's typical knack for conflating the sexual with the political, Justina, mother of the ousted young western emperor, now spied an opportunity. Having sought sanctuary with her son and three daughters at Theodosius's palace in Thessalonica, she begged him not to accept Maximus as co-ruler, but to restore her son Valentinian II to the throne, and, in return, accept her daughter Galla as a replacement bride for Aelia Flaccilla. Given that Maximus was a fellow Spaniard with impeccable Nicene credentials, in contrast to the Arianism of Justina and her son, there were those who urged Theodosius privately to reject Justina's plea and brush the illegality of Maximus's coup under the carpet. But Galla's beauty, so said Zosimus, was too tempting a prospect for Theodosius, though the historian neglected to mention that the circuitous family ties she provided to Constantine would have proved equally alluring, and the marriage would give Theodosius a moral excuse to replace Maximus with a novice emperor he could manipulate to his own ends more easily. Theodosius duly made Galla his second wife, and honoured his obligations to his new in-laws by defeating Maximus and restoring Valentinian II to power in the west in 388, although Theodosius, the shorter-serving yet elder of the two *Augusti*, retained the more senior role.[19] A year or two into his marriage to Galla, while Theodosius was still away on campaign, their daughter Galla Placidia was born.[20]

Though Galla Placidia was born in the eastern half of the empire, her future lay west. Four years after his restoration by Theodosius, Valentinian II was found dead in Gaul and his place was taken by yet another usurper, Eugenius. Senior emperor Theodosius now stubbornly refused to delegate control of the west to a more threatening partner, having already earmarked it for one of his sons, and he secured a famous battle victory over Eugenius at the River Frigidus in September 394. Months later, Theodosius died of illness in Milan on 17 January 395 at the age of forty-nine, after entrusting his close aide and *magister militum* Stilicho – another Roman officer of barbarian origins, who had been married to Theodosius's niece Serena since 384 – with the guardianship of his children, eighteen-year-old Arcadius, ten-year old Honorius, and their half-sister Galla Placidia, aged around seven. That at least was the arrangement according to Stilicho, whose word was the only guarantee of Theodosius's last wishes.[21]

Arcadius and Honorius now became joint-emperors, Arcadius ruling from Constantinople and the much younger Honorius from the western court in Milan, with Stilicho acting as de-facto regent for the latter. Galla Placidia herself was also based in Milan, where she had been summoned to visit her father on his deathbed.[22] But when Milan no longer provided the required protection against the sabre-rattling of increasingly troublesome Goth invaders on the empire's Rhine–Danube frontier, the city of Ravenna was chosen as a replacement capital, all in all a more secure stronghold protected by marsh on three sides and a sea coast on the other. In 402, when Galla Placidia was approximately thirteen years old, the entire court decamped to a palace in Ravenna's south-eastern quarter. Where Constantinople had been a city of dreams, its vast imperial palace on the shore buffeted by warm sea breezes, heavily fortified Ravenna was a malodorous and utilitarian headquarters, more like a military base than a capital, and there was moreover little prospect for its new young imperial residents of leaving its perimeters.[23]

For the days when Roman soldier-emperors and their entourages had travelled from imperial capital to imperial capital, province to province, campaign post to campaign post, were gone. Galla Placidia's half-brothers were to some extent passive bystanders in their own courts. Too young and inexperienced to lead their armies on campaign, kept firmly under the thumb of their senior advisers, Honorius, Arcadius and their respective families at Ravenna and Constantinople, lived sheltered lives compared to their predecessors, holed up in their palaces, venturing out only for occasional public appearances or summer holiday trips to cooler climes. Access to the emperor's presence was carefully regulated by the eunuchs and civil servants who staffed his private quarters, and a thick, suffocating veneer of ceremonial procedure clogged up the channels of everyday palace life.[24]

As a result, the imperial women of this era were a far more sedentary and closeted bunch than their many itinerant predecessors unless, like Helena, they were given permission to embark on pilgrimages to Christian sites. Although Theodosius had promoted a greater separation between the emperor and his court, his wife Aelia Flaccilla's purple and gold travelling wagon was at least sometimes seen abroad, and greeted on her return journey by a guard of honour and a dutifully cheering crowd.[25] After 395 though, the emperor's female dependants, like their youthful brothers, sons and husbands, were largely confined to the rarefied palace environment, probably seeing few other human beings save a few close female attendants who waited on them in their own carefully segregated apartments. This was testified in a speech by John Chrysostom in praise of the conduct of Arcadius's wife Eudoxia when she took part one night in a candlelit procession of some relics out of Constantinople. He commented that it was probably the first time even some of the eunuch chamberlains who haunted the palace corridors had actually seen the empress.[26]

Though Galla Placidia was compelled to live a more cloistered life, the template for rearing a girl in her position had nonetheless changed little since the salad days of Julia, Livilla and the other girls of the Julio-Claudian household. A letter written in around 400 by the Christian ascetic scholar Jerome to his high-ranking female friend Laeta, advising her on the education of her daughter Paula, advocated much of the same pedagogical prescription as written down by educational theorist Quintilian in the first century. A child should learn to read and write in Latin and Greek, by being given alphabetical 'blocks', and being taught an 'ABC' song. Hints in the compositions of Claudian, a contemporary poet and observer of fourth-century court life, suggest that Serena's and Stilicho's daughters Maria and Thermantia were tutored in Latin and Greek. It is thus a safe assumption that Placidia received a similar education – even more likely given that the principal language of the eastern court at least was Greek.[27] She also seems to have assisted at one stage in the embroidery of a girth for her big brother Honorius's horse, chiming with Jerome's recommendation to Laeta that Paula should cultivate enough skill with the spindle to make her own clothes, and proving that wool-working was as desirable an accomplishment for well-brought-up Roman girls as it had been in the day when Augustus broadcast the fact that his female relatives wove his tunics.[28] Any ambitions on Paula's part to dress herself in the latest silk fashions should be squashed, warned Jerome, and make-up, jewellery and pierced ears forbidden, recalling Augustus's reproofs of Julia for her vanity, and praise of Livia for her lack of adornment. The only thing that was fundamentally different about the education being prescribed by Jerome for Paula to that of one of her upper-class Roman forebears was that it was aimed at training her up for a life committed to virginal asceticism, rather than a position as someone's wife.[29]

Jerome's letter also advised that care should be taken over the choice of Paula's companions and domestic attendants. One of the few surviving pieces of evidence about Placidia's early life is that her nurse was called Elpidia, and was a trusted confidante who would remain a member of her household into adulthood. Farming out one's babies for breast-feeding was frowned upon just as much by Christian writers as it had been by Tacitus, but Elpidia's companionship suggests that Placidia's mother Galla had, like most mothers of her class, ignored such recriminations.[30]

Placidia's closeness to her nurse Elpidia contrasts sharply with the picture of her relationship with her foster mother Serena. While a coterie of influential and ambitious courtiers pulled the strings of power for Placidia's brother Arcadius in Constantinople, Serena and her Vandal-born husband Stilicho were unquestionably the new power couple of the western empire, a pose realised visually in a famous ivory diptych from the cathedral of Monza carved in around 400. Its left panel frames a standing portrait of Serena, her hair arranged in a thick roll around her head, her person adorned in the high-necked voluminous tunic layered over a tighter-fitting under-dress which had become the prevailing fashion for women of late antiquity. Although a looser and shorter ankle-exposing style of tunic called the dalmatic had begun to appear on portraits of some Christian women from the third century onwards, Serena's robe is tightly wrapped under her bust with a jewelled belt, and pebble-sized precious stones decorate her ears and throat, an example of the increasing tendency towards lavish personal adornment, though still modest compared to the astonishingly ornate bejewelled and diademed representations of women from the later Byzantine era.[31]

To the right of Serena, barely reaching her waist, hovers the neatly cropped head of her small son Eucherius, enveloped in a child-size version of the military *paludamentum* worn by his father in the diptych's right-hand panel. Stilicho, whose short narrow tunic and breeches proclaim his barbarian origins, stands leaning on a shield while curling the fingers of his other hand around a long spear.[32] It is a portrait of assured combined authority, Serena the traditional Roman *matrona* holding a plucked bloom in her hand as a symbol of her guardianship of the fertility of the state, Stilicho the hard-nosed military protector at the ready. Their ambition was obvious and understandable – by 398, they had succeeded in marrying their elder daughter Maria to thirteen-year-old Honorius, making them not just guardians but grandparents to a potential heir to the western empire. The symbolism of the marriage was underlined by the fact that Honorius gave his bride a wedding gift of some of the jewels once worn by Livia and subsequently by other imperial women. When the union failed to produce any children after six years and was ended by the bride's death in 404, Thermantia was ushered into her sister's shoes in a bid to see if the younger girl could do any better – though this marriage also remained childless.[33]

In a poem written in honour of Stilicho's consulship in 400, Claudian coyly alluded to the future prospect of another marriage in the family one day – between Stilicho's and Serena's little son Eucherius and Honorius's sister Placidia: 'the winged Loves throng the affianced bride, daughter and sister of an emperor . . . Eucherius now lifts the veil from the bashful maiden's face . . .' But the veil in question – still the crocus-yellow affair worn by brides in Livia's day, though now encrusted by jewels as befitted the fifth-century imperial aesthetic – was never worn.[34] While Honorius was being put to stud with first Maria and then Thermantia in a vain bid to produce children, Placidia remained resolutely unwed throughout her teenage years, a highly unusual state of affairs among girls of the elite and almost unheard-of in the close female relative of an emperor, the exception of Hadrian's sister-in-law Matidia Minor notwithstanding. Vows of celibacy were of course newly in vogue among girls of Rome's noble families, but no Christian writer claims Placidia as a devotee to the monastic movement, like Jerome's protégée Paula. Was Placidia refusing, as has been claimed, to play her foster parents' game? It is far more likely, given that girls in her position evidently had little say in the matter, that Stilicho was still hoping that Honorius would provide them with an heir through one of their daughters. For this half-Vandal officer to have blatantly set up his own son as a rival to Honorius by marrying him to Placidia when the young emperor's wives were still having trouble conceiving, would have been unwise. In the meantime, Stilicho would have good reason for fearing that were Placidia to marry and produce children in the interim, they would one day have a strong claim to the throne and spoil his ambitions for a Roman dynasty in his own name. So Placidia was kept on the shelf for the time being, her marginalisation reflected in the fact that she was the only imperial member of the western court not to be named on an extraordinary gold locket found in the sixteenth century in the jewel-filled sarcophagus of her sister-in-law Maria.[35]

Stilicho's mettle had been severely tested from day 1 of his guardianship of the western Roman Empire. Since the reign of Valens in 376, when a mass of Goth refugees, under pressure from a surging Hun migration from the north, had attempted to seek asylum inside Roman borders, the Romans had been struggling to deal with the territorial aspirations of these marauding newcomers. Theodosius had adopted a relatively successful containment policy, giving them land in return for their military aid, but between 405 and 408, the Danube and Rhine frontiers of the western empire took a series of hits from yet more raiding parties, comprised both of Goths and of other barbarian groups. To add to Stilicho's problems, a usurper presumptuously calling himself Constantine III was leading a mutiny of troops in Britain and Gaul and the Balkans were being treated as a looters' playground by a separate 20,000-strong group of migrant Goths led by Alaric, who had been trying for some years to force either the western or eastern Roman Empire to give them a settlement of land. In 406, an olive branch was extended to Alaric by Stilicho himself who promised an agreement in return for the barbarians' military assistance in asserting western control over territory in Illyricum, an offer that Alaric duly accepted. But Stilicho's problems on the frontiers were soon surpassed by the dangers he faced closer to home, specifically at Honorius's court, where he had made too many enemies. After the death of Honorius's brother Arcadius at Constantinople in 408, a rumour spread that Stilicho was scheming to set his own son Eucherius on the eastern throne, a rumour which Honorius was apparently willing to believe. On 22 August 408, Stilicho was cornered in a church in Ravenna and murdered.

Alaric's deal was in the dust. He decided to gamble. In November 408, he arrived with an army of around 40,000 warriers outside Rome – still the symbolic jewel in the imperial crown for all its political isolation – and held the city to ransom. After a two-year siege, frustrated at Honorius's constant prevarication, the Goths marched through the Salarian Gate and sacked the city in August 410, shaking it until its pockets rattled. In the fallout, people asked themselves who had opened the gate and let the barbarians in. Fingers were pointed by several ancient chroniclers at a woman, though they could not agree on which woman. The sixth-century account of Procopius pinned the blame on a noblewoman named Proba. But others asserted that even before the barbarians had entered the city, the Roman Senate had already weeded out the real culprit – Stilicho's widow Serena.

Serena and her surviving daughter Thermantia had found themselves outcasts after Stilicho's death. Thermantia had been summarily divorced and sent back to her mother, while Serena had been left with nothing, her husband's assets all confiscated. Mother and daughter sought refuge in Rome – conceivably even attempting to make a home for themselves in the old imperial residence on the Palatine. Also living in Rome that summer was Galla Placidia, now aged around twenty, still unmarried and evidently still left out in the cold by her brother's court in Ravenna. But when Serena was accused of secretly parleying with Alaric, the Roman Senate – according to the account of Zosimus – decided to consult Serena's cousin and former foster daughter Placidia, the only member of the imperial family available, on the decision of whether the former regent's wife should be put to death for her crimes. Placidia's answer was yes. A sentence of strangulation was passed on Stilicho's widow.[36]

The notion that any Roman woman could be responsible for such a dereliction of her traditional duty as helpmate and guardian of the household as to betray it to barbarian invaders was anathema even to its early chroniclers, who condemned a Vestal Virgin named Tarpeia for treacherously opening the gates of Rome to the Sabines in exchange for gold. This negative stereotype was also grist to the mill of writers like Zosimus, who used such failures of female character as proof both that the traditional gods had abandoned their protection of Rome and that the new religion of Christianity had softened the backbone of the Roman Empire.[37] Yet Zosimus himself admitted that he did not think Serena had had any such intention to conspire with Alaric. Naturally, his report of Placidia's acquiescence in Serena's death sentence fuels questions about their relationship over the years. Whether she thought her former foster mother was guilty or not, it is hard not to suspect that her condemnation of Serena was the bitter culmination of years of dislike.

After three days of filling their boots, Alaric and his Goths left, heading south in a renewed search for a permanent homeland. But a new member had now joined their touring party. Among the sacks of gold and silver, silks, skins and spices that the Goths had acquired from their siege and loaded on to their travelling convoy, they had procured a valuable human souvenir – the emperor's sister, Galla Placidia herself. Placidia's feelings on finding herself hostage to a many-thousand-strong band of barbarian migrants can only be imagined. But ahead of her lay six years in their company, the bargaining chip in repeated diplomatic haggling between her captors and the Romans over the Goths' continued demands for a land settlement. As the Goth convoy disappeared from Roman view, her future looked dangerous and uncertain.[38]

* * *

While Honorius and his western advisers grappled with the problem of his sister's abduction, which may not have been high on his list of priorities given the continuing problems presented by the usurper Constantine III and barbarian raiding parties, the court in Constantinople had been having a relatively less troublesome time. While Stilicho cracked the whip in the west, the reign of Galla Placidia's elder half-brother Arcadius had been stage-managed for him by a coterie of eunuch courtiers, one of whom – Eutropius – had arranged the young emperor's marriage on 27 April 395 to Eudoxia, the daughter of a Frankish general who, like Stilicho and Magnus Magnentius, had graduated from barbarian origins to become *magister militum* of the Roman army. Eudoxia's public image on coins expressed devout allegiance to the memory of Helena, featuring as it did depictions of a cross on a wreath – a clear nod to Helena's associations with the True Cross. A hand appeared from the ether above the empress's head to crown her with a wreath on other coins. This image, known as the *manus Dei* or *dextera Dei* – the hand of God – denoted divine approval and was already a common sight on the coinage of Arcadius. Like her role models Helena and Aelia Flaccilla, Eudoxia was also praised for busying herself in support of the orthodox Nicene faith, her efforts initially earning her accolades from the bishop of Constantinople at the time, John Chrysostom. But a tempestuous falling-out between the empress and the bishop over her objections to one of his sermons, and his to the noise from a crowd of her supporters while he was conducting a service in the church of Hagia Sophia, drew accusations from John's supporters that Eudoxia was an emissary of the devil. When she died of a fatal miscarriage on 6 October 404, it was said to have been brought on by her trauma over this affair.[39]

Arcadius never remarried and when his own death came in 408, he left his throne to their seven-year-old son Theodosius II, who would rule for forty-two years, nose-led by a series of powerful court insiders. Internal, rather than external, quarrels continued to be the chief source of strife at court, typically between rival civil servants vying with each other for greatest authority over the pre-pubescent emperor. Between 405 and 414, praetorian prefect Anthemius assumed guidance of eastern imperial strategy, while the day-to-day supervision of the boy-emperor and his sisters Pulcheria, Marina and Arcadia was delegated to a plump eunuch named Antiochus, who arranged tutors for the children, found them playfellows and so forth.[40] Their religious education meanwhile was attended to by John Chrysostom's replacement as the bishop of

Constantinople, Atticus, who affected a paternalistic concern for the young princesses, for whom he composed a pamphlet, 'On Faith and Virginity'.

Theodosius II's senior by two years, Pulcheria was just nine when she and her siblings were orphaned by Arcadius's death in 408. It was not long, however, before she assumed the role of bear-leader to her sisters and brother, and from an early age exhibited all the signs of an intractable and imperious force of will. A quarrel between her and the eunuch Antiochus led to the latter's dismissal from his post in 412. Two years later, at the age of fifteen, Pulcheria was proclaimed *Augusta*. On 30 December of the same year, a bust of her was reportedly dedicated in the Senate House alongside those of the male *Augusti*.[41] Yet it is not so much her precocious assumption of the rank of *Augusta* that conveys the image of her as a young woman of unusual single-mindedness, but her decision the same year, 414, to pledge herself to the ascetic Christian ideal of lifelong celibacy and insist that her sisters do the same.[42]

By taking such a vow, Pulcheria was gouging a deep line in the sand between herself and her female predecessors, though at the same time establishing an ideological link to that paragon of recent empresses, Helena. In a dynastic ruling culture where a woman's principal usefulness to her male relatives was still as a symbol of wifely or maternal virtue, for a woman to opt out of that equation completely just as she reached her fertile years, and moreover publicly proclaim her intention of doing so, was unheard of. Pulcheria's choice reflected the radically changing nature of the options open to fifth-century women seeking to live a virtuous life, and how deeply these rebellious new Christian values had seeped into elite Roman culture. John Chrysostom's close friend Olympias and the famous Melania the Younger, for example, had both been forced into early wedlock but stubbornly rejected their families' choices of second husbands, instead using their inherited wealth to build monasteries in Constantinople and Jerusalem and therefore giving a strong religious legitimacy to their independent status. For Pulcheria, a member of the ruling dynasty, to join their number without ever marrying and co-opt her sisters as well was a remarkable victory for the ascetic wing of Christianity.[43]

Daily life in the palace of Theodosius II reflected the family's new religious sympathies, assuming an appearance similar to a monastery. The boy-emperor and his sisters were said to have risen at the crack of dawn and chanted antiphonal hymns together, learning holy scriptures by heart. Theodosius II barely moved without his sister's say-so. Pulcheria made all her brother's decisions for him, trusting to others to teach him the art of horsemanship, fighting and letter-writing, but assuming personal control of his education in princely etiquette, instructing him how to carry his robes, how to sit down elegantly and how to walk. She made him refine his over-raucous laugh, taught him to school his expression into seriousness as befitting the occasion, and showed him how to affect a polished manner in audi-ences with his petitioners. Above all, she insisted that he pray and attend church regularly.[44]

The image of Pulcheria clucking around her little brother trying to groom him into acting the part of emperor is not incompatible with a traditional imperial woman's job description – part of any Roman woman's duty had of course always been the supervision of the upbringing and education of her son. But such duties fell less commonly to a sister. What is truly remarkable, however, is that the description of Pulcheria's activities does not stop there – by contem-porary church historian Sozomen's reckoning, Pulcheria was the effective ruler of the Roman Empire, a state of affairs with which he apparently saw nothing amiss:

> The Divine Power which is the guardian of the universe, foresaw that the emperor would be distinguished by his piety, and therefore deter-mined that Pulcheria, his sister, should be the protector of him and his government. This princess was not yet fifteen years of age, but had received a mind most wise and divine above her years. She first devoted her virginity to God . . . after quietly resuming the care of the state, she governed the Roman Empire excellently and with great orderliness . . .[45]

Had Tacitus been writing Pulcheria's obituary, he would not have been so complacent. As it was, there were those who were less inclined to be complimentary. Writing in the seventh century, John of Nikiu lambasted Pulcheria for publicly chastising her brother and for usurping the responsibilities of a man – directly echoing the criticisms of 'unwomanly' imperial women like Agrippina Minor, almost five centuries earlier.[46]

The rules had nevertheless changed for the imperial woman of late antiquity. No longer was it only the successes and follies of one's husband that determined the kind of reputation she received in later centuries. Now, her religious beliefs could make or break her in the eyes of her critics. By linking her status to a vow of virginity, Pulcheria was able to forge a powerful identity for herself independent of a husband, one that the Virgin Queen Elizabeth I herself adopted centuries later. Over the next forty years of her life, it was a pose that the young Theodosian princess perfected.[47]

While Pulcheria was being credited for reforming her family's way of life in Constantinople, over 1,000 miles (1,600 kilometres) away, her half-aunt Galla Placidia was taking a vow of her own. The Goths were under new management. Alaric had died of fever in Italy not long after the Goths' sack of Rome, and his place was taken by his deputy Athaulf. In his ongoing bid to secure the elusive land deal for his people, Athaulf first attempted to ransom Galla Placidia back to the court in Ravenna, which was itself under the influence of a new strong-man – Stilicho's replacement Flavius Constantius. But with Honorius still dragging his feet and Flavius Constantius unable to bring the two camps to the negotiating table, Athaulf decided on a different tack. In January 414, he married his Roman prisoner in the town of Narbonne in southern Gaul, an area well known to Roman epicures for its production of rosemary-flower honey.[48]

A description of the wedding between Athaulf and Placidia survives in a history written by a contemporaneous eastern diplomat named Olympiodorus. He relates that the ceremony took place at the town-house of a leading local citizen of Narbonne named Ingenuus, and was attended by a mixture of both barbarian and Roman guests, including the senator Priscus Attalus who had been taken hostage by the Goths at the same time as Placidia although released early in a plea bargain. The bride was dressed in 'royal raiment' and sat in a hall 'decorated in the Roman manner' to receive her guests. The groom had also cast aside his barbarian garb and instead had donned 'a Roman general's cloak' and other Roman clothing. Among the wedding gifts was Athaulf's personal offering to Placidia, a line-up of fifty handsome young men, clothed in silk and each carrying two vast dishes piled high with gold and precious stones, glittering souvenirs of the Goths' sack of Rome. This last detail is the only discomfiting flicker in this eye-witness account – otherwise it seems that this wedding was nothing more unusual than the contented union of two well-heeled subjects of the Roman Empire. Not a hint of coercion or reluctance on the part of the bride spoils the picture.[49]

The romantic possibilities of the union between a Roman princess and a Gothic king acknowledged by a witness to be handsome and well built are almost too good to be true.[50] But even if we give in to the temptation of believing that Placidia had fallen in love with her barbarian captor as they wandered across western Europe – and there are ancient witnesses willing to confirm that the partnership was a harmonious one, and that Athaulf was attracted by Placidia's 'nobility, beauty and chaste purity' – Olympiodorus's description of their wedding alludes to more prosaic motives as well.[51] The very Roman-ness of the wedding, from Athaulf's choosing to array himself in the uniform of a Roman general to the presence of several important Roman dignitaries who even took part in singing traditional Roman wedding songs, testifies to Athaulf's political ambitions. Marriage to Placidia made him the Roman emperor's brother-in-law, an emperor whose own childlessness gave Athaulf another trump card. For Placidia then fell pregnant, after the Goths had temporarily established themselves in Barcelona, and she was there delivered of a son, provocatively named Theodosius after the bride's father. For all the pomp, woman had once again served her most important and basic use in the eyes of every dynasty. The king of the Goths was now father to the potential heir of the western Roman Empire. Now, Athaulf must have thought, he had Honorius and Flavius Constantius over a barrel.[52]

The death of his baby son, however, weakened Athaulf's hand, and the western court proved intransigent. Rather than breaking bread with Athaulf, they blockaded him, squeezing the life out of the Goths' supply line. The atmosphere inside the Gothic camp turned ugly, and in the summer of 415, little more than a year after the festivities in Narbonne, Athaulf was assassinated by a Goth in his employ, and Placidia left a widow at the age of twenty-six. Her husband's successor Segeric showed a humiliating lack of regard for the Roman emperor's sister, forcing her to walk in front of his horse in convoy with the Goths' less exalted prisoners. But Segeric's regime lasted only a week before he himself was killed, and the Goths' new leader, Vallia, had little stomach for renewed bartering with Flavius Constantius and the Romans over this troublesome hostage. He agreed to trade her back to the Romans in return for grain and a corner of Gaul to cultivate, between Toulouse and Bordeaux. In 416, six years after she had been abducted from Rome, Galla Placidia was home again.[53]

She returned to a more confident political set-up than the one she had left. Flavius Constantius was a formidable politician who had stamped his authority on the western court over the decade since Stilicho's death, not only securing the return of Placidia from the Goths but using the latter's military assistance to decimate barbarian intruders in Spain and finally bringing the head of troublesome British usurper Constantine III back to Ravenna on a pole. He could be forgiven for fancying himself a good catch for any prospective bride. Placidia, however, did not apparently see it that way. When it was suggested to her that Constantius should become her second husband, she dug her heels in, causing great annoyance to her suitor, and it took her brother's intervention to force her unwillingly into matrimony.[54]

Galla Placidia's second marriage took place on 1 January 417, and was celebrated with great fanfare. But the marital harmony that characterised her union with Athaulf is markedly absent from accounts of her life with Constantius. Why she should have been so reluctant to marry again is a tantalising question. Some have suggested lingering affection for Athaulf, whose dashing reputation formed an awkward contrast with a description of Constantius as 'downcast and sullen, a man with bulging eyes, a long neck and a broad head, who always slumped over the neck of the horse he was riding, darting glances here and there out of the corners of his eyes'. While Athaulf and Placidia had presented a united front, weeping together for their baby son when they buried him in a silver coffin in a chapel outside of Barcelona, Placidia's and Constantius's relationship was described as cold and distant. He was portrayed as an increasingly sour and penny-pinching tyrant as a result of his wife's influence, and Placidia as a controlling nag who threatened to divorce him on one occasion if he did not execute a cocksure travelling conjurer named Libanius, who claimed he could magic away the barbarians, a boast Placidia stonily regarded as blasphemous.[55]

The marriage met at least one of the criteria by which Roman dynasties assessed marital unions. It produced two children – a daughter, Justa Grata Honoria, born in 419, and the all-important son and heir, Valentinian III, born in 421. The latter's birth in the face of Honorius's own continued childlessless left Honorius with little option but to share the title of *Augustus* with Flavius Constantius on 8 February 421. At the same time, he extended the title of *Augusta* to his sister which gave Placidia the honour of being the first woman of the western empire since Constantine's wife Fausta to receive Livia's old sobriquet.[56] But the promotions were greeted with displeasure by the court of Theodosius II in Constantinople, whose leading officials resented not being consulted and refused to acknowledge the new *Augustus* and his family.[57] Before Flavius Constantius could square up to his eastern critics in Constantinople, however, he died unexpectedly on 2 September that year, leaving Ravenna without an effective strong-man and precipitating a bun-fight for political supremacy in the west.

The removal of Flavius Constantius's protection, however fractious their personal relationship might have been, left Placidia and her son Valentinian III exposed. She was not without allies, among the most loyal of whom were a circle of Gothic retainers who had remained with her since her restoration to Ravenna, and the recently appointed *comes* ('Count') of North Africa, Boniface. Honorius was another obvious source of support and for a time, brother and sister banded together. Yet that old political slander – incest – soon polluted the relationship. Familiar-sounding rumours germinated that there was more than sibling affection in all of Honorius's and Placidia's constant kissing. Eventually a rift developed between brother and sister, reportedly causing their respective entourages to come to blows in the streets of Ravenna. Finally, the cord of family unity was permanently snapped, and in the spring of 423, little more than a year after Constantius's death, Placidia was cut off from her home and family for the second time in her life, forced to withdraw to the eastern court in Constantinople.[58]

It was thus that Placidia found herself on a boat heading out to sea, presumably pondering what her reception would be in the court of her eastern relatives and contemplating the tumultuous past decade of her life. She had buried two husbands, lost one child and now faced a lonely and uncertain future, which seemed even more uncertain when a tempest blew up during her sea-crossing, threatening her vessel. A miniature illustration preserved on a dark blue background in a fourteenth-century manuscript in Ravenna's Biblioteca Classense, imagines the scene as the crowned *Augusta* and her children Honoria and Valentinian III clung to their little boat as it was buffeted on the waves against a menacing sky.[59] In despair, she later claimed, she uttered a prayer to St John the Evangelist, promising to build him a church if he would save her and her children from the storm. Her prayer was heard, and her ship made land safely.

It was the first time Placidia had set foot in Constantinople since she was a child in the court of her father Theodosius I, and as far as the imperial family set-up was concerned, she found it changed in several ways, from the strict daily routine of prayer observed by her nephew and nieces to the prominent way in which Pulcheria and her sisters were represented in imperial iconography. A vast column erected in the city's parade ground in honour of Theodosius II's recent victory over the Persians contained an acknowledgement of the role played by 'the vows of his sisters' in the triumph, while gold coins minted since the beginning of that decade showed images of Pulcheria backed by a personification of Victory, holding a long cross.[60]

That Pulcheria was credited by contemporaries with great influence in the court of her brother is not in doubt. But in a repeat of judgements passed on Livia, Julia Domna and other imperial women, opinions in late antiquity were sharply divided over the benefits of that influence. Some wrote approvingly of her management of her brother's affairs. Others were critical that 'in the time of Pulcheria', corruption was rife, with political offices being sold to the highest bidder. One firm conclusion at least can be drawn. Pulcheria's decision to withdraw herself from the marriage market and devote herself to God, was a hugely profitable stratagem politically and personally, even if driven by genuine religious conviction. It gave her access to a rich seam of praise and kudos for her pious conduct both from contemporaries and later commentators that could potentially even survive the disgrace or downfall of a husband or brother, a luxury that many of Pulcheria's female predecessors would have been grateful for.[61]

She had chosen moreover to ally herself to the cult of the Virgin Mary – known as *Theotokos* ('Mother of God') – a red rag to those religious leaders who believed that to say that God had been born of a human womb amounted to sacrilege, but winning her great popularity among a growing number of fellow 'Mariologists'. Their number included Atticus, the serving bishop of Constantinople, and a popular local preacher and protégé of Atticus named Proclus, whose sermons often evoked the image of Mary weaving at her loom – a religious paragon practising Rome's favourite domestic female pastime, an ideal mental picture for Pulcheria to identify herself with. Those who voiced criticism of Pulcheria would have to do so in the knowledge that they risked being seen as attacking not just the sister of the emperor, but the Virgin Mary herself.[62]

Pulcheria, who had of course held the title of *Augusta* since the age of fifteen, had been joined recently on her pedestal by a newcomer to the imperial family. By the summer of 421, two years before Placidia's arrival in Constantinople, Theodosius II had reached the age of twenty and was ready for a wife. Sixth-century Byzantine chronicler John Malalas tells the story of how Pulcheria embarked on the task of finding her brother a bride. Living in Constantinople at the time, so Malalas wrote, was a girl named Athenais, a native of Athens and the orphaned daughter of a prominent Greek sophist named Leontius, who had once held the chair of rhetoric at Athens. Thanks to her father, she had been educated to an unusually high level for a female, tutored in astronomy and geometry, as well as Greek and Latin literature and philosophy. However, after the death of Leontius, Athenais's brothers had refused to increase the meagre portion she had been allocated in her father's will, and so, driven from her home, she was accompanied by her two aunts to Constantinople in order to ask Pulcheria to intervene and compel the brothers to pay up.[63]

When Pulcheria saw Athenais, who combined extraordinary beauty with wit and intelligence, it immediately struck her that here was the perfect wife for her brother, who had specified good looks as an essential quality in his prospective bride. Theodosius II came to steal a viewing of the girl for himself and was instantly smitten – a seventh-century adaptation of Malalas's version of the tale added the details that she was 'a pure young thing, with slim and graceful figure, a delicate nose, skin as white as snow, large eyes, charming features, blonde curly tresses and dancing feet'.[64] The only argument against her was her paganism, but that obstacle was removed when Athenais agreed to be baptised a Christian under a new name – Eudocia. Thus, the story of how an obscure girl from Athens was catapulted into the role of wife to the Roman emperor crept into legend.

Modern scholarship has understandably sought to water down some of the more florid details of this rags-to-riches tale, suggesting that Eudocia was not as obscure as she seemed and that she was in fact the choice of Pulcheria's enemies at court, who included Eudocia's uncle Asclepiodotus, praetorian prefect of the east that year. These conspirators, so one theory goes, were bent upon prising young Theodosius II away from the controlling grip of his sister. Nevertheless, Eudocia's original name and parentage, and her baptism into the Christian faith by Bishop Atticus, do chime with the testimony of other ancient commentators – though they omit Pulcheria's role in fostering the marriage. The intellectual pretensions of Theodosius II's bride come through strongly as well, with the survival of several compositions attributed to her authorship or editorship, including the Homeric Centos, a 2,400-line adaptation of the poetry of Homer to fit a biblical theme which was later read by poet Elizabeth Barrett Browning, among others.[65]

The marriage between Theodosius II and Eudocia took place on 7 June 421, and the bride was made *Augusta* in January 423, by which time the first of three children to be born of the union had arrived – a daughter, Licinia Eudoxia. Shortly afterwards, Galla Placidia turned up on the eastern court's doorstep with her two children in tow. Precious few glimpses survive of Placidia's brief sojourn in Constantinople. Given the hostility with which Theodosius II had greeted the news that she and Flavius Constantius had been made *Augusta* and *Augustus* earlier that year without his say-so, she could not have been certain of a warm reception at his court.

Barely had Placidia arrived and reacquainted herself with her surroundings, however, than fate took a hand once more. On 27 August 423, only months after she had left Ravenna, the death was announced of her brother Honorius, a victim of dropsy at the age of thirty-nine, his legacy as an ineffectual puppet-emperor assured. On 20 November, a senior civil servant named John secured the backing of enough of the western top brass – with the notable exception of Placidia's old friend Boniface – to declare himself *Augustus*. Emissaries from John arrived at the court in Constantinople seeking an accommodation with Theodosius II. After some deliberation, though, the eastern emperor decided to restore the dynastic status quo, perhaps daunted by Boniface's refusal to recognise John and permit the departure of the critical grain supply shipments which serviced Rome from North Africa or else moved by a sense of familial duty. He therefore appointed two generals, the father-and-son team of Ardaburius and Aspar, to head up a military taskforce charged with the mission of ousting John and installing Galla Placidia's five-year-old son Valentinian III as the rightful heir to Honorius's throne. Placidia and Valentinian III were given an escort to Thessalonica, where on 23 October 424, Valentinian III was declared Caesar in preparation for his planned inauguration.

The campaign to depose John began, with Placidia and Valentinian III as anxious spectators. While John dispatched his palace curator Flavius Aetius to try and enlist the auxiliary assistance of the Huns as mercenaries against the formidable force marching against him, Ardaburius and Aspar captured the port of Salona, near modern Split, and from there led their troops into Italy. The prospective emperor and his mother were left in Aquileia while the armies of the east clashed with their opposite numbers from the west. Despite setbacks,

by the summer of 425, John had been captured and brought before
Placidia and Valentinian III at Aquileia, where he had his hand cut off
– the traditional punishment for a thief – and was subjected to
degrading treatment before a crowd in the town's hippodrome, before
finally being decapitated. From Aquileia, the imperial party proceeded
triumphantly to Rome, where on 23 October 425, Placidia witnessed
the investiture of her now six-year-old son as *Augustus* without equal
in the west.[66]

From sister to one Roman emperor, to wife of another, Galla Placidia
was now mother to a third, all within the space of little more than a
decade. From that year on, and for the first time since the reign of
Constantine almost a century previously, the mints of the western
empire again recognised an *Augusta* on their coinage, and despite his
earlier objections, Theodosius II now acknowledged Placidia in that
role too. Indeed it was the coins of Aelia Flaccilla, Eudoxia and
Pulcheria to whom western die-cutters looked for inspiration, depicting
a bejewelled Placidia with a diadem set over her wavy hair, her
paludamentum cloak secured by a fibula brooch and the sleeve adorned
by the Christian chi-rho monogram. A 'hand of God' hovered, ready
to crown her, while the reverses featured the same profile of the
goddess Victory holding a tall Christian cross as seen on the eastern
empresses' coins. The eastern mints too paid tribute to Valentinian
III's mother with their own issues, though referring to her as AEL[IA]
PLACIDIA in the tradition of Aelia Flaccilla's descendants, rather than
GALLA PLACIDIA as she was known in the west.[67]

Her fortunes had come full circle, and she did not forget her debt
to St John the Evangelist for answering her prayers during the stormy
crossing to Constantinople three years before. Not long after her son
had been crowned emperor, she commissioned a basilica dedicated to
St John in Ravenna. The original church, which has undergone many
reconstructions during its lifetime, was obliterated in 1944 by air-raid
bombs aiming for Ravenna's nearby railway station, but thanks to the
observations of ninth-century historian Andrea Agnello, we know that
its commemorative inscription once read: 'To the holy and most blessed
apostle John the evangelist, Galla Placidia *Augusta*, with her son Placidus
Valentinianus *Augustus* and her daughter Justa Grata Honoria *Augusta*,
fulfil a vow for their deliverance from the danger of the sea'.[68]

Our only visual clue of what the inside of the church once looked
like comes from the tiny aforementioned medieval manuscript

illustration of Placidia's boat being tossed over stormy seas, whose illustrator had access to the famous mosaics that lined the church walls.[69] Further help, however, is at hand from a visitor of the sixteenth century, Girolamo Rossi, who described the mosaics in detail. His account proves that as well as commemorating her sea rescue, the brief for Placidia's church was to celebrate and legitimate the restoration of her family to the Roman throne. Around the apse of the church were placed portraits of all the key members of the Constantinian and Valentinian houses, all with a firm or plausible blood connection to Placidia. On the right was her father Theodosius, her half-brothers Arcadius and Honorius, her dead son Theodosius from her marriage to Athaulf, and the emperor Constantine himself, to whom she could claim a distant connection through her half-uncle Gratian's first marriage to Constantine's granddaughter Constantia. On the left face were Gratian himself, Placidia's grandfather Valentinian I, images of two of her little brothers – Gratian and John – who had died in infancy, and finally one 'Divus Constantinus', whose name is assumed to be a misspelling by Rossi denoting Placidia's second husband Flavius Constantius. Rossi also noticed inscriptions near a choir bench acknowledging Placidia's Constantinople-based relatives, her nephew Theodosius II and his wife Eudocia, and their children Arcadius and Licinia Eudoxia.[70] It is interesting to note that no mention of Pulcheria appears. This may just be because Rossi could not find one. Or it may be a delicately pointed message that as far as Placidia and the western court was concerned, an *Augusta* without a husband or chance of providing an heir did not count.

By publicly linking her gesture of thanks to St John with a reminder of the roll-call of distinguished emperors through whom her family could trace its lineage right back to the great Constantine himself, Placidia was issuing a strong message to anyone who might challenge the right to rule of her newly enthroned son Valentinian III. And it needed to be strong. The summary elevation of a six-year-old to the most powerful job in the west did not draw a line in the sand as far as those who had recently backed John were concerned. Placidia was to have an important and testing role to play in protecting her son from attempts both to influence him and oust him from power. There was no such thing in Roman law as a 'regent', but Theodosius II nevertheless saw fit to entrust Placidia with a mandate to look after the administration of her son's affairs.[71]

Her first crisis in this role followed on almost immediately from the usurper John's defeat, when the latter's aide Flavius Aetius returned from his embassy to the Huns with 60,000 of them at his back. The Huns, though not yet under the leadership of their famous figurehead Attila, possessed formidable military talents. This rendered them useful soldiers of fortune to do business with, but also dangerous enemies to cross. When Aetius returned with an expectant army of them in 425, they had to be bribed to avert the prospect of attack. For his part in persuading the Huns to accept the deal and in return for not causing trouble, Aetius was bought off with a senior command post in Gaul.

Over the next decade, three principal rivals emerged seeking to exert influence over the young emperor – the increasingly formidable Aetius, Placidia's old protector Boniface, and *magister militum praesentalis* (senior field-army general) Flavius Felix. It fell to Placidia to try and prevent one from upsetting the equilibrium of power between them and thus threaten her son. In the meantime, she busied herself in publicising the names of herself and her children in connection with the legacy of Helena, as part of the same stratagem that sought to reinforce Valentinian III's inarguable right to the throne. During the late 420s, church-building began in the name of the empress and her children, including the refurbishment of Helena's own chapel of Santa Croce in Gerusalemme. New mosaics were added to the chapel interior, with an inscription recording that by this donation, 'Valentinian, Placidia and Honoria, *Augusti*, have paid their vow to the Holy Church Hierusalem'.[72]

By the early 430s, though, Placidia could not any longer restrain the different egos competing to control her son in Ravenna. In May 430, Felix and his wife Padusia, a one-time confidante of Placidia, were executed on the order of Aetius, who had earned back enough credit since his support of John's bid for power to have been promoted to the rank of *magister militum*. Placidia recalled Boniface from North Africa and promoted him above Aetius in a bid to check the latter's momentum. Soon afterwards, Boniface and Aetius clashed in battle near Rimini in late 432 and although Boniface came off the better of these two titans, he died soon afterwards of his injuries. Thus by 433, Aetius had established an unassailable foothold by the canny courting of support from poachers-turned-gamekeepers the Huns, and succeeded in establishing an iron grip on the western court which Placidia and Valentinian were powerless to loosen.[73]

Aetius's peremptory assumption of the reins of power in the west met with no objection from Constantinople, which even sent him the benefit of military expertise in the person of Aspar, who had led the army that forced John to make way for Valentinian III. They were well used to a model of government where a young emperor ceded all but symbolic authority to more experienced advisers around him. Among those jostling for position in this pack at the eastern court during the 430s and early 440s were *magister officiorum* Paulinus (the head of palace administration), praetorian prefect Cyrus and the eunuch Chrysaphius, all three of whom were agents in an emerging rivalry between the emperor's wife and sister.

Pulcheria might have been expected to take more of a back-seat role in the imperial set-up since the marriage of her brother to Eudocia in 421. She was certainly spending more time in the imperial family's secondary palaces in the suburbs of Constantinople, such as the palace of Rufinianae on the shore of the Sea of Marmara. This was one of numerous accommodation choices available to her, she and her sisters being the owners of a string of impressive private properties within the city, so many in fact that districts of Constantinople were named after them – the 'Pulcherianiai' quarter, for example. Yet Pulcheria did not fade into the background completely after her brother's marriage, a fact that is underlined by his allocation to her of a *praepositus augustae* – a counterpart to the eunuch major-domo who served as his own chief of staff – and her own armed escort for trips out into the city streets.[74]

Pulcheria also continued to be a staunch advocate for Marianism, and in 431, had scored a sweet triumph over the new bishop of Constantinople, Nestorius, with whom she had a relationship as antagonistic as her mother Eudoxia's with John Chrysostom. Nestorius had been appointed in 428, two and a half years after the death of Pulcheria's old mentor Atticus, and was outraged when he discovered only five days into his new post that Pulcheria had been allowed regularly to enter the sanctuary of the Great Church to receive communion along with the priests and her brother Theodosius II. Wading boldly into the increasingly fractious relationship between church and state in late antiquity, Nestorius apparently ordered Pulcheria to be turned away at the gate in future, and from that day on, it was open warfare between the empress and the bishop, who vehemently objected to the practice of calling Mary the 'Mother of God', rather than the 'Mother of Christ'. Urged on by his sister, Theodosius II reluctantly convened an ecumenical council at Ephesus in June 431, to settle the matter, and Nestorius's arguments were defeated by a close ally of Pulcheria's,

Bishop Cyril of Alexandria. Four years later, Nestorius was banished to an Egyptian monastery on Theodosius's order. Nestorius himself, though, was in no doubt who was really behind his defeat, nor were the empress's supporters, who had crowded into the Great Church after the triumph at Ephesus, chanting support for her championing of the Mariologists' view:

> Long live Pulcheria! It is she who has strengthened the faith! . . . Long live the orthodox one![75]

Pulcheria's sister-in-law Eudocia was perhaps a less enthusiastic endorser of the latter sentiment. Court tittle-tattle about the frosty relationship between the two women was so widespread that a story of how Pulcheria, in a black humour, had once tricked her gullible brother into signing his wife into slavery was still doing the rounds in the Byzantine court centuries later.[76] Such tales did the imperial mantra of *concordia* no favours, so the arrival in Constantinople of Galla Placidia's eighteen-year-old son Valentinian III in October 437 for his wedding to Eudocia's fifteen-year-old daughter Licinia Eudoxia was an opportunity for the Theodosian dynasty to put on a display of family loyalty. To celebrate the union between the western and eastern imperial houses, the father of the bride appeared next to his daughter and new son-in-law on a special gold wedding coin, inscribed *feliciter nuptiis* ('happy nuptials'). Theodosius II and Valentinian III were depicted holding an orb, to promote the image of an empire united, and after being joined in marriage, the young couple headed off on a honeymoon tour equally divided between their home territories, wintering in Thessalonica and then arriving the next spring in Ravenna, where they were greeted by the groom's sister Honoria and Galla Placidia, who had remained there to deter any attempt by Aetius to take advantage of her son's absence.[77]

While Valentinian III and Licinia Eudoxia were receiving the congratulations of their western subjects in 438, the bride's mother, Eudocia, set off on a trip of her own. A new friendship was the catalyst behind her sudden departure, though if things were as bad between her and Pulcheria as sources indicate, she surely welcomed the opportunity to put some distance between herself and her sister-in-law. The previous year, Eudocia had made the acquaintance of Melania the Younger, the famous ascetic heiress who, thirty years previously, had sought the help of Stilicho's wife Serena in an inheritance dispute, triggering a slight altercation over Melania's refusal to remove her veil in Serena's presence.[78] Driven from Rome after the Goths sacked the city, Melania had eventually wound up in Jerusalem, where she founded a women's monastery on the Mount of Olives, and another one for men near the Church of the Ascension. In 436, she went to visit her uncle, who was in Constantinople in anticipation of Valentinian's and Licinia's wedding, and during her stay she was permitted audiences with the emperor and empress. The connection between the two women was so auspicious that Melania urged Eudocia to come and stay with her in Jerusalem.[79]

The opportunity to emulate Helena in making a journey to the Holy Land was an obvious priority for Eudocia in accepting Melania's invitation. As with Helena's own pilgrimage, it was the ancient equivalent of a good photo-opportunity for the ruling dynasty, the chance to court popularity with a display of religious devotion and generous munificence on the part of the empress. So Eudocia set off, armed with gifts and donations for the churches in Jerusalem and elsewhere in the region, and after being met by Melania at Sidon, was duly installed as a guest in the Mount of Olives monastery. From here, she sallied forth to embark on an itinerary of carefully chosen public appearances, no doubt distributing money and taking an interest in the construction of various church-building programmes, following the example of Helena, whose Church of the Ascension was just up the hill from her monastery accommodation.[80]

Many ancient tourists to the Holy Land brought back mementoes of their travels. When Eudocia made a triumphant return to Constantinople in the summer of 439, she brought with her a particularly impressive souvenir. During her visit, she had specially requested to attend the dedication of a vast church, built to house the relics of St Stephen, the first martyr, whose bones had been identified on the say-so of a Palestinian priest in 415. Melania's loyal biographer presented her as the mastermind behind the shrine, but that Eudocia had some stake in the shrine's construction is strongly suggested by reports that Eudocia brought Stephen's relics back to Constantinople with her. To be the guardian of holy relics conferred a powerful distinction in antiquity. It was a satisfying coup for Eudocia to return to Constantinople with her own, admittedly more modest, version of Helena's True Cross, and perhaps she permitted herself a smug satisfaction in being their courier rather than Pulcheria, though it was Pulcheria who was the one to actually deposit the relics in the church of St Lawrence in Constantinople. An ivory panel of uncertain date and subject matter preserved in Trier may well be a representation of the actual moment of the relics' arrival at their destination, greeted by an elaborately dressed Pulcheria, who stands at the centre of the scene, holding a cross as though the master of ceremonies.[81]

Eudocia did not long bask in the glow of her achievement. Within a year, her relationship with her husband had deteriorated drastically. A new supremo was calling the shots in Theodosius's court, the eunuch chamberlain Chrysaphius, who, thanks to his closeted access to the emperor's inner sanctum, was said to have usurped even Pulcheria in her brother's confidence. He set about exploiting that influence to the full. Not long after Eudocia returned from Jerusalem, Chrysaphius reputedly began aggravating the problematic relationship between the two empresses, fanning the flames of Eudocia's jealousy of her sister-in-law, slyly reminding her that Pulcheria had her own *praepositus*, while she, the emperor's wife, did not. That Pulcheria soon stopped appearing in public in Constantinople, confining herself to one of the imperial palaces, seems to confirm that Chrysaphius's baiting had the desired effect. Within two years, Eudocia too had fallen victim to the poisonous palace atmosphere, accused of having committed adultery with the *magister officiorum*, Paulinus. Theodosius was outraged and ordered Paulinus's execution. Eudocia fled back to Jerusalem, where she would live out the last eighteen years of her life.[82]

Writing from exile in 451, the embittered bishop Nestorius put the whole affair down as divine punishment on Theodosius and Eudocia for their heretical behaviour.[83] Christian authors of the sixth and seventh centuries, however, remembered Eudocia more warmly and dismissed the charges against her as the fabrication of heretical historians, asserting that Eudocia was 'wise and chaste, spotless and perfect in all her conduct'. Describing Eudocia's retirement years in Jerusalem, one sixth-century historian wrote that he was sceptical of the rumours that surrounded her flight, and pointed out that she continued to endow churches and monasteries just as she had while staying with Melania. Theodosius's anger over the supposed affair did not fade, though, and he dispatched his domestic equerry Saturninus to execute two clerics in his ex-wife's service. Eudocia retaliated by ordering the death, tit for tat, of Saturninus, a piece of impertinence for which Theodosius deprived her of the services of an imperial staff.[84]

With Eudocia's old ties to the imperial court severed, she was able to establish a new, second life for herself in Jerusalem, with her own household rules and an identity separate to that of her husband and the imperial court. She thus joined an elite roll-call of Roman empresses such as Livia and Domitia Longina who had also contrived to forge relatively independent lives in retirement. Eudocia's example proved an inspiration for her own granddaughter by Licina and Valentinian III, who was named after her. This younger Eudocia would endure several unhappy betrothals and dynastic marriages, before fleeing her Vandal husband Huneric in 471, and trekking to Jerusalem, where she is said to have fallen on her knees before the resting place of her grandmother and embraced her tomb, which had lain in the empress's beloved shrine of St Stephen since her death in 460. One hundred years later, an anonymous Italian traveller known simply to historians as the Piacenza Pilgrim, who was undertaking a religious tour of the holiest eastern sites, wrote of visiting the tomb of Eudocia and remarked on the way in which the memory of both she and Helena still lived on in the Holy Land, Helena as a charitable guardian of the poor, and Eudocia as a friend of Jerusalem, the construction of whose city walls she had helped to fund. To be compared with Helena was the best epitaph Eudocia could have asked for.[85]

While Eudocia forged a new life for herself in Jerusalem, Pulcheria was plotting to get her old one back. In 450, her chance came, thanks to a fatal horse-riding accident suffered by Theodosius II on 28 July, and the execution that same year of the powerful Chrysaphius. Into her brother's shoes stepped a grey-haired junior staff officer named Marcian, whose candidacy was heavily backed by military bigwigs Aspar and Zeno, both hoping to secure powerful positions of influence for themselves by parachuting Marcian on to the throne. The other key player in Marcian's elevation was Pulcheria herself, who apparently realised that with Theodosius II having failed to provide a male heir, there was only one way to keep imperial power in the family. Having spent the past thirty-six years of her life carving an identity for herself on the back of her public vow of virginity at the age of fifteen, Pulcheria now bowed to the inevitable and married for the first time at the age of fifty-one. On 25 August 450, she and Marcian appeared at the Hebdomon parade ground on the coast outside of Constantinople, and in view of the troops, Pulcheria personally bestowed the diadem and the purple military *paludamentum* upon her new husband, effectively crowning him the new *Augustus*. Not since Agrippina Minor was immortalised in marble at Aphrodisias, placing the laurel crown on her son Nero's head, had a woman been seen directing the coronation of an emperor.[86]

Pulcheria had compromised her vow of chastity but not broken it. Marcian agreed to her condition that the union would not be consummated, and to silence the cynics, gossipmongers and critics who surely spotted comedic and political ammunition in Pulcheria's U-turn, gold coins were commissioned showing Marcian's and Pulcheria's union being blessed by Christ himself, who stood like a father-figure between them. It was a striking departure from previous imperial coin iconography. A near identical format was used again some forty years later to commemorate the marriage of a Byzantine emperor and empress – Anastasios and Ariadne – where once again, it was the empress who legitimised the imperial succession of the emperor in question. But for at least another 400 years after that, no such portrait appeared again in imperial art.[87]

Marcian's leadership was tested almost immediately by the pressing diplomatic and military problem presented by the Huns. Under the leadership of their new leader Attila, the Huns had been bent on terrorising both the eastern and western courts for the past decade. Uninterested, as the Goths had been, in acquiring a permanent settlement within the empire, and with their services as mercenaries no longer required by Aetius in the west, the Huns' principal demand was money, and Attila adopted a policy of effectively blackmailing the Romans to give him enough gold in return for not attacking their fortresses and pillaging their territories. Attila adopted a highly aggressive strategy towards Theodosius II's court in particular, and after a bungled Roman assassination attempt against the Hunnic king, in 450 the Constantinople court adopted a more conciliatory tack, and enough gold was stumped up to persuade Attila to go away.

The rise of the Huns had meanwhile created problems of a different kind for Galla Placidia, now aged in her early sixties. The past seventeen years since Aetius had exploited Hunnic military might to assume authority over her son's affairs, seem to have been spent quietly by comparison to the domestic turbulence affecting Pulcheria and Eudocia in the east. Ever since the death of Flavius Constantius in 421, Placidia had remained unmarried, and though there is no evidence that she adopted the monastic way of life favoured by her nieces in Constantinople, she had nevertheless proved herself a committed servant of the Christian God. She exchanged letters with Pulcheria and Theodosius II on the controversy over miaphysitism – the ongoing debate over the true nature of Christ.[88] She was also a regular correspondent of Pope

Leo I, and during the 440s had teamed up with the pontiff to assist with repairs of the church now known as the Basilica of St Paul-outside-the Walls, built by her father on the site of St Paul's tomb in Rome. A heavily restored inscription on the triumphal arch pays tribute to her efforts.[89]

Most of her time was now spent in Ravenna, but in February of 450, Placidia came again to Rome with other members of her family to take part in celebrations in honour of St Peter and also preside over the reburial of the remains of her infant son with Athaulf, little Theodosius, whose silver coffin had been exhumed from its resting place in Barcelona and brought to Rome for reinterment in the family mausoleum next to St Peter's.[90]Around the same time, a scandal involving her daughter Honoria was brewing. Thirty-two-year-old Honoria had grown up into a recalcitrant imperial princess, causing enormous embarrassment to her mother in 434 by getting pregnant by her estate manager, Eugenius, at the age of sixteen. Eugenius was executed, and Honoria packed off in disgrace to Constantinople to live in the conventlike surroundings of her cousin Pulcheria's palace, where she gave birth to the baby who would be heard of no more. On being allowed to return to Ravenna, now demoted from the imperial rank of *Augusta*, a respectable but dull husband was found for her, Herculanus Bassus, who would not object to her tainted past and could be trusted not to use the marriage as a stepping stone to power. But rebelling furiously against her relatives' marriage plans for her, Honoria took the drastic and melodramatic step of writing to Attila and offering him money to intervene in her predicament. She enclosed her ring with the letter and sent it via her eunuch Hyacinthus, whom Valentinian later tortured and beheaded on discovering his sister's treachery.[91]

Attila's emotions on receiving Honoria's letter must have been something to behold. Having recently come to a peace deal with Constantinople, his eyes were already swivelling greedily to the riches potentially on offer from Ravenna, and Honoria's letter unwittingly showed him how to play his ace. Interpreting the message and the enclosure of the ring as a de-facto offer of marriage, he pledged, mock-heroically, to avenge his bride, and provocatively dispatched several Hun embassies to Ravenna between 450 and 451, insisting that Honoria and her share of imperial power – what he called the 'sceptre of empire' – should be delivered to him forthwith. A curt response was issued by Valentinian III, who pointed out that it was not within Honoria's power to receive the so-called sceptre, since the rule of the Roman Empire belonged not to females but to males. Attila of course had no expect-ation of his demand being met, but planned to use it in any case as an excuse to declare war on the west. Honoria herself meanwhile had been handed over to her mother for punishment, but instead of imposing a sentence of death as Antonia once had on her wayward daughter Livilla, Galla Placidia contented herself with insisting that Honoria marry Herculanus, whereupon presumably she retired to a quiet life on one of his estates, and was heard of no more.[92]

Attila continued to press his claim to Honoria, even after he suffered a devastating defeat at the hands of Aetius in the French region of Champagne in 451. It was not the end of Attila's ambitions in the west. He managed to milk Valentinian's territories of at least another year's worth of plunder after the setback of 451. But he found in Marcian, the new husband of Pulcheria, a much more tight-fisted proposition than his predecessor Theodosius II, and once Attila had committed himself to a western campaign, all pay-outs from Constantinople were stopped completely. Attila lived only another two years before dying ignominiously in 453 of a nosebleed which choked him while he lay in a drunken sleep on his wedding night.[93]

The scandal caused by her daughter's folly was also to bring down the final curtain on Galla Placidia's life. While Pulcheria went on to be acclaimed publicly as a 'New Helena' for her part at the seminal, faith-defining meeting of the Council of Chalcedon in 451, and died at the age of fifty-four in July 453 to an outpouring of grief from the faithful in Constantinople, Galla Placidia's own passing seems to have passed almost unnoticed in the reportage of the tense disintegration of her son's government. She died a few months after her daughter Honoria's disgrace and hasty marriage to Herculanus Bassus, on 27 November 450 at the age of around sixty-two. No details of her last days survive, nor the cause of her death, nor the place of her burial.[94]

Almost exactly 1,000 years later, on 25 June 1458, gravediggers were toiling on the Vatican hill in Rome at the chapel of St Petronilla – a female martyr said to have been converted to Christianity by St Peter during the first century and whose remains had been housed in this chapel, next door to the Church of St Peter's, since the sixth century. They found a marble sarcophagus containing two silver-coated cypress caskets, one large, one small. Inside the two caskets, the bodies of an adult and a child were found. Gold cloth, weighing a total of 16 pounds (7.25 kg) shrouded the pair. Otherwise, nothing to denote their identity was preserved, save an inscribed cross.

The mistaken assumption at the time was that the bodies were of Constantine and one of his sons. This was despite there being nothing even to indicate whether the individuals found in this instance were male or female, and historical tradition having long since established Constantine's burial in Constantinople. But there was another reason to be excited by the gravediggers' discovery. For before its redesignation as the resting place for the remains of the saint, the chapel of St Petronilla was formerly the imperial mausoleum of Honorius. During the sixteenth century, when the building was knocked down to make room for the reconstruction of St Peter's, more sarcophagi were discovered in the foundations, including, on 3 February 1544, that of Honorius's wife Maria – daughter of Serena and Stilicho – whose marble coffin was filled with almost 200 precious objects, including gold, agate and crystal vessels, and precious jewellery including an emerald engraved with a bust of the empress's husband. A pendant inscribed with a cross-shaped inscription listing the names of Honorius, Maria, Stilicho, Serena, Thermantia and Eucherius – all that remains now of the treasure – assisted with the identification of the casket's occupant. But whose were the bodies found by the gravediggers?

The clue lies in the smaller of the two caskets. Only one child is known from our literary sources to have been buried in the mausoleum – Galla Placidia's and Athaulf's infant son Theodosius, whose reinterment here by his mother in a silver coffin is recorded and dated to the year 450. In spite of the sixteenth-century legend of the children playing in the mausoleum of Galla Placidia and setting fire to the woman's corpse, the body lying next to little Theodosius in the mausoleum beneath St Peter's – which has never since been excavated – must be that of Galla Placidia herself.[95] It is both a thrilling and poignant realisation. For all the elusiveness of their characters, the gloss and gossip of their public personae, Galla Placidia and the entire female imperial cohort were flesh-and-blood women who once lived, breathed and felt. A discovery such as the one below St Peter's can only make us feel the loss of their voices from history all the more keenly.

Epilogue

Galla Placidia and Pulcheria were the last women to make a significant impact on the annals of Roman history before the respective murders of Aetius and Placidia's son Valentinian III, in 454 and 455, precipitated the spasmodic breakup of the western empire. Under pressure from barbarian groups such as the Vandals, the Franks and the reinvigorated Goths, emperor after emperor was sworn in at Ravenna, and then almost immediately eliminated, until the last Roman emperor, Romulus Augustulus, was deposed and replaced in 476 by the German Odoacer, son of one of Attila's followers. In the interim, women continued to be deployed as marital bargaining chips, lending a seal of legitimacy to the ambitions of the western empire's new political order. Valentinian III's widow, Licinia Eudoxia, and daughters, Eudocia and Placidia – the daughter-in-law and granddaughters of Galla Placidia – were given a taste of their immediate forebear's fate when they were abducted from Rome in 455 by Geiseric, leader of the Vandals, after he had subjected the city to its second sack in recent memory. On reaching their destination of Carthage, the Vandals' stronghold on the North African coast, Eudocia was married off to Geiseric's son Huneric, to whom she bore a son who would later become king of the Vandals. Licinia Eudoxia's and the young Placidia's release was eventually negotiated by eastern emperor Leo I in 462, and through the children of Placidia, who married Olybrius, the very short-lived western emperor of 472, the blood of Galla Placidia continued to flow through the veins of the nobility in the eastern empire.[1]

For the Roman Empire was not quite dead. The east survived the breakup of its western wing, and lived on under the banner of the Byzantine Empire, the history of which is littered with the colourful stories of empresses such as Theodora – the former circus-entertainer who became the wife of sixth-century emperor Justinian; her niece

Sophia, who was said to have taken over the reins of empire when her husband Justin II went insane during the 570s; and Irene, who ruled on behalf of her son Constantine VI in the eighth century. All of them in turn became pathfinders for the medieval queens of Europe. And for the Byzantine empresses themselves, there was no uncertainty about whom they were expected to look to in history for inspiration. Statues of Constantine's mother Helena continued to outnumber those of all other women honoured throughout Constantinople. A survey taken of the city's antiquities in the eighth century tells us that of the twenty-eight imperial statues identified throughout Constantinople at that time, Pulcheria, Eudoxia, even Constantine's disgraced wife Fausta were all accounted for, immortalised with two or three images apiece. But no fewer than six of the statues – almost a quarter, in other words – were of the first Christian *Augusta*.[2]

Not surprisingly, the names of Livia, Messalina, Agrippina and Julia appeared nowhere in the document. To all intents and purposes, the wives and women who had established the behavioural blueprint for Rome's first ladies almost 500 years earlier were little more than a distant memory now – the Roman buildings to which they had once lent their patronage stripped or broken up to provide construction material for the Christian empire; many of their dedicated statues recycled and remodelled to assume the facial features of new female icons; a large proportion of the literary works responsible for the preservation of their names facing the threat of extinction, thanks to the heavily biased allocation of copying resources to the great wave of biblical and liturgical literature produced during late antiquity and the early Middle Ages. It would be many centuries, in fact, before the attention of authors or artists returned to the women of the early Roman Empire, and then, as we have seen, almost invariably with hostile intent in mind.

The ghosts of these women nevertheless loomed large over the political landscape out of which the empresses and queens of early medieval and modern Europe were born. Though anxieties about the power of women to corrupt the political process had existed long before the arrival of Livia on the Palatine, those concerns had crystallised around her and her successors, and in turn became integral to the moral criteria by which female sovereigns and consorts would be judged for generations to come.

It is a legacy that we live with today. Never before have the wives of prime ministerial and presidential candidates been subject to so much public scrutiny – fêted and mocked for their fashion choices, criticised for their political pronouncements, and called upon to give speeches and interviews promoting their spouses as caring family men. All the while, back-room spin doctors scrutinise their personal and professional backgrounds, looking for weaknesses to exploit. In March 2009, a frenzied media reaction greeted the arrival of the wives of world heads of state attending the G20 conference in London – resulting in more attention being paid to them than the economic agenda of the meeting. In today's personality-driven political culture, no politician's wife – or indeed, in certain cases, husband – can expect to escape such scrutiny altogether. Some will embrace it – a few may even prove guilty of taking advantage of their proximity to the political process. Others will hide from it, yet reluctantly allow themselves to be pushed into the spotlight if it will help their partner's personal approval ratings. The question of what the proper role of a politician's spouse or family members should be in his or her campaign and administration is one that elicits many different responses. And in that respect, the 'first ladies' of the Roman Empire still speak powerfully to us today.

Acknowledgements

Most of my time researching this book has been spent either in the library of the Faculty of Classics in Cambridge, or in the Cambridge University Library. I would like to express my gratitude to the librarians of both these institutions, and to the Classics faculty for affording me the generous borrowing and access privileges of a Visiting Scholar. I am grateful as well to the staff of the British Library and the British Museum for their help with various queries.

I am indebted to Duncan Fowler-Watt for inspiring me with an early enthusiasm for Classics, and encouraging me to apply to study at Newnham College, Cambridge – where I was incredibly lucky to be taught by Mary Beard, Simon Goldhill and John Henderson. Collectively, they have done the most to shape my ideas about the ancient world. All three were also kind enough to read and comment on individual chapters of this book, as did Christopher Kelly and Caroline Vout. I very much appreciate their time and help – any errors that remain are entirely my own. I would also like to express my thanks to Ronnie Ancona, Franco Basso, Paul Cartledge, Pam Hirsch, Daniel Orrells, Adrian Poole and Agnes Schwarzmaier for their assistance with individual queries, and to the two delightful and informative guides, Ulisse and Evan, who respectively shepherded myself and various members of my family around Rome on visits in May 2008 and October 2009.

The Leys School in Cambridge has been my place of work for five of the last ten years. I am grateful for the patience and support of all my colleagues there, especially those in the Classics Department: Elaine Culshaw, Alex Welby - and, above all, Caroline Wiedermann. Thank you also to another friend and former teaching colleague Rod Jackson, who invited me to talk to his pupils at Cranleigh School, allowing me to road-test a few ideas for this book. Many of my own pupils have asked me to mention them individually here – I'm so sorry that I can't, but, more than you know, you have kept me sane by giving me something to think about other than my own work, and by making me laugh. I am very much obliged to you all.

I owe a huge debt to my indefatigable agent, Araminta Whitley, to Ellah Allfrey, my original commissioning editor at Jonathan Cape, and to Alex Bowler, who has edited the manuscript with calm intelligence and insight. Thank you also to everyone at Cape who worked on the production. At Free Press in the United States, I would like to thank Leslie Meredith and her assistant Donna Loffredo for their faith in the book and invaluable editing contributions. I am grateful also to my American agent Melissa Chinchillo, and must add a big thank-you to Bettany Hughes, who gave me my entrée into publishing, and has been a generous source of encouragement and advice since.

Aude Doody, Katie Fleming, Miriam Leonard and Daniel Orrells are not just the best of Classicists, but the best of friends, and I couldn't do without their support. Julian Alexander has heroically put up with a writer's questions out of hours, and I owe him for a great deal, not least the use of a kitchen table on which to write, and shrewd advice on when it was time to open the wine.

Lastly, my heartfelt thanks go to my family, both here in England and in Bermuda – above all my parents, for their love, support and extraordinary generosity, without which none of this would mean anything.

A Postscript: During the writing of this book, I acquired a new nephew and a new goddaughter. By a purely happy coincidence, their parents chose to christen them, respectively, Augustus and Livia. I am not sure whether or not I should hope that they follow in their name-sakes' footsteps. But I certainly wish them well in their endeavours.

The author is grateful to copyright holders for permission to use lines from the following texts: Suetonius, *The Twelve Caesars*, translated by Robert Graves (1957). London: Penguin. Reproduced by permission of Carcanet Press Limited. *The Annals of Imperial Rome* by Tacitus, translated with an introduction by Michael Grant (Penguin Classics 1956, sixth revised edition 1989). Copyright © Michael Grant Publications Ltd, 1956, 1959, 1971, 1973, 1975, 1977, 1989. Reproduced by permission of Penguin Books Ltd. *Agrippa's Daughter* (1964) by Howard Fast. Reprinted by permission of SLL/Sterling Lord Literistic, Inc. Copyright by Howard Fast Literary Trust.

A Note on Naming and Dating Conventions

Names:

Imperial Roman genealogies are labyrinthine affairs. I have done everything I can to avoid confusion for the reader in trying to give everyone in the book distinct names, though inevitably there are still several female characters with variants on the name 'Julia', for example. The family trees I have provided will hopefully prove useful here.

Under the republic, most Roman women used only one name. During the Imperial age, however, it became more common for a freeborn woman to have two names. The first was usually a feminine form of her father's *nomen*, or clan name; the second was a version of his *cognomen* – which identified which branch of the clan he was from. So, for example, Livia Drusilla was the daughter of Marcus Livius Drusus Claudianus, and Valeria Messalina was the daughter of Marcus Valerius Messala Barbatus. However, in a break from convention, certain imperial women were also named after dynastic female predecessors. For example, Livia Julia (known by her nickname of 'Livilla') was named after her paternal grandmother Livia, rather than in tribute to her father Drusus's *cognomen* of Claudius, emphasizing Livia's unusual importance in the Julio-Claudian dynasty.

Women did not change their names at marriage. Former slave women who had been freed kept their old slave name, and added on the 'clan' name of the family they had served. Thus Antonia Minor's scribe-woman Caenis later became known as Antonia Caenis.

Families with more than one daughter of the same name distinguished them by using comparative or ordinal adjectives – so Antonia Minor ('Antonia the Younger') was the younger sister of Antonia Maior ('Antonia the Elder'). In the case of the two Agrippinas, however, 'Maior' distinguishes the elder Agrippina from her more notorious daughter, Agrippina Minor. It is perhaps more conventional to use the anglicized form 'Major', rather than 'Maior', but I made the amendment after one of my readers pointed out that Agrippina Major and Agrippina Minor sounded like two pupils at an English public school.

Dates:
If a BC date is not indicated, all dates may be considered AD.

Notes

Introduction: I, Claudia . . .

1 Plutarch, *Caesar* 10.8. Mrs Landingham, secretary and doorkeeper to the president, utters this line in the episode '18th and Potomac', series 2 of *The West Wing*. • 2 On the way in which we read portraits of emperors, see Vout (2009), 262. This bust of Faustina Minor is a copy of an original in the Vatican, Braccio Nuovo, 2195. Museum of Classical Archaeology, Faculty of Classics, Cambridge: no. 601. • 3 On the writing of *I, Claudius*, see Spivey (1999), vii, and Seymour-Smith (1995), 227–33. On the reception of the television drama, see Joshel (2001), *passim*, and 159, n. 35 on the portrayal of Livia in particular. In both the book and television version, Nero's mother is actually called Agrippinilla, to distinguish her from her mother Agrippina Maior. • 4 Jonathan Stamp, the creative director of *Rome*, is on record as stating that the Republican Roman matron Clodia Metelli was actually the inspiration for Atia, but the legacy of *I, Claudius* seems to be clearly apparent in her portrayal: see also Ragalie (2007), 5–7. On Graves's acknowledged debt to ancient historians, see Spivey (1999), ix. • 5 An 1893 publication on the physiognomy and pathology of female criminals by Italian doctor Cesare Lombroso and historian Guglielmo Ferrero – the latter of whom was responsible eighteen years later for a history of the Roman empresses titled *The Women of the Caesars* – was fronted by a title-page illustration of a Roman portrait bust of Claudius's wife Messalina, whose facial proportions were claimed to match those of nineteenth-century prostitutes: see Wyke (2002), 328–30. • 6 On the literary tradition of 'female worthies' and their roots in Roman history, see Winterer (2007), 41f; Hicks (2005a) and (2005b); McLeod (1991). On Messalina's modern reception history, see chapters 9 and 10 of Wyke (2002), for a full and fascinating account. • 7 See recent revisionist readings of Nero too; for example, Elsner and Masters (1994). • 8 See Elsner and Masters (1994), 2, on the problem with regard to Nero's story; also Edwards (2000), xvi and D'Ambra (2007), 160. • 9 On the preoccupations of biography as a genre, see Lee (2009) and (2005). • 10 Literary references to individual imperial women as *princeps femina* include Ovid, *Epistulae ex Ponto* 3.1.125, Ovid, *Tristia* 1.6.25 and the anonymous

Consolatio ad Liviam 303 (all referring to Livia) and Macrobius, *Saturnalia* 2.5.6 (referring to both Livia and Julia). See also Purcell (1986), 78–9 on the term; and Barrett (2002), on the analogy of 'first lady' as applied to Livia. • **11** On the habits of America's first ladies, see Caroli (1995), 5–7 (on Martha Washington); 148 (on Edith Wilson); 56 (on Martha Johnson Patterson); 90 (on Lucy Hayes); 71–2 (on Mary Lincoln); 275–6 (on Nancy Reagan). • **12** See Caroli (1995), 35.

1 *Ulysses in a Dress: The Making of a Roman First Lady*

1 The opening to Hays's entry on Livia, in Vol. 2 of *Female Biography*. • **2** This dramatised portrait of Livia's flight is based on Suetonius, *Tiberius* 6; also Cassius Dio, *Roman History* 54.15.4 and Velleius Paterculus 2.75. • **3** An admittedly loose translation of Caligula's reported nickname for his great-grandmother: Suetonius, *Caligula* 23.2. See Purcell (1986), 79 on translating this epithet. • **4** Livia's birth is commonly dated to either 59 or 58 BC: see appendix 5 in Barrett (2002) for a full summary of the arguments. I have abided by the more orthodox date of 58. • **5** Suetonius, *Tiberius* 1. On Livia's genealogy, see Barrett (2002), 4–8. • **6** The year of Livia's and Tiberius Nero's marriage is uncertain, but see Barrett (2002), 11 on 43 BC being the most likely date. • **7** Cicero, *Letters to his Friends* 13.64.2: trans. Treggiari (1991), 129. • **8** Barrett (2002), 11 on Tiberius Nero's likely age. • **9** Treggiari (2007), 95; see also D'Ambra (2007), 73. On Cicero's letter, and on women's consent to marriage in general, see Gardner (1986), 41f. • **10** On women, marriage and the law, see Gardner (1986), 5 and 13. • **11** Gardner (1986), 42–3 on limited opportunities for acquaintanceship. • **12** The use of a spear in this context has long proved difficult to interpret. It may, as Plutarch suggests, have been intended to recall the warlike claiming of the Sabine brides by the Romans: see Olson (2008), 21f for more on this. • **13** I have reconstructed this scene based on modern scholarship on Roman weddings, chiefly that of Treggiari (1991), 161ff. For specific details, see also Hemelrijk (1999), 9 on the putting-away of toys; Lefkowitz and Fant (1992), no. 271 for a third-century wedding invitation specifying the time of day; Croom (2000), 95–6, citing Pliny the Elder's *Natural History* 9.56–114, for pearl-embroidery on *socci*; Shelton (1998), no. 56 for Catullus's take on the wedding song with its 'dirty Fescennine jokes'.• **14** Suetonius, *Tiberius* 5 on Tiberius's date and place of birth. • **15** Barrett (2002), 177. • **16** Suetonius, *Tiberius* 14.1; Pliny the Elder, *Natural History* 10.154. • **17** Rawson (2003), 101–2. • **18** Kleiner and Matheson (1996), 92, cat. no. 56, for illustration of the speculum from Pompeii; Lefkowitz and Fant (1992), no. 355 on instructions for the midwife: Soranus, *Gynaecology* 1.67–9. • **19** Rawson (2003), 106. • **20** See the Favorinus episode described in Aulus Gellius, *Attic Nights* 12, as below. • **21** On the *lustratio*, or cleansing ritual, see Rawson (2003), 110–11. • **22** Aulus Gellius, *Attic Nights*

12. • **23** Hemelrijk (1999), 66, citing Tacitus, *Dialogue* 28 which also states that Aurelia, the mother of Julius Caesar, and Atia, the mother of Augustus, nursed their own children. See also Gardner (1986), 241f on breast-feeding, which briefly discusses a fragmentary third-century letter from a parent apparently requesting their son-in-law to provide their daughter with a wet-nurse: 'I do not permit my daughter to suckle.' • **24** Suetonius, *Tiberius* 6. • **25** Suetonius, *Tiberius* 4; Cassius Dio, *Roman History* 48.15.3. • **26** *Inscriptiones Latinae Liberae Rei Publicae* 1106 and 1112: translated P. J. Jones (2006), 98; see also Hallett (1977), 151–7. • **27** On Fulvia's reputation, see Delia (1991). • **28** Martial, 11.20.3–8 preserves the poem. On Fulvia's pleasure in Cicero's death, see Cassius Dio, *Roman History* 47.8.3–4. See Wyke (2002), 170 and Pelling (1988), 141 on the abuse and function of Fulvia. • **29** See Milnor (2009), 277–8 on women acting virtuously in the public sphere. On Rome's republican female heroines and villainesses, see Hillard (1992) and Joshel (1992). On their adoption by British and American women in the eighteenth century, see Hicks (2005a) and (2005b). • **30** Cicero also implied an incestuous relationship between Clodia Metelli and her brother, a standard theme of Roman political invective that would also be levelled at Caligula and Drusilla; Nero and Agrippina Minor; Berenice and Agrippa II; Domitian and Julia Flavia; Julia Domna and Caracalla; and Galla Placidia and Honorius. • **31** Plutarch, *Life of Antony* 10.5. • **32** See Fischler (1994), 117: *Inscriptiones Latinae Selectae* 8403. • **33** Cartledge and Spawforth (1989), 94 on Claudian connections in region: see also Barrett (2002), 17. • **34** Lefkowitz and Fant (1992), no. 179. • **35** Tacitus, *Histories* 1.3.1. There are also references to mothers supporting their sons' political candidacies; for example, in the cases of Helvia and Seneca, or Servilia and Brutus: see Dixon (1988), 5. On the concept of *sui iuris*, see Gardner (1986), 6. • **36** Plutarch, *Life of Antony* 31: see also Wallace-Hadrill (1993), 32, and Wood (1999), 30-1. Octavia was born around 69 BC and was Octavian's full sister – he had another elder half-sister named Octavia too. In his account, Plutarch confuses the two sisters. For reasons of clarity, I have omitted any mention of the half-sister Octavia from the main narrative. • **37** *Antony and Cleopatra*, II. vi.119–23. The television drama in question is HBO's *Rome*. • **38** Plutarch, *Life of Antony* 87 on Antony's and Octavia's children. • **39** There is an argument that Fulvia was the first woman to be depicted on a coin, but the identification is too insecure for comfort: see Wood (1999), 41–3, and Wallace-Hadrill (1993), 32 in support of theory that Octavia is the first woman. • **40** Kleiner (2005), 262, suggests that Octavia and her hairdressers invented the *nodus*. • **41** Wood (1999), 44 on acceptability of royal couples appearing on Hellenistic coinage. • **42** For a complete survey of Octavia's coin portraits, see Wood (1999), 41–51. • **43** Barrett (2002), 18–19 on the date of Livia's and Tiberius Nero's return. • **44** On the marriage to Claudia, see Suetonius, *Augustus* 62; and Plutarch, *Life of Antony* 20. See Barrett (2002), 22 on the argument that the marriage to Claudia never actually went

ahead. • **45** On Livia moving in with Augustus, see Barrett (2002), 26. • **46** Suetonius, *Augustus* 62.2. • **47** Suetonius, *Augustus* 69. For the arguments over whether this wife was Livia or not, see Barrett (2002), 24 and Flory (1988), 352–3. On Augustus falling in love with Livia: Cassius Dio, *Roman History* 48.34. • **48** Velleius Paterculus, 2.79 and 2.94. • **49** Barrett (2002), 26 on arguments over the relationship of Drusus's birth to the wedding. The discovery of a calendar at Verulae in Lazio in 1922 revealed the date of the wedding: Flory (1988), 348. • **50** Suetonius, *Claudius* 1.1. See also Cassius Dio, *Roman History* 48.44.5. • **51** On the historiographical tradition of this episode, see Flory (1988). • **52** See also Vout (2007), 1–3 on this episode. • **53** Gardner (1986), 146–7 and Pomeroy (1975), 158 on guardianship and custody of children – children do sometimes seem to have been allowed to remain with their mothers, however. • **54** Fantham (2006), 23. • **55** Seneca, *Epistulae Morales* 70.a2; Propertius 4.11.65. Scribonia's genealogy is extremely complicated. We do need to be a little cautious about the term *'gravis'*, to which translators react differently: see Severy (2003), 149. • **56** On Catherine Macaulay and Hortensia, see Winterer (2007), 44f. On the house of Hortensius, see Tamm (1963), chapter iv; Kleiner (1996), 34; Claridge (1998), 128–30; Barrett (2002), 177f. • **57** For a close-up of the women of Cicero's family, see Treggiari (2007). • **58** Ovid, *Amores* 3.2. • **59** Some soirées were evidently men-only affairs, save for females hired to provide entertainment. On women drinking, see Treggiari (2007), 19. See Cicero's contemporary Cornelius Nepos on the custom of Roman women dining out, in the prologue to the *Lives of the Foreign Generals*, 6. • **60** Hemelrijk (1999), 10; see also Treggiari (1991), 414. • **61** See Hemelrijk (1999), 42–4 on women's presence at dinner parties. • **62** See Treggiari (2007), 7; also Treggiari (1991), 420 on women's *salutatio*. • **63** Casson (1974), 139. • **64** On the discovery of the Prima Porta villa, and its identification, see Zarmakoupi (2008), 269–70; also Reeder (2001), 13f. The identification is now widely accepted, although there is still room for reasonable doubt. It is certainly reflective of the kind of property Livia would have owned, at the very least. • **65** Reeder (2001), 84 on naming of the villa. The villa was also possibly known just as *ad gallinas*. • **66** Casson (1974), 145. • **67** Reeder (2001), 12. • **68** Reeder (2001), 84. See Pliny the Elder, *Natural History* 15.136 on the story of the hen-chick, and Macaulay-Lewis (2006), on the discovery of perforated pots at the villa. • **69** The story has slight variations according to different accounts: compare Pliny the Elder, *Natural History* 15.136–7; and Suetonius, *Galba* 1.1. See Flory (1995) on the omen. • **70** Plutarch, *Life of Antony* 35. There is a possibility that Octavia was not actually pregnant with Antonia Minor here, who was born in January 36, but another daughter, who did not survive: see note by Philip Stadter in the translation of Plutarch's *Life of Antony* by Waterfield (1999), 525. • **71** Plutarch, *Life of Antony* 31; Barrett (2002), 30 on the epithet being inspired by the occasion of Tarentum. • **72** See Wood (1999), 50, and figs 9 and 10; Zanker (1988), 61. • **73** Plutarch,

Life of Antony 36. • **74** Cicero, *Letters to Atticus* 15.15. • **75** There are countless books on Cleopatra and her legend, and I have no intention of trying to muscle in on their territory. For the essentials of Cleopatra's biography and her artistic representation, see Walker and Higgs (2001) and Kleiner (2005); on her afterlife, see Hamer (1993) and Wyke (2002), 195–320. • **76** Bondanella (1987), 215 on the exorbitant costs of making the film. • **77** See Walker and Higgs (2001), cat. 381–2 for watch-casings; cat. 390–1 for figurines, and Hamer (2001), 306, on Tiepolo's paintings, one of which can be seen in the National Gallery in London: cat. no. 6509: *The Banquet of Cleopatra*. • **78** See Pelling (2001), 298, on Plutarch's role in the creation of 'the Cleopatra legend'; and Pelling (1988), 37, on Shakespeare's reliance on North's translation of Plutarch, which was in itself indebted to a French translation of 1559. • **79** Pelling (1988), 33–6 on truth, fiction and reconstruction in Plutarch's account. • **80** Plutarch, *Life of Antony* 28–9. • **81** Plutarch, *Life of Antony* 53–4. See Fischler (1994), 118 on this passage. • **82** Cassius Dio, *Roman History* 49.38.1. • **83** On the grant of *sacrosanctitas* and *tutela* see Hemelrijk (2005); Flory (1993) and Purcell (1986), 85–7. On the concept of *tutela*, see Gardner (1986), 14f. • **84** This statue is discussed in more detail in Chapter 2 of this book. Flory (1993) cites several references in Roman literature to other women said to have been granted public statues, none of which survive, but they were virtually all women from Rome's mythical history; cf. Hemelrijk (2005). The only notable exception is a gilded statue of Cleopatra herself, reputed to have been set up by Julius Caesar in the temple of Venus Genetrix. On the statues of Livia and Octavia as a possible propagandistic reaction to this statue, see Flory, 295–6, and also Hemelrijk, 316, for the argument that it may in fact have been placed there by Octavian, not Julius Caesar. • **85** On statues and inscriptions honouring women in the Greek east, see Flory (1993), 296 and Hemelrijk (2005), 309; for more detail, see Smith (1987), Kajava (1990) and Van Bremen (1996). • **86** Positioning based on last visit in 2008. • **87** On the Velletri head (Museo Nazionale Romano inv. 121221), see Wood (1999), 52ff. • **88** Wood (1999), 96 on Livia's 'Claudian' overbite. • **89** Wyke (2002), 217–18, and Kleiner (1992), fig. 3. Cleopatra in turn put Antony on her own coins. • **90** Suetonius, *Augustus* 69. • **91** Ibid. • **92** Edwards (1993), 47. • **93** See Hamer (1993), 60ff on the episode in art. • **94** Pliny the Elder, *Natural History* 12.84 and 9.120–1. Edwards (1993), 186–91 on attacks on food and expenditure. • **95** On use of asses' milk in women's cosmetics, see Richlin (1995), 198f. • **96** Plutarch, *Life of Antony* 57. Interestingly, Plutarch in fact goes on to note that people pitied Antony rather than the tearful Octavia, because Cleopatra was no more beautiful than she was. • **97** Cassius Dio, *Roman History* 50.3 and Plutarch, *Life of Antony*, 58. • **98** Plutarch, *Life of Antony* 58–9 and Cassius Dio, *Roman History* 50.4. See Zanker (1988), 57–8 on the identification of Antony with eastern god Dionysus. • **99** Plutarch, *Life of Antony* 60; Cassius Dio, *Roman History* 50.4–6. • **100** Plutarch, *Life of Antony* 60; Cassius Dio,

Roman History 50.8. • **101** It may of course be that this was a story put about to make Octavian's victory seem even greater: see Pelling (1996) 55, n. 297. • **102** Plutarch, *Life of Antony* 65. • **103** Virgil, *Aeneid* 8.678–708. • **104** Plutarch, *Life of Antony* 85. Shakespeare, *Antony and Cleopatra*, 'It is well done, and fitting for a princess, / Descended from so many royal kings' (V.ii.325–6). • **105** See Flory (1987), on the criteria for awarding the name *Augusta*, throughout the Julio-Claudian period. • **106** D. Kleiner in K. Galinsky, ed. (2005) *The Cambridge Companion to Augustus* (Cambridge: Cambridge University Press), 203.

2 First Family: Augustus's Women

1 *I, Claudius*, Episode 2: 'Waiting in the Wings'. • **2** Michael Bloomberg, mayor of New York, famously maintains a public telephone directory listing. • **3** Suetonius, *Augustus* 72. On the oak crown and laurel trees decorating the front doorway, see Ovid, *Fasti* 4.953–4 and Augustus, *Res Gestae* 34; cf. Favro (1996), 203. • **4** Richardson (1992), 73; cf. obituary for Pietro Rosa in the 13 September 1891 edition of the *New York Times*. • **5** The lead pipe was stamped with the name Julia Aug[usta], Livia's honorary name in later life: see more in chapter three. This has led to the current identification of the house as the Casa di Livia, or the House of Livia. There is no conclusive evidence otherwise that Livia had her own separate residential quarters. Yet literary evidence does suggest that different members of the imperial household had their own quarters, and their own staff even. On the 'House of Livia', and the subsequently discovered 'House of Augustus', identified with Catulus's old home, see Tamm (1963), chapter iv; Richardson (1992), 73; and Claridge (1998), 128–31. • **6** Cassius Dio, *Roman History* 54.16.5; Ovid, *Epistulae Ex Ponto* 3.1.142. • **7** On Cornelia's dictum, see Valerius Maximus 4.4 pr.: Lefkowitz and Fant (1992), no. 259. • **8** On the empresses' toothpaste recipes, see Levick and Innes (1989), 17–18. • **9** See D'Ambra (2007), 60. • **10** Edwards (1993), 166 on use of local stone. Suetonius, *Augustus* 64 on the emperor's taking care that his daughters and granddaughters were taught spinning. • **11** Treggiari (1975), 54 and 74. • **12** For all of the above, see the seminal article by Treggiari (1975). On Roman women's footwear, see Croom (2000), 107 and Olson (2008), 56. • **13** This competition began in 1992 after Hillary Clinton provoked hostility by telling an interviewer she had chosen not 'to stay at home and bake cookies' – and was forced to atone by pitting her recipe against Barbara Bush's in a contest sponsored by *Family Circle* magazine. • **14** Suetonius, *Augustus* 64. Edwards (2000), 313, n. 76 suggests this explanation for the 'daily chronicles'. • **15** Octavia had five children of her own in all: her son Marcellus and two daughters Claudia Marcella Maior and Claudia Marcella Minor; and her two daughters by Antony: Antonia Maior and Antonia Minor. In the interests of clarity, I have omitted to go into detail about the lives of the two Claudia Marcellas, or the elder Antonia. • **16** Hemelrijk (1999), 17 on lack of information about Roman girls' childhoods; D'Ambra (2007), 62, and figs 25 and 26 on the ivory doll from the second-century sarcophagus of Crepereia Tryphaena in the Capitoline Museum in Rome. • **17** Olson (2008), 16; cf. Croom (2000), 91–3. • **18** Treggiari (1975), 52 and 56 on Dorcas and education of members of Livia's household. • **19** See Hemelrijk (1999), 79–88. • **20** Hemelrijk (1999), 22. • **21** Macrobius, *Saturnalia* 2.5.2. On Agrippina Maior's education, see Chapter 3 of this book. • **22** On the production and dissemination of ancient portraits, see Fittschen (1996), 42 and Wood (1999), 6. • **23** On Julia's *nodus*, see Wood (1999), 64 and figs. 20 and 21; also Wood (1999), 1–2 on portraits as ideals for other women of empire. • **24** Plutarch, *Peri tou Ei tou en delphois* 385F; cf. Barrett (2002), 37. • **25** Casson (1974), 180 on emperors' travelling style. • **26** Cassius Dio, *Roman History* 54.7.2. For a detailed account of Livia's and Augustus's travels, see Barrett (2002), 34–8. • **27** See Reynolds (1982), 104–6: Document 13. Inscriptions suggest her family had a patron-client relationship with the island: see Barrett (2002), 37. • **28** On the dates of their stay on Samos, see Barrett (2002), 37–8. On the statues on Samos, see Flory (1993), 303, n. 27. See also Reynolds (1982), 105 on the grant of freedom to the Samians. • **29** Fischler (1994), 118 and n. 10 for more examples. See also Dixon (1983). On Cleopatra: see Plutarch, *Life of Antony* 83. • **30** Excerpted from Cassius Dio, *Roman History* 55.16–21. • **31** Augustus's habit of consulting Livia on matters such as this calls to mind the modern parallel of Harry and Bess Truman. He publicised the fact that he consulted his wife on important decisions, and their lifetime's correspondence was published in 1983: see Caroli (1995), 203–4. • **32** D'Ambra (2007), 77–8 discusses this; cf. Lefkowitz and Fant (1992), nos. 242–6 for epistolary examples, and also the letters of second-century rhetorician Fronto on his relationship with his wife Cratia. • **33** Cassius Dio, *Roman History* 54.19.3 on Augustus's affair with Terentia; Suetonius, *Augustus* 62 on the emperor's love for Livia and *Augustus* 71 on her finding virgins for him. See also Aurelius Victor, *de Caesaribus* 1.7 and the anonymous *Epitome de Caesaribus* 1.23: the first says that Augustus was unlucky in marriage, the other that Livia was passionate about her husband. • **34** Pierre d'Hancarville (1787), *Monumens du culte secret des dames romaines*, no. IV, *Auguste et Livie*. My thanks to Daniel Orrells for drawing my attention to this work. • **35** Cassius Dio, *Roman History* 58.2.5. • **36** On Livia as a successor to women of the golden age, see *Consolatio ad Liviam* 343; on the naked men, see Cassius Dio, *Roman History* 58.2.4. • **37** Cassius Dio, *Roman History* 55.16.2. • **38** Suetonius, *Augustus* 63; Pliny the Elder, *Natural History* 7.13. • **39** See Barrett (2002), 35. • **40** His eldest son with Fulvia, Iullus Antyllus, had been put to death by Octavian after the latter's victory; but the younger son Iullus Antonius ended up marrying Octavia's daughter Claudia Marcella Maior. Antony also had three children with Cleopatra: the twins Alexander Helios and Cleopatra Selene, and a son Ptolemy Philadelphus. • **41** Suetonius, *Augustus* 28. • **42** See Kleiner

(1996), 32. On the portico's history, see Ridley (1986), 179–80. • **43** Pliny the Elder, *Natural History* 34.31. See Flory (1993), 290, and Plutarch, *Caius Gracchus* 4 on the statue. • **44** On the inscription, see Flory (1993), 290–2 and Hemelrijk (2005), 312f on the possibility that Augustus had a Greek statue of a goddess recycled to depict Cornelia. • **45** Marcellus's qualities: Velleius Paterculus 93. On Tiberius's appearance and demeanour, see Suetonius, *Tiberius* 68. • **46** It was not Julia's first betrothal – a former engagement when she was two years old to Antony's eldest son Antyllus was dissolved when the two men's brief rapprochement of 37 BC collapsed. • **47** Fantham (2006), 29. • **48** On Marcellus's death and tributes: Fantham (2006), 29f. Seneca, *Consolatio ad Marciam* 2 reports that Octavia never recovered from Marcellus's death. • **49** Donatus, *Life of Virgil* 32. The work was based on one by Suetonius. • **50** Siegfried and Rifkin, eds. (2001) 16–22, on Ingres's *Virgil* compositions. • **51** Graves (1934), 37; BBC's *I, Claudius*, episode 1. • **52** See note 50. • **53** Currie (1998), 147. On Cleopatra, see Plutarch, *Antony* 71. • **54** Juvenal, *Satires* 6.629–33. • **55** Marcellus Empiricus, *De Medicamentis liber* 15.6 and 35.6: see Barrett (2002), 111–12 for a translation. On Octavia's toothpaste, see Levick and Innes (1989), 17–18. • **56** Seneca, *Consolatio ad Marciam* 2. • **57** On marrying after being widowed, see Severy (2003), 53; on marriage laws, in general, see Gardner (1986), chapter three. • **58** Cassius Dio, *Roman History* 54.6.5 on Maecenas's advice to Augustus; for Octavia's role in the affair see Plutarch, *Antony* 87. Agrippa's birthdate is not certain, but thought to have been around 63 BC. • **59** On the Villa Boscotrecase, see Crawford (1976) and von Blanckenhagen and Alexander (1962); on Agrippa owning a house in the region see Cassius Dio, *Roman History* 54.28.2. Matteo della Corte, who published the only record of the finds and floor plan of the villa in 1922, believed that it belonged to Julia's and Agrippa's son Agrippa Postumus, thanks to the discovery of a tile bearing his name. He was challenged in 1926 by Michael Rostovtzeff, whose theory that the house originally belonged to Agrippa before passing to his son's hands, is now widely accepted. • **60** For more on the Boscotrecase paintings, see Ling (1991), 55–6; and Fantham (2006), 77. • **61** D'Ambra (2007), 96; Wallace-Hadrill (1988), 50–2 on the absence of upstairs floors from Pompeii houses, which may be significant. • **62** Treggiari (1975), 52 on Livia's *cubicularii*. Note that although 'bedroom' is the usual translation for *cubiculum*, it does not quite have the same connotations as our modern notion of that room. The key point is that it is the most private room in the house. • **63** Suetonius, *Augustus* 72 on Julia Minor's palace and Augustus's country residences. • **64** The act was called *adoptio* when the person being adopted – who could be male or female – was previously in the *patria potestas* of another; when, however, the male being adopted was himself not under paternal power (*sui iuris*) or even a *paterfamilias* himself, it was called *adrogatio*. Women could not be adopted under this latter arrangement, nor could they initially adopt themselves although later emperors seem to have permitted it, in cases where a woman had lost children. • **65** C. B. Rose (1997), 225, n. 154. • **66** The exact date of Julia's and Agrippa's marriage is unknown, as are the years of the births of their daughters Julia and Agrippina Maior, but based on an estimate of the years of their marriages, and the birth dates of their own children, a birth date before 16 BC is probably accurate for Julia – who may in fact have been born before Lucius – and after 16 BC for Agrippina: see Fantham (2006), 108. • **67** C. B. Rose (1997), 13: I. Priene 225. See Fantham (2006), 66 for more inscriptions honouring Julia. • **68** On senators being banned from marrying women from certain classes, see Gardner (1986), 32. On inheritance to anyone beyond sixth degree of relation, see Gardner (1986), 178. • **69** *Lex Papia Poppaea* of AD 9. See Edwards (1993), 40. • **70** Gardner (1986), 77. These figures were later revised to a period of two years' grace for widows, and eighteen months' grace for divorcees. There was some form of redress for women who could prove they had been wrongly accused of adultery, or whose husbands had cheated on them with married women: see Gardner (1986), 90. • **71** Gardner (1986), 178. • **72** On the *ius trium liberorum*, see Gardner (1986), 20. Women still *in patria potestas*, in other words women whose fathers were still alive, had to wait until those fathers' deaths before the law could apply to them. On the statue, see Zanker (1988), 157. • **73** Edwards (1993), 34. This translation of *Res Gestae* 8.5 is hers. • **74** Edwards (1993), 56. On the unlikelihood of the law being enforced very often, see Gardner (1986), 121 and 124. • **75** Suetonius, *Augustus* 34.2 on the public demonstrations; Vistilia's case actually came to trial during the reign of Augustus's successor Tiberius: see Tacitus, *Annals* 2.85. • **76** Ovid, *Amores*, 1.4. On Augustus's new seating laws, see Rawson (1987), 85, 89 and 113; also Edmondson (1996), 88–9. • **77** See Richlin (1992), 76 and Fantham (2006), 81. • **78** Macrobius, *Saturnalia* 2.5.9. On Domitius Marsus as a source, see Fantham (2006), 81; and Richlin (1992), 69 and n. 7. On the alleged affair with Sempronius Gracchus while married to Agrippa, see Tacitus, *Annals* 1.53. • **79** Macrobius, *Saturnalia* 2.5.2. • **80** Macrobius, *Saturnalia* 2.5.3–5. • **81** Croom (2000), 74 and 87, and Olson (2008), 32. • **82** On colours, see Ovid, *Ars Amatoria* 3.169; on vulgar colours, see, for example, Martial *Epigrams* 10.29.4; cf. Olson (2008), 11–12. • **83** Olson (2008), 55–7 and Croom (2000), 104–7 and Stout (1994) on women's accessories. • **84** On cost of clothes-making, see Croom (2000), 21; on Coan silk, see Olson (2008), 14 and Croom (2000), 121. • **85** Macrobius, *Saturnalia* 2.5.7. • **86** Olson (2008), ch. 2 *passim* on the cosmetic arts employed by Roman women, and 73 on the treatment for grey hair. • **87** D'Ambra (2007), 115 on the jar of face cream, and the health of the cosmetics industry. • **88** On the rhetoric of female self-adornment, see Wyke (1994). • **89** Seneca, *Consolatio ad Marciam* 2.3–4 on Octavia's behaviour after Marcellus's death. • **90** Richardson (1992), 248. • **91** See Flory (1998), 491 on the role of Roman women in a triumph. • **92** Suetonius, *Tiberius* 7. • **93** Fronto, *De Nepote Amisso, ii* (Haines. Vol. 2. 229–9). • **94** On Drusus's banquet, see Cassius Dio,

Roman History 55.2.4; and Flory (1998), 491. • **95** *Consolatio ad Liviam*, 133–7. My own translation. Suetonius, *Claudius* 1 reports that Augustus was suspected of having a hand in Drusus's death, on the grounds of his stepson's reputation for favouring republicanism, although Suetonius himself dismisses these allegations. For more on this sequence of events, see Barrett (2002), 42–4. • **96** See Flory (1993), 299. • **97** Seneca, *Consolatio ad Helviam*; cf. Lefkowitz and Fant (1992), no. 261. • **98** See Flory (1993), 297–300. • **99** See Kleiner (1996), for a reassessment of women's roles in this regard; also Purcell (1986), 88–9 on Livia's contribution. • **100** Cassius Dio, *Roman History* 55.8.4 on Vipsania Polla's racetrack. • **101** On the festival of Bona Dea, see Beard, North and Price (1998), Vol. 1: 296–7 and Takács (2008), 101; cf. Juvenal, *Satires* 6.314–41. See Takács (2008), 23 on provenance of temple of Fortuna Muliebris. • **102** Kleiner (1996), 32–3. • **103** Strabo 5.3.8. Barrett (2002), 200–1 for more detail on the portico. • **104** The portico has long since vanished, but a surviving fragment of a marble plan of Rome dating from the era of the Severan dynasty has preserved for us the existence, location and general floor plan of the building. It was built in the shape of a rectangle 115 m by 75 m (377 feet by 246 feet) around a courtyard garden. Ovid, *Ars Amatoria* 1.71–2, tells us there was an art gallery there, and Pliny the Younger mentions meeting friends there: *Epistulae* 1.5.9. • **105** Kleiner (1996), 33–4 on Eumachia's portico, and other women who commissioned their own buildings. • **106** Severy (2003), 131f on the cult of *Concordia*, and 134 for the idea of Mother's Day and the festival of the *Matralia*. • **107** See Suetonius, *Tiberius* 10; Tacitus, *Annals* 1.53; Velleius Paterculus 2.99; Cassius Dio, *Roman History* 55.9.5–8. • **108** See previous note, and Fantham (2006), 83 on Tiberius's possible motives. • **109** Macrobius, *Saturnalia* 2.5.3; 2.5.6; 2.5.8. • **110** See Ovid, *Fasti* 2.127f on this event. On Julius Caesar's consecration, see Beard, North and Price (1998), Vol. 1, 208. • **111** Velleius Paterculus, 2.100; Seneca, *de Beneficiis* 6.32; Pliny the Elder, *Natural History* 21.8–9; Tacitus, *Annals* 3.24; Suetonius, *Augustus* 64–5; Cassius Dio, *Roman History* 55.10.12–16. See also Syme (1984) on 'the crisis of 2 BC'. • **112** Cassius Dio, *Roman History* 55.10.14. • **113** See Ferrill (1980) for an overview of scholarship on the reasons for Julia's downfall. • **114** Seneca, *De Brevitate Vitae* 4.5: translation from Richlin (1992), 68. • **115** Edwards (1993), 42–7 and Fischler (1994), 118–19 on adultery and political invective. • **116** Varner (2004), 46. • **117** Linderski (1988), 190. See Suetonius, *Augustus* 65 and 101; Cassius Dio, *Roman History* 56.32.4. • **118** Wood (1999), 30. • **119** Wood (1999), 30 and 74; C. B. Rose (1997), 21 and Varner (2006), 86–8 on possible treatment of Julia's portraits after her exile. • **120** Wood (1999), 69–70, and Fantham (2006), 137. • **121** On subsequent judgements of Julia, see Fantham (2006), chapter 10. • **122** Suetonius, *Tiberius* 11 and 15; Barrett (2002), 52. • **123** See Olson (2008), 15, on the *toga virilis*. • **124** C. B. Rose (1997), 18. • **125** Barrett (2002), 53 for a summary. • **126** Potter (2007), 55. An obvious exception of course was Britain, conquered by Claudius in AD 43.

• **127** Suetonius, *Augustus* 97–9; Velleius Paterculus 2.123. • **128** Cassius Dio, *Roman History* 56.42–6 • **129** Tacitus, *Annals* 1.5–6: Cassius Dio, *Roman History* 56.30. • **130** These questions rear their heads again in chapters four and six with regard to Agrippina Minor and Plotina: see Barrett (1996), 24–5 on the Agrippina comparison. • **131** *My Turn: The Memoirs of Nancy Reagan* (1989), 216, cited by Caroli (1995), 279.

3 Family Feud: The People's Princess and the Women of Tiberius's Reign

1 *Les femmes illustres, or Twenty heroick harangues of the most illustrious women from history*. London: Dormand Newman (1693), trans. James Innes. • **2** This description of Agrippina's homeward journey is based on and excerpted from Tacitus, *Annals* 3.1. • **3** On Scribonia's age and longevity, see Fantham (2006), 17–18 and 158, n. 30. We know that she was still alive in 16, two years after Julia's death, as Seneca (*Epistulae Morales* 70, 12) refers to her giving counsel to her relative Scribonius Libo, when he was implicated in a conspiracy against Tiberius. • **4** Germanicus's birth date was 24 May, in either 15 or 16 BC. I have opted for the later date here. • **5** On the journey between Brundisium and Rome along the Appian Way, see Casson (1974), 194f. • **6** For description of Tiberius, see Suetonius, *Tiberius* 21. • **7** Suetonius, *Augustus* 101. • **8** Cassius Dio, *Roman History* 56.10 and 56.32. He mistakenly refers to the sum of 100,000 sesterces, rather than the 100,000 asses specified by the *Lex Voconia*. See Barrett (2002), 175 on this, and on the *Lex Papia Poppaea* of 9, which curbed the inheritance rights of women with less than three children, with a handful of special exceptions, including Livia herself: see Cassius Dio, *Roman History* 55.2.5–6. On the value of different forms of Roman currency: *Oxford Classical Dictionary*, 3rd edn, s.v. 'Roman coinage'. • **9** Crawford (1976), 39; Barrett (2002), 174–5 and 183. • **10** Tacitus, *Annals* 1.8; Suetonius, *Augustus* 101; Cassius Dio, *Roman History* 56.46.1. Cf. Barrett (2002), 151; C. B. Rose (1997), 22. • **11** See Flory (1987), 113 and *passim*, on the history and meaning of the name *Augusta*, and for an overview of who was granted the title during the Julio-Claudian era. • **12** Flory (1987), 114 on the prevalence of this belief in the nineteenth century; also Barrett (2002), 154. • **13** Tacitus, *Annals* 1.14; Suetonius, *Tiberius* 50. Cf. Flory (1987), 121. • **14** Wood (1999), 90. • **15** Cassius Dio, *Roman History* 57.12.2; Tacitus, *Annals* 2.42; Josephus, *Antiquities* 17.1.1; C. B. Rose (1997), 23 on Tiberius's response to the ambassador from Gytheum, in Sparta. • **16** Barrett (2002), 164–5. • **17** See Treggiari (1975) on these individuals. • **18** Ovid, *Epistulae ex Ponto* 3.1, my own translation. • **19** *Senatus Consultum de Cn. Pisone Patre*: see Griffin (1997), 252. • **20** Cassius Dio, *Roman History* 57.12.2. • **21** Cassius Dio, *Roman History* 57.12.5: cf. Purcell (1986), 90. • **22** Suetonius, *Augustus* 50. Cf. Cassius Dio, *Roman History* 61.33.12 on Agrippina Minor accompanying Claudius to supervise fire-fighting efforts in a display of her overbearing desire to share in his power. This indicates that this was very much one of the duties of concerned emperors and their families, yet also that it could be seen as evidence of a woman becoming too visible. • **23** I follow the line taken by Susan Wood, who in turn subscribes to the theory of Rolf Winkes on the dating of Livia's portraits: see Wood (1999), 91–5; cf. Winkes (2000) and Bartman (1998). • **24** Virgil, *Aeneid* 1.279. • **25** See Fejfer (2008), 345 on male and female portraits. • **26** Purcell (1986), 91–2, and nn. 76–7. • **27** See Caroli (1995), chapter two, on first ladies of the nineteenth century. • **28** Kokkinos (2002),11. • **29** *Consolatio ad Liviam* 299–328. • **30** Kokkinos (2002), 15–16. On *univirae* and opinions about the remarriage of divorcees, see Gardner (1986), 51. • **31** Kokkinos (2002), 16 and 148: cf. Valerius Maximus 3.3. • **32** On Antonia's staff, see Kokkinos (2002), 57–65 and Treggiari (1973). • **33** Crawford (1976), 43; see also Kokkinos (2002), 71–2. • **34** Kokkinos (2002), 75–7. • **35** On women's management of business and own affairs, see Gardner (1986), 21–2, and 234–5. On the raising of children under Livia's and Antonia's aegis, see, for example, Suetonius, *Otho* 1. • **36** Kokkinos (2002), 25. • **37** Josephus, *Antiquities* 18.143; cf. 18.165. • **38** See Suetonius, *Claudius* 2–4. • **39** Suetonius, *Claudius* 2. • **40** Suetonius, *Claudius* 4. • **41** Suetonius, *Claudius* 3. • **42** Suetonius, *Claudius* 41. • **43** *Senatus Consultum de Cn. Pisone Patre*: see Griffin (1997), 253. • **44** Wood (1999), 160 and 175. • **45** Erhart (1978), 194. • **46** Antonia's Wilton House portrait: see Erhart (1978); Wood (1999), 158–62; Kokkinos (2002), 122–5; Kleiner and Matheson (1996), 60. • **47** On the statue group at Lepcis Magna: Kokkinos (2002), 109–10; Wood (1999), 110–11; Barrett (2002), 208; C. B. Rose (1997), 29. Drusus Minor was flanked by his own mother Vipsania, and his wife Livilla. • **48** C. B. Rose (1997), 30. • **49** On Agrippina Maior's date of birth, see Chapter 2. • **50** Suetonius, *Augustus* 86. The *Senatus Consultum de Gn. Pisone Patre* also comments on Augustus's esteem for his granddaughter Agrippina: see Griffin (1997), 253. • **51** Hicks (2005a), 68; Rendall (1996). Tacitus, *Annals* 1.33. • **52** See Tacitus, *Annals* 2.43.6, on Agrippina's celebrated fertility. • **53** Suetonius, *Caligula* 8–9. • **54** Tacitus, *Annals* 1.41. See O'Gorman (2000), 71–2 on similarities between this and Velleius Paterculus 2.75.3 when Livia flees with her infant son Tiberius in her arms. Cf. Suetonius, *Augustus* 48 and Cassius Dio, *Roman History* 57.5.2 for alternative versions of the story. • **55** Barrett (1996), 27 on Agrippina's pregnancy. • **56** Tacitus, *Annals* 1.69. • **57** Tacitus, *Annals* 3.33. • **58** Tacitus, *Annals* 3.34. • **59** See Santoro L'hoir (1994). • **60** Tacitus, *Annals* 1.69. • **61** Tacitus, *Annals* 2.41. See Flory (1998) on the presence of women at Roman triumphs, esp. 491–2 on Germanicus's triumph. • **62** Tacitus, *Annals* 2.42. • **63** Kokkinos (2002), 17 and 43. • **64** Wood (1999), 145 on this notion. • **65** Tacitus, *Annals* 2.59. • **66** C. B. Rose (1997), 24–5. • **67** Wood (1999), 217–37 on Agrippina's portrait types. On curly hair and fertility, see Wood (1999), 130–1 and 228. • **68** Tacitus, *Annals* 1.33 and 2.43. • **69** *Das Senatus Consultum de Cn. Pisone Patre*: see Griffin (1997), 253. See also Tacitus, *Annals* 4.12. • **70** Josephus is our source for this story, although he gives slightly different versions of it in the *Antiquities* (17.1.1) and in the *Jewish War* (1.28.6): in the latter, Livia is actually the go-between for Salome's request to Herod that she be allowed to marry Syllaeus, but Salome is then forced to marry Herod's choice, Alexas, against her will. • **71** Tacitus, *Annals* 2.34. • **72** Tacitus, *Annals* 4.22. • **73** See Fischler (1994), 126f on attitudes to women's interference in the judicial process. • **74** Tacitus, Annals 2.43 and 2.55 • **75** Tacitus, *Annals* 2.71–75. • **76** Tacitus, *Annals* 2.82; 3.3 and 3.6. • **77** Tacitus, *Annals* 3.10–15. • **78** On the discovery of the tablet, see Eck, Caballos and Fernández (1996); also Griffin (1997), 249–50, and the review of Eck, Caballos and Fernández by Harriet Flower, in *Bryn Mawr Classical Review* 97.7.22. • **79** See Griffin (1997), 258 and Flower (2006), 250 on Tacitus's factual accuracy; also Kokkinos (2002), 38. • **80** Tacitus, *Annals* 3.17. • **81** Trans. M. Griffin (1997), 252: lines III–120. • **82** See also the *Consolatio ad Liviam* 47–50 for the repetition of the same idea. • **83** C. B. Rose (1997), 26 on the arch marking a milestone for women; see also Flory (1998), 491–2; and Kokkinos (2002), 37–9. • **84** Trans. M. Griffin (1997), 253: lines 136–146. I have amended the translation of 'Livia' here to make clear it refers to Germanicus's sister Livilla. • **85** Tacitus, *Annals* 3.4, • **86** Drusus Minor's son Tiberius Gemellus was the fourth possible contender, though see Tacitus, *Annals* 4.3 where Tiberius claims he would now call on Germanicus's sons to provide him with support during his rule. • **87** Tacitus, *Annals* 4.12. • **88** Barrett (2002), 172. • **89** I concur with Wood (1999), 109, who argues that this is indeed a portrait of Livia and not a personification: cf. Barrett (2002), 93. • **90** C. B. Rose (1997), 28. • **91** Wood (1999), 209 on forms of transportation for women; Flory (1987), 119 on accumulation of Vestals' honours. • **92** Cassius Dio, *Roman History* 57.12.6 on people saying Livia's bullying had driven Tiberius to Capri; Tacitus, *Annals* 4.57 for alternative that it was Sejanus's intriguing that compelled him to go. • **93** Suetonius, *Tiberius* 51. • **94** Tacitus, *Annals* 4.52; cf. Suetonius, *Tiberius* 53 on Agrippina saying more than was wise about her husband's death. • **95** My own translation of Suetonius, *Tiberius* 53; same line quoted in Tacitus, *Annals* 4.52. • **96** Tacitus, *Annals* 4.53. • **97** Tacitus, *Annals* 4.54. See Barrett (2002), 98 on Agrippina's being placed under house arrest. • **98** See Treggiari (1975). • **99** First World War veteran Henry Allingham, who died in 2009 at the age of 113, put his longevity down to 'whisky and wild women', while port was said to have featured heavily in the diet of Jeanne Calment, the world's oldest woman before her death in 1997 at the age of 122. On the diet and the satirical treatment of the elderly, see Parkin (2002), 253. On Livia's love for Pucine wine, see Pliny the Elder, *Natural History* 14.8. • **100** See Barrett (2002), Appendix 5 on Livia's birth date and death date. • **101** Velleius Paterculus, 2.130; cf. Suetonius, *Tiberius* 51 and Tacitus, *Annals* 5.1. • **102** Davies (2000), 103. • **103** Cassius Dio, *Roman History* 58.2. See Barrett (2002), 188f on Livia's benefactions. • **104** Cassius Dio, *Roman History* 58.2; also Cassius Dio, *Roman History* 54.35.5 and Flory (1993), 305–6 on Octavia's and Livia's funeral honours. Tacitus, *Annals* 5.2

on rejection of deification for Livia. • **105** Caligula and Nero were descendants of Augustus through Agrippina Maior, daughter of Julia; Claudius was linked to Augustus only through his grandmother Octavia. • **106** See Wood (1999), 121–2 on the Lepcis Magna example. • **107** Barrett (2002), 223. • **108** See Claudian, *Epithalamium* 10, on the marriage of the Emperor Honorius and Maria, whereby the groom gave the bride some of Livia's jewels; discussed later in chapters four and nine. • **109** Tacitus, *Annals* 5.1. • **110** Tacitus, *Annals* 5.3. • **111** Tacitus, *Annals* 5.4; 6.23; Suetonius, *Tiberius* 53. • **112** Staley (1965), 10; Duffy (1995), 212. • **113** Hicks (2005a), 45–6. • **114** *The Gentleman's Magazine*, 28 December 1800. See Flora Fraser (1986), *Beloved Emma: The Life of Lady Emma Hamilton* (London: Weidenfeld & Nicolson), 276–8 on this episode. • **115** Tacitus, *Annals* 6.26. • **116** Tacitus, *Annals* 5.3. • **117** Josephus, *Antiquities* 18.181–2. • **118** Cassius Dio, *Roman History* 58.11.3–7. Tacitus, *Annals* 4.11 on Apicata's role. See Wood (1999), 181–4 on Livilla's death. • **119** Tacitus, *Annals* 6.2. On Livilla as the first, see Kleiner (2001), 49–50. On *damnatio memoriae* generally, see Flower (2006), Elsner (2004) and Varner (2001) and (2004).

4 Witches of the Tiber: The Last of the Julio-Claudian Empresses

1 A description of Livia in a review of the BBC's *I, Claudius* by Gerald Clarke, in *Time* magazine, Monday 14 November 1977: cited in Joshel (2001), 153. • **2** Charlotte Brontë, *Jane Eyre* (1847), 338 (Penguin Classics). • **3** Tacitus, *Annals* 14.9.3. • **4** See D'Arms (1970), 134ff on the attractions of the Bay of Naples. • **5** Suetonius, *Augustus* 64.2, on the letter to L. Vinicius: 'You were very ill-mannered to visit my daughter at Baiae'. • **6** On the fishpond, see Pliny the Elder, *Natural History* 9.172. On Antonia's inheritance of the villa, see d'Arms (1970), 68–9. On the identification of Bauli as Bacoli, and the location of Antonia's villa, see D'Arms (1970) 181, and Kokkinos (2002), 153. • **7** Suetonius, *Nero* 5. • **8** Suetonius, *Tiberius* 75. • **9** Suetonius, *Caligula* 23; cf. Cassius Dio, *Roman History* 58.7. • **10** Suetonius, *Caligula* 27; 32; 37; on death of Tiberius, see *Caligula* 12; cf. *Tiberius* 73 for alternative version. • **11** Suetonius, *Caligula* 15; Cassius Dio, *Roman History* 59.3.3–5. The inscription from Agrippina's ash cist has been recovered from the mausoleum: illustration in Kokkinos (2002), 29, fig. 18. • **12** C. B. Rose (1997), 32. • **13** C. B. Rose (1997), 33: on personifications of *Securitas*, *Concordia* and *Fortuna*. • **14** Suetonius, *Caligula* 15 and *Claudius* 11.2. See Flory (1993), 123–4 on evidence for posthumous conferral of the title, and the evolving meaning of *Augusta* throughout the early imperial period. • **15** On Junia Claudilla, see Suetonius, *Caligula* 12; on Livia Orestilla, Lollia Paulina and the birth of Julia Drusilla, see Suetonius, *Caligula* 25; on Caesonia, see Cassius Dio, *Roman History* 59.23.7 and Suetonius, *Caligula* 25. • **16** See Wood (1999), 211. On promiscuity, incest and poisoning reflecting anxieties about queenship throughout the ages, see Hunt (1991), 123; also Heller (2003). • **17** See C. B.

Rose (1997), 35–6. • **18** Kokkinos (2002), 36. • **19** Suetonius, *Caligula* 23. • **20** On Agrippina Minor's and Julia Livilla's exile, see Cassius Dio, *Roman History* 59.22.8. On Caesonia's murder, see Josephus, *Antiquities* 19.2.4. • **21** Suetonius, *Claudius* 10. • **22** Suetonius, *Claudius* 11; Cassius Dio, *Roman History* 60.5.2. See Flory (1995) on the deification of Roman women. • **23** Barrett (1996), 84 on Passienus Crispus's estate. • **24** Claudius had two children by his first marriage, a son who died in an accident, and a daughter, Claudia, whom he disowned after his divorce from the child's mother. Claudia Antonia, his daughter by Aelia Patina, was banished during Nero's reign after refusing to marry the emperor in the wake of Poppaea's death. • **25** Messalina's mother Domitia Lepida Minor was the daughter of Antonia Minor's elder sister Antonia Maior. Messalina's father Marcus Valerius Messala Barbatus was the son of another daughter of Octavia's, Claudia Marcella Minor. • **26** Cassius Dio, *Roman History* 60.22.2 and Suetonius, *Claudius* 17. On Messalina at Claudius's triumph, see Flory (1998), 493. • **27** Cassius Dio, *Roman History* 60.12.5. • **28** Juvenal, *Satires* 6.117; cf. Wyke (2002), 325, n. 6. • **29** On Dumas, see Wyke (2002), 324, n. 3; on Sade, see Cryle (2001), 283, citing Sade, *Oeuvres complètes* 9:44; on anti-venereal propaganda, see Kidd (2004), 343-4. See also Wyke (2002), 390 and n. 82 on Messalina as a star of adult films. • **30** Juvenal, *Satires* 6.117–32. • **31** Cassius Dio, *Roman History* 60.18.1–3. Augustus too is said to have indulged in similar practices of course. • **32** Pliny the Elder, *Natural History* 10.172. The world record entry is in A. Klynne, C. Klynne and H. Wolandt (2007) *Das Buch der Antiken Rekorde* (C. H. Beck Verlag, Munich). I have not seen the volume in question, but its publication was covered in the British press. • **33** Cassius Dio, *Roman History* 60.8.5; Tacitus, *Annals* 14.63.2; Suetonius, *Claudius* 29 and Seneca, *Apocolocyntosis* 10.4. On Livilla's urn, see Davies (2004), 103: Braccio Nuovo inv. 2302. On the episode as a whole, see Barrett (1996), 81–2. • **34** On Appius Silanus, see Cassius Dio, *Roman History* 60.14.2–4; on Marcus Vinicius, see Cassius Dio, *Roman History* 60.27.4. Other victims included Catonius Justus, a praetorian guard who threatened to inform Claudius of Messalina's scandalous exploits: see Cassius Dio, *Roman History* 60.18.3. On Antonia's granddaughter Julia, the daughter of Drusus Minor, see Cassius Dio, *Roman History* 60.18.4. See Bauman (1992), 170 on the echoes of Fulvia's sexually aggressive behaviour in Messalina. • **35** My thanks to Simon Goldhill for pointing this detail out to me. • **36** Cassius Dio, *Roman History* 60.14.3–4; 60.15.5–16.2 on the machinations of the freedmen; Suetonius, *Claudius* 29 and Cassius Dio, *Roman History* 60.18 on the emperor's being at the mercy of freedmen and wives. • **37** Her reported lovers included the actor Mnester and the freedman Polybius. • **38** Barrett (1996), 88. • **39** Tacitus, *Annals* 11.11. • **40** Tacitus, *Annals* 11.1–3; cf. Cassius Dio, *Roman History* 60.27.2–4. The fact that other women from imperial history, for example, Pulcheria, are said to have eliminated opponents for the sake of a garden or vineyard implies some recycling of stereotypes across the centuries. • **41** According to a news report from *The Times*, 17 May 2007, mosaic remains of the gardens have been brought to light in excavations 30 feet (9 metres) below the ground, near the Spanish Steps. • **42** This account is based principally on Tacitus, *Annals* 11.26–38, which gives the fullest account of the episode. See also Cassius Dio, *Roman History* 60.31.1–5, and Suetonius, *Claudius* 36–7. • **43** Tacitus, *Annals* 11.27. • **44** Fagan (2002), and Wood (1992), 233–4 on the possible reasons for Messalina's fall. • **45** Hunt (1991), 122 on Marie-Antoinette and Messalina. • **46** Flower (2006), 185 and C. B. Rose (1997), 41. • **47** See Wood (1992) and (1999), 276f. • **48** Robert Graves (1934), *I, Claudius*, 381 (London: Penguin, 2006). • **49** *Octavia* 266–8. • **50** Ps-Seneca, *Apocolocyntosis* 11. • **51** Wyke (2002), 335–43 on Cossa's play, and see also chapters 9–10 *passim* for further examples of Messalina's reception during the late nineteenth and twentieth centuries. • **52** See Ginsburg (2006), 17 on this meeting. • **53** On the incest law, see Gardner (1986), 36–7; and Bauman (1992), 180. • **54** C. B. Rose (1997), 42; Ginsburg (2006), 57. • **55** On Agrippina's coin portraits, see Wood (1999), 289–91 and C. B. Rose (1997), 42. • **56** Wood (1999), 306–7; Ginsburg (2006), 91f. • **57** Tacitus, *Annals* 12.7.3, • **58** Tacitus, *Annals* 12.26. Flory (1987), 125–6 and 129–31 on the changing meaning of *Augusta*. On Agrippina publicising her son as heir, see, for example, Cassius Dio, *Roman History* 60.33.9. • **59** Tacitus, *Annals* 12.27.1. See Barrett (1996), 114–15. • **60** Barrett (1996), 124. • **61** On Agrippina's sculpture types, and the resemblance to her parents, see Ginsburg (2006), 81; Wood (1999), 297. • **62** Tacitus, *Annals* 12.37.4; Cassius Dio, *Roman History* 60.33.7. • **63** Suetonius, *Caligula* 25. • **64** On Agrippina as a *dux femina*, see Santoro l'hoir (1994), 21–5, and *passim*; also Ginsburg (2006), 26–7. • **65** Suetonius, *Claudius* 18; Tacitus, *Annals* 12.43 on the grain shortages; Barrett (1996), 121–2 on this period. • **66** Tacitus, *Annals* 12.56–57; Cassius Dio, *Roman History* 60.33.3. • **67** Pliny the Elder, *Natural History* 33.63; Tacitus, *Annals* 12.56.3. • **68** Tacitus, *Annals* 12.57. • **69** Tacitus, *Annals* 12.7.2. • **70** Tacitus, *Annals* 12.22.1–3; Cassius Dio, *Roman History* 60.32.4. • **71** See O'Gorman (2000), 71–2 and 129–32 on parallels between Livia and Agrippina Minor in Tacitus's account. • **72** Claudius's death: Suetonius, *Claudius* 43–5; Tacitus, *Annals* 12.66–9; Cassius Dio, *Roman History* 60.34.1–3; Josephus, *Antiquities* 20.8.1. • **73** On the Sebasteion at Aphrodisias, see Smith (1987); also Ginsburg (2006), 89; and C. B. Rose (1997), 47–8, and Gradel (2002), 21. • **74** C. B. Rose (1997), 47. Wood (1999), 293 notes that although Antony and Octavia had been featured in a similar pose, those were issues from Antony's eastern mints, not Rome. • **75** Cassius Dio, *Roman History* 61.3.2. • **76** Tacitus, *Annals* 13.2.3. • **77** Ibid. • **78** Suetonius, *Vespasian* 9. Gradel (2002), 68: the temple was later destroyed again, though the Forma Urbis gives us an idea of its ground plan. • **79** Tacitus, *Annals* 13.5.1. Barrett (1996), 150: the practice of the Senate meeting on the Palatine was not without precedent, but certainly such arrangements had never been made for the convenience of a woman.

• **80** Tacitus, *Annals* 13.5.2. There is a striking modern parallel here in that Julia Tyler, the vivacious second wife of tenth US President John Tyler (1841–5) apparently caused offence by receiving guests seated on a raised platform: Caroli (1995), 46. • **81** Tacitus, *Annals* 13.6.2. • **82** Suetonius, *Nero* 52. Santoro L'hoir (1994), 17–25 for more on a woman's unsuitability for power. • **83** Tacitus, *Annals* 13.12.1. • **84** Tacitus, *Annals* 13.12–13; Suetonius, *Nero* 28 says that Agrippina and Nero consummated passion in a litter, and that he even chose a mistress who looked like her. • **85** Tacitus, *Annals* 13.1.3. • **86** Cassius Dio, *Roman History* 61.7.3; Tacitus, *Annals* 14. • **87** Tacitus, *Annals* 13.15–16. • **88** Tacitus, *Annals* 13.18–19. Suetonius, *Nero* 34. • **89** Tacitus, *Annals* 13.21.5. • **90** Tacitus, *Annals* 13.19–22 on whole episode. • **91** On Agrippina's ownership of Antonia's villa, see Tacitus, *Annals* 13.18.5; Bicknell (1963); Kokkinos (2002), 154–5. • **92** Tacitus, *Annals* 13.45–6; cf. Suetonius, *Otho* 3. • **93** Juvenal, *Satire* 6.462. On Poppaea's reputed habits, see Griffin (1984), 101; on the coincidence of Claudia Octavia's name, see Vout (2007), 158. • **94** See Vout (2007), 158–9. • **95** The following is closely based on Tacitus, *Annals* 14.3f; see also Cassius Dio, *Roman History* 62.12–13. • **96** Tacitus, *Annals* 14.4.4. • **97** Cassius Dio, *Roman History* 62.13.5. • **98** Jean de Outremeuse, 14th century: cited in G. Walter (1957), *Nero*, 264 (London: Allen & Unwin). See also Elsner and Masters (1994), 1. • **99** Tacitus, *Annals* 14.12.1. • **100** Suetonius, *Nero* 39. Greek numbers are expressed by letters. If you convert the letters of Nero's name when written in Greek, into numbers, they add up to 1,005, as do the letters for the Greek for 'murdered his own mother': see note to Graves's translation. • **101** Suetonius, *Nero* 34. • **102** *Octavia*, 629–45. The subject of the play is the fate of Claudia Octavia, Nero's first wife, who was divorced and banished to Pandateria in order that Nero might marry Poppaea. She was later put to death. • **103** *Octavia*, 609–11. On Seneca's disputed authorship and the afterlife of the play, see Kragelund (2007), 24f. • **104** Kragelund (2007), 27. • **105** Ginsburg (2006), 80; see also Wood (1999), 251–2. • **106** Moltesen and Nielsen (2007), esp. 9–10, 113 and 133. • **107** See Dean and Knapp (1987), 114–19 on Handel's opera. • **108** Wood (1999), 302–4 on Agrippina's posthumous sculptural tradition. • **109** Tacitus, *Annals* 14.9.1. • **110** *Letters Written in France in the Summer 1790: Helen Maria Williams*, ed. N. Fraistat, and S. S. Lanser, (2001), 173 (Peterborough, Ontario Broadview Press). • **111** Tacitus, *Annals* 4.53.3; Pliny the Elder, *Natural History* 7.46. • **112** See Hemelrijk (1999), 186–8 on Agrippina's 'memoirs'. • **113** William Wetmore Story, *Poems* 1:16 cited by W. L. Vance (1989), in *America's Rome* (New Haven and London: Yale University Press).

5 Little Cleopatra: A Jewish Princess and the First Ladies of the Flavian Dynasty

1 'Kleopatra im kleinen': Theodor Mommsen, *Römische Geschichte*, V, 540 (1885). • 2 *Bérénice*, Act IV, lines 1208–9, trans. R. C. Knight (1999). • 3 On the simultaneous appearance of the two works and the tale's popularity in 17th-century France and Britain, see Walton (1965), 10–16; on the theme of Rome in early modern Europe, see Schroder (2009), 390. See also the appendix of Jordan (1974) for a thorough review of Berenice's appearances in literature post-antiquity. • 4 Walton (1965), 12. Marie Mancini: see Antonia Fraser (2006) *Love and Louis XIV: The Women in the Life of the Sun-King*, 52 (London: Weidenfeld & Nicolson); also Schroder (2009), 392. For Henrietta's involvement, see L. Auchincloss (1996), *La Gloire: The Roman Empire of Corneille and Racine* (Columbia, SC: University of South Carolina Press), 61–2, citing Voltaire's preface to *Tite et Bérénice*. • 5 This account of Agrippa's activities is based on Josephus, *Antiquities* 18.6. See also Jordan (1974), 30–48. • 6 Josephus, *Antiquities* 19.5.1. • 7 Josephus, *Antiquities* 18.8.2; 19.4.1; 19.5.1. • 8 Josephus, *Antiquities* 19.5.1. • 9 Josephus, *Antiquities* 19.8.2 and 20.5.2. • 10 Josephus, *Antiquities* 20.78.3. On the incest rumour, see *Antiquities* 20.145; Juvenal, *Satires* 6.157–8. The marriage with her uncle Herod produced two sons, Bernicianus and Hyrcanus, but little more is known about them. • 11 Macurdy (1935), 246 and Jordan (1974), 113. • 12 The plea for clemency on behalf of Justus dates from the period of the Jewish Revolt: Josephus, *Life* 65. On the audience with St Paul: *Acts* 25–6. On Berenice as a woman of wealth, see Jones (1984), 61. • 13 Josephus, *Jewish Wars* 2.15.1. • 14 Josephus, *Jewish Wars* 2.16–17.1. • 15 Suetonius, *Vespasian* 4; Josephus, *Jewish Wars* 3.1–2. • 16 Josephus, *Jewish Wars* 3.7. • 17 *Agrippa's Daughter*, 234–5 (1981 edition). • 18 *The Jew of Rome* (1935), 94–5. • 19 Tacitus, *Histories* 2.2. • 20 Vout (2007), 158. • 21 Suetonius, *Nero* 35; Tacitus, *Annals* 16.6.1–2. • 22 Suetonius, *Nero* 49; Cassius Dio, *Roman History* 63.29.2. • 23 Suetonius, *Galba* 5; Barrett (2002), 223. • 24 Suetonius, *Otho* 1 on links to Livia. • 25 Tacitus, *Histories* 2.81. • 26 Cf. Crook (1951), 163. • 27 Suetonius, *Galba* 1. • 28 Suetonius, *Vespasian* 20–2 on the new emperor's character and favoured pastimes. • 29 Boyle and Dominik (2003), 4–5 and 10–11 on Vespasian's populist behaviour and the creation of a new aristocracy of power. • 30 Suetonius, *Otho* 10. • 31 Tacitus, *Histories* 2.64 on Galeria Fundana, and 2.89 on Sextilia. Cf. Suetonius, *Vitellius* 14 where it is said that Vitellius either starved or gave poison to his mother, thus casting him as another Nero. Flory (1993), 127–8 on award of title of *Augusta*. • 32 Suetonius, *Vespasian* 3; Cassius Dio, *Roman History* 65.14. • 33 Cassius Dio, *Roman History* 65.14 on Caenis's influence and wealth. • 34 Richardson (1992), 48. • 35 Trans. Kokkinos (1992), 58. The altar was displayed in an exhibition on Vespasian at the Colosseum in 2009. • 36 Lindsey Davis's official website, referring to

her 1997 novel *The Course of Honour*. • **37** Suetonius, *Domitian* 12. • **38** See Kleiner (1992b), 177–81 and (2000), 53 on Flavian female portraiture and the absence of a tradition under Vespasian and Titus. • **39** See Varner (1995), 188. • **40** McDermott and Orentzel (1979), 73. Phyllis: Suetonius, *Domitian* 17. • **41** Cassius Dio, *Roman History* 65.15.3–4 on Berenice's arrival at Rome. For arguments over chronology of her arrival and departure, see Braund (1984) and Keaveney and Madden (2003). • **42** Cassius Dio, *Roman History* 65.15.4; see also Braund (1984). • **43** Juvenal, *Satires* 6.156–7. Croom (2000), 128 and Roussin (1994), on lack of representation for Jewish costume. • **44** We should not infer that Juvenal was buying wholesale into such disapproving tendencies, but rather parodying the reaction itself. • **45** See Livy, 5.50.7; 34.1–8; Olson (2008), 106. For later citations of the fourth-century Roman matrons, see Hicks (2005a), 43 and 65. • **46** Treggiari (1975), 55. • **47** On Roman jewellery and attitudes to display, see Fejfer (2008), 345–8; Wyke (1994) and Olson (2008), 54–5 and 80f. • **48** Jordan (1974), 212. • **49** Quintilian, *Institutio Orationis* 4.1.19. • **50** See Crook (1951), 169–70 and Young–Widmaier (2002) for readings of this episode. • **51** Cassius Dio, *Roman History* 65.15.5. • **52** The *Epitome de Caesaribus* 10.4 claims that Titus in fact had Caecina killed on the suspicion that he had raped Berenice. This runs contrary to the accounts of Suetonius and Cassius Dio: see Crook (1951), 167. On the reaction to Berenice's stay in Rome as a whole, see Braund (1984). • **53** Suetonius, *Titus* 7; also Boyle (2003), 59, n. 180. • **54** Suetonius, *Titus* 7. • **55** On Berenice's possible return, see Cassius Dio, *Roman History* 66.18.1; also B. W. Jones (1984), 91. • **56** Our only possible clue to her movements after this point lies in the 1920s discovery of an inscription in Beirut, recording the dedication there by Berenice of a colonnade: see Boyle (2003), 59, n. 180; Macurdy (1935), 247 and Hall (2004), 63. • **57** *Daniel Deronda*, chapter xxxvii, 392–3 (New York, Oxford World Classics, 1998). • **58** Cassius Dio, *Roman History* 66.26.3 and Suetonius, *Titus* 10. Burns (2007), 93 on the line as a possible lament for Berenice. • **59** Suetonius, *Domitian* 3.1. Poppaea and her baby daughter Claudia Octavia were both given the appellation *Augusta*, but there is no evidence that Statilia Messalina, Nero's third and final wife, received the title. See Flory (1987), 126. • **60** Varner (1995), 194. • **61** Flory (1987), 129–31. • **62** Varner (1995), 194. • **63** Suetonius, *Domitian* 8. Temple of Minerva: Loven (1998), 90. • **64** Ummidia Quadratilla: D'Ambra (2007), 134; and Pliny the Younger, *Letters* 7.24. • **65** Boyle (2003), 24f. • **66** Martial, *Epigrams* 8.36. See Tomei (1998), 45–53 on the Domus Flavia. • **67** Matheson (2000), 73 and 216. • **68** See also Bartman (2001), 10 on how a loosely woven fabric stiffened with beeswax or resin could be used as a mould through which to pull the sitter's hair. • **69** Ovid, *Amores* 1.14.1–2 and 42–3. On dyes used in women's hairdressing, see also Olson (2008), 72–3. • **70** See plates section for an illustration of such a comb from the British Museum. • **71** Juvenal, *Satires* 6.490. • **72** Lefkowitz and Fant (1992), no. 334 (8959). • **73** Juvenal, *Satires* 6.502–4. See Fittschen (1996), 42 and 46 on women emulating the empresses' styles. • **74** Bartman (2001), 7–8. • **75** Bartman (2001), 5f. • **76** See Matheson (2000), 132 and n. 52. See Varner (1995) for full details of Domitia's portrait tradition. • **77** Kleiner and Matheson (1996), 169 and cat. no. 125. San Antonio Museum of Art: 86.134.99. • **78** Bartman (2001), 8–9. • **79** Cassius Dio, *Roman History* 67.3.2. • **80** Julia and Demosthenes: Macrobius, *Saturnalia* 1.11.17; Claudia Octavia and the flute-player: Tacitus, *Annals* 14.60. See Varner (2004), 86-7 and Vinson (1989), 440 on sexual misconduct as a pretext for political attack. • **81** D'Ambra (1993), 9. • **82** Wood (1999), 317 on comparison to Livia's portraits; Kleiner (1992b), 178 on the diadem; cf. Varner (1995), 194–5, who says that Domitia was the first woman to have the diadem as part of official type. • **83** See Wood (1999), 21, n. 35. • **84** Suetonius, *Domitian* 22. • **85** Cassius Dio, *Roman History* 67.3.2. • **86** Cassius Dio, *Roman History* 67.4.2. • **87** Suetonius, *Domitian* 3.1; cf. *Domitian* 22. Cassius Dio, *Roman History* 67.3.2 claims that Julia's and Domitian's relationship continued even after Domitia's recall. • **88** McDermott and Orentzel (1979), 93. • **89** Wood (1999), 318. • **90** Juvenal, *Satires* 2.29–33. See also Pliny the Younger, *Letters* 4.11.7. • **91** The sainthood was withdrawn from her by the Roman Catholic Church in 1969. This Flavia Domitilla was the daughter of Vespasian's daughter of that name. • **92** Cassius Dio, *Roman History* 67.15.2–4; Suetonius, *Domitian* 14; Aurelius Victor, *de Caesaribus* 11. On Domitian's reflective walls, see Tomei (1998), 48. • **93** Suetonius, *Domitian* 1 and 17. The bodies of Vespasian and Titus, which had initially been placed in the mausoleum of Augustus, were later transferred here: Johnson (2009), no. 8 in appendix A. • **94** Procopius, *Secret History* 8.15–20. • **95** Pliny the Younger, *Panegyricus* 52.4–5, trans. in Varner (2004), 112–13. • **96** Varner (1995), 202–5 and fig. 13, and Matheson (2000), 132. • **97** Varner (1995), 205; McDermott and Orentzel (1979), 81f. For more on brick-stamps as evidence of female wealth, see Setälä (1977).

6 *Good Empresses: The First Ladies of the Second Century*

1 Marguerite Yourcenar, *Memoirs of Hadrian* [1951] (2000), 5, Trans. Grace Frick. • **2** Colossus of Memnon: Brennan (1998), 215–7; Hemelrijk (1999), 164–70. • **3** Trans. Lefkowitz and Fant (1992), 10, no. 26. • **4** Hemelrijk (1999), 164 and n. 87 on the erosion of the poems. • **5** For a useful summary of the history of Roman imperial conquest, s.v. 'Rome' in the *Oxford Classical Dictionary*, 1329. • **6** On the *Historia Augusta*'s unreliability: see Goodman (1997), 4–5. • **7** See Pliny the Younger, *Panegyricus* 7–8; and Griffin (2000), 94–5. • **8** Boatwright (2000), 61; Keltanen (2002), 140f. • **9** Her birthplace is deduced from the fact that after her death, Hadrian erected a basilica at Nemausus in her honour: see McDermott (1977), 195 and Keltanen (2002), 109f on Plotina's background. • **10** Boatwright (1991), 518 on the *arriviste* status of Plotina and her cohort. • **11** Cassius Dio, *Roman History* 68.5.5.

• **12** See Roche (2002), 41–2. • **13** Feldherr (2009), 402 points out that Pliny's panegyric cannot be taken as a straightforward homage to Trajan, but the point about Plotina representing the ideal Roman woman remains the same. • **14** Pliny the Younger, *Panegyricus* 83. • **15** Roche (2002), 48–9. • **16** Pliny, the Younger, *Panegyricus* 84.2–5. See McDermott (1977), 196. • **17** Boatwright (1991), 521–3. Note the slight uncertainty over Matidia Minor's and Vibia Sabina's full names. • **18** Keltanen (2002), 111 on *Pudicitia* as a first and Vesta as an unusual association. • **19** Although they do not tend to appear on state monuments: Kleiner (2001), 53. • **20** Fittschen (1996), 42. • **21** Fittschen (1996), 42 on Marciana's style, and on other female hair-styles from the period not sported by imperial women. Cf. Kleiner and Matheson (1996), cat. no. 21. • **22** Boatwright (1991), 515 and 532. • **23** Cassius Dio, *Roman History* 69.1; Aurelius Victor, *de Caesaribus* 13; *Historia Augusta* (Hadrian) 4.10. • **24** See Bauman (1994), on the tradition in literature and history, beginning with Livia. • **25** Caroli (1995), 148–9 on the Edith Wilson affair; and 164 on the Florence Harding controversy; the book in question was *The Strange Death of President Harding: From the Diaries of Gaston B. Means as Told to May Dixon Thacker* (New York: 1930). • **26** *Historia Augusta* (Hadrian) 2.10. • **27** Trans. P. J. Alexander (1938), 'Letters and speeches of the Emperor Hadrian', *Harvard Studies in Classical Philology* 49: 160–1, with modifications after Hemelrijk (1999), 117. • **28** Trans. J. H. Oliver (1989), *Greek Constitutions of Early Roman Emperors from Inscriptions and Papyri*, 177 (Document 73), (Philadelphia: American Philosophical Society) • **29** See also Boatwright (1991), 531. • **30** Lucian, *de Mercede Conductis* 33–4. • **31** Hemelrijk (1999), 37–41 and 51–2 on attitudes to philosophy and women's learning. • **32** Boatwright (1991), 521 on Plotina's brickworks. For her coins, see Keltanen (2002), 113. • **33** Cassius Dio, *Roman History* 69.10.3. Plotina's ashes: Kleiner (1992b), 262. • **34** Keltanen (2002), 114, n. 55; Boatwright (1991), 533; Opper (2008), 211–12. • **35** Opper (2008), 211. See Davies (200), 118; Opper (2008), 211 • **36** See Davies (2000), 118; Opper (2008), 211. • **37** Boatwright (1991), 522 and Hemelrijk (1999), 120–1. • **38** Opper (2008), 242f. • **39** *Historia Augusta* (Hadrian) 11.3; *Epitome de Caesaribus* 14.8. • **40** Lefkowitz and Fant (1992), no. 186. • **41** Boatwright (1991), 523. • **42** *Historia Augusta* (Hadrian) 11.3. • **43** Burns (2007), 135. For more modern verdicts on Sabina, see Burns (2007), 125–6, citing M. Grant (1975), *Twelve Caesars*, 2 (New York: Charles Scribner's Sons); also Perowne (1974), 117; Royston Lambert (1984), *Beloved of God: the Story of Hadrian and Antinous*, 39 (London: Phoenix). My thanks to Carrie Vout for pointing out this last example to me. • **44** Keltanen (2002), 118 and Kleiner (1992b), 241–2. • **45** Brennan (1998), 233 and n. 73 on number in entourage. On sources for Hadrian's and Antinous's relationship, see Vout (2007), 54f. • **46** Vout (2007), 18 on the power differential in male sexual relations. • **47** On same-sex emperor relationships, such as that of Nero and Sporus, see Vout (2007), 18 and 138, and chapter two on Hadrian and Antinous and the creation of the latter's legend. • **48** Brennan (1998), 221 and n. 34. • **49** See Vout (2007), 54–6 on various explanations for Antinous's death. • **50** Cassius Dio, *Roman History* 69.11.5. • **51** On dating of the poems, see Hemelrijk (1999), 164–8. • **52** We should note that Sulpicia's authorship is disputed. • **53** Hemelrijk (1999), 177 and n. 134. • **54** Hemelrijk (1999), 168, citing E. Bowie (1990) 'Greek Poetry in the Antonine Age', in D. A. Russell, ed., *Antonine Literature* (Oxford: Clarendon Press), 62. • **55** Brennan (1998), 229f suggests Damo could have been Claudia Damo of Athens and that she was one of Hadrian's entourage. • **56** Hemelrijk (1999), 118. • **57** *Historia Augusta* (Hadrian) 23.9. • **58** On this relief, see Davies (2000), 105–6; Kleiner (1992b), 254; Beard and Henderson (1998), 213–14. • **59** Keltanen (2002), 124. • **60** Opper (2008), 59 on this theory. • **61** Davies (2000), 109. • **62** S. Perowne (1960), *Hadrian* (London: Hodder & Stoughton), 117. • **63** *Historia Augusta* (Antoninus Pius) 5.2 and 6.4–6; Birley (2000a), 47. • **64** Birley (2000a), 28f on the family background of the *gens Annia*, including on possible family links to Scribonia and Salonia Matidia. • **65** Birley (2000b), 151. • **66** See Freisenbruch (2004), for an overview of Fronto's letters. • **67** Fronto to Marcus Aurelius: Vol. 1, p. 183 of Haines. • **68** Marcus Aurelius to Fronto: Vol. 1, p. 197 of Haines. • **69** Marcus Aurelius to Fronto: Vol. 1, p. 115 of Haines. • **70** Fronto to Marcus Aurelius: Vol. 1, p. 125 of Haines. • **71** *Discourse on Love*, 9: Vol. 1, p. 29 of Haines. Domitia Lucilla on philosophy: *Historia Augusta* (Marcus Aurelius) 2.6. See Hemelrijk (1999), 68–9 on role of mothers in sons' education. • **72** Van den Hout (1999), 56, n. 21.15. • **73** Marcus Aurelius, *Meditations* 1.3 • **74** Fronto to Marcus Aurelius: Vol. II, pp. 119–20 of Haines. On Marcus's and Faustina's children, see Appendix 2F in Birley (2000a). • **75** *Historia Augusta* (Antoninus Pius) 6.7–8 and 8.1; Keltanen (2002), 128; Davies (2000), 109. • **76** Keltanen (2002), 126–7; cf. Beard and Henderson (1998), 217. • **77** Keltanen (2002), 128–32 on Antoninus's and Annia Galeria's marriage as a model. Antoninus's letter to Fronto: Vol. 1, p. 129 of Haines. • **78** On the apotheosis relief, see Kleiner (1992b), 287–8; Beard and Henderson (1998), 193–4 and 217–19. • **79** Fittschen (1996), 44. • **80** Keltanen (2002), 135. • **81** Cassius Dio, *Roman History* 71.1.3. • **82** Boatwright (1991), 522 on possible location of Matidia's residence. Marcus Aurelius to Fronto on his daughters staying with Matidia: Vol. 1, p. 301 of Haines. • **83** *Historia Augusta* (Marcus Aurelius) 9.4–6 and 20.7; *Historia Augusta* (Verus) 7.7. • **84** *Historia Augusta* (Marcus Aurelius) 20.6–7; Cassius Dio, *Roman History* 73.4.5. • **85** Cassius Dio, *Roman History* 72.10.5; *Historia Augusta* (Marcus Aurelius) 17.4; 26.8. • **86** *Historia Augusta* (Marcus Aurelius) 26.5; Cassius Dio, *Roman History* 71.29.1. On Faustina's probable age, see Birley (2000), 34–5. • **87** Cassius Dio, *Roman History* 72.29; *Historia Augusta* (Marcus Aurelius) 19.1–9; *Historia Augusta* (Verus) 10.1. • **88** Keltanen (2002), 138–40; Davies (2000), 109. • **89** Cassius Dio, *Roman History*, 73.4.5–6; Herodian 1.8.3–5.

7 *The Philosopher Empress: Julia Domna and the 'Syrian Matriarchy'*

1 Syrian matriarchy: Balsdon (1962), 156; I. Shahid (1984) (Washington, D.C.: Dumbarton Oats Research Library and Collection), *Rome and the Arabs*, 42; W. Ball (2000), 415; Burns (2007), 201. • 2 Caracalla's last words to his mother Julia Domna: Cassius Dio, *Roman History* 78.2.3. • 3 See Varner (2004), 177. • 4 Philostratus, *Lives of the Sophists* 622. • 5 Gorrie (2004), 66, n. 25 citing the publications by A. von Domaszewski which form the original basis for this view; see also Levick (2007), 1 and 167, n. 3. Gibbon's view: *The Decline and Fall of the Roman Empire* (ed. J. B. Bury) Vol. 1, 139 and 171 (London: Methuen) • 6 Bowersock (1969), 102, n. 5, citing M. Platnauer (1918) *The Life of Emperor Lucius Septimius Severus*, 128. (Oxford; Oxford University Press) • 7 On Severus's arrival in Emesa, and the general locale, see Birley (1971), 68–71; also Ball (2000), 36f and Levick (2007), chapter one, *passim*. • 8 Levick (2007), 18; Birley (1971), 72 and 222. • 9 Levick (2007), 19 on Julia Domna's probable age. • 10 See Birley (1971), 73–6; Levick (2007), 28–9 on this sequence of events. • 11 See Zwalve (2001) and Birley (1971), 72 on legal dispute concerning one Julius Agrippa. • 12 Cassius Dio, *Roman History* 75.3; *Historia Augusta* (Severus) 3.9. • 13 Levick (2007), 34 on their property portfolio. • 14 Cassius Dio, *Roman History* 72.21.1–2. • 15 Marcia: Cassius Dio, *Roman History* 72.22.4; Herodian 1.17.7–11. • 16 Birley (1971), 97. • 17 Flavia Titiana: *Historia Augusta* (Pertinax) 6.9. • 18 *Historia Augusta* (Albinus) 9.5; *Historia Augusta* (Severus) 11.9. • 19 See E. Doxiadis, (1995) *The Mysterious Fayum Portraits: Faces from Ancient Egypt* (London: Thames & Hudson), 88 and 225a on the Berlin tondo. It is housed today in the Staatliche Museen, in Berlin, where it was acquired in the 1930s. • 20 *Historia Augusta* (Severus) 19.7–9 on Severus's appearance. • 21 Fejfer (2008), 348. • 22 Baharal (1992), 114. • 23 Gorrie (2004), 63–4 and n. 14. See also Lusnia (1995), 123 on Commodus's wife Crispina also holding this title. • 24 Cascio (2005), 137–9. • 25 Cassius Dio, *Roman History* 77.9.4. See Cooley (2007), 385–6. • 26 See Newby (2007), 224 and Cooley (2007), 385–7 on Severus's attempts to link himself to the Antonines. • 27 Newby (2007), 222–4 on Severan dynastic portraits; Lusnia (1995), 138–9 on Julia's key role in imperial propaganda. • 28 Birley (1971), 107. • 29 Cassius Dio, *Roman History* 79.30.3. On promotion of Domna's relatives, see Birley (1971), 134; Levick (2007), 48. • 30 Birley (1971), 76 and 35. • 31 *Historia Augusta* (Severus) 18.8. • 32 See Hemelrijk (1999), 306, n. 130. • 33 Cassius Dio, *Roman History* 77.1.2. • 34 Cassius Dio, *Roman History* 76.15. • 35 Herodian 3.10.8; Cassius Dio, *Roman History* 77.3. • 36 Varner (2004), 164–5 on Plautilla's portrait typology. • 37 Cassius Dio, *Roman History* 76.15. • 38 Philostratus, *Life of Apollonius* 1.3,. • 39 Whitmarsh (2007), 33 on talk of a 'salon' culture; see also Bowersock (1969), 101–2. • 40 Philostratus, *Lives of the Sophists* 622. See also Hemelrijk (1999), 124. • 41 Bowersock (1969), 101–9, on Victor Duruy's *Histoire de Rome* of 1879 as the root of speculation

about Julia Domna's circle; cf. Hemelrijk (1999), 122–4. • **42** Philostratus, *Epistle* 73: trans. Penella (1979), 163; cited in Hemelrijk (1999), 125. • **43** Hemelrijk (1999), 25 and 233, n. 38 on Julia Domna being the first woman since Cornelia known to have studied rhetoric; see also Levick (2002) on rarity of women philosophers. • **44** Lucian, *De Mercede Conductis* 36. • **45** Martial, *Epigrams* 11.19. • **46** Birley (1971), 149. • **47** Kampen (1991), 231. • **48** Croom (2000), 79–80. On the Severan arch at Lepcis Magna, see Newby (2007), 206–11; Varner (2004), 178–9. • **49** Lusnia (1995), 138. • **50** Kleiner and Matheson (1996), 152. • **51** Gorrie (2004), 69. • **52** Lusnia (1995), 120–1. • **53** Kleiner and Matheson (1996), 85–6, no. 46. • **54** Cassius Dio, *Roman History* 76.16. • **55** Cassius Dio, *Roman History* 77.4. • **56** Varner (2004), 163–8 on the mutilation of Plautinaus's and Plautilla's portraits; see also Kleiner and Matheson (1996), 86. • **57** Cassius Dio, *Roman History* 77.7. • **58** Birley (1971), 170. • **59** Cassius Dio, *Roman History* 77.12. • **60** Herodian 3.14.2 and 3.14.9. • **61** Cassius Dio, *Roman History* 77.16.5. • **62** Lusnia (1995), 131–2 on Domna as *mater Augustorum*, and on the new coin issue; see also Gorrie (2004), 64. • **63** Cassius Dio, *Roman History* 77.14.7. • **64** Cassius Dio, *Roman History* 77.15.2. • **65** Herodian 3.15.6–7. • **66** Herodian 4.1.5; 4.3.5. • **67** Herodian 4.3.8. • **68** See Lusnia (1995), 133–4. • **69** Cassius Dio, *Roman History* 78.2.2–6. • **70** Varner (2004), 176–7. • **71** Varner (2004), 182. • **72** Varner (2004), 184. • **73** Cassius Dio, *Roman History* 78.2.5–6. • **74** Herodian 4.6.3. • **75** Cassius Dio, *Roman History* 78.10. • **76** Herodian 4.9.3. • **77** Hemelrijk (1999), 306, n. 130 on 'Neronisation' of Caracalla, as discussed by R. J. Penella (1980), in 'Caracalla and his Mother in the *Historia Augusta*', *Historia* 29: 382–5. • **78** Cassius Dio, *Roman History* 79.4.3. • **79** Cassius Dio, *Roman History* 79.23.1. • **80** Cassius Dio, *Roman History* 79.24; Herodian 4.13.4. • **81** Cassius 79.24. See Levick (2007), 145, and Varner (2004), 168, n. 116. • **82** Levick (2007), 145 on Julia Domna's deification. • **83** Herodian 5.3.2–3; *Historia Augusta* (Macrinus) 9; Cassius Dio, *Roman History* 79.30. See Kosmetatou (2002), 401 and Birley (1971), 191–3 on this sequence of events. • **84** Herodian 5.4.1–4; Cassius Dio, *Roman History* 79.30f. A rumour was apparently planted that Avitus was actually the product of an affair between Soaemias and Caracalla: Herodian 5.3.10. • **85** Cassius Dio, *Roman History* 78.38. On destruction of portraits, see Varner (2004), 185. • **86** *Historia Augusta* (Elagabalus) 4.1. • **87** Icks (2008), 175. • **88** *Historia Augusta* (Elagabalus) 2.1. • **89** *Historia Augusta* (Elagabalus) 21.4; Herodian 5.5.5–7. • **90** Herodian 5.7–8. • **91** Cassius Dio, *Roman History* 80.20; cf. Herodian 5.8.9. Varner (2004), 199. • **92** Fragment of Zonaras 12.15. Trans. E. H. Cary (in translation of Cassius Dio, *Roman History*) • **93** Kosmetatou (2002), 399–400 and 414. • **94** *Historia Augusta* (Elagabalus) 18.3. • **95** Kosmetatou (2002), 402–11 on the public image of Mamaea in particular. • **96** Herodian 6.1.9–10; *Historia Augusta* (Alexander) 20.3; Kosmetatou (2002), 409–10. • **97** *Historia Augusta* (Alexander) 26.9; Eusebius, *Ecclesiastical History* 6, 21, 3f. • **98** Kosmetatou (2002), 412. • **99** Herodian 6.8.3. • **100** Herodian 6.9.6–7.

8 The First Christian Empress: Women in the Age of Constantine

1 Speech at the Edinburgh Rectorial Election, *The Times*, 8 November 1951: cited by Drijvers (2000), 28, from Donat Gallagher, ed. (1983) *The Essays, Articles and Reviews of Evelyn Waugh* (London: 1983), 407. • 2 See Pohlsander (1995) and Harbus (2002) for detailed overviews. • 3 Drinkwater (2005), 28. • 4 Zenobia: Drinkwater (2005), 51–3 and Sartre (2005) 513–15. • 5 The key sources on Helena's early background are Ambrose, *De Obitu Theodosii* 42; Eutropius, *Breviarum* 10.2; the anonymous *Origo Constantini* 2.2; Philostorgius, *Ecclesiastical History* 2.16; and Zosimus 2.8.2 and 2.9.2. See also Drijvers (1992), Pohlsander (1995) and Harbus (2002). • 6 See McClanan (2002), 180 on narrative patterns of redemption in the lives of female saints. In the sixth century, for example, the humble background of Justinian's wife Theodora morphed into the story of the reformation of a born courtesan. • 7 See Lieu (1998), 149f on this tradition. • 8 Pohlsander (1995), 15. • 9 See Drijvers (1992), 17–18 on legality of the marriage and use of the term *uxor*; also Leadbetter (1998), 78–9 on concubinage and legitimacy. • 10 Gardner (1986), 58 on imperial use of concubines; see also Arjava (1996), 205–10. • 11 On Constantine's need to prove his legitimacy and discourage unfavourable rumours about Helena's and Chlorus's relationship, see Leadbetter (1998), 79–81. For the suggestion that Constantine deliberately suppressed details about his and Helena's background, see Harbus (2002), 10. • 12 On the arrangement of the tetrarchy: see Bowman (2005), 74–6, and Rees (2004), 76–80. • 13 Leadbetter (1998), 77–82 for more on links between the marriages and the creation of the tetrarchy; see also Pohlsander (1995), 17, Harbus (2002), 19 and Lenski (2006), 59–60. • 14 See Lancon (2000), 18, and *Panegyrici Latini* 12.19.3. • 15 See Rees (2004), 46–51. • 16 Elsner (1998), 84–6. • 17 Croom (2000), 101. • 18 Lactantius, *On the Deaths of the Persecutors* 7.9. • 19 For conclusions on this point, see Pohlsander (1995), 14–15 and Drijvers (1992), 21. E. D. Hunt (1982), 30 suggests she would have accompanied her son to Nicomedia, however. • 20 Zosimus 2.9.2. • 21 Drijvers (1992), 22–3; see also Harbus (2002), 44f and Pohlsander (1995), 7–8, and chapter 4, *passim*, on Helena's links to Trier. • 22 Trier ceiling: M. E. Rose (2006); Ling (1991), 186f, Pohlsander (1995), 37–46. • 23 On changing attitudes to jewellery in late antiquity, see Fejfer (2008), 349–51 and M. E. Rose (2006), 101. • 24 *Panegyrici Latini*.6.2; see also R. Rees (2002), *Layers of Loyalty in Latin Panegyric, AD* 289–307 (Oxford: Oxford University Press), 168–171 on the 'truth' of the panegyricist's claim. • 25 On the deaths of Prisca and Valeria in the summer of 314: see Lactantius, *On the Deaths of the Persecutors* 39–41 and 50–1. • 26 The key accounts are Eusebius, *Life of Constantine* 1.28: Lactantius, *On the Deaths of the Persecutors* 44. See Cameron and Hall (1999), 204–6. • 27 See Lenski (2006), 72–3 for an overview of Licinius's downfall; Eusebius, *Life of Constantine* 3.47 on Helena's receiving title of *Augusta*. • 28 Beard, North and Price (1998), 298–9 on the female principle

and Christianity, and on elite female adherents to the new faith. Augustine, *City of God* 1.19 scrutinises the example of Lucretia to reproach those critics of Christian women who did not commit suicide after the sack of Rome in 410. • **29** Constantine's laws: see Gardner (1986), 120; Cameron (1993), 58; G. Clark (1993), 21–36; Evans-Grubbs (1995), 317-21. • **30** Elsner (199), 40–1 and 96 on the imagery of the Proiecta casket. • **31** Cameron (1992), 177; also Clark (1986), 25–6. • **32** On the new ascetic vogue and tension with traditional Roman values, see the excellent monographs of Cooper (1996) and Clark (1986). • **33** Gardner (1986), 78. • **34** G. Clark (1993), 51. Evans-Grubbs (1995), 137–8 on the political stratagem behind Constantine's laws. • **35** E. A. Clark (1986), 47–52. • **36** E. A. Clark and Richardson (1996), 3; E. A. Clark (1986), 46–52. • **37** Cooper (1996), 113–15. • **38** Cooper (1996), 144, on prevailing importance of kinship; Elsner (1998), on art and imperial power in late antiquity. • **39** Brubaker (1997), 57–8. On *nobilissima femina*, see Pohlsander (1995), 20. • **40** On Helena's and Fausta's coin portraits, see Walter (2006), 20f, and Pohlsander (1995), 179–84. For reasons of time and clarity, I have omitted further mention of the younger Helena, but she went on to marry Julian the Apostate, and died in 360. • **41** It may, admittedly, represent another empress of the period, but I have leaned towards the interpretation of C. Kelly (1999), in G. W. Bowersock, P. Brown and O. Grabar, eds., *Late Antiquity: a Guide to the Postclassical World* (Cambridge, MA and London: Belknap Press), 173. • **42** On Constantine's rhetoric of legitimacy, see Leadbetter (1998), 80–1; on the inscriptions, see Drijvers (1992), 45–54. • **43** McClanan (2002), 16. On the evidence for Helena's portraits, see Drijvers (1992), 189–94 and Pohlsander (1995), 167–78. • **44** Haskell and Penny (1981), 133 and fig. 69; C. M. S. Johns (1998) *Antonia Canova and the Politics of Patronage in Revolutionary and Napoleonic Europe* (Berkeley: University of California Press), 112–16. • **45** McClanan (2002), 185. • **46** Mango (1994), 146 and Pohlsander (1995), 3–4. • **47** Helena and Rome: Drijvers (1992), 30–4; Pohlsander (1995), 73f; Brubaker (1997), 57–8. • **48** On the plundering of Rome's artistic treasures for the beautification of Constantinople, see Elsner (1998), 73; on the refusal to make the sacrifice to Jupiter, see Lenski (2006), 79. The practice of sacrifice was finally outlawed by Theodosius I, in 391. • **49** Eusebius, *Ecclesiastical History* 10.9.4, trans. Pohlsander (1984), 98. On confusion of the two Helenas, see Drijvers (1992), 29. • **50** Pohlsander (1984), 98. • **51** For an overview of accounts of Crispus's and Fausta's deaths, see Pohlsander (1984) and Woods (1998). • **52** Frakes (2006), 94 on the Potiphar scenario. • **53** Woods (1998), 77. • **54** Lefkowitz and Fant (1992), no. 355. • **55** On the inscription from Sorrento, see Brubaker (1997), 59; McClanan (2002), 16–17; Frakes (2006), 94–5. • **56** Eusebius, *Life of Constantine* 3.44. For Eusebius's full account of Helena's journey, see *Life of Constantine* 3.42–7. See also E. D. Hunt (1982); Drijvers (1992), chapter 5, *passim*; Pohlsander (1995), chapter 8, *passim*. • **57** E. D. Hunt (1982), 33; Lenski (2004), 16. • **58** Drijvers (1992), 34–7; Pohlsander (1995), 24; Lieu (2006),

303–4 • **59** Helena as a trailblazer: see E. D. Hunt (1982), 49; Brubaker (1997), 58–62; Holum (1999), 70–5. • **60** Eusebius, *Life of Constantine* 3.30–2. • **61** Helena's involvement: see Pohlsander (1995), 102f; Harbus (2002), 20–1. • **62** E. D. Hunt (1982), 39. • **63** Ambrose, *De obitu Theodosii* 45. • **64** See E. D. Hunt (1982), 42–7; Drijvers (1992), 4–6; Pohlsander (1995), 107. • **65** For an overview of the arguments as to whether Helena really discovered the Cross, see Pohlsander (1995), chapter 9, *passim*. • **66** Drijvers (2000), 47–8; Harbus (2002), 20–2; Lieu (2006), 304–5 • **67** Pohlsander (1995), 228. • **68** Pohlsander (1995), 217. Walter (2006), 37–52 on development of this type in art. • **69** Pohlsander (1995), 117 and E. D. Hunt (1982), 48. • **70** Eusebius, *Life of Constantine* 3.46.2. • **71** Drijvers (1992), 73. • **72** Pohlsander (1995), 155. • **73** See Johnson (1992), 148–9 for argument as to why Rome must be indicated. • **74** Johnson (2009), 110–17 for further details on Helena's mausoleum; also Elsner (1998), 21. • **75** Pohlsander (1995), 152–60; Drijvers (1992), 75–6. • **76** Pohlsander (1995), 160ff; Johnson (2009), 149. • **77** On Helena's sainthood, see Pohlsander (1995), chapter 15, *passim*. • **78** Helena's feast days: E. D. Hunt (1982), 28–9 and Harbus (2002), 3. Helena and King Coel: Harbus (2002), 1; Helena and Henry VIII: Harbus (2002), 120f. • **79** Pohlsander (1995), 11. • **80** Drijvers (2000), 44. • **81** Drijvers (2000), 31–6 on genesis and reception of Waugh's *Helena*. • **82** E. D. Hunt (1982), 29, for example, on Pulcheria being hailed as a 'New Helena'.

9 Brides of Christ, Daughters of Eve: The First Ladies of the Last Roman Dynasty

1 Thomas Nugent (2004) [1756] *The Grand Tour: a Journey through the Netherlands, Germany, Italy and France*, Vol. 3: 192. • **2** Rizzardi (1996), 106 on the poem by Gabriele D'Annunzio, *Le città del silenzio* (*The Cities of Silence*): cf. Dante, *Paradise* XXXI, 130–2. • **3** Ricci (1907), 14–15. • **4** Richlin (1992), 81. Technically, Galla Placidia was Pulcheria's half-aunt, by virtue of Pulcheria being the daughter of Placidia's half-brother Arcadius. • **5** See Brubaker (1997), 54 and 60, and Oost (1968), 38. • **6** See Tougher (1998) on this speech; also James (2001), 11–12. • **7** Socrates Scholasticus, *Ecclesiastical History* 4.31. My thanks to Christopher Kelly for his help on this point. • **8** See Richlin (1992), 81f. • **9** Paulinus, *Life of Ambrose*; Sozomen 7.13. See James (2001), 93–4; E. A. Clark (1990), 24. • **10** See MacCormack (1981), 263–4 on new virtues of empresses. • **11** James (2001), 128. • **12** Sozomen 7.6. • **13** Theodoret 5.18. See also McClanan (2002), 18–19. • **14** Eusebius, *Life of Constantine* 3.44. • **15** See Holum (1982), 32–4; Brubaker and Tobler (2000), 580; Brubaker (1997), 60; James (2001), 101–2; McClanan (2002), 26. • **16** Stout (1994), 86–7. • **17** Brubaker and Tobler (2000), 573 on appearance of 'Victory'; Holum (1982), 28 on *paludamentum*. See also James (2001), 26 on similarities to the mosaic of Theodora in San Vitale in Ravenna. • **18** *The Chronicle of John, Bishop of Nikiu*, 83.44–52. See Holum (1982), 41 and Mayer (2006), 205. • **19**

Justina: Zosimus, 4.43. See Holum (1982), 44–6, Oost (1968), 46–50 and Curran, 105–7 on this sequence of events. The family tie to Constantine was through Constantia, wife of Gratian, who was in turn the half-brother of Valentinian II, Galla's father. See James (2001), 60–1. • **20** Oost (1968), 1 on Galla Placidia's probable year of birth. For a challenge to this, see Rebenich (1985), 384–5, who places her date of birth in 392 or 393. • **21** See Heather (2005), 216–17 on Stilicho's rise to power. • **22** Her mother Galla had died in childbirth ten years earlier in 384. • **23** McCormick (2000) 136. • **24** McCormick (2000), 156f. • **25** Holum (1982), 25 on Flaccilla's *adventus*, as described in Gregory of Nyssa's *Oratio*. • **26** Holum (1982), 57. McCormick (2000), 141 on rarefied atmosphere for empresses. • **27** McCormick (2000), 135. Maria's education: see Claudian, *Epithalamium of Honorius and Maria* 231–7. • **28** Placidia's education: Oost (1968), 63–4. Girth: see Claudian, *Carmina Minora* 47–8. • **29** On the education of girls in late antiquity, as discussed in Jerome, see Nathan (2000), 152; on Jerome's advice, see Hemelrijk (1999), 63 and 262, n. 23. • **30** Elpidia: see Olympiodorus, fragment 38, in Blockley (1983), 201. Nathan (2000), 150 on *nutrices*. Olympiodorus refers to Elpidia as a *'trophos'* – which usually indicates a 'wet-nurse', like the Latin *nutrix*. • **31** See Harlow (2004a), 207–12 on Serena's dress and its future imitators. • **32** Harlow (2004a), 214–15 on Stilicho's dress. • **33** Livia's jewels: Claudian, *Epithalamium of Honorius and Maria* 13. • **34** Claudian, *On Stilicho's Consulship* 2. 356–9 on the suggestion of Eucherius's and Placidia's betrothal; and *Epithalamium of Honorius and Maria* 13, 211 and 285 on the bride's *flammeum*. • **35** I have followed the line taken by Oost (1968), 72–4 on the reasons for Galla Placidia remaining unmarried. On the discovery of Maria's tomb, see Johnson (2009), 173–4. • **36** Olympiodorus, fragment 7.3, in Blockley (1983), 159; Zosimus 5.38. • **37** Cooper (2009), 187–8. • **38** Olympiodorus, fragment 6, in Blockley (1983), 153. See Heather (2005), 224 and 239. • **39** Socrates Scholasticus, *Ecclesiastical History* 6.18. For more on Eudoxia's life, see McClanan (2002), 19–20 and Mayer (2006). • **40** Antiochus: Holum (1982), 80–1. • **41** See James (2001), 42 and Holum (1982), 97 on this dedication. The source is the *Chronicon Paschale*. • **42** Sozomen 9.1. • **43** See E. A. Clark (1990), 26f on the significance of such a choice. • **44** Sozomen 9.1. • **45** Sozomen 9.1. • **46** *The Chronicle of John, Bishop of Nikiu* 87.36: cited in James (2001), 18. • **47** Richlin (1992), 66. • **48** M. Toussaint-Samat (1992) *A History of Food* (Oxford: Blackwell), 26. See Olympiodorus, fragment 22, in Blockley (1983), 185. • **49** Olympiodorus, fragment 24, in Blockley (1983), 187–9. • **50** Oost (1968), 104, for example, coyly describes Athaulf as being 'not without his masculine charms'. • **51** Jordanes, *Getica* 160. See Harlow (2004b), 142; also Orosius 7.40.2 and 7.43. • **52** Olympiodorus, fragment 26, in Blockley (1983), 189. See Heather (2005), 240. • **53** Olympiodorus, fragment 26 and fragment 30, in Blockley (1983), Vol. 2: 189 and 195. • **54** Olympiodorus, fragment 33, fragment 36 and fragment 37, in Blockley (1983), 197–201. • **55** Olympiodorus, fragment 23, fragment 26 and fragment 36, in Blockley (1983),

187, 189 and 201. • **56** See James (2001), 119–22 on the women who received the title *Augusta* in late antiquity. • **57** See Oost (1968), 165–6. • **58** Olympiodorus, fragment 38, in Blockley (1983), 201–3. • **59** See Rizzardi (1996), 121, fig. 14 and 127, n. 66. Also Rebenich (1985), 372–3. • **60** Holum (1982), 109–11; Brubaker and Tobler (2000), 579–80. • **61** On reactions to Pulcheria's influence, see Holum (1982), 100–1 and James (2001), 66–8. • **62** Pulcheria and Mariology: Constas (1995), 169 and 188–9. • **63** *The Chronicle of John Malalas* 14.3–4, 191–3. This is the first and fullest account of Theodosius II and Eudocia's marriage: see Holum (1982), 114, n. 2 for others. • **64** *Chronicon Paschale* a. 420, trans Holum (1982), 114. • **65** Eudocia: see Cameron (1981), 270–9; Holum (1982), 112f and Herrin (2001), 134–5. On Eudocia and Elizabeth Barrett Browning, see M. D. Usher (1998) *Homeric Stitchings: the Homeric Centos of the Empress Eudocia* (Lanham, MD and Oxford: Rowman & Littlefield), 1. • **66** Olympiodorus, fragment 38, fragment 39 and fragment 43, in Blockley (1983), 203–7. • **67** Holum (1982), 129–30; Rizzardi (1996), 114. See also MacCormack (1981), 228. • **68** My translation. On the church, see Oost (1968), 274. • **69** Rebenich (1985), 373. • **70** See Brubaker (1997), 54, and 67, n. 14–17. • **71** Socrates Scholasticus, *Ecclesiastical History* 7.24.3. On Placidia's 'regency', see Oost (1968), 194–5 and Heather (2005), 260–1. • **72** Brubaker (1997), 61. • **73** Heather (2005), 261–2. • **74** Holum (1982), 131–2; McCormick (2000), 137–9. • **75** Modified from the translation of Holum (1982), 170: translation of *Acta conciliorum oecumenicorum* I, 1, 3, 14. See also Constas (1995), 173–6 on this episode, and Elsner (1998), 224–5 on the relationship between the Church and the emperor in this period. • **76** Theophanes AM 5941: see Holum (1982), 130. • **77** Oost (1968), 246. • **78** Cooper (2009), 198, on Gerontius, *Life of Melania the Younger*. • **79** Dietz (2005), 125; E. A. Clark (1982), 148; Brubaker (1997), 61–2; Lenski (2004), 117. • **80** Holum (1982), 186–7 for more details of Eudocia's trip. • **81** See Holum (1982), 104f; E. A. Clark (1982), 143 and Elsner (1998), 231. • **82** See Cameron (1981), 263–7 and Holum (1982), 176f. I have omitted to give details of the elaborate 'apple' story here, but the original version comes from *The Chronicle of John Malalas* 14.8: see Cameron (1981), 258–9 for details. • **83** Cameron (1981), 259, citing Nestorius, the *Bazaar of Heracleides*: 2.2. • **84** See James (2001), 15–16 and 23, nn. 36–7, citing *The Chronicle of John, Bishop of Nikiu* 87.1 and Evagrios, *Ecclesiastical History* 1.21–2. Saturninus: see Priscus, fragment 14, in Blockley (1983), 291 and 388, n. 86 and Lenski (2004), 118. • **85** Dietz (2005), 147 and Lenski (2004), 118. • **86** Holum (1982), 208–9. • **87** Brubaker and Tobler (2000), 580–1. • **88** Richlin (1992), 82–3: *Patrologia Latina*, J.P. Migne (ed.), 54.859–62, 863–6, 877–8. • **89** Brubaker (1997), 55 and Oost (1968), 270. • **90** See Oost (1968), 290–1. • **91** Priscus, fragment 17, in Blockley (1983), 301–3. Honoria's age: I follow Holum (1982), 1 on the date of Honoria's affair with Eugenius. Cf. Oost (1968), 282–3. • **92** Priscus, fragment 17 and fragment 20, in Blockley (1983), 303–5. • **93** Attila's death: Priscus, fragment 21, in Blockley (1983), 309. • **94** Pulcheria's death: Holum (1982), 216 and

226; Galla Placidia's death: Oost (1968), 291–2. • **95** Johnson (2009), 167–71. I am convinced by his reasoning that Galla Placidia and Theodosius are the two bodies found in 1458. See also the wistful words of Oost (1968): 'whatever is mortal of her may well still to this day rest beneath the transept floor of Michelangelo's mighty basilica' (p. 1).

Epilogue

1 Oost (1968), 307. • **2** See Cameron and Herrin (1984), 48–51 for a list of the works of art in the *Parastaseis Syntomoi Chronikoi*; also James (2001), 14–15 on Helena as the primary role model for Byzantine empresses.

Select Bibliography

Texts and Translations

Unless otherwise stated in the notes, all quoted translations of Greek and Roman works are taken from the following:

Ambrose, *De Obitu Theodosii*
Sister Mary Dolorosa Mannix, trans. *Sancti Ambrosii Oratio de obitu Theodosii.* Washington: Catholic University of America, 1925.

Anon, *Historia Augusta*
David Magie, trans. *Scriptores Historiae Augustae.* 3 vols. London: Heinemann, 1921–23.

Aulus Gellius, *Attic Nights*
J. C. Rolfe, trans. *The Attic Nights of Aulus Gellius.* 3 vols. London: Heinemann; Cambridge, MA: Harvard University Press, 1927.

Cassius Dio, *Roman History*
E.H. Cary, trans. *Dio's Roman History.* 9 vols. London: Heinemann, 1914–1927.

Cicero, *Letters to Atticus.*
D. R. Shackleton-Bailey, trans. *Letters to Atticus.* 4 vols. Cambridge, MA; London: Harvard University Press, 1998.

Claudian, *On the Consulship of Stilicho*
M. Platnauer, trans. *Works.* 2 vols. London: Heinemann, 1922.

Eusebius, *Life of Constantine*
Averil Cameron and S. G. Hall, trans. *Eusebius, Life of Constantine.* Oxford: Clarendon Press, 1999.

Fronto
C. H. Haines, trans. *The Correspondence of Marcus Cornelius Fronto with Marcus Aurelius Antoninus, Lucius Verus, Antoninus Pius and various friends.* 2 vols. London: Heinemann, 1919–20.

Herodian, *History of the Empire*
C. R. Whittaker, trans. *Herodian.* 2 vols. London: Heinemann; Cambridge, MA: Harvard University Press, 1969.

Jordanes, *Getica*
C. C. Mierow, trans. *The Gothic History of Jordanes*. Princeton, NJ; London: Princeton University Press, 1915.

Juvenal, *Satires*
S.M. Braund, trans. *Juvenal and Persius*. Cambridge, MA; London: Harvard University Press, 2004.

Macrobius, *Saturnalia*
P V. Davies, trans. *Macrobius: The Saturnalia*. New York: Columbia University Press, 1969.

Marcus Aurelius, *Meditations*
A. S. L. Farquharson, trans. *The Meditations of Marcus Aurelius Antoninus*. Oxford: Oxford University Press, 1989.

Martial, *Epigrams*
D. R. Shackleton-Bailey, trans. *Epigrams*. 3 vols. Cambridge, MA; London: Harvard University Press, 1993.

Olympiodorus
C. Blockley, trans. *The Fragmentary Classicising Historians of the Later Roman Empire*, Vol. 2 of 2. Liverpool: Cairns, 1983.

Ovid, *Amores*
P. Green, trans. *The Erotic Poems*. Harmondsworth: Penguin, 1982.

Philostratus, *Life of Apollonius*
C.P. Jones, trans. *The Life of Apollonius of Tyana*. 3 vols. Cambridge, MA; London: Harvard University Press, 2005.

Philostratus, *Lives of the Sophists*
W.C. Wright, trans. *Philostratus and Eunapius: The Lives of the Sophists*. London: Heinemann; Cambridge, MA: Harvard University Press, 1968.

Pliny the Elder, *Natural History*
H. Rackham, trans. *Natural History*. 10 vols. Cambridge, MA: Harvard University Press; London: Heinemann Press, 1938–1963.

Pliny the Younger, *Letters*
B. Radice, trans. *Letters and Panegyricus*. 2 vols. London: Heinemann Press, 1969.

Pliny the Younger, *Panegyricus*
B. Radice, trans. *Letters and Panegyricus*. 2 vols. London: Heinemann Press, 1969.

Plutarch, *Life of Antony*
R. Waterfield, trans. *Plutarch: Roman Lives*. Oxford: Oxford University Press. 1999.

Ps-Seneca, *Octavia*
J. G. Fitch, trans., *Seneca: Oedipus, Agamemnon, Thyestes, Hercules on Oeta, Octavia*. Cambridge, MA; London: Harvard University Press, 2004.

Sozomen, *Ecclesiastical History*
C. Hartranft, trans. *A Select Library of Nicene and Post-Nicene Fathers of the Christian Church*. Second series. Vol. 2. Oxford: Parker and Company; New York: The Christian Literature Company, 1891.

Suetonius, *Lives of the Caesars*
R. Graves, trans. *The Twelve Caesars*. London: Penguin, 1957.

Tacitus, *Annals*
M. Grant, trans. *The Annals of Imperial Rome*. London: Penguin, 1956.

Tacitus, *Histories*.
C. H. Moore, trans. *Histories*. Cambridge, MA: Harvard University Press; London: Heinemann, 1914–1937.

Theodoret, *Ecclesiastical History*
The Revd. Blomfield-Jackson, trans. *A Select Library of Nicene and Post-Nicene Fathers of the Christian Church*. Second series. Vol. 3. Oxford: Parker and Company; New York: The Christian Literature Company, 1892.

Velleius Paterculus
F. W. Shipley, trans. *Velleius Paterculus: Compendium of Roman History*. London: Heinemann; Cambridge, MA: Harvard University Press, 1967.

Virgil, *The Aeneid*
D. West, trans. *Virgil, The Aeneid: A New Prose Translation*. London: Penguin.

Secondary Reading

Archer, L. J., Fischler, S. and Wyke, M. (eds.), (1994) *Women in Ancient Societies: 'An Illusion of the Night'*. Basingstoke.
Arjava, A. (1996) *Women and Law in Late Antiquity*. Oxford.
Baharal, C. (1992) 'The Portraits of Julia Domna from the Years 193–211 A.D. and the Dynastic Propaganda of L. Septimius Severus', *Latomus* 51: 110–18.
Ball, W. (2000) *Rome in the East: The Transformation of an Empire*. London.
Balsdon, J. P. V. D. (1962) *Roman Women: Their History and Habits*. London.
Barrett, A. A. (1996) *Agrippina: Sex, Power and Politics in the Early Empire*. London.
——(2002) *Livia: First Lady of Imperial Rome*. New Haven. CT and London.
Bartman, E. (1998) *Portraits of Livia: Imaging the Imperial Women in Augustan Rome*. Cambridge.
——(2001) 'Hair and the Artifice of Roman Female Adornment', *American Journal of Archaeology* 105: 1–25.
Bauman, R. A. (1992) *Women and Politics in Ancient Rome*. London and New York.
——(1994) 'Tanaquil-Livia and the Death of Augustus', *Historia* 43.2: 177–188.

Beard, M. and Henderson J. (1998) 'The Emperor's New Body: Ascension from Rome', in Wyke (ed.).

——(2001) *Classical Art: From Greece to Rome.* Oxford.

Beard, M., North, J. and Price, S. (1998) *Roman Religion.* 2 vols. Cambridge.

Bicknell, P. J. (1963) 'Agrippina's Villa at Bauli', *Classical Review* 13: 261–3.

Birley, A. R. (1971) *The African Emperor: Septimius Severus.* London.

——(2000a) *Marcus Aurelius: A Biography.* London.

——(2000b) 'Hadrian to the Antonines', in Bowman, Garnsey and Rathbone (eds.).

Blockley, C. (1983) *The Fragmentary Classicising Historians of the Later Roman Empire.* 2 vols. Liverpool.

Boatwright, M. (1991) 'The Imperial Women of the Early Second Century A.D.', *American Journal of Philology* 112: 513–40.

——(2000) 'Just Window Dressing? Imperial Women as Architectural Sculpture', in Kleiner and Matheson (eds.).

Bondanella, P. (1987) *The Eternal City: Roman Images in the Modern World.* Chapel Hill, NC.

Bowersock, G. (1969) *Greek Sophists in the Roman Empire.* Oxford.

Bowman, A. K. (2005) 'Diocletian and the First Tetrarchy, AD 284–305', in Bowman, Garnsey and Cameron (eds.).

Bowman, A. K., Champlin, E. and Lintott, A. (eds.) (1996) *The Augustan Empire, 43BC–AD 69.* The Cambridge Ancient History, Vol. 10. Cambridge.

Bowman, A. K., Garnsey, P. and Cameron, A. (eds.) (2005) *The Crisis of Empire, AD 193–337.* The Cambridge Ancient History, Vol. 12. Cambridge.

Bowman, A. K., Garnsey, P. and Rathbone, D. (eds.) (2000) *The High Empire, AD 70–192.* The Cambridge Ancient History, Vol. 11. Cambridge.

Boyle, A. J. (2003) 'Reading Flavian Rome', in Boyle and Dominik (eds.).

Boyle, A. J. and Dominik, W. J. (eds.), (2003) *Flavian Rome: Culture, Image, Text.* Leiden.

Braund, D. C. (1984) 'Berenice in Rome', *Historia* 33: 120–23.

Brennan, T.C. (1998) 'The Poets Julia Balbilla and Damo at the Colossus of Memnon', *Classical World* 91.4: 215–34.

Brubaker, L. (1997) 'Memories of Helena: Patterns in Imperial Female Matronage in the Fourth and Fifth Centuries', in L. James (ed.), *Women, Men and Eunuchs: Gender in Byzantium.* London.

Brubaker, L. and Smith, J. M. H. (eds.), (2004) *Gender in the Early Medieval World: East and West, 300–900.* Cambridge.

Brubaker, L. and Tobler, H. (2000) 'The Gender of Money: Byzantine Empresses on Coins (324–802)', *Gender and History* 12.3: 572–94.

Burns, J. (2007) *Great Women of Imperial Rome: Mothers and Wives of the Caesars.* London and New York.

Cameron, Alan (1981) 'The Empress and the Poet: Paganism and Politics at the Court of Theodosius II', *Yale Classical Studies* 27: 217–89.

Cameron, Averil (1992) *Christianity and the Rhetoric of Empire: The Development of Christian Discourse*. Berkeley and London.

——(1993) *The Later Roman Empire: A.D. 284–430*. London.

Cameron, A. and Garnsey, P. (eds.) (1998) *The Late Empire, AD 337–425*. The Cambridge Ancient History, Vol. 13. Cambridge.

Cameron, A. and Herrin, J. (eds.), (1984) *Constantinople in the Early Eighth Century: the Parastaseis syntomoi chronikai*. Leiden.

Cameron, A., Ward-Perkins, B. and Whitby, M. (eds.) (2000) *Late Antiquity: Empire and Successors, AD 425–600*. The Cambridge Ancient History, Vol. 14. Cambridge.

Caroli, B. B. (1995) *First Ladies*. New York and Oxford.

Cartledge, P. and Spawforth, A. (1989) *Hellenistic and Roman Sparta: A Tale of Two Cities*. London.

Cascio, E. Lo (2005) 'The Emperor and his Administration: The Age of the Severans', in Bowman, Garnsey and Cameron (eds.).

Casson, L. (1974) *Travel in the Ancient World*. London.

Claridge, A. (1998) *Rome*. Oxford.

Clark, E.A. (1982) 'Claims on the Bones of Saint Stephen: The Partisans of Melania and Eudocia', *Church History* 51.2: 141–156.

——(1986) *Ascetic Piety and Women's Faith: Essays on Late Ancient Christianity*. Lewiston, N Y.

——(1990) 'Early Christian Women: Sources and Interpretations', in L. L. Coon, K. J. Haldane and E.W. Sommer (eds.), *That Gentle Strength: Historical Perspectives on Women in Christianity*. Charlottesville, VA and London.

Clark, E. A. and Richardson, H. (eds.), (1996) *Women and Religion: the Original Sourcebook of Women in Christian Thought*. New York.

Clark, G. (1993) *Women in Late Antiquity: Pagan and Christian Lifestyles*. Oxford and New York.

Constas, N. P. (1995) 'Weaving the Body of God: Proclus of Constantinople, the Theotokos, and the Loom of the Flesh', *Journal of Early Christian Studies* 3.2: 169–194.

Cooley, A. (2007) 'Septimius Severus – the Augustan Emperor', in Swain, Harrison and Elsner (eds.).

Coon, L. L. (1997) *Sacred Fictions: Holy Women and Hagiography in Late Antiquity*. Philadelphia.

Cooper, K. (1996) *The Virgin and the Bride: Idealized Womanhood in Late Antiquity*. Cambridge, MA and London.

——(2007) 'Poverty, Obligation, and Inheritance: Roman Heiresses and the Varieties of Senatorial Christianity in Fifth-century Rome', in K. Cooper and J. Hillner (ed.), *Religion, Dynasty, and Patronage in Early Christian Rome*. Cambridge.

——(2009) 'Gender and the Fall of Rome', in P. Rousseau (ed.), *A Companion to Late Antiquity*. Oxford.

Crawford, D. J. (1976) 'Imperial Estates', in M. I. Finley (ed.), *Studies in Roman Property*. Cambridge.

Crook, J. A. (1951) 'Titus and Berenice', *American Journal of Philology* 72: 162–75.

Croom, A. T. (2000) *Roman Clothing and Fashion*. Stroud, Glos.

Cryle, P. (2001) *The Telling of the Act: Sexuality as Narrative in Eighteenth- and Nineteenth-century France*. Newark and London.

Curran, J. (1998) 'From Jovian to Theodosius' in Cameron and Garnsey (eds.)

Currie, S. (1998) 'Poisonous Women and Unnatural History in Roman Culture' in Wyke (ed.).

D'Ambra, E. (1993) *Private Lives, Imperial Virtues: The Frieze of the Forum Transitorium in Rome*. Princeton, NJ.

——(2007) *Roman Women*. Cambridge.

D'Arms, J. H. (1970) *Romans on the Bay of Naples: A Social and Cultural Study of the Villas and their Owners from 150 B.C. to A.D. 400*. Cambridge, MA.

Davies, P. J. E. (2000) '*Damnatio memoriae* and Roman architecture', in Varner (ed.).

——(2004) *Death and the Emperor: Roman Imperial Funerary Monuments from Augustus to Marcus Aurelius*. Austin, TX.'

Dean, W. and Knapp, J. M. (1987) *Handel's Operas: 1704–1726*. Oxford.

Delia, D. (1991) 'Fulvia Reconsidered', in S. B. Pomeroy (ed.), *Women's History and Ancient History*. Chapel Hill, NC.

de Serviez, J. R. (1752) *The Roman Empresses*. London.

D'Hancarville, Baron [pseud. of Pierre François Hugues] (1780) *Monumens de la vie privée des douze Césars, d'après une suite de pierres gravées sous leur règne*.

——(1787) *Monumens du culte secret des dames romaines*.

Dietz, M. (2005) *Wandering Monks, Virgins, and Pilgrims: Ascetic Travel in the Mediterranean World AD 300–800*. University Park, AP.

Dixon, S. (1983) 'A Family Business: Women's Role in Patronage and Politics at Rome', *Classica and Mediaevalia* 34: 91–112.

——(1988) *The Roman Mother*. London.

——(1990) *Reading Roman Women: Sources, Genres and Real Life*. London.

——(1992) *The Roman Family*. Baltimore, MD.

——(2007) *Cornelia: Mother of the Gracchi*. London.

Drijvers, J. W. (1992) *Helena Augusta: The Mother of Constantine the Great and the Legend of Her Finding of the True Cross*. Leiden.

——(2000) 'Evelyn Waugh, Helena and the True Cross', *Classics Ireland* 7: 25–50.

Drinkwater, J. (2005) 'Maximinus to Diocletian and the "crisis"', in Bowman, Garnsey and Cameron (eds.).

Duffy, M. H. (1995) 'West's *Agrippina*, *Wolfe* and the Expression of Restraint', *Zeitschrift für Kunstgeschichte* 58.2: 207–25.

Eck, W., Caballos, A. and Fernández, F. (1996) *Das Senatus Consultum de Cn. Pisone Patre*. Munich.

Edmondson, J. C. (1996) 'Dynamic Arenas: Gladiatorial Presentations in the City of Rome and the Construction of Roman Society During the Early Empire', in W. J. Slater (ed.) *Roman Theater and Society*. Ann Arbor, MI.

Edwards, C. (1993) *The Politics of Immorality in Ancient Rome*. Cambridge and New York.

——(2000) *The Lives of the Caesars: Suetonius. Translated with an introduction and notes*. Oxford.

Elsner, J. (1998) *Imperial Rome and Christian Triumph: The Art of the Roman Empire AD 100–450*. Oxford.

——(2003) 'Iconoclasm and the Preservation of Memory', in R. S. Nelson and M. Olin (eds.), *Monuments and Memory, Made and Unmade*. Chicago and London.

Elsner, J. and Masters, J. (eds.), (1994) *Reflections of Nero: Culture, History and Representation*. London.

Emmanuel, M. (1994) 'Hairstyles and Headdresses of Empresses, Princesses, and Ladies of the Aristocracy in Byzantium', *Deltion tes Christianikes Archiologikes Hetaireias* 17: 113–20.

Erhart, K. (1978) 'A Portrait of Antonia Minor in the Fogg Art Museum and its Iconographical Tradition', *American Journal of Archaeology* 82: 193– 212.

Evans Grubbs, J. (1995) *Law and Family in Late Antiquity: The Emperor Constantine's Marriage Legislation*. Oxford and New York.

Fagan, G. (2002) 'Messalina's Folly', *Classical Quarterly* 52.2: 566–79.

Fantham, E. (2006) *Julia Augusti: The Emperor's Daughter*. London.

Fantham, E., Foley, H., Kampen, N. B., Pomeroy, S. B. and Shapiro, H. A. (eds.), (1994) *Women in the Classical World: Image and Text*. New York and Oxford.

Favro, D. G. (1996) *The Urban Image of Augustan Rome*. Cambridge.

Feldherr, A. (ed.) (2009) *The Cambridge Companion to the Roman Historians*. Cambridge.

Fejfer, J. (2008) *Roman Portraits in Context*. Berlin.

Ferrero, G. (1911) *The Women of the Caesars*. London.

Ferrill, A. (1980) 'Augustus and his Daughter: A Modern Myth', in C. Deroux (ed.) *Studies in Latin Literature and Roman Society*, II, vol. 332–66.

Fischler, S. (1994) 'Social Stereotypes and Historical Analysis: The Case of the Imperial Women at Rome', in Archer, Fischler and Wyke (eds.).

Fishwick, D. (1987–92) *The Imperial Cult in the Latin West: Studies in the Ruler Cult of the Western Provinces of the Roman Empire*. 2 vols. Leiden.

Fittschen, K. (1996) 'Courtly Portraits of Women in the Era of the Adoptive Emperors (AD 98–180) and their Reception in Roman Society', in Kleiner and Matheson (eds.).

Flory, M. B. (1984) 'Sic Exempla Parantur: Livia's Shrine to Concordia and the Porticus Liviae', *Historia* 33 (1984): 309–30.

——(1987) 'The Meaning of *Augusta* in the Julio-Claudian Period', *American Journal of Ancient History* 13.2: 113–38.

——(1988) '*Abducta Neroni Uxor*: The Historiographical Tradition on the Marriage of Octavian and Livia', *Transactions of the America Philological Association* 118: 343–59.

——(1993) 'Livia and the History of Public Honorific Statues for Women in Rome', *Transactions of the American Philological Association* 123: 287–308.

——(1995) 'The Deification of Roman Women', *Ancient History Bulletin* 9.3: 127–34.

——(1998) 'The Integration of Women into the Roman Triumph', *Historia* 47: 489–94.

Flower, H. I. (2006) *The Art of Forgetting: Disgrace and Oblivion in Roman Political Culture*. Chapel Hil, NC.

Frakes, R. M. (2006) 'The Dynasty of Constantine down to 363', in Lenski (ed.).

Fraschetti, A. (2001) *Roman Women*, trans. L. Lappin. Chicago and London.

Freisenbruch, A. (2004) 'The Correspondence of Marcus Cornelius Fronto'. Dissertation. (unpublished). Cambridge.

Frost, H. (1983) 'The Nymphaeum at Baiae', *International Journal of Nautical Archaeology* 12: 81–3.

Gabriel, M. M. (1955) *Livia's Garden Room at Prima Porta*. New York.

Gardner, J. F. (1986) *Women in Roman Law and Society*. London.

Garlick, B., Dixon, S. and Allen, P. (eds.) (1992) *Stereotypes of Women in Power: Historical Perspectives and Revisionist Views*. London and New York.

Ginsburg, J. (2006) *Representing Agrippina: Constructions of Female Power in the Early Roman Empire*. New York and Oxford.

Goodman, M. (1997) *The Roman World 44 BC–AD 180*. London.

Gorrie, C. (2004) 'Julia Domna's Building Patronage, Imperial Family Roles and the Severan Revival of Moral Legislation', *Historia* 53: 61–72.

Gradel, I. (2002) *Emperor Worship and Roman Religion*. Oxford.

Graves, R. (1934) *I, Claudius*. London.

Griffin, M. (1984) *Nero: The End of a Dynasty*. London.

——(1997) 'The Senate's Story', *Journal of Roman Studies* 87: 249–63.

——(2000) 'Nerva to Hadrian', in Bowman, Garnsey and Rathbone (eds.).

Hall, L. J. (2004) *Roman Berytus: Beirut in Late Antiquity*. London.

Hallett, J. P. (1977) 'Perusinae Glandes and the Changing Image of Augustus', *American Journal of Ancient History* 2: 151–71.

—— (1984) *Fathers and Daughters in Roman Society: Women and the Elite Family*. Princeton.

——(2002) 'Women Writing in Rome and Cornelia, Mother of the Gracchi', in L. J. Churchill, P. R. Brown and J. E. Jeffrey (eds.), *Women Writing Latin: From Early Antiquity to Early Modern Europe*, Vol. 1. New York and London.

Hamer, M. (1993) *Signs of Cleopatra: History, Politics, Representation*. London and New York.

——(2001) 'The Myth of Cleopatra since the Renaissance', in Walker and Higgs (eds.).

Harbus, A. (2002) *Helena of Britain in Medieval Legend*. Cambridge.

Harlow, M. (2004a) 'Female Dress, Third–Sixth Century: The Messages in the Media?', *Antiquité Tardive* 12: 203–15.

——(2004b) 'Galla Placidia: Conduit of Culture?' in F. McHardy and E. Marshall (eds.), *Women's Influence on Classical Civilization*. London and New York.

Haskell, F. and Penny, N. (1981) *Taste and the Antique: The Lure of Classical Sculpture, 1500–1900*. New Haven, CT and London.

Heather, P. (2005) *The Fall of the Roman Empire: A New History*. London.

Heller, W. (2003) *Emblems of Eloquence: Opera and Women's Voices in Seventeenth-Century Venice*. Berkeley.

Hemelrijk, E. H. (1999) *Matrona Docta: Educated Women in the Roman Elite from Cornelia to Julia Domna*. London.

——(2005) 'Octavian and the Introduction of Public Statues for Women in Rome', *Athenaeum* 93.1: 309–17.

Henderson, J. G. (1989) 'Satire writes Woman: Gendersong', *Proceedings of the Cambridge Philological Society* 35: 50–80.

Herrin, J. (2001) *Women in Purple: Rulers of Medieval Byzantium*. London.

Hicks, P. (2005a) 'The Roman Matron in Britain: Female Political Influence and Republican Response ca. 1750–1800', *Journal of Modern History* 77.1: 35–69.

——(2005b) 'Portia and Marcia: Female Political Identity and the Historical Imagination, 1770–1800', *The William and Mary Quarterly* 62.2: 265–94.

Hillard, T. (1992) 'On the Stage, Behind the Curtain: Images of Politically Active Women in the Late Roman Republic', in Garlick, Dixon and Allen (eds.).

Holum, K. (1982) *Theodosian Empresses: Women and Imperial Dominion in Late Antiquity*. Berkeley and London.

——(1999) 'Hadrian and St Helena: Imperial Travel and the Origins of Christian Holy Pilgrimmage', in R. Ousterhout (ed.), *The Blessings of Pilgrimage*. Urbana.

Hopkins, M.K. (1965) 'The Age of Roman Girls at Marriage', *Population Studies* 18: 309–27.

Hunt, E.D. (1982) 'Constantine and the Holy Land: Helena – History and Legend', in E.D. Hunt, (ed.), *Holy Land Pilgrimage in the Later Roman Empire AD 312–460*. Oxford.

Hunt, L. (1991) 'The Many Bodies of Marie Antoinette: Political Pornography and the Problem of the Feminine in the French Revolution', in L. Hunt (ed.), *Eroticism and the Body Politic*. Baltimore, MD.

Icks, M. (2008) *Images of Elagabalus*. Nijmegen.

James, L. (2001) *Empresses and Power in Early Byzantium*. London.

Johnson, M.J. (1992) 'Where were Constantius I and Helena Buried?', *Latomus* 51: 145–50.

——(2009) *The Roman Imperial Mausoleum in Late Antiquity*. Cambridge.

Jones, B.W. (1984) *The Emperor Titus*. London.

Jones, P.J. (2006) *Cleopatra: A Sourcebook*. Norman, OK.

Jordan, R. (1974) *Berenice*. London.

Joshel, S. R. (1992) 'The Body Female and the Body Politic: Livy's Lucretia and Verginia', in A. Richlin (ed.), *Pornography and Representation in Greece and Rome*. New York and London.

——(1995) 'Female Desire and the Discourse of Empire: Tacitus' Messalina', *Signs: Journal of Women in Culture and Society* 21.1: 50–82.

——(2001) 'I, Claudius: Projection and Imperial Soap Opera' in S. R. Joshel, M. Malamud and D. McGuire, Jr (eds.), *Imperial Projections: Ancient Rome in Modern Popular Culture*. Baltimore, MD and London.

Kajava, M. (1990) 'Roman Senatorial Women and the Greek East: Epigraphic Evidence from the Republican and Augustan Periods', in H. Solin and M. Kajava (eds.), *Roman Eastern Policy and Other Studies in Roman History*. Helsinki.

Kampen, N. B. (1991) 'Between Private and Public: Women as Historical Subjects in Roman Art', in S. B. Pomeroy (ed.), *Women's History and Ancient History*. Chapel Hill, NC.

Kaplan, M. (1979) 'Agrippina semper atrox: A Study in Tacitus' Characterization of Women', in C. Deroux (ed.), *Studies in Latin Literature and Roman History*, Vol.1. Brussels.

Keaveney, A. and Madden, J. (2003) 'Berenice at Rome', *Museum Helveticum* 60: 39–43.

Kelly, C. (2006) *The Roman Empire: A Very Short Introduction*. Oxford.

——(2008) *Attila the Hun: Barbarian Terror and the Fall of the Roman Empire*. London.

Keltanen, M. (2002) 'The Public Image of the Four Empresses: Ideal Wives, Mothers and Regents?', in P. Setälä, R. Berg, R. Hälikkä, M. Keltanen, J. Pölönen and V. Vuolanto (eds.), *Women, Wealth and Power in the Roman Empire*. Rome.

Kidd, W. (2004) 'Marianne: from Medusa to Messalina: Psycho-sexual imagery and political propaganda in France 1789–1945', *Journal of European Studies* 34.4: 333–48.

Kleiner, D. E. E. (1992a) 'Politics and Gender in the Pictorial Propaganda of Antony and Octavian', *Echos du Monde Classique* 36: 357–67.

——(1992b) *Roman Sculpture*. New Haven, CT and London.

——(1996) 'Imperial Women as Patrons of the Arts in the Early Empire', in Kleiner and Matheson (eds.).

——(2000) 'Family Ties: Mothers and Sons in Elite and Non-Elite Roman Art', in Kleiner and Matheson (eds.).

——(2001) 'Now you See Them, Now You Don't: The Presence and Absence of Women in Roman Art', in Varner (ed.).

——(2005) *Cleopatra and Rome*. Cambridge, Mass. and London.

Kleiner, D. E. E. and Matheson, S. B. (eds.), (1996) *I Claudia: Women in Ancient Rome*. New Haven, CT.

——(2000) *I, Claudia II: Women in Roman Art and Society*. Austin, TX.

Knight, R. C. (1999) *Berenice: Jean Racine*. A translation by R. C. Knight, completed and edited by H. T. Barnwell. Durham.

Kokkinos, N. (2002) *Antonia Augusta: Portrait of a Great Roman Lady*. London.

Kosmetatou, E. (2002) 'The Public Image of Julia Mamaea: An Epigraphic and Numismatic Enquiry', *Latomus* 61: 398–414.

Kragelund, P. (2007) 'Agrippina's Revenge' in M. Moltesen and A.-M. Nielsen (eds.), *Agrippina Minor: Life and Afterlife*. Copenhagen.

Lancon, B. (2000) *Rome in Late Antiquity: Everyday Life and Urban Change, AD 312–609*, trans. A. Nevill. Edinburgh.

Leadbetter, B. (1998) 'The Illegitimacy of Constantine and the Birth of the Tetrarchy', in Lieu and Montserrat (eds.).

Lee, H. (2005) *Body Parts: Essays on Life Writing*. London.

——(2009) *Biography: A Very Short Introduction*. Oxford.

Lefkowitz, M. R. and Fant, M. B. (1992) *Women's Life in Greece and Rome: A Sourcebook in Translation*. London.

Lenski, N. (2004) 'Empresses in the Holy Land: The Creation of a Christian Utopia in Late Antique Palestine', in L. Ellis and F. L. Kidner (eds.), *Travel, Communication and Geography in Late Antiquity: Sacred and Profane*. Aldershot.

——(ed.), (2006) *The Cambridge Companion to the Age of Constantine*. Cambridge.

Levick, B. (2002) 'Women, Power, and Philosophy at Rome and Beyond', in G. Clark and T. Rajak (eds.), *Philosophy and Power in the Graeco-Roman World: Essays in Honour of Miriam Griffin*. Oxford.

——(2007) *Julia Domna: Syrian Empress*. London.

Levick, B. and Innes, D. (1989) 'Luxurious Dentifrice in Rome', *Omnibus* 18: 17–18.

Lieu, S. N. C. (1998) 'From History to Legend: The Medieval and Byzantine Transformation of Constantine's *Vita*', in Lieu and Montserrat (eds.).

—— (2006) 'Constantine in Legendary Literature', in Lenski (ed.).

Lieu, S. N. C. and Montserrat, D. (eds.) (1998) *Constantine: History, Historiography and Legend*. New York.

Linderski, J. (1988) 'Julia in Regium', *Zeitschrift für Papyrologie und Epigraphik* 72: 181–200.

Ling, R. (1991) *Roman Painting*. Cambridge.

Loven, L. L. (1998) 'Lanam fecit – Woolworking and Female Virtue', in Loven and Stromberg (eds.).

Loven, L. L. and Stromberg, A. (eds.) (1998) Aspects of Women in Antiquity: Proceedings of the First Nordic Symposium on Women's Lives in Antiquity. Jonsered.

Lusnia, S. (1995) 'Julia Domna's Coinage and Severan Dynastic Propaganda', Latomus 54: 119–40.

Macaulay-Lewis, E. (2006) 'The Role of Ollae Perforatae in Understanding Horticulture, Planting Techniques, Garden Design and Plant Trade in the Roman World', in J. P. Morel, J. T. Juan and J. C. Matamala (eds.), The Archaeology of Crop Fields and Gardens. Bari.

MacCormack, S. (1981) Art and Ceremony in Late Antiquity. Berkeley, CA and London.

MacDonald, W. L. (1965) The Architecture of the Roman Empire. New Haven, CT and London.

Macurdy, G. H. (1935) 'Julia Berenice', American Journal of Philology 56: 246–53.

Mango, C. (1994) 'The Empress Helena, Helenopolis, Pylae', Travaux et Mémoires 12: 143–58.

Matheson, S. B. (2000) 'The Elder Claudia: Older Women in Roman Art', in Kleiner and Matheson (eds.)

Mayer, W. (2006) 'Doing Violence to the Image of an Empress: The Destruction of Eudoxia's Reputation', in H. A. Drake (ed.), Violence in Late Antiquity: Perceptions and Practices. Aldershot.

McClanan, A. (2002) Representations of Early Byzantine Empresses: Image and Empire. London.

McCormick, M. (2000) 'Emperor and Court', in A. Cameron, B. Ward-Perkins and M. Whitby (eds.), Late Antiquity: Empire and Successors AD 425–600. Cambridge Ancient History, Vol. 14. Cambridge.

McDermott, W. C. (1977) 'Plotina Augusta and Nicomachus of Gerasa', Historia 26: 192–203.

McDermott, W. C. and Orentzel, A. E. (1979) Roman Portraits: The Flavian-Trajanic Period. Columbia and London.

McLeod, G. (1991) Virtue and Venom: Catalogs of Women from Antiquity to the Renaissance. Ann Arbor.

Milnor, K. (2005) Gender, Domesticity and the Age of Augustus: Inventing Private Life. Oxford.

——(2009) 'Women in Roman Historiography', in Feldherr (ed.).

Moltesen, M. and Nielsen, A.-M. (eds.) (2007) Agrippina Minor: Life and Afterlife. Copenhagen.

Nathan, G. S. (2000) The Family in Late Antiquity: The Rise of Christianity and the Endurance of Tradition. London.

Newby, Z. (2007) 'Art at the Crossroads? Themes and Styles in Severan Art', in Swain, Harrison and Elsner (eds.).

Nixon, C. E. V. and Rodgers, B. S. (1994) *In Praise of Later Roman Emperors: The Panegyrici Latini*. Berkely; Oxford.

O'Gorman, E. (2000) *Irony and Misreading in the Annals of Tacitus*. Cambridge.

Olson, K. (2008) *Dress and the Roman Woman: Self-Presentation and Society*. Abingdon.

Oost, S. I. (1968) *Galla Placidia Augusta: A Biographical Essay*. London and New York.

Opper, T. (2008) *Hadrian: Empire and Conflict*. London.

Parkin, T. G. (2002) *Old Age in the Roman World: A Cultural and Social History*. Baltimore, MD.

Pelling, C. (1988) *Plutarch: Life of Antony*. Cambridge.

——(1996) 'The Triumviral Period', in Bowman, Champlin and Lintott (eds.).

——(2001) 'Anything Truth Can Do, We Can Do Better: The Cleopatra Legend', in Walker and Higgs (eds.).

Penella, R. J. (1979) 'Philostratus' Letter to Julia Domna', *Hermes* 107: 161–8.

Perowne, S. (1974) *Caesars' Wives: Above Suspicion?* London.

Pohlsander, H. (1984) 'Crispus: Brilliant Career and Tragic End', *Historia* 33: 79–106.

——(1995) *Helena: Empress and Saint*. Chicago.

Pomeroy, S. B. (1975) *Goddesses, Whores, Wives and Slaves: Women in Classical Antiquity*. London.

Potter, D. (2007) *Emperors of Rome: The Story of Imperial Rome from Julius Caesar to the Last Emperor*. London.

Price, S. (1984) *Rituals and Power: The Roman Imperial Cult in Asia Minor*. Cambridge.

Purcell, N. (1986) 'Livia and the Womanhood of Rome', *Proceedings of the Cambridge Philological Society* 32: 78–105.

Ragalie, M. (2007) 'Sex and Scandal with Sword and Sandals: A Study of the Female Characters in HBO's *Rome*', *Studies in Mediterranean Antiquity and Classics*:Vol. 1: Iss. 1, Article 4.

Rawson, B. (1987) 'Discrimina Ordinum: The Lex Julia Theatralis', *Papers of the British School at Rome* 55: 83–113.

——(ed.) (1991) *Marriage, Divorce, and Children in Ancient Rome*. Canberra.

——(ed.) (1992) *The Family in Ancient Rome: New Perspectives*. Ithaca, New York.

——(2003) *Children and Childhood in Roman Italy*. Oxford.

Rebenich, S. (1985) 'Gratian, a Son of Theodosius, and the Birth of Galla Placidia', *Historia* 34: 372–85.

Reeder, J. C. (2001) *The Villa of Livia Ad Gallinas Albas: A Study in the Augustan Villa and Garden*. Providence, RI.

Rees, R. (2004) *Diocletian and the Tetrarchy*. Edinburgh.

Rendall, J. (1996) 'Writing History for British Women: Elizabeth Hamilton and the Memoirs of Agrippina' in C. Campbell-Orr (ed.), *Wollstonecraft's Daughters: Womanhood in England and France 1780–1920*. Manchester.

Reynolds, J. (1982) *Aphrodisias and Rome*. London.

Ricci, C. (1907) *Ravenna*. Bergamo.

Richardson, L. (1992) *A New Topographical Dictionary of Ancient Rome*. Baltimore, MD.

Richlin, A. (1992) 'Julia's Jokes, Galla Placidia, and the Roman Use of Women as Political Icons', in Garlick, Dixon and Allen (eds.).

——(1995) 'Making up a Woman: The Face of Roman Gender', in H. Eilberg-Schwartz and W. Doniger (eds.), *Off With her Head! The Denial of Women's Identity in Myth, Religion and Culture*. Berkeley, CA.

Ridley, R. T. (1986) 'Augusti Manes Volitant per Auras': The Archaeology of Rome under the Fascists', *Xenia* II: 19–46.

Rizzardi, C. (ed.) (1996) *Il Mausoleo di Galla Placidia a Ravenna*. Modena.

Roche, P. A. (2002) 'The Public Image of Trajan's Family', *Classical Philology* 97: 41–60.

Rose, C. B. (1997) *Dynastic Commemoration and Imperial Portraiture in the Julio-Claudian Period*. Cambridge.

Rose, M. E. (2006) 'The Trier Ceiling: Power and Status on Display in Late Antiquity', *Greece and Rome* 53.1: 92–109.

Roussin, L. A. (1994) 'Costume in Roman Palestine: Archaeological Remains and the Evidence from the Mishnah', in Sebesta and Bonfante (eds.).

Santoro L'hoir, F. (1994) 'Tacitus and Women's Usurpation of Power', *Classical World* 88: 5–25.

Sartre, M. (2005) 'The Arabs and the Desert Peoples', in Bowman, Garnsey and Cameron (eds.).

Schmitt-Pantel, P. (1992) *A History of Women in the West*, Vol. 1: *From Ancient Goddesses to Christian Saints*. Cambridge, MA and London.

Schroder, V. (2009) 'Re-Writing History for the Early Modern Stage: Racine's Roman Tragedies', in Feldherr (ed.).

Sebesta, J. and Bonfante, L. (eds.) (1994) *The World of Roman Costume*. Madison, WI.

Setälä, P. (1977) *Private Domini in Roman Brick Stamps of the Empire: A Historical and Prosopographical Study of Landowners in the District of Rome*. Helsinki.

——(1998) 'Female Property and Power in Imperial Rome', in Loven and Stromberg (eds.).

Setälä, P., Berg, R., Hälikkä, R., Keltanen, M., Pölönen, J. and Vuolanto, V. (eds.) (2002) *Women, Wealth and Power in the Roman Empire*. Rome.

Severy, B. (2003) *Augustus and the Family at the Birth of Empire*. New York and London.

Seymour-Smith, M. (1995) *Robert Graves: His Life and Work*. London.

Sharrock, A. (1991) 'Womanufacture', *Journal of Roman Studies* 81: 36–49.

Shaw, B. D. (1987) 'The Age of Roman Girls at Marriage: Some Reconsiderations', *Journal of Roman Studies* 77: 30–46.

Shelton, J-A. (1998) *As the Romans Did: A Sourcebook in Roman Social History*. New York and Oxford.

Siegfried, S. (2001) 'Ingres's Reading – The Undoing of Narrative', in Siegfried, S. and Rifkin, A. (2001) *Fingering Ingres*. Oxford.

Smith, R. R. R. (1987) 'The Imperial Reliefs from the Sebasteion at Aphrodisias', *Journal of Roman Studies* 77: 88–138.

——(1988) *Hellenistic Royal Portraits*. Oxford.

Spivey, N.J. (1999) 'Introduction' to *Robert Graves, The Claudius Novels*. London.

Staley, A. (1965) 'The Landing of Agrippina at Brundisium with the Ashes of Germanicus', *Philadelphia Museum of Art Bulletin* 61: 10–19.

Stout, A. M. (1994) 'Jewelry as a Symbol of Status in the Roman Empire', in Sebesta and Bonfante (eds.).

Supple, J. J. (1986) *Racine: Berenice*. London.

Swain, S., Harrison, S. J. and Elsner, J. (eds.) (2007) *Severan Culture*. Cambridge.

Syme, R. (1984) 'The Crisis of 2 BC', in A. Birley (ed.), *Roman Papers*, Vol. 3. Oxford.

Takács, S. A. (2008) *Vestal Virgins, Sibyls and Matrons: Women in Roman Religion*. Austin, TX.

Tamm, B. (1963) *Auditorium and Palatium: A Study on Assembly-Rooms in Roman Palaces During the First Century BC and the First Century AD*. Stockholm.

Tomei, M. A. (1998) *The Palatine*, trans. L. Guarneri Hynd. Milan.

Tougher, S. (1998) 'In Praise of an Empress: Julian's Speech of Thanks to Eusebia', in M. Whitby (ed.), *The Propaganda of Power: The Role of Panegyric in Late Antiquity*. Boston, MA.

Treggiari, S. (1973) 'Domestic Staff in the Julio-Claudian Period', *Histoire Sociale* 6: 241–55.

——(1975) 'Jobs in the Household of Livia', *Papers of the British School at Rome* 43: 48–77.

——(1991) *Roman Marriage: Iusti Coniuges from the Time of Cicero to the Time of Ulpian*. Oxford.

——(2007) *Terentia, Tullia, and Publilia: The Women of Cicero's Family*. London.

Van Bremen, R. (1983) 'Women and Wealth', in A. Cameron and A. Kuhrt (eds.), *Images of Women in Antiquity*. London.

——(1996) *The Limits of Participation: Women and Civic Life in the Greek East in the Hellenistic and Roman Periods*. Amsterdam.

Van den Hout, M. P. J. (1999) *A Commentary on the Letters of M. Cornelius Fronto*. Leiden.

Varner, E. R. (1995) 'Domitia Longina and the Politics of Portraiture', *American Journal of Archaeology* 99.2: 187–206.

——(ed.) (2001a) *From Caligula to Constantine: Tyranny and Transformation in Roman Portraiture*. Atlanta, GA.

——(2001b) 'Portraits, Plots and Politics: *Damnatio Memoriae* and the Images of Imperial Women', *Memoirs of the American Academy in Rome* 46: 41–93.

——(2004) *Mutilation and Transformation: Damnatio Memoriae and Roman Imperial Portraiture*. Leiden.

Vinson, M. (1989) 'Domitia Longina, Julia Titi and the Literary Tradition', *Historia* 38: 431–50.

Von Blanckenhagen, P. H. and Alexander, C. (1962) *The Augustan Villa at Boscotrecase*. Mainz.

Vout, C. (2007) *Power and Eroticism in Imperial Rome*. Cambridge.

——(2009) 'Representing the Emperor', in Feldherr (ed.).

Walker, S. and Higgs, P. (eds.) (2001) *Cleopatra of Egypt: From History to Myth*. London.

Wallace-Hadrill, A. (1988) 'The Social Structure of the Roman House', *Papers of the British School at Rome* 56: 43–98.

——(1993) *Augustan Rome*. London.

——(1994) *Houses and Society in Pompeii and Herculaneum*. Princeton, NJ.

——(1996) 'The Imperial Court', in Bowman, Champlin and Lintott (eds.).

Walter, C. (2006) *The Iconography of Constantine the Great: Emperor and Saint*. Leiden.

Walton, C. L. (ed.) (1965) *Berenice*. London.

Whitmarsh, T. (2007) 'Prose Literature and the Severan Dynasty', in Swain, Harrison and Elsner (eds.).

Winkes, R. (2000) 'Livia: Portrait and Propaganda', in Kleiner and Matheson (eds.)

Winterer, C. (2007) *The Mirror of Antiquity: American Women and the Classical Tradition 1750–1900*. Ithaca, NY and London.

Wood, S. (1988) 'Agrippina the Elder in Julio-Claudian Art and Propaganda', *American Journal of Archaeology* 92: 409–26.

——(1992) 'Messalina, wife of Claudius: Propaganda Successes and Failures of his Reign', *Journal of Roman Archaeology* 5: 219–34.

——(1999) *Imperial Women: A Study in Public Images, 40BC–AD 68*. Leiden.

Woods, D. (1998) 'On the Death of the Empress Fausta', *Greece and Rome* 45.1: 70–86.

Wyke, M. (1994) 'Woman in the Mirror: The Rhetoric of Adornment in the Roman World', in Archer, Fischler and Wyke (eds.).

——(ed.) (1998) *Parchments of Gender: Deciphering the Body in Antiquity*. Oxford.

——(2002) *The Roman Mistress: Ancient and Modern Representations*. Oxford.

Young-Widmaier, M. R. (2002) 'Quintilian's Legal Representation of Julia Berenice', *Historia* 51.1: 124–29.

Zanker, P. (1988) *The Power of Images in the Age of Augustus*, trans. A. Shapiro. Ann Arbor.

Zarmakoupi, M. (2008) 'Designing the Landscapes of the Villa of Livia at

Prima Porta', in D. Kurtz, H. C. Meyer and E. Hatzivassiliou (eds.), *Essays in Classical Archaeology for Eleni Hatzivassiliou 1977–2007*. Oxford.

Zwalve, W. J. (2001) 'In Re Iulius Agrippa's Estate: Q. Cervidius Scaevola, Iulia Domna and the Estate of Iulius Agrippa', in L. de Blois (ed.), *Administration, Prosopography and Appointment Policies in the Roman Empire*. Amsterdam.

Index